Contemplating Marriage

Reader

Edited by Gloria Blanchfield Thomas

Sheed & Ward
Kansas City

Sheed & Ward™ is a service of The National Catholic Reporter Publishing Company.

◆

Library of Congress Cataloguing-in-Publication Data
Contemplating marriage : reader / edited by Gloria Blanchfield Thomas.
       p.   cm.
   ISBN: 1-55612-817-7 (pbk. : alk. paper)
    1. Marriage—Religious aspects—Catholic Church. 2. Catholic
Church—Doctrines. I. Thomas, Gloria Blanchfield.
BX2250.C595 1995
248.4'82—dc20   95-24019
                                                    CIP

◆

Published by: Sheed & Ward
               115 E. Armour Blvd.
               P.O. Box 419492
               Kansas City, MO 64141-6492

To order, call: (800) 333-7373

Contents

Topic 12 – Choosing a Lifestyle—Coping with Life

Acknowledgments

Grateful acknowledgement is given for copyright reprint permissions as follows:

"Three Perspectives," from *In Her Image,* by Kathie Carlson ©1989. Reprinted by arrangement with Shambahala Publications, Inc., 300 Massachusetts Ave., Boston MA 02115.

"Fathers and Daughters," from *Fathers and Daughters,* by William S. Appleton. Copyright© 1981 by William S. Appleton, M.D. Used by permission of Doubleday, a division of Bantam Doubleday Dell Publishing Group, Inc.

"Confessions from Four Mother's Sons," by Nyta Mann and Francis Elliott, from *New Statesman & Society.* ©1993 Statesman and Nation Publishing Company. Permission in via.

"Father Hunger," by Andrew Merton, and "What Makes Love Last?," by Alan Atkisson, from *New Age Journal.* ©1986, 1994 by Rising Star Associates. Permission in via.

"Expectations," "Communication," and "The First Child" reprinted from *The First Two Years of Marriage,* by Kathleen Fischer Hart and Thomas N. Hart ©1983, by Thomas N. Hart and Kathleen Fischer Hart. "Marriage in the Old Testament," "Marriage in the New Testament," and "The Search for Intimacy" reprinted from *The Challenge of Christian Marriage,* by Thomas M. Martin ©1990 by Thomas M. Martin. "Sexual Intimacy" reprinted from *Partners in Intimacy,* by Challon O'Hearn Roberts and William P. Roberts, ©1988 by William P. Roberts and Challon O'Hearn Roberts. "Careers and Money, Committments and Frugality," reprinted from *Love and Destiny,* by Anthony Padovano, ©1987 by Anthony Padovano. Used by permission of Paulist Press.

"Two Reasons Marriages Fail," taken from the book, *The Joy of Committed Love,* by Gary Smalley. Copyright ©1984 by Gary Smalley. Used by permission of Zondervan Publishing House.

"The Meaning of Marriage," "Identity: Vocation and Marriage," "Marriage as a Sacramental Passage," and "Marriage as a Sacramental Passage," from *Marrying Well: Stages on the Journey of Christian Marriage,* by Evelyn Eaton Whitehead and James D. Whitehead. New York: Image Books, Doubleday, copyright ©1981. Reprinted with permission of the authors.

"The Extrovert/Introvert Marriage," by K.J. Eppes (April 1991), "Scapegoating: The Phony Equalizer in Marriage," by A.H. Smith, Jr. (February 1991), "Of Apples, Serpents, and Sex," by David M. Thomas (July 1986), "Spirituality of the Difficult Marriage," by Thomas Fitzpatrick (August 1991), "Annulment: The Process and Its Meaning," by Patrick R. Lagges (April 1991), and "Ten Ingredients of Parenting," by Victor M. Parachin (August 1991), reprinted with permission from *Marriage and Family* magazine. Published by Abbey Press, St. Meinrad Archabbey, St. Meinrad, IN 47577.

"Can We Get Real About Sex?," by Lisa Sowle Cahill, from *Commonweal* (September 14, 1990). Reprinted with permission of Commonweal Foundation ©1990.

"I Knew My Marriage Was a Sacrament When. . ." by Anna C. Erhart, Nancy Forest-Flier, John Garvey, Jo McCowan, and Linus Mundy (February 1992),

Teaching Marriage in a Catholic College

CERTAINLY MARRIAGE THEOLOGY IN THE ROMAN CATHOLIC TRADITION IS evolving. Theologians are once again examining sacramentality and the permanence of the sacramental bond. The theology and canonical law concerned with the validity of the sacramental rite and the indissoluable bond are consuming much scholarly energy and fine-tuned research. This phenomenon evidences an alive and Spirit-filled church. In the meantime, however, Catholic marriages are failing at the same dismal rate as American marriages in general. And Catholic college students are looking for some meaningful, concrete guidance. Many of our students are the children of painful divorces. Their fears are real. They have many pointed and often difficult questions for their Church.

The marriage course at a Catholic college is, indeed, a challenge, for there are no easy answers available. The format of this course suggests a process for teaching marriage. Its approach asks the students and the professor to do marriage theology together. The experience of this author suggests this method as a way of honoring our Catholic tradition and our Scriptures, as well as the wisdom, joy, and pain of married people's experience. It also honors the experience of the students, most of whom have observed at least one marriage up close.

Married teachers have an opportunity to witness from their own lives concerning their sexual relationships in marriage. Although their own decisions and present sexual activity may differ considerably, students do listen carefully to personal testimony. Discussing the enormous impact of sexual experience will help students understand the reasons and/or motivations for their own choices. This discussion should include a clear statement about the misuse of sexual intimacy that does not celebrate and affirm genuine intimacy, love and commitment. A witness to belief in the appropriateness of sexual intercourse as an expression of exclusive love and commitment is effective only if the teacher listens deeply to their perspectives. Students are usually more than surprised that a greater percentage of the marriages of couples who have lived together end in divorce than of those who had not.

Much of the learning in this course is accomplished within the method itself. It is a type of hermeneutical praxis. Interpreting one's experience, much reading and reflection and exposure to the wisdom of people in happy marriages and even those in failed marriages are essential components. The Catholic doctrinal tradition, the history of Catholic Christian marriage, the sacramentality of marriage, the wedding liturgy and symbols and Scripture passages from the Hebrew and Christian Scriptures are considered through the lens of the students' experience and expectations.

Using this method requires great flexibility. It is often messy, but it works. It is necessary to constantly rethink and reevaluate as the learning continues. This whole hermeneutical approach depends on real communication and a willingness to change and grow. It depends on the honoring of everyone's experience. This process of learning models the very openness and ongoing acceptance of change and growth that is required in marriage itself. Students have the opportunity to reflect on their learning and its relevance in their present relationships. They also are able to understand themselves as part of the Church's evolving theological process. It is an adult approach, requiring of the teacher and students alike an openness to differences and to real and sometimes painful change. It demands faith in the presence of divine possibility within all relationships.

Additional Suggestions

Throughout this course the class is considering the meaning of Catholic Christian marriage. The voices of our tradition and the voice of Scripture are reflected upon, along with many modern voices of today's Church and society. Participants are asked to carefully consider these voices in light of their own reflected-upon experience.

It is a most worthwhile addition to invite guest speakers into the classroom. These speakers can offer personal testimony concerning their experience and expertise. Students should prepare questions for the guests and reflect upon their contributions in their journals.

Suggestions for guest speakers:
- Married couples of all ages
- Divorced individuals
- Clergy people
- Marriage counselors
- Leaders of marriage help-groups:
  - Engaged Encounter
  - Marriage Encounter
  - pre-Cana, Cana

- local parish groups
- Retrouvaille

During a final class discussion have all participants share in the making of a list of Topics which they will thoroughly discuss with their intended partners before engagement. Hopefully the list they develop together will include all of the following:

- expectations of their families
- habits of drugs, alcohol
- importance of their separate friends
- careers, career plans
- children — when? how many?
- inability to have children
- childcare / parenting styles
- where we will live
- religious values
- religious practice
- God's part in our marriage
- sexual expectations
- methods of birth control
- our communication skills
- finances / budget
- feelings about counseling
- wedding celebration plans
- roles of husband and wife — before children and after children

Additional and Related Topics

Students, working alone or in small groups, can offer written papers and/or oral reports on related subjects. It is effective to give all class members an opportunity to present questions concerning these Topics which the students can research and answer for the class.

Suggestions for Student Research:

- Alternative Lifestyles — gay and lesbian
- Marriage customs from other countries
- Wedding rituals and symbols
- Adoption and foster care
- Abortions within marriage
- Childless marriages
- "Mommy track"
- Second marriages, stepfamilies and stepchildren
- Surrogate mothers
- In vitro fertilization, test-tube babies, fertility problems

- Natural family planning
- AIDS within marriage and family

The Influence of Parenting

1.1   Three Perspectives
by Kathie Carlson

SEVERAL PERSPECTIVES ARE NECESSARY TO GAIN A FULL VISION OF THE MOTHER-daughter relationship. The perspectives I have found to be most helpful in teaching and doing therapy with women are those centered in a child, a feminist, and a transpersonal point of view. These three perspectives articulate successively broader and deeper visionings of the mother. Each one has its merits and limitations and each is vital to the daughter's comprehension of her inner and outer experience of her mother.

In the first vision, the daughter sees her mother through the eyes of a child, and through the dependency dynamics that existed in her early relationship with her mother. Most women see their mothers through this perspective at some level, even if through subsequent learning and reflection they have acquired a more adult viewpoint that takes a larger picture into account.

The daughter who is looking through a child's eyes makes several assumptions about her mother. First, she assumes that her mother is really powerful or could be if she wanted to be. Secondly, she believes that her mother has control over her life because she is an adult. Even a woman who has learned to see the personal and collective factors that shaped her mother's parenting style and capacity may go back to this earlier view when thinking about her own childhood. Thus, one of the college students I worked with in therapy, a gifted, mature young woman, who got along well with both of her parents and was particularly empathic with her mother, was baffled at her mother's newly emerged resentment at "never having done what I wanted to do in life." She told me that it seemed to her that her mother always did *exactly* what she wanted to do. Further reflection on her reactions led her to realize that a part of her was hurt and frightened by her mother's statement and wanted to maintain the belief that her mother had always had the power to do whatever she wanted. If the full-time mothering that the mother had done was not what she wanted to do in life, where did this leave the daughter, particularly since her experience was one of feeling well-cared-for and loved? The security of her childhood experience was threatened by her mother's revelation, and secretly she feared that if her mother resented having been a full-time mother, she must resent her daughter as well. Maintaining the image of her mother as all-powerful also preserved a sense of her child self as having deserved the care she had been given.

The child's view is egocentric; it evaluates the mother in terms of how her behavior affected the child, how the daughter's needs and longings were met or not met. All positive experience is seen as good and "right," and there is a truth in that, for it *was* right for the child. All negative experience (e.g., the mother's absence, preoccupations, or angers) is perceived as aimed at the daughter and personally motivated even when this is obviously not the case (as, for example, when a mother is absent because she is hospitalized due to mental or physical illness). In addition, the child view believes that it was (and is) possible for all the daughter's legitimate needs to have been met by the mother "if only — ." Many an adult daughter has a whole list of "if onlys" to bolster her child belief that the mother could give her most or all of what she needs. "If only I had been a better daughter"; "if only she hadn't gone to work full-time"; "if only she would stop lecturing me"; "if only she were less concerned with appearances. . . ." And the final clause to all of these "if onlys" is: *"then* she would be the mother I wanted" or *"then* we could finally have a relationship."

The child's perspective, on the one hand, is the outgrowth of taking seriously and valuing the *true* needs of the child, needs that are legitimate and vital for us to be aware of even as adults. Valuing these needs and this part of ourselves contributes to a healthy ego and to a sense of wholeness and self-worth as an adult; women who suppress or deny their child perspectives lose a vital part of themselves. Such women are often unable to care well for themselves or to receive care from others. On the other hand, the child perspective on the mother is steeped in the dependency dynamics inherent in patriarchal child-rearing arrangements in which the mother tends to be the sole caretaker of the child or is expected to be and is therefore seen consensually as the "all-fulfiller." (We tend to let up on grandmothers, aunts, and even fathers, who may have played vital roles in our lives but were not expected to be emotionally responsible for all of our needs.) Thus, this perspective is also supported by cultural stereotypes and expectations of what the mother can and is supposed to be: supportive, nurturing, unselfish, infinitely caring of the child, etc.

The problem is that *no one* can be all that; the expectations placed on mothers are inhuman, yet we've had nowhere else to refer them. A man who has been disappointed or hurt in relationship with his personal father can sometimes find his way to a "heavenly" Father, a God image that can carry the greater-than-human expectations. As daughters in a culture that offers no feminine God image, we've had no place else to turn.

Many of us have not had even adequate mothering, much less the ideal; many of our mothers have been too depleted themselves. We end up disappointed in our mothers, hurt, angry, blaming, needy, raging, yet unable to let go of our need for them. We feel starved emotionally and try to cover that over. We feel terrified of becoming like our mothers and vow to be different with our children. We end up estranged from our mothers and estranged from ourselves. We carry around an unhealed child, a sense of woundedness and of longing that seems to have nowhere to go. Identifying with this child in ourselves, expanding her vision, and connecting her with healing possibilities are the underlying themes of this book.

The child's view of the mother-daughter relationship is both valuable and limited. It is valuable because it allows preservation of legitimate needs for attention, nurturance, care, and primary bonding; these needs are true even for the adult and should not be dismissed. Also preserved by this perspective is a sense of oneself as important and central, a birthright not easily claimed by women in a culture that has so often exhorted them to put others first. The child's position counters and compensates both personal and cultural experiences of the devaluation and psychological "decentralization" of women and focuses attention on the self. Even the rage and blaming that often emerge when the unhealed child comes into consciousness may be necessary, not as an end point (and unfortunately, many daughters get stuck here), but as a way of separating out and claiming oneself vis-à-vis one's mother, and as a basis for legitimate self-interest and self-assertion. All of this focus on oneself and assertion of one's true needs are necessary to sustain a healthy ego that can feed and maintain the adult woman.

At the same time, the child's viewpoint is limited. It does not see the mother in herself, as a person with her own needs, interests, and concerns separate from the child. Nor does it take into account important factors affecting the mother's life and ability to parent, factors such as economics, what kinds of supports the mother herself had available, what her own experience of being mothered was. It also overlooks the effects that cultural expectations and stereotypes of mothers have on the mother's parenting (e.g., she may be living a false self because she's doing what she thinks she's "supposed" to do). And finally, the child's perspective envisions the mother inhumanly, assumes she is somehow "matched" to the daughter's needs, does not have needs of her own that conflict with her daughter's, and has nearly infinite resources.

A second perspective — seeing our mothers through feminist eyes — expands the child's vision. This extremely valuable and necessary viewpoint is an adult perspective rooted in a different power dynamic than that of the child's. From this vantage, the mother is seen as an equal, a "sister," a woman like oneself. In addition, an attempt is made to separate out the cultural image of "mother" and the institution of motherhood from this particular human being. Cultural and environmental factors are taken into account and the mother's parenting is seen as a response to these factors as well as being the creation of her own personality and abilities. Remembering her mother's literal or emotional absence, for example, which she may have felt keenly as a child, the daughter is now able to take into account a broader picture of the mother's life. She may understand, as an adult, the economic pressure that necessitated that her mother work long hours away from home. She may recognize the submission to a collective ideal that may have led her mother to have had more children than she had time and energy for. She may also come to realize that some of her mother's pattern of mothering was a replica of her grandmother's and that both women's styles were in part a reflection of the culture, which has an investment in reproducing itself and its values in the socialization process mothers are expected to undertake with regard to their children (i.e., the preparation for and induction into the society's values).

Many a mother has gone against her own instincts and preferences in deference to the so-called "experts" because she genuinely wanted to raise her child "right" and was not expected to be able to determine what was right from her own instinct or authority. I still remember the time when my daughter was very little and had great difficulty sleeping whenever she was sick. I'd be up and down all night with her, growing progressively more irritable and exhausted as the night wore on. I thought of taking her into bed with me, which seemed the natural thing to do, but recalled Dr. Spock's admonition against this, his warning about what a bad habit would be formed as a consequence. Unsure of myself as a parent, reasoning that I didn't "know" anything about children since I had been an only child myself, I followed his dictum. (It never occurred to me to question whether Spock himself had ever been up all night with a sick baby and had a two-year-old as well to cope with in the morning.) Finally one night I could barely function and put Rachele next to me in bed, just so I could lie down. Comforted by my presence and by being close to my body, she immediately went to sleep and, though still ill, continued to sleep through the night.

The feminist perspective is valuable because it allows the daughter to extend an empathic concern to her mother, seeing her as a limited adult instead of an ideal. It takes into account multiple cultural and environmental, as well as personal, factors that affect her mothering. The feminist view has also given weight and value to women who have served as "counter-mothers" in the daughter's life: grandmothers, aunts, nannies, teachers, and other women who have provided an adjunct or alternative care to the mother's. The presence of such women in our lives allows the needs of the unhealed child to be spread out among many "mothers" and addressed by several different sources of care. One woman in one of my mother-daughter classes whose mother had often been mentally ill while she was growing up suddenly realized how much nurturing one of her aunts had provided; she had never thought of this as "mothering" before and immediately got in touch with her aunt to thank her.

The limit of this perspective lies in the possibility that other truly personal factors in the mother-daughter relationship that are not caused by the environment may be overlooked, factors such as differences in temperament or psychological type (e.g., problems of the extroverted mother raising an introverted daughter or vice versa). In addition, in spite of the fact that feminism has encouraged and facilitated self-care, some women may use their feminist views to split off from the unhealed child within themselves, extending their empathy only toward their mothers and excluding the validity of their own unmet needs.

Sometimes women who have relinquished their child perspective on their experiences with their mothers have to be encouraged to reclaim it, in order to bring up and work through the precious parts of themselves that got locked away when the child self was suppressed. One woman, who had been severely abused by her father with her mother's knowledge, resisted seeing her mother negatively in any way. Her mother was also being abused, she said; they were poor and her mother held down a job to try to support the family when the father wouldn't or was unable to. All of this was admirable on the part of the mother and, from my patient's strong feminist perspective, an empathic vision of the forces her mother struggled to contend with. What was missing from this picture was the same kind of empathy for herself, empathy for the unmothered and abused child, feeling for her own needs and pain as deeply as she felt for her mother's.

It is not necessary to denigrate one's mother to hold many points of view simultaneously, even when the foci inherent in these points of view clash. It is possible to learn to have deep compassion, concern, and even outrage on behalf of the child one was, regardless of how legitimate or inevitable the factors were that led to abusive or neglectful behavior. The child's passion and egocentrism don't care about what is going on with the mother in her own life and shouldn't be asked to; her rage at being mistreated or having her needs unmet should be valued as part of her claiming her importance in the world, her intrinsic worth as a human being. When a woman holds down or denies these feelings, a great deal else is lost: an intrinsic sense of self-worth, an ability to identify what in the environment or in other people is dangerous to her and to respond with self-protection, and much of the child's spontaneity and passionate interest in herself. A person who has suppressed her child's needs and viewpoint will find it almost impossible to adequately care for herself or to care about herself. Her perceptiveness and empathic concern for others may be extremely well developed; she may be a fine caretaker of everyone except herself. Championing her mother's worth at the expense of her own reflects exactly what was true in the first place: that there is no adequate *mother* in the situation. There was not in the past, and is not internally in the present. The person who has suppressed her child self and cannot stand for her own experience grows into an adult who must continue to be unmothered, who cannot take in support and love from others because she cannot claim her right to have them or to have had these things in the past.

Seeing only through a feminist view skews the picture. What was missing from my patient's tale were other aspects of her mother's behavior. The mother made no attempt to stop the father from beating and raping his daughter; and, in addition, when the daughter tried to intervene in her mother's beatings, the mother would turn against her and join the father in beating the daughter. No one can dismiss the pressures in this mother's life which underlay her inability to be empathic and protective of her daughter; yet to fail to feel alarm and concern for the battered child is to collude in dismissing her own legitimate needs for more of a mothering presence than she could manage for herself.

While a woman who has only the child's point of view of her mother may need to add a feminist view in order to expand her picture and understanding of her mother, a woman who claims only a feminist view may need to find or reclaim the child's. I am not trying to set these views against each other, only to point out that *both* are necessary to work toward a whole picture in which both mother and daughter are adequately seen and valued but neither at the expense of the other. Holding both views simultaneously involves a certain level of tension, since it is quite hard (and, from a therapeutic perspective, not necessarily useful) to feel compassion for another and outrage on one's own behalf at the same time. In experiences less extreme than the example given, it may be possible to take both viewpoints into account at the same time. At any rate, both are vital if one is not to lose some very precious aspects of the daughter's reality.

A third view of the mother-daughter relationship revisions mother and daughter from a transpersonal orientation. In this perspective, the child's needs are taken very seriously and seen and carried as legitimate, but no longer put on the personal mother alone. They are also referred to the transpersonal level, to the spiritual entity of the Great Mother, as She manifests Her various aspects in other human beings and appears in both ancient and modern visions and dreams. This perspective adds to and extends the feminist awareness that there are other resources available and that "mother" is bigger than personal experience with one woman. If we have other sources to turn to and our needs are not devalued, it is easier to put our personal mothers in perspective; we can accept their limits more easily because we have more than "one chance."

The transpersonal perspective also allows us to revision the cultural stereotype of "mother" and to preserve it, not as a realistic ideal that one human being should be expected to live up to, but as part of a vision of the Feminine as Deity that has existed for thousands of years and is part of our inner and outer heritage. The woman who is infinitely supportive, nurturing, unselfish, and caring, who can feed others without needing to feed herself — the image of that great abundance — is an archetypal image. It resides in the deepest and most collective layers of the psyche and found its most vivid expression in the imagery of prepatriarchal religions, thousands of years ago.

The mistake that we make as a culture is to expect one human woman to *be* the archetype and, further, to be only that aspect of the mother archetype we want, that we see as positive. The cultural stereotype of the "good mother" is but one part of a much larger entity; the archetype is more complicated and bi-valent than we would choose. The Great Mother has both a benevolent and a terrible side, and either or both may come through our personal mothers as well as through ourselves and other women. We don't get to choose and, to a very real extent, neither do our mothers. A woman can't *make* herself into the good archetypal mother simply by willing herself to be it, no matter how hard she tries. The fact that women are expected to do this, to have this power, is one of the major problems in human relationships today, and differentiating themselves from such expectations poses a central individuation task for modern women. To know that one carries the archetype and can relate to it but not control it — and to know that one is also *not* the archetype, not that powerful or full or unlimited — is the cultural lesson that mothers and daughters alike need to learn.

What we can choose to do is to *relate* to the archetypal Mother in a conscious, voluntary way, to get in touch with a heritage of spiritual vision that belongs to all of us but that has been stamped out of our collective awareness by the destructive aspects of patriarchal culture. Contacting this heritage enables us to reconnect with a time, uninfluenced by patriarchal views of women, when "feminine" was experienced as vast, multifaceted, and valuable — so valuable that it appeared as a God image. Whether we look at this heritage and its reappearance in modern times as a history we can draw from for images and inspiration, as the mirror of forces within and between us, or as a spiritual image — a living Goddess whose children we are — we can, by connecting with this perspective, come to see our mothers and ourselves differently. We can come to see what of the Great Mother came through our personal mother experiences, what of Her radiance and Her terror, and raise questions of deeper meaning. Further, we can seek out aspects we haven't experienced that we need for healing and for wholeness. Through this vision, we can eventually become daughters of ourselves, of each other, and of a Mother as vast as our vision can stretch. It is true that in the process, something will also be lost; our personal mothers can no longer carry the "bigness" we've attributed to them, or be expected to be the only carrier of the Mother our bodies and souls need; but, in exchange, we can gain all the richness of the transpersonal world.

Knowledge of the Great Mother's images and stories provides pictures, models, and connections across time and culture to female sources and to a multiplicity of "styles" of being female. Through meditation, imaginal play, art, and worship, the Great Mother can give us what our personal mothers often could not.

Each perspective depicted in this chapter gives us access to the mother. The childhood perspective gives us each a personal connection to one human being as mother. The feminist perspective relates us to other women in our culture and puts our mothers in cultural context. The transpersonal perspective expands this to include connection with a spiritual source and people across time.

To summarize: The child perspective sees the mother egocentrically, believing her to be all-powerful and able to fulfill the daughter's needs. The mother is not seen as individual, or as limited by circumstances within and without. The great expectations surrounding her from this perspective are rarely met; this gives rise to the unhealed child full of rage, blame, hurt, and need. Although frustrating and too narrow, the unhealed child is a true inner experience; it is valuable for finding and claiming the importance of oneself. The feminist perspective places the mother in a social and cultural context, and takes into account both her personal difficulties and the environmental impact on her. The feminist perspective may lead to an objective understanding of the mother as a limited human being, but risks losing connection with the unhealed child. The transpersonal perspective sees both mother and daughter against the backdrop of a rich spiritual heritage. The mother is no longer asked to carry the archetype alone; resources are found in other women, history, and spiritual connections.

All three of these perspectives minister to our need for wholeness.

1.2 Fathers & Daughters
William Appleton

THREE FACTS ABOUT TODAY'S WOMEN TROUBLE ME. THE FIRST IS THE LARGE number of women unhappy in their careers and in their private lives. The second is that most of them think they understand their father's role in their adult dissatisfactions but in reality do not. And the third is how hard it is for them to understand and change unproductive patterns in their personal lives and in their careers.

The more a woman understands her father's effect on her the more she will be able to enjoy her husband or lover sexually, emotionally, and intellectually, the freer she will be to pursue and advance in her career, the better mother she will be to her own children, and the richer her life will be.

Two life cycles. The double-life cycle approach is a method I devised to create order out of the years of confusion, complexity, and emotional interaction between father and daughter. This approach enables the daughter to see how they have loved, hurt, and helped one another and what effect this continues to have on her life.

The father-daughter model. This model divides the first thirty years of interaction between father and daughter into three parts, each of which is ten years long. It assumes father is in his late twenties or early thirties when she is born and focuses on the main characteristics of each of them during the three decades. The first decade, the *Oasis,* occurs during her childhood and his thirties; the second, the *Conflict,* during her adolescence and his forties; the third, *Separation,* during her twenties and his fifties. The pleasures and conflicts of each stage will be described below in brief detail.

Think back over the years. How did you and your father interact when you were a child, an adolescent, and now, as an adult? The model's structure will minimize emotional distortions from any one decade and put each into the perspective of all three. Stormy adolescent reactions can be softened by memories of the oasis of childhood. As extreme feelings calm and take their place in the total picture, a realistic view of father will emerge, uncolored by worship or anger. This balanced comprehension of how your male parent has affected you will help you improve your present and future love life.

The Oasis

This first stage includes the girl's childhood and her father's thirties. Now that it seems well established that infants develop attachment, behavior to *both* parents during the first nine months of life, the importance of the father-daughter relationship from the beginning is greater than previously suspected. Attachment is the preference for or desire to be close to a specific person, usually conceived of as stronger or wiser.

Intense emotions arise during the formation, maintenance, and disruption of attachment relationships. Maintenance of the bond is experienced as a source of security.

Adult attachments are influenced by the experiences one has had with similar figures in childhood. There is a strong causal relationship between an individual's experiences with her parents and her later capacity to make affectional bonds. Past psychoanalytic theory had girls discovering their fathers between the ages of three and six as a result of disappointment in their mothers and in themselves for not possessing a penis. Present knowledge shows father's influence to be earlier and even more significant, or in the words of the theory, *not just oedipal but preoedipal.*

Father. Typically father is in his third decade when his daughter is in her first. He is usually preoccupied with career building. Often this is at the expense of his marriage, his leisure, his friendships, his sex drive, and his time for introspection. He can be a relatively sexless, working machine, and in this sense, he is in a kind of latent period akin to the latency of childhood, which occurs between the ages of six and the onset of puberty. The latency period is one of emotional quiescence between the turmoil of childhood and adolescence. This period in the child is associated with the acquisition of skills. The thirties of father is a period during which he strives for the position he will achieve in his forties and fifties. While his child acquires skills he gains job status.

During this time in their lives his daughter may not see a lot of him and this is one reason why father's importance has been overlooked by researchers and theoreticians. What has only recently been noticed is that in many cases she sees *enough* of him to form an attachment in infancy. It is not certain what the minimum number of hours or quality of interaction is necessary for this attachment to occur. Frequently it is assumed that because mother is there more hours it only occurs with her. But mothers may be in the same house with babies and spend very little time actually interacting with them. Several researchers have observed that even when mother is in the same room or carrying the child, social interaction may be minimal and infrequent. Furthermore, it is not the amount but the quality of time between parents and children that is more important. Daily separations from mothers in day-care centers do not hurt the infant-mother attachment. Daily separations from a working father are no more harmful.

The busyness of the latent-period father in his thirties, far from destroying his impact on his daughter's development, may heighten the quality of the time they spent together, since he allows himself few other pleasures and emotional outlets as he strives to get ahead and build his career. The time spent together by fathers and infants is very enjoyable and elicits highly positive emotions on both sides. It is this delight that has made me call this period an oasis for him from his cold, competitive world of striving for success. It is a time of pure pleasure and deep emotional attachment for him and as a consequence for her as well.

Of course this oasis is not always such a romantic, positive interlude. Often a tired man is called upon by his equally tired wife for child care, which is no longer a delight but a chore. An irritable, overworked father forced to change diapers is not a desirable attachment figure, at least for the moment. But, nonetheless, he loves his pretty little girl and usually the over-all picture is positive.

Daughter. It is not very long before the baby to whom he has become at-tached becomes a little girl. From then on, throughout the first six years of her life father and daughter emotionally provide each other with a happy respite from the rigors of daily life, he from the workaday world and she from mother's discipline and demands. This special holiday from care con-tinues as one aspect of their attachment all their lives. He is usually tougher on his sons as mother is on her daughters. From age six to puberty, *her* latency period, he becomes more involved with her intellectual development and begins to be interested in her schoolwork and to teach her.

The Legacy of the Oasis

The way a father treats his daughter in the oasis period makes an indel-ible impression on her. For some women the delight of the oasis is etched forever after and interferes with all adult love relationships. No man is as attentive and caring as her doting father.

If there was none or too little happiness with father in the oasis period, her femininity suffers. Their first decade together not only includes her need to form an infant's attachment but if the father is absent or angry and reject-ing, the girl is left completely discouraged in her beginning and most impor-tant efforts with a man. She has no experience of flirting with, gaining atten-tion from, being worshipped by or delighting the man who means the most to her at the most impressionable time in her life. Four studies in the 1960s found that paternal masculinity was consistently associated with the feminin-ity of daughters and inconsistently with the masculinity of sons. It is surpris-ing that fathers affect their daughters' femininity more than their sons' mas-culinity. Researchers, theorists, and my own clinical and research experience all concur that a good relationship with a warm and accepting father who is not too frightened of her sexuality is extremely important to a little girl. Someone who can enjoy her beauty, her smile, her pretty dress, her first efforts at makeup and jewelry helps her gain the confidence that she can attract, charm, and interest a man. A father who is made nervous by and ridicules her little feminine gestures or who is always too tired or angry to be pleased by them or who is absent too much can cause his daughter to be insecure about her body and her ability to attract a man.

Too little or no childhood closeness to an accepting father can leave a woman with various kinds of scars; insecurity is one of the deepest. Detach-ment is another because she does not know how to be close to a man and feels cut off. Not frightened necessarily, she simply does not expect love, closeness, warmth, or intimacy from a male. Anger is another unhappy leg-acy from this period. If the most important man in her life, her father, has not given her the love and attention she needed, she is left deeply enraged. Later, then, as soon as her husband or lover lets her down her fury bursts forth. Her rageful, righteous indignation at his social slip, drinking, crudeness, wandering eye, dullness is too great, fueled by her anger at her father's neglect. Her hostility drives men away, while punishing any who remain.

Some women, deprived in their childhood of father's warmth, may be sexless as adults. Sexless does not necessarily mean spinsterish virginal, or even unorgasmic, although it can exhibit itself in these ways. Rather it means the absence of desire for men. A girl who has not been aroused by her father's attention is unlikely to feel strong sexual passions as a women. She grows into a wife who can perform sexually for her husband but has no interest in him or anyone else. Adult sexual fantasies and desires have their basis in childhood experiences and longings. Modified through the years, they represent a women's lifelong story and her father played a key role in what excites her years later.

The absent or rejecting father can also leave a woman with excessive hunger for male attention, very demanding that her lover be totally devoted and quick to anger and throw her partner out should he fail her. Another manifestation of father deprivation is addiction to the excitement of the courtship and intolerance of the calmness of the long term. These women crave the daily flowers and phone calls, lust for the new man but become bored and depressed once the affair calms down. Unreasonably quick to feel ignored and hurt, as the veneer of excitement wears off, their childhood pain resurfaces and they rush off to the narcotic of a new love.

If the poisoned or absent oasis is harmful, then equally dangerous is the overbearing one. Fathers who are too needful of the worship of their little girls, who are too disappointed in the real world and revel in this escape, cling too long and try to stunt the growth and independence of their developing child can bring up women who never love psychologically. Some women, when interviewed, are quite open about saying how none of their men measure up to father who is brighter, more considerate, and better company than any of them.

The effect of the disturbed oasis is not everlasting, however. Women can get over it if they recognize what their oasis was like and how it currently affects them and try to change their pattern. Childhood unhappinesses are harder to overcome than those from adolescence or adulthood. Knowledge of the self, determination to change and the courage to try different behavior is what is required.

Conflict: His Forties, Her Teens

The period of midlife has been compared to adolescence. For both father and daughter it is a time of separation as she leaves the oasis they shared. For each it is a time of questioning. She asks, "Who am I?" He wonders who he will continue to be. She rebels against authority and convention, he wonders if he can stand one more board meeting or dinner party. Both may be moody. Each may be concerned with questions of life and death, the brevity of time and the inevitability of age. Both may be restless and discontent.

Father in his forties is reevaluating his existence and wondering if he will continue his career and private life as it is in the time left to him, which he now sees as limited. Would it be wise for him to change jobs or careers? Does he still love his wife? Should he remain married to her? Does he have friends and does he see them enough? Is he using his talents and being creative? Does he enjoy his life or has it become an empty shell?

But father does not have the leisure to reflect. There are financial pressures. Concerned about the young men coming up the ladder behind him, he may fear losing his job or failing to get an important promotion. He worries about his health and aging. And he watches his little girl grow to womanhood and prepare to leave him.

The adolescent daughter, however, *does* have time to reflect. She sees her father differently because she is no longer a little, worshipful girl and also because he has in fact changed. Typically, in his thirties he worked constantly to build his career and resembled an emotionally quiescent latency child. Now in his forties, he is more like an adolescent himself, more sexual, harder drinking, moodier, and likelier to get into trouble with work or women.

Although adolescent girls become upset as they discover the flaws in their fathers, it is a disturbance that is ultimately good for them. They see that he, like all of us, is not perfect. This discovery may bring about his fall from grace, which in turn if too severe or too abrupt may have lasting effects. The father who deserts his family suddenly and never sees them again can have a daughter forever afraid to allow herself to be vulnerable to a man, sure that he too will leave her. But if the fall from grace is reasonable and not too severe, and if he accepts the anger and criticism arising from her disappointment in him, it will help her to separate from him, and it will encourage her to have reasonable, adult expectations of her lovers, rather than unrealistic and childish ones.

Most fathers struggle to maintain their hero image with their daughters and become too upset about revealing their human weaknesses. This reluctance is akin to the daughter's wish to remain a pure virgin in his eyes. Each wants to hold onto the happy childhood days and not face the realities of life.

Angry, tired fathers seem more available to daughters for fighting than for joy. Rebellion is flamed as a contest of wills ensues over rules, growing independence, excessive concern about safety, and too often ultimately over whether to let her grow and go or keep her with him. She struggles to get away but also wants to continue to please him so he will still love and care for her.

Their second decade together can leave lifelong scars that can harm her relationships with men due to anger, rebellion, and excessive fighting. Unable to be a fully functioning separate woman when involved in a love affair, she longs for the childhood oasis. But if a father takes pleasure in his adolescent daughter, talks to her about philosophical, aesthetic, or material matters, sharing the growth, ideas, sensitivities, and intelligence of her youth, she can be a source of joy to him. Good memories of long talks and beautiful walks from this era allow a woman to enjoy her lover's mind, to be close to him philosophically, romantically, sexually and to forgive his faults and permit him to be human.

Separation

When a woman reaches her twenties, if she has successfully grown through her childhood and adolesence she is ready physically and emotionally to leave her family. The geographical step is easier than the psychological. In every adult there is within a helpless child afraid of being alone. Separation, therefore, causes everyone anxiety.

The question is what is she leaving? Is it someone who is necessary for her survival or parents who have helped her be able to confidently care for herself? No daughter leaves home without fear, ambivalence, and mourning. The process takes varying amounts of time depending upon the strength of the woman, her psychological maturity, and the support of her parents.

In the process of separation the daughter *detaches* her feelings from her father. This is accomplished by moving physically and emotionally away from him. As they come in contact less frequently the strength of their psychological attachment subsides. This is aided by her increasing involvement with others in her intimate life and in her work. The process is not always smooth and gradual. Sometimes father and daughter fight as they break apart and they may speak to each other rarely, if at all. Their parting of company is accompanied by distress on each side. When the pain becomes too great they may totally withdraw, fight, or slip back to a closer, childlike way for a time. But once the emotional sadness and mourning are over, the daughter is able to take her feelings from her father and reinvest them in others. She is then free to find a man and a life of her own.

During her twenties a woman modifies her needs and emotions. The swings of mood, characteristic of the adolescent, become less extreme. She evolves from the *a*ffective (emotional) state of the adolescent to the *e*ffective (masterful) status of the adult. She is less inclined to get upset about events and more willing to do something about them.

In this process, during which she becomes the master of her feelings, her anger matures. From the temper tantrum of the two year old who cannot stand frustration to the argumentative adolescent who engages in critical battles with the restricting parent, she becomes able to feel the appropriate angry response of the adult. She is able to feel her wrath, control it, and express it at the appropriate time when it is in her own interest.

The resolution within the woman in her twenties of her feelings about the *fall of Father* helps her gain control of herself and be able to separate. She has behind her, in adolescence, the feeling of anger toward and disappointment in him which helped her begin to leave him. The process of reconciliation between them releases her feelings. If adolescent anger toward him continues throughout her twenties and on into complete adulthood, her emotions, though negative, will continue to be tied up with him. By forgiving him and accepting him with his faults she finds it much easier to leave.

The father and separation. Father is in his fifties as his daughter is leaving. If his career and marriage are going well he is able to tolerate it much better. Nonetheless, he is saddened and goes into a state of depression. Psychologically mature men accept the pain, suffer it, get over it, and go on with a new phase of their lives. Others attempt to hold on to their daughters or may create emotional scenes. If a woman is lucky her father will help her leave. He will calm her fears and encourage her to live her independent life, remaining available to her should she need him. All this adjusting takes time and rarely proceeds smoothly. Emotions are strong and few men are perfect. There may be tears, anger, and attempts to cling. It takes fathers years to adjust to the adult status of their daughters.

The daughter and separation. A young woman in her twenties knows her parents are no longer necessary for her survival yet she is not always quite certain. She feels anxious about going out on her own and dreads leaving the father capable of protecting her and relieving her fears. Her attempt to go may be counteracted by anxiety, which completely paralyzes her. She may pick a fight with her father and depart in a rage.

Once physically away from her father, she must work on her part of the emotional separation from him. If she relies on him too much, turns to him with every problem, the necessary work of mourning and detaching her feelings from him will be interfered with. Some young women go to the opposite extreme and have nothing to do with their fathers. In assuming that any turning to him is a total surrender, they tightly close off their dependent wishes without working on them. Thus, they avoid experiencing the sadness of losing him, but they also subvert the emotional process of separation. They are unable to freely interact with their fathers as equal adults and their feelings are not truly freed up for others.

The young woman who tolerates the pain of separation from her father and recognizes his loss becomes a true adult who wants to see her father and is not afraid of being overwhelmed by his care or her desire for it. No longer afraid of being a dependent child in his presence, she is able to share her life generously with him. This is a source of continuing pleasure to both of them.

Anxiety and confusion are rampant in America for both sexes. Our society is evolving and changing so fast women do not know whether to be virgins, promiscuous, sex objects, brains, mothers, housewives, workaholics, married, divorced, single, faithful, adulterers, or to try to do it all at once in a high-powered seventy-hour-a-week career combined with attentive motherhood and warm wifeliness.

Should daughters be brought up to live close? What if they marry a corporate man who has to move a dozen times as his career advances? How will such a woman do with him? Or should she be brought up ready to move and travel? Does this mean preparing for separation and independence too early with the resulting cold and distant family that never truly enjoys one another?

How much should fathers and daughters separate in her twenties? Should a woman be prepared to stand on her own two feet, to adjust to a modern, lonely reality or alternatively be held in the warmth and support of the extended family with its emotional and economic interdependence? The upbringing for modern corporate life, for frequent moves and adjustments, is not the same as that for the woman who will live her whole life around the corner from her family. Yet both are normal and American.

There are two ways to look at normal — one is healthy, with an absence of psychopathology, while the second encompasses the ideal, the optimal in functioning.

There are no universal rules regarding how fathers and daughters should treat each other. But if their relationship prevents her from finding a man of her own, if it unduly influences her in the kind of man she finds or makes her relate badly to him, then something is wrong.

Self-awareness

All of us carry vestiges of youth that leave parts of us psychologically undeveloped. Even the most grown-up person retains elements of childhood and adolescent emotional and behavioral patterns. Since we like to think of ourselves as responsible we find our continuing immaturities embarrassing and difficult to face.

For a woman to understand herself she must be fully aware of the child, adolescent, and adult facets of her personality. She has to know when her immaturities are most likely to cloud her reasoning and to guard against their excessive sway. No one is able to eliminate all of the irrational elements within herself. Even if possible it would be unfortunate since emotions color our lives and make them more exciting and worthwhile.

Childlike and adolescent attributes are more likely to trouble us at home with our intimates than out in the world. (Sometimes the reverse is true and an oasis girl is comfortable with her autocratic husband but cannot cope with a promotion at work.) Our youthful traces show in different parts of our lives at various times. Understanding how and why a particular circumstance threatens rationality makes us more able to cope with it effectively.

For a woman to comprehend herself and overcome her difficulties, she must know what it is in herself that perpetuates them and under what circumstances they arise. Her problems may occur mainly with her long-term relationships, be primarily sexual, restricted to her career, or affect her overall self-esteem.

Hundreds of interviews, scores of them over prolonged periods, reveal that most women do not and cannot see their fathers accurately. They are unaware of the many ways he has shaped and continues to shape their lives long after they have left home. Thinking about their effect on each other, however, at different stages in their relationship, helps women clarify their fathers' continuing influence. Previously unnoticed paternal powers over the mind and actions become obvious. Only by the wisdom gained through calmly reviewing the touching of their two life cycles will she be able to free herself successfully of his hold.

1.3   Confessions from Four Mothers' Sons
Nyta Mann and Francis Elliott

Greg,[1] 38, is a carpenter

I do love my mother, but I only say that because I haven't seen her for a good few months. I love her intensely from a distance. As soon as she's actually *there*, with me, it's bearable for about half an hour, but then I can't stand it. I can't stand *her*. I turn into a 14-year-old again, and start resenting her clinging on to me — I know that isn't the truth, but it always feels like that. So whenever I do see her, I end up racked with guilt for being so horrible — but only after she's gone and it's too late.

All the time I was growing up, my father used to put me down a lot, so I relied on my mother to give me a sense of worth. But I don't think she ever realized that, which meant she could be very cruel without realizing it. Even now, I'm enormously affected by her opinions, although I fight against it.

My mum didn't often tell me she loved me when I was a kid. But that changed after my older brother died — he drowned in a boating accident when I was 25. Suddenly, I became the only son, and that made her more

---

1. All four names have been changed.

receptive to me. Since then, she's always telling me she loves me. She doesn't need an excuse.

But by then I'd got married and in a way it was too late. I think my wife filled the gap of love that my mum hadn't been able to show me, and I didn't need her so much any more.

I think that's got a lot to do with her becoming more open about showing affection towards me, and wanting me to do the same. But I've got my own life now, and I don't think you can suddenly change a relationship that's been built up over so long — for better or worse.

Tom, 21, is a sound engineer

She's quite a strong matriarchal figure; she's got a short temper and she's pretty moral. But she is very supportive of what I do. Of course, she doesn't know all that I do!

My relationship with her is getting much better. In my rebellious teens it was pretty bad. She was distraught that she didn't seem to be able to do anything right for me. But since I *was* rebelling, she couldn't possibly do anything right.

She asked me to leave home when I was 19. We stopped clashing then. The problem is that we are quite similar. Our tendency is to fly off the handle and exaggerate a lot; we are both artistic people.

Until I was seven, I was in a creche at the architectural college where my mother taught. I went to work with her; I saw her all day. But she gave up teaching for a while because my younger brother and I were quite a handful. He's got quite a good relationship with her — where I was always rebelling, he was always fulfilling her expectations.

All the things my parents argue about have arisen in my relationship with my girlfriend. She says she sees all my dad's faults in me.

I do talk to my mother about my relationships with women. It's easy because she takes my side — not very constructive, really. She tries to get involved, but in a hands-off way. She once vetoed a girlfriend of my brother's, but I think she was probably right. She tends to be a bit over-friendly to my girlfriends.

I do tell her I love her once in a while. I once stayed with a family in the US, and I remember them telling each other that they loved one another all the time. That has never happened in my family — only in making up after huge rows. It's not in my mother's personality to say it casually: she's far too objective.

David, 25, is a campaign manager for a PR company

We're very close and affectionate but it's not a very honest relationship. I don't show her all sides of myself. I never allow her to see my anger.

I'm her only son, and I'm much more tolerant of her than my sisters are. I spent an awful lot of time with her when I was younger. I was definitely her favorite.

She tries to have a good relationship with my girlfriends, which is weird, considering how affectionate she is with me. But at least she takes an interest. My father takes the view that no girl I bring home could be good enough for me and makes no effort to know them. Subconsciously, having a doting mother means I look for doting girlfriends.

As for being protective, the other night I was out at a comedy club with a couple of friends and their mother, and the compere made some remark about her. They had to be restrained from storming the stage. I would behave in exactly the same way.

It's just a part of the unconditional love thing. I don't try to impress her. When I was going through some rough times recently, she was the only one I broke down in front of. But you don't want them to see your weaknesses. There is that sense of sexual distance you want to retain: your dignity.

You are her little boy, then you are her young man, her handsome young man, her eligible young man, her "anyone would be crazy not to want to marry you" young man. It's not an expectation in the way a father has expectations of you; but a certain image of you. That's where the dishonesty comes from; presenting this image, protecting her from worrying about you. Unconditional love can be quite suffocating. You don't want to show her everything, for fear she will soak it all up and throw it back at you later.

John, 25, is unemployed. His mother was a single parent.

The only time I actually tell my mother I love her is when I sign a Christmas card, "Love from John." Otherwise I've never told her, and I can't ever remember her telling me. I suppose I have to say I *do* love her, in the sense that I'd do anything for her. I'm obliged to, as well as for love.

It's difficult to say what my mother's like, because first and foremost I think of her as "my mum," not as a separate personality. I've always thought of her as strong — a single mother having to make sure she could feed us, coping with financial worries. But she doesn't show *love*; she shows affection, in that she'd take care of me even now if need be. She never shows that she *needs* you, which is what love is really.

Everybody thinks their mum could've been a better mother. But from an early age, I understood the financial predicament she was in. When I was at school, I did hanker after the straight-up family unit, mum and dad, like all my friends had. The only family pride *I* had then was that my mum worked, and at a job — nursing — that wasn't as menial as some other mothers'.

I can't say we really get on together. We get on better since I left home, though. Now we sometimes have conversations, whereas before we hardly communicated at all. If she got a phone bill, she's just put it down in front of me, and I might get a rant, at the most. I was the same back.

Even now, I don't visit her for a chat or anything — I couldn't. When I went home the other day, I just went up to my old bedroom and read the paper. She was in the kitchen and pottering about the lounge. But we didn't talk to each other. That's quite normal for us.

It's always at the back of my mind that no matter how bad things are between us, if I was in deep trouble and shunned by everyone I knew, I could always go back home to mum.

1.4   Father Hunger

Andrew Merton

I AM GOING TO TELL YOU A SECRET ABOUT MEN. BUT FIRST LET ME REMIND you of something you already know, although, if you are a woman, part of you keeps denying it — the part that takes over late at night as you are drifting off to sleep, alone, and whispers things like, *How come I never have any luck with men? How come the only guys I ever meet are insensitive louts or oversensitive wimps or both rolled into one?* The implication being that everybody else is meeting men who are wonderful.

Here is the good news: There's nothing wrong with *you.*

The bad news (and this is what you already knew) is that the kind of man you want — one who is strong yet sensitive, virile, yet faithful, decisive yet considerate — really is in short supply. When it comes to intimacy — sustained, egalitarian intimacy — men are incompetent.

Maybe not *all* men. But a lot of them. Probably most of them. And (this may or may not comfort you) this condition is not confined to available men. A lot of married men are afflicted as well. Unfortunately, the same problems that prevent them from becoming truly intimate with their wives also frustrate their attempts to establish close relationships with their children — and this is true even if the men intend to take active roles in child rearing.

Now, here is the secret. It has two parts. Part one is dark, so dark that a lot of tough guys, men with well-developed pectorals and lots of notches on their bedposts, will go to great lengths to deny it, but it is true nonetheless: In terms of psychological development, there is not much difference between a macho and a wimp.

Oh, I know. On the surface they are opposites. Sylvester Stallone and Woody Allen. One uses force to achieve his goals, while the other manipulates through weakness. The wimp may be harder to spot, because he does seem genuinely concerned about *you:* only later do you realize that when he asks about your feelings, it's a cue to answer quickly and then ask him about *his.*

They have this in common: Both are incapable of dealing with a woman as an equal. Therefore, neither is able to enter into an intimate, stable partnership with a woman.

Experts have been telling us about men's inability to connect with women for a while now. In *The Seasons of a Man's Life,* psychologist Daniel J. Levinson warns, "Most men in their twenties are not ready to make an enduring inner commitment to wife and family, and they are not capable of a highly loving, sexually free, and emotionally intimate relationship." His studies show that, in this regard, a lot of men never *leave* their twenties. In her book *In a Different Voice,* psychologist Carol Gilligan pinpoints the different qualities men and women value in establishing relationships: "male and female voices typically speak of the importance of different truths, the former of the role of separation as it defines and empowers the self, the latter of the ongoing process of attachment that creates and sustains the human community." Levinson, Gilligan, and others point out that from the day he is born a boy is conditioned to be strong, stoic, and independent. Little in the culture at large tells him he should value intimacy or nurturing. The male cartoon heroes on television are lone warriors. (Voltron? He-Man? Tom Selleck? You might as well share your feelings with a B-52.) Girls' and women's magazines are full of articles about relationships. But you will not find articles on "How to Make This Relationship Last" in *Playboy.*

But here is something that, from experience, you may have trouble believing: A lot of men, deep down, want intimacy as much as you do. The trouble is, they don't know how to go about achieving it. And while the culture around them has a lot to do with this, some researchers are concluding that for an enormous number of men the inability to form intimate relationships may be traced to flawed relationships with their own fathers.

Which brings us to the second part of the secret: It is likely that both wimp and macho behavior are different manifestations of the same underlying psychological problem: the yearning for a father who never was.

Four years ago Harvard University psychoanalyst James Herzog invented the term *father hunger to* describe the psychological state of young children who had been deprived of their fathers through separation, divorce, or death. In his study, "On Father Hunger," published in *Father and Child,* he found that children thus affected — particularly boys — tended to have trouble controlling their aggressive impulses. He speculated that on a long-term basis "father hunger" appears to be a critical motivational variable in matters as diverse as caretaking, sexual orientation, moral development, and achievement."

In that study Herzog applied the term *father hunger to* men whose fathers had been physically absent. But based on recent work by psychoanalyst John Munder Ross and psychologist Samuel Osherson, as well as on my own interviews with fifty men, the term can be expanded to include the offspring of fathers who were physically present, but *psychologically* absent or inadequate. We can define "father hunger" as a subconscious yearning for an ideal father that results in behavior ranging from self-pity to hypermasculinity and frustrates attempts to achieve intimacy.

If a father is bad enough, he can short-circuit his daughter's capacity for intimacy as well. But that's another story. And while inadequate fathering may do damage to a daughter, it is more likely to wound a son and the wound is likely to be deeper and longer lasting.

And this is for the simple reason that a daughter can identify with her mother, while a son, at least beyond the age of two, can't. For it is at that age a boy begins to understand that he cannot be a woman. That is to say, he learns he cannot satisfy his creative and nurturing instincts directly by bearing a child. He must separate his own identity from that of his mother. He needs someone else to identify with.

According to John Ross of Cornell Medical College, the boy lucky enough to have a good father will develop a broad and flexible concept of what being a man is all about — a concept that includes tenderness, vulnerability, and open displays of feelings, alongside strength and fortitude. He will be secure enough to "expand and deepen his concept of manhood to encompass a variety of affects and activities that might otherwise become associated with the mother's exclusive province, with being womanly."

But chances are that if you are an adult between twenty and fifty-five, your father was not a big part of your childhood, or big only in a negative way; remote, angry, repressed, vindictive.

Maybe you have met a guy like Paul O'Shea. The image that comes to Paul's mind when he thinks of the pace of his life just before his breakdown in 1967 is the collage on the cover of the Beatles' *Sgt. Pepper* album: All those faces! Early Beatles, middle Beatles (John, somber in his epaulets, carrying a French horn), Diana Dors in gold lamé, the Mona Lisa, fifty, sixty faces jammed in next to one another. And the vaguely funereal floral arrangement on the foreground, with BEATLES spelled out in red hyacinths. An album cover to linger over, yet one must keep one's eyes moving, the way O'Shea himself was moving, trying to ward off failure and death.

Always he was extraordinarily handsome in an ascetic way, with a lean face softened by dark, liquid eyes. He grew up in New England, the son of a contractor. What went on between father and son was unspoken and horrible. The irregular beatings were the least of it. There was a house rule in matters involving the father: "You had to lose. Whatever it was. If you won, it was a violation of the family rule, and you don't . . . the consequences are too terrible to contemplate." He fixed a toaster once and was beaten for his troubles. His father had been unable to fix the toaster, had declared the toaster unfixable, and had been shown up. When things got unbearable, Paul took refuge with his mother, a stolid woman willing to deflect some of her husband's rage from her son to herself.

Paul had a high IQ, but he barely made it through college. At twenty-five, he found work teaching math and science at a private high school in Washington, D.C. The year was 1967. Antiwar fever was rising quickly. O'Shea plunged in — to the politics and the counterculture that went along with them. A new drug, a new woman every night. He was learning firsthand what Camus knew about debauchery: "One plays at being immortal, and after a few weeks one doesn't even know whether one can hang on till the next day." One night at a party he took LSD laced with angel dust. He was babbling, out of his head. The women he was with fled. But another woman stayed and talked him down. Her name was June. She took him home, and for two months she nursed him through seizures, out-of-body experiences, paranoia. At night, when he woke up screaming, she held him. At the end of it they were married. "She took over as my mother," says O'Shea.

A boy with an inflexible, authoritarian father might go one of two ways: He might rebel against his father with such rage that, in his rebelling, he becomes just as macho as the father. Or like Paul, he might succumb to his father's bullying, take shelter with his mother, and perpetually seek women who will mother him.

A boy with a father who is not a strong presence in the home is likely to have a dominant, if not domineering, mother. He, too, can go one of two ways: If he is strong, he will strive to become the man his father is not and in doing so, become overly aggressive, macho. Or he can succumb to his mother's will and perpetually seek women who will give him direction.

Terry Leonard's father was not a bad man — just a weak one with a tendency to exaggerate his abilities. Terry found this out early, with the help of the Brooklyn Dodgers. It was on a summer day in 1952, Ebbets Field, with the Cubs leading 5-2 in the eighth inning. Terry's father said, "Let's get out of here and beat the traffic."

"But the meat of the order is coming up," Terry said. "Furrillo, Snider, Campanella!"

"I know this game," said the father. "They won't score."

"Are you sure?"

"I'm sure."

Reluctantly, Terry accompanied his father out of the stadium.

One of the worst feelings in the world happens when you are walking away from the ballpark before the game is over and from inside you hear a roar. Campy hit one over the wall with two men on, and the Dodgers went on to win. Terry, thirteen, turned to his father and said, "You promised! You promised!" He hasn't forgiven the old man yet.

The father was a wholesale furrier who worked most of the time and spent the rest promoting himself. Once when the family was vacationing at the beach, Terry overheard his father chatting with a man. "My father was talking about his business, and he said, 'I have forty employees.' He had four. I couldn't believe it. Later I said, 'How come you told him you have forty employees?' He just smiled. 'Did I say that?' He disappointed me. I felt something profound. My father let me down."

Terry's father had a coronary when Terry was thirteen and subsequently began to drink and womanize. In 1964 his parents were divorced after thirty-seven years of marriage. Terry sought situations and relationships that would be unlike his parents' in any respect. The idea of marriage appealed to him in the abstract, but "when I was in high school I just thought about fucking as much as I could." In college and later as an administrator for a city welfare program, he made it a point to go to bed with women of every ethnic and religious background he could find. "It was a smorgasbord. Orientals, blacks. . . . I also came into contact with gays and lesbians." And his career changed almost as often as his girlfriends. He left social work to manage a motel. Then he became a stockbroker. Nor was this to be the final change.

And then suddenly, a few weeks before this thirtieth birthday, he married. It was time. He married a nice, quiet woman who he thought would be a good wife. And she thought he would be a good husband. It was as though they had read each other's resumes and each had thought, "Yeah, this ought to work." And it worked for a while, the way a machine works. But there is no intimacy in resumes or machines. After one child, they were divorced. They arranged joint custody of their son. Terry's wife became a radical feminist who wore bib overalls. Terry became a psychologist. In the process he learned that in trying to be someone other than his father — in trying to be first a stud and then a model husband and father — he was actually trying to *re-create* his father through himself in ideal form, which never works. He also learned this about both his father and himself: You cannot develop intimacy while attempting to project an image. The two are mutually exclusive, since image is concerned only with what is on the surface, while intimacy depends on the ability to share what is beneath.

Terry yearned for a father strong enough not to have to lie about his accomplishments. But even when a father has enough self-esteem to be honest with his children, "father hunger" is possible.

Frank Snyder, thirty-six, a successful lawyer, remembers worshipping his father and is happy with many of the values his father preached. "The force that drove him forward was not to make money, but to do the right thing. And to make a mark. I translated that into seeking justice. My father was an athlete, a big-time college football coach, and an air-force pilot. He came from the slums and made good. He was gone a lot. I remember him coming home from trips. . . . He had the right stuff, like Chuck Yeager. Trying to live up to him was a crushing feeling, although it might have been easier for me because I was not a good athlete, so there was no possibility of competing."

But intimacy was not something Frank thought about. "As a kid I didn't see getting married and having a family as a positive value. The things I did were masculine kinds of things. . . . Women were always interesting to me. I liked them. But I had difficulty with relationships. I always thought women needed relationships, settling down, more than men did." Frank's father's world was different from his own, remote and abstract. There was casual affection between father and son, but no intimacy in the sense of sharing their lives with one another. And Frank perceived this same relationship between his father and mother. The main business of the father's life was not here with the family, but somewhere else, somewhere outside, where life was played out in a broader sphere, which in his son's imagination was much more fascinating, much more exciting. But intimacy is not something that can be learned from an abstraction.

And this is why father hunger tends to be passed from generation to generation — why the son of a father-hungry father will be father hungry himself. For a man who fails to develop an intimate relationship with his wife has an extremely poor chance of doing so with his children. James Herzog is certain that, with men (but not necessarily with women), "adult-adult interaction predicts adult-child interaction" — that is, if a man is in touch with his own feelings and those of his wife, he is likely to be attuned to his children as well, but if his relationship with his wife is poor to begin with, the odds of his becoming a good father are long. Which is why the idea of having a baby to solidify a relationship is almost always a bad one. Even for a well-adjusted man, the transition from husband to husband-and-father, starting with pregnancy, can be daunting. Suddenly he is no longer the center of his wife's attention. He has fulfilled his biological function in reproduction and is reduced to a supporting role. His wife may become moody. Lovemaking is likely to become less frequent. "There's just some existential pain in becoming a father," Samuel Osherson says. "You're a deeply feeling person who's on the periphery."

Herzog studied a group of men whose wives had recently given birth and found that those who had been most supportive of their wives during pregnancy tended to be able to come to terms with their feelings about their own fathers (living or dead), while men who had never resolved these feelings "seemed to become progressively less able to participate in their expectant fatherhood." During the third trimester, many of these men, he says, "seemed . . . to make a career of the pursuit of . . . maleness." And he stresses again "that the male's caretaking line of development is fatefully affected by the presence of a good-enough male mentor-father, who helps the boy grieve the loss of his earlier identification [with his mother] and helps him see what a man is and what a man does."

Once the child is born, the problems are likely to intensify. The father, already insecure, feels displaced by the child. Ed Wyzanski, a computer technician in his late thirties, said his relationship with his wife deteriorated dangerously following the birth of their first child: "I remember being very angry at times. Holding the baby, trying to get him to stop crying, bouncing him, being so mad I wanted to do something violent. That was scary. I had never seen that in myself. I'd swing him around out of desperation, slam him back into the crib."

"I saw him as a rival for my wife's affections. Here was someone else getting the affection I had gotten. . . . I pushed myself on her sexually shortly after the birth. I regret that."

Wyzanski, who is in therapy, describes his own father as an insecure manipulator and misogynist. "If my mother was saying something he didn't like, he would glare and purse his lips. 'Shut up.' It was a very destructive relationship. I learned insecurity from him."

In his new book, *Finding Our Fathers,* Samuel Osherson sums up persuasive evidence of the psychological gap "between men and their fathers":

> Shere Hite's survey of 7,239 men revealed that "almost no men said they had been or were close to their fathers." Judith Arcana writes that in interviews for her book on mothers and sons only "about 1 percent of the sons had good relations with their fathers."

> The psychologist Jack Sternbach examined the father-son relationship in seventy-one of his male clients. He found fathers were physically absent for 23 percent of the men; 29 percent had psychologically absent fathers who were too busy with work, uninterested in their sons, or passive at home; 18 percent had psychologically absent fathers who were austere, moralistic, and emotionally uninvolved; and 15 percent had fathers who were dangerous, frightening to their sons, and seemingly out of control. Only 15 percent of Stenbach's cases showed evidence of fathers appropriately involved with their sons, with a history of nurturance and trustworthy warmth and connection.

Osherson adds that his own interviews with men in their thirties and forties convinced him "that the psychological or physical absence of fathers from their families is one of the great underestimated tragedies of our times."

The American man who grew up with a father who was affectionate, strong, and significantly involved in the upbringing of his children is so rare he is a curiosity. It has not always been this way. At the turn of the century the average father, whether affectionate or not, at least provided a concrete role model for his sons. Typically he worked on a farm or ran a store or business near home; typically, as a matter of course, he included his sons in his affairs. They went to work with him and were expected to follow in his footsteps or urged to do better.

But a series of historical events beginning with World War I altered this state of affairs dramatically. Beginning in 1917 and again in 1941, millions of U.S. men went off to war, leaving their families for as long as four years. They came home to sons who had grown up in their absence. And they came home to a changed society.

For a sizable portion of American men, the nature of work itself changed drastically after 1946. The ideal living situation was no longer an apartment next to the store but a house in the suburbs. In addition to spending eight or more hours away from his family at work, a man now spent an additional two, three, or even four hours commuting to and from his job. He came home to sleep. And on weekends he went bowling or golfing with his buddies. To his family he was a phantom.

And the nature of his job had changed from something that his son could identify with to something rendering the father even more remote, mysterious, and abstract than he already was. No longer could a boy say with confidence that his father was a cobbler or a merchant; now he might scratch his head and say, "Well, he deals in futures," or "He's a consultant," with no understanding of what that meant. In his 1968 book, *Fatherhood: A Sociological Perspective,* Leonard Benson declared the separation of the father from the rest of the family complete and self-perpetuating:

> Mother is the primary parent. She is first by popular acclaim, in actual household practice, and in the minds of students of family life. . . . The fact that the father is assigned the role of breadwinner rather than that of caring for the children guarantees that boys will not develop and cultivate skills appropriate to child care. The primary skills of fathers are often beyond the understanding or even appreciation of contemporary children, and their style in social relations is usually conditioned by the demanding, singularly adult world of "work."

Today's adult males grew to maturity under those conditions. But Benson was wrong to predict that the situation would remain unchanged forever, because even when a man is pigeonholed as the worker, the achiever, the distant voice of authority, he has creative and nurturing instincts: to the extent that they are suppressed in the service of a macho image, he is not whole. All it takes are the right conditions to bring these instincts to the surface. And those conditions now exist.

The women's movement was in its infancy when Benson wrote his book. Women were only beginning to discover that they were not whole, that they too possessed traits encouraged only in men: assertiveness, independence, aptitudes for an enormous variety of occupations outside the home. During the intervening eighteen years they have done something about it — in schools, in consciousness-raising groups, in therapy. In unprecedented numbers women have tapped these previously latent reserves, have made themselves whole. And men in large numbers are beginning to understand: whole women want whole men. Macho men and wimps need not apply.

Despite Rambo, values are changing. In 1970 only 30 percent of Americans believed that it was important for fathers to spend as much time with their children as mothers do. In 1986 the figure is 91 percent, according to the Ethan Allen Report on the Status of the American Family. Another recent study by *USA Today* found that 65 percent of men think they are closer to their kids than their fathers were. Within the past fifteen years scholars and the media have pronounced men's private and family lives fit subjects for investigation. The pressure is on for men to change. And men who grew up in the sixties and seventies have a hunger to *be* the father they never had.

Were it not for this pressure, father hunger as a concept probably would not exist. The raw material was supplied by men going into therapy, talking about their difficulties in forming and maintaining relationships and with fathering.

Fortunately, once a man discovers that his unresolved frustrations about his relationship with his father are causing some of his distress, he is in a position to change. Terry Leonard, Paul O'Shea, Frank Snyder, and Ed Wyzanski are among thousands of men who are working to come to terms with these feelings. They have had varying degrees of success, but in each case the recognition of a problem and the desire to resolve it has forced the man to move and to change.

By coming to terms with their feelings about their fathers, men are becoming better fathers themselves. And in doing so, they are breaking the cycle of father hunger.

Paul O'Shea no longer treats June like his mother. The change has been recent, and June is not sure she trusts it yet. But she says she's enjoying it while she can. They have a son and a daughter now, and Paul is working hard to be the kind of father his own father was not. The transition has not been simple. He's been in and out of therapy for years. And he's come to an understanding with his father.

Shortly before Christmas, Paul sat in his small apartment with his two children in his arms. "I have been a little-boy husband for a lot of years. Never again. I have made it. With a little boy of my own and a baby girl sleeping on my shoulder." He sat silently for a while. Then he said, "My father is over seventy now. He's mellowed a bit. He told me that when *his* father was dying, he wanted to tell him he loved him, but he couldn't. He cried about that. I took a chance, sitting with him at the kitchen table." He paused, took a deep breath. "I told him I loved him."

Marriage: What Are My Expectations?

2.1 Expectations

Kathleen Fischer Hart and Thomas N. Hart

BILL AND CINDY HAD A DREAM ABOUT HOW THEIR MARRIAGE WAS GOING to be. Bill had started dreaming about marriage already in high school, when he was experiencing loneliness and all relationships seemed superficial and phony. Someday he would have a very special friend and lover, and they would do everything together. He had visions of laughter and much physical affection, of sitting close and watching TV in the evenings, or just talking, of making love often and with great tenderness. He would share all of himself, honestly and without fear, and so would she. They would be intensely interested in one another, and feel, probably for the first time in their lives, completely happy.

Cindy's dream was similar. All her life she had longed for someone to whom she could be special, who would treat her with respect and be gentle and tender to her. She had visions of going places and doing exciting things with her husband, of being told frequently that she was beautiful and that she looked nice, of really being Number One in somebody's life. Her vision of marriage with Bill did not include fighting. Her parents had fought a great deal, but she saw that as her mother's fault and she did not plan on being like her mother. And she and Bill had a very good record on that score in their year and a half of going together. Bill and Cindy shared their dreams, and found that they agreed. Anticipation ran high.

The disillusionment that came in the first year of marriage was awful. Cindy cried a lot, and Bill walked with a heavy heart. Both had outside jobs

29

that first year. Bill would come home stressed out, looking for warmth and affection from Cindy. But Cindy would be tired too, and, if things had not gone well during the day, irritable besides. Bill would want to share, but Cindy showed less interest than before. She accused him of not listening to her. They watched TV all right, but the warmth was missing. Bill would be looking forward to ending the day with lovemaking, but Cindy seemed more concerned with getting a good night's sleep. It bothered Bill that Cindy showed so little sexual interest in him. What surprised Cindy was that Bill was no longer as affectionate as he used to be, no longer looked at her in the same way or told her she was beautiful. He didn't embrace her as often, and failed to notice many of the little things she did to make their home more attractive. He came on, it seemed, only when he wanted sex.

There were other problems too. The cost of renting and furnishing a place and keeping two cars going took all the money they had, and there were no trips and few dinners out. They had much difficulty finding other couples they both enjoyed being with, and who seemed to be comfortable with both of them. And Cindy had trouble getting along with Bill's mother, who showed them a lot of attention and freely shared her advice with Cindy about what Bill needed and about how to manage a household. Bill was not particularly fond of his mother, but he tended to defend her against Cindy's criticisms. The result of all these unexpected developments was a lot of arguing in that first year, and much more silence than either of them was comfortable with. Cindy could hardly believe that her marriage showed some of the same patterns her parents' marriage did, and she was doing some of the very things she hated her mother for doing. Bill, for his part, was haunted with the question: Have I made a big mistake?

Bill and Cindy's experience is not at all unusual. Probably most couples expect more of marriage than it can deliver, and have to undergo a painful disillusionment. We need our dreams, or we might settle for less than we could have. But in the area of romantic love especially, an unreality can creep into our dreaming, setting us up for acute disappointment. Bill's and Cindy's dreams flow from deep longings in the human heart. All of us want more intensity and excitement in life, and more love. But these longings of the heart may more suggest what awaits us in the next life than what we will find in marriage. Perhaps if we look at some of the most common unrealistic expectations for marriage, and revise them, we will feel better about what we actually have in marriage and see more possibilities in it.

1. We will do everything together. This might be nice, but it cannot be. My interests are bound to diverge from yours, and yours from mine, in various areas. I will want male companionship at times, and you female, without each other's company. We will not share all the same activities because we do not share all the same interests. In fact, in the same way that we used to escape together from the routine of our individual lives, we will probably want to escape singly at times from the routine of being together.

2. *We will always feel the same way about things.* About some things, yes. About other things, no. We are unique individuals. The families in which we were raised were different "culturally," and we are stamped by those differences. When we marry, two "cultures" come together under the same roof. Seeing eye to eye with one another may be as difficult at times as it is for Israelis and Arabs or Westerners and Orientals. Values are different. Customs are different. You make little of birthdays; to me, my birthday is the most important day of the year. You express anger openly and strongly; I avoid conflict and hold angry feelings in. You are physically affectionate; I was raised in a home in which we very rarely touched each other. Each of us brings a different pair of glasses and a different set of habits to the unfolding drama of life. The key is going to be learning to live and let live, accepting and blessing our diversity, and not trying to establish who is right and who is wrong.

3. *You will always be intensely interested in me, and I in you.* One of the marvelous things about being in love is that this is the way things are for a while. I am intensely interested in you, and you in me. You may be the first person I have ever known in such depth. You are most certainly the first person who has ever found me so fascinating. And when we are together, it is usually a special time, a temporary escape from our humdrum separate existences at home, at school, or at work. But we get used to each other. If we are not careful, we may even begin to take each other for granted. In the best of circumstances, I hear you say the same things many times over, and you reach a stage where you can give my whole speech on any subject if I provide but the cue. Each of us will continue to give birth to new things as our lives unfold, and it would be a shame not to notice. But there will never be so much so fast as there was at the beginning. So we had better be sure we have each other's attention before beginning to speak.

4. *There will be a lot of sex and warm physical closeness.* If you are driving down the freeway and the couple in the car ahead of you is sitting so close that you wonder if they are one person or two, they are probably not married. This is not because married couples do not love each other, but only because they are a little more relaxed about it most of the time. Being together has become a way of life. And sex is just a part of it. Somebody has to go out and buy food once in a while, and walk the dog. Even the intensity of the first sexual encounters is a little hard to sustain. For sex lives in a total context and varies with feelings and energy. It is almost impossible to have a very accurate picture of all this before marriage. But one can safely expect that things will not be as expected.

5. You will meet all my deeper needs, and I yours. Actually, the first part of this expectation is the more common one, and it is not fully conscious. So when I feel misunderstood in the marriage, or still lonely at times, or unable to get you interested in my favorite activity, I feel as if you have let me down. But am I being fair? Did you promise that you would meet all my deeper needs? Could you possibly? No. Each of the parties to a marriage needs to live in a larger social world and to draw on resources outside the marriage, as well as inside, for life and love. When we try to get our mates to do it all, we imprison and drain them, and sooner or later they will probably run for their lives.

6. The character defects I now see in you will disappear under the influence of my love. This would be wonderful. But it is most unlikely. Alcoholics do not usually recover by marriage. Neatniks remain neatniks. Those who tend to be lazy are not suddenly energized. And moody folks tend, alas, to remain moody. In fact, you may have seen less of your mate's undesirable qualities during courtship, when both of you were on your good behavior.

People do change in life, especially if they work at it and are loved well. Marriage is a growthful state. But if you want a sense of how hard it is to change habits that are rooted deeply in our personalities, look at yourself and how many years you have struggled to change some of the things you don't like about yourself. Most likely, the "character defects" you see in your mate will persist a good long time, even if the two of you genuinely love one another.

7. The details of our living will fall naturally into place. Alas, it is precisely the details that stick in the machinery. It is the wet towel in the middle of the bathroom floor, the near empty gas tank, and the dirty dishes in the sink that test the durability of the bond. If you would close your mouth when you chew, refrain from profanity, and close the door quietly when you come and go, we would have no problems. If we could agree on the arrangement of the furniture, a comfortable temperature, and a proper time to go to bed, we might make fifty years. It is precisely the details that call for tolerance and negotiation.

8. We will probably never fight. We know a couple who were terribly surprised, even shocked, when they had their first fight. They had never fought before they got married, and were sure they never would. And their first fight was not a quiet little one; it was a noisy big one that left them nursing their wounds and still arguing in their heads in separate beds.

Why the dreadful eruption? They had not dealt with occasions as they arose, but allowed irritations to build up. Each was feeling, below the level of immediate offenses, some painful disillusionments with how their life together was actually shaping up. And they were as yet unskilled at expressing negative feelings and working through differences. Do good couples fight? Yes, in some way or other. Some have dramatic flareups, go apart and think about it, and come back and make up, closer for the conflict. Others deal with their differences in quieter exchanges and get the message just as well. What is important is that differences be dealt with. It is better to "fight it out" in some way than to try to bury things. Even between those who love each other deeply and truly, anger and conflict are inevitable. They can be very growthful.

9. *We enter this marriage with pretty much the same expectations.* Actually we do not. We have some of the same expectations, and we have talked about them. But we have many different ones too, unspoken because largely unconscious. A man's sexism, for instance, is usually unconscious; it is in the culture, and he has simply absorbed it. And culture, as we have said, is the key to understanding this whole matter. Both parties to a marriage were raised in a family "culture," and from it they learned many things about what a man's and woman's role are, how the house is kept up, children raised, time spent separately or together. Many of these expectations will appear in the present marriage only as circumstances unfold. They cannot all be declared beforehand because they are simply taken for granted.

There is another unsettling thing about expectations. They are fluid, and some of them change even in the first two years. A man may have entered marriage thinking he wanted children, and his feelings change. A woman may have thought she wanted to be mother and homemaker, only to find her inclinations moving toward more education or a job outside the home. In this respect, marriage is like a young sapling which has to bend with the wind and keep adapting to changing conditions. The key to longevity in marriage too is flexibility.

10. *Our marriage will be different from all the bad ones we have seen.* It probably will, being both better and worse. It could be much better than many, but that depends on a lot of hard work and some favorable breaks rather than on the simple fact that it is we, not they. All those other folks too started out very much in love and full of dreams. Human sinfulness and limitation wore them down. And these things, like the air we breathe, are in every household.

Where do all these unrealistic expectations come from? They come partly from the deep longings of the human heart, as we have said. They are born also of the experience of falling in love. Falling in love is wonderful, and much of the world's great poetry and music have been spun from the experience. People in love need no one and nothing else. There is discovery, excitement, and a feeling of fullness. Here is someone I can talk with, be genuinely myself with, be understood and accepted by. Here at last is a friend and lover. My world is tremendously expanded, my daily life marvelously enlivened. Being apart leaves a terrible ache, and we languish and yearn to be together again. When together, I am reflected back to myself with warmth and enthusiasm, and I can hardly help feeling whole. And I suddenly have something to do in life: to love and be loved by you. There is someone to go places with, someone to hold and be held by, someone with whom to be lifted above the dullness and difficulties of life. For a time, the experience is all-absorbing.

Unfortunately, it does not last. What is substantial in it can endure, but there are elements of unreality in it which must gradually yield to the harsher light of day. When we are in love, more sober folk indulge us with patience. Psychologists warn us that we project a lot. We impose an idealized image on our partners so that we cannot see them as they are. The wisdom of the ages tells us that love is blind, and people who are in love are often "madly" in love. But reality gradually regains the ascendancy, and we discover that our partner is an ordinary mortal, and a sinner at that. If this happens after marriage, the awakening is an added part of the difficulty of adjusting. If we have been together long enough before marriage that we are no longer in love, at least not so madly, the adjustment will be easier.

Loving someone over the years is a very different matter from being in love. It is much less an emotional state, much more a choice. Falling in love is something that *happens* to a person; loving someone is something a person *chooses* to do or not do. And so, in most marriages, there dawns a morning when one finds oneself in sober reflection. One man we know put it down this way in his journal.

> I know you pretty well now. I used to think I understood you completely; now I wonder if I understand you very much at all. There are many things I can share with you, but some I find it hard to. I think the same holds true for you, so our communication has its gaps.

> I haven't gotten all I hoped for when I married you. There are some things you just cannot be for me. There are also some things about you that really bother me. I wasn't fully aware of them when I married you. Sometimes I look around and wonder if I wouldn't be happier with someone else. That is probably an illusion though. And I realize that you could say all the same things about me.

> I am going to go on loving you. You are a good person, and I love many things about you. You have loved me, as best you can. I need that. I think you need my love too. I know I have a lot to learn about loving, about getting outside myself, about acceptance. I'd really like to do it with you. We've shared so much. I know that any marriage I would get into would eventually come down to this same thing: the choice to love or to move out in quest of greener pastures. I am going to work at the relationship we've got. I'm going to keep trying to listen and understand, to meet your needs insofar as I can, to be there for you. You can count on me.

Lord, help me to do this. Teach me to love Ginger the way you do.

At this, the marriage takes a large growth-step forward. It becomes mature. As the years go on, it will keep coming into question from time to time. The commitment will have to be made over again, especially at critical junctures. From a religious standpoint, these crises or passages are moments when the mystery of death/resurrection is experienced. The marriage as it was dies, and it rises again to new life. It takes courage and surrender to go through it, and hope in God's power to regenerate and renew. But this is the law of growth, the only access to deeper, richer levels of living.

If the ideas with which this chapter opened are unrealistic expectations of marriage, what might we more realistically expect? Perhaps some metaphors can help us get at the reality of it.

1. The German philosopher Nietzsche mused that marriage is a long conversation. So marry a friend, he said.

2. Marriage is not gazing at one another, but looking outward together in the same direction.

3. Marriage is a long walk two people take together. Sometimes the terrain is very interesting, sometimes rather dull. At times the walk is arduous, for both persons or for one. Sometimes the conversation is lively; at other times, there is not much to say. The travelers do not know exactly where they are going, nor when they will arrive. But they share everything they have. And they find that it is a lot more fun, and also a great help, to walk with a companion rather than alone.

4. Marriage is a continual compromise, with life and with each other.

5. Marriage is a covenant of love and fidelity, in good times and in bad. It mirrors the covenant of love and fidelity, in good times and in bad, which God has with each human being. This is the New Testament's metaphor for marriage.

If I am married, and find myself with an expectation which is not being met, what can I do? I can examine it and see if it might fall into the category of the unrealistic. If so, I can quietly let go of it. If it seems realistic to me, I can share it with my mate. I make my needs and wants known. Sometimes this is all it takes to make new things happen. Sometimes the situation is more difficult.

A woman came for marriage counseling who had been married some fifteen years. She was deeply frustrated because her husband would not share his feelings with her, but would only talk about his business, the weather, and other matters of fact. He loved her. But no matter how hard she tried, and she had been doing it for fifteen years, she could not get him to share his feelings. Deeply frustrated, she had finally moved out, and then come for counseling. A few joint sessions with both husband and wife convinced us that even though the man had good will, given his background, his habits, and his age, this man was simply not going to become a sharer of feelings. So we asked the woman to come in alone, and we reviewed her options with her: (1) She could leave this man and look for someone who would share his feelings with her. (2) She could go back to him and keep working on him (though fifteen years of this had been fruitless). (3) She could go back to him and love him as he was. But if she chose this last, it would mean renouncing the deepest dream she had had for her marriage.

Those three options are always the options, in one form or another, in situations of dissatisfaction. (1) You can leave the situation and look for a better one. (2) You can remain in the situation and keep striving for what you want. (3) You can remain in the situation, accepting it, and letting part of your dream go.

The woman in the story chose the last option, because she could not conceive of living the rest of her life without this man, whom she loved, and because she realized that she was not going to change this thing in him. And the sequel was a happy one. When she stopped pressuring him to deliver what he scarcely could, he began to show her love in new and unexpected ways. In making the choice she did, she died a painful death, a death to her own expectations. And they both rose to new life.

2.2 Two Reasons Marriages Fail
Gary Smalley

1. Men and women enter marriage with "storybook" expectations and limited training.

I once asked a college girl what kind of man she would like to marry. "I'd like for him to be able to tell jokes, sing and dance, and stay home at night."

"You don't want a husband," I told her. "You want a television set."

Her visions of a husband reveal one of the most common reasons marriages fail. We marry with unrealistic expectations and few, if any, caring skills. In fact, most of us are rather fuzzy when it comes to our mates' real needs.

Isn't it ironic that a plumber's license requires four years of training, but a marriage license requires nothing but two willing bodies and sometimes a blood test? Since most of us bounce through the educational corridors without any basic communication courses, many men marry with absolutely no knowledge of how to build a meaningful relationship. In short, most men have no idea how to love their wives in a way that makes both of them happy.

Recently I asked five divorced women, individually, "If your husband began treating you in a consistently loving manner, would you take him back?"

"Of course I would," each replied. But, unfortunately, none had hope that her husband would ever be like that.

Because I knew one of the men personally, I had to concur with his wife's hopelessness. If he were willing to try, he could win her back. Unfortunately, he wasn't interested in learning.

"What he doesn't realize is that a lot of women are as responsive as puppies," one woman explained to me. "If he'd come back and treat me with tenderness, gentleness, and understanding, I'd take him back tomorrow."

How sad that we men don't know how to win our wives back or even how to keep from losing them. How can we win their affection, their respect, their love and cooperation when *we don't even know where to begin*? Instead of trying to learn what it takes to mend a cracked marriage, most of us would rather jump on the divorce bandwagon. We violate the relationship laws inherent in marriage, and then we wonder why it all goes sour. But we wouldn't wonder if the law of aerodynamics sent a one-winged airplane plummeting to the earth.

Imagine yourself an aerospace engineer working for NASA. Your job is to put several men on the moon, but something goes wrong halfway through their flight. You wouldn't dream of walking out on the entire project because something went wrong. Instead, you and the other engineers would put your heads together, insert data into the computer, and . . . *voilà*! You would work night and day to try to discover the problem and make all the vital adjustments to get that spacecraft back on course or help the men return to earth. If the project had failed altogether, you still wouldn't forsake it. You would study what happened and modify it to avoid similar problems in the future.

Like the spacecraft, your marriage is subject to laws that determine its success or failure. If any of these laws are violated, you and your wife are locked into orbits, destined to crash. However, if during the marriage you recognize which law or principle you are violating and make the necessary adjustments, your marriage will stay on the right course.

2. Men and women lack understanding about the general differences between men and women.

I would venture to say that most marital difficulties center around one fact — men and women are TOTALLY different. The differences (emotional, mental, and physical) are so extreme that without a *concentrated effort* to understand them, it is nearly impossible to have a happy marriage. A famous psychiatrist once said, "After thirty years of studying women, I ask myself, 'What is it that they really want?'" If this was his conclusion, just imagine how little we know about our wives.

You may already be aware of some of the differences. Many, however, will come as a complete surprise. Did you know, for instance, that virtually every cell in a man's body has a chromosome makeup entirely different from those in a woman's body? How about this next one? Dr. James Dobson says there is strong evidence indicating that the "seat" of the emotions in a man's brain is wired differently than in a woman's. By virtue of these two differences alone, men and women are miles apart emotionally and physically.

2.3   The Meaning of Marriage
Evelyn Eaton Whitehead and James D. Whitehead

THE WORD "MARRIAGE" REFERS TO MANY THINGS. WE CAN USE THE WORD TO mean our own experience of the day-to-day relationship we share. The word can also mean the social institution of matrimony, which has legal definition and rights and duties that are regulated by the state and sanctioned in many religious traditions through special rites and ceremonies. Between these two senses of the word — marriage as my experience and marriage as a social institution — there are other meanings as well. Marriage is a relationship; marriage is a commitment; marriage is a lifestyle.

When we speak of marriage as a *relationship* we focus on the quality of the bond that exists between us, our mutual love. The *commitment* of marriage refers to the promises we make to do "whatever is necessary" to deepen and develop this love and, in this love, to move beyond ourselves in creativity and care. The *lifestyle* of marriage describes the patterns that we develop as we attempt to live out these promises — our choices among values and activities, the organization of our daily life, our patterns in the use of time and money and the other resources we have. These three facets of marriage are overlapping and interrelated. Each contributes richly to the complexity of our life together and to the satisfaction we experience in marriage. And, as we are becoming more aware, none of these aspects of our marriage is ever finished or static. Each is in movement, in an ongoing process of realization and development or decline.

The Relationship of Marriage — Mutual Love

Mutual love is the heart of the process of marriage as we envision it today. This has not always been the case. In patriarchal understandings of marriage the wife is more property than partner. Vestiges of this "wife as possession" are still to be found (often embodied in laws and customs surrounding sexuality in marriage) but the movement toward mutuality continues in the way many married people choose to live and, gradually, in the larger social definitions of marriage as well.

The expectations for love in marriage today are high. The "ideal" of married love for most people includes romance, sex, friendship and devotion. Romance: we want the emotional and physical attraction that we experienced early in our relationship to continue through our married years. Sex: we want our lovemaking to be lively and mutually satisfying, enhanced by a deepening responsiveness to each other's preferences and needs. Friendship: we want to continue to like each other, to enjoy each other's company, to find in each other the sources of comfort and challenge, of solace and stimulation that we need for continuing growth. Devotion: we want to be able to "count on" one another, to give our trust in the deep conviction that it shall not be betrayed, to experience the awesome responsibility and transforming power of holding someone else's well-being as important to us as our own and to know that we, too, are held in such care.

These are not easy accomplishments. With these high expectations come equally high demands. In a relationship that is mutual, I must be ready to give these benefits as well as to receive them. And for many of us these emotional benefits are sought and expected only in marriage. We have no other so serious or so sustained an adult relationship.

Marriage did not always carry such high emotional demands. Wives and husbands did not generally expect to be one another's chief companion or best friend. Each could be expected to develop a range of social relationships — in the extended family, in the neighborhood, in the workplace, in clubs and churches and associations — that provided support and a sense of belonging to complement the marriage relationship. Today our involvement in these wider circles seems to have slipped. Economic and geographic mobility can cut into, even cut off, ties with family and neighborhood. The workplace is increasingly competitive; our relationships there seem of necessity to remain superficial. No one wants to take the risk of deeper friendship with a potential rival. And here, too, mobility plays a part in keeping these relationships light. We know it is likely that one or both of us may move to another job. Many associations — political parties, civic groups, churches — seem to have lost the consensus they formerly enjoyed. In these groupings today we are likely to experience polarization rather than a sense of belonging. Now it is often only from my spouse and, perhaps, my children that I expect any deep or continuing emotional response. This expectation has enriched the experience of mutuality in marriage, but it has also added to its strains. There are few of us today who would choose a style of marriage that did not include friendship and mutuality among its chief goals. But we have not given much attention to pressures that are inevitable in the companionate marriage or to the resources that may be required for us to live well this style of mutual love.

Marriage brings us in touch with our incompatible hopes for human life. It is useful to look at some of these incompatibles — the tensions and ambiguities that are inevitable as we attempt to live as complex a relationship as marriage. These tensions exist not simply because I am "selfish" or my spouse is "unreasonable" or "immature." These tensions are built into the experience of relationship — most relationships, but especially relationships as encompassing as marriage.

Security and adventure are both significant goals in adult life. We seek the stability of established patterns, and yet we are attracted by the new and the unknown. Often we sense these goals in opposition; life seems to force our choice of one over the other. To seek adventure means to risk some of the security I have known; to be secure means to turn away from some of life's invitations to novelty and change. Most of us learn to make these choices, but an ambivalence remains. At times, when the pull of security is strong, change may be seen as uninviting or even dangerous. A preference for stability is then easy to sustain. But at other times the appeal of change will be compelling and stability will seem a synonym for boredom and stagnation.

One of the ongoing tensions of marriage concerns this conflict between freedom and security, adventure and stability. I want to deepen the love and life we share, and I want to be able to pursue other possibilities that are open to me, unencumbered by the limits that come with my commitment to you. I need change and novelty and challenge; I need what is predictable and familiar and sure. I want to be close to you in a way that lets me share my weaknesses as well as my strengths, and I want to be strong enough to stand apart from you and from the relationship we share. Again, the presence of these incompatibles is not, of itself, cause for concern. These are normal, expectable, inevitable. But, then, neither is it surprising that the process of mediating among these needs generates considerable stress.

The commitment of marriage takes us to the heart of this ambivalence between stability and change. In marriage we say both "yes" and "no" — "yes" to each other and to the known and unknown possibilities that will be a part of our life together as it unfolds, "no" to the known and unknown possibilities that our life together will exclude. Marriage for a lifetime demands both stability (that we hold ourselves faithful to the promises we have made) and change (that we recognize the changing context in which our promises remain alive). We can anticipate that at different points in our marriage we will experience this ambivalence — sometimes celebrating the new developments in our life together, sometimes resisting these changes; sometimes grateful for the stability of our love, sometimes resenting its "sameness."

Marriage invites me to recognize these ambiguities of my own heart as I attempt to choose a style of life and love in which both to express myself and to hold myself accountable. Without commitment and choices, I know I remain a child, but that realization seldom makes the process of choice any easier.

The Commitments of Marriage — Priority and Permanence

The commitments of marriage are the promises we make. In many ways it is these mutual promises that transform our experience of love into marriage — an enduring relationship of mutual care and shared life-giving. Both by our choice and by the momentum of its own dynamics, marriage takes us beyond where we are now. It projects us into the future. Through the hopes we hold for our life together we condition the future — we begin to mold and shape it. We open ourselves to possibilities, we make demands, we place limits, we hold each other in trust.

Our commitments, of course, do not control the future. We learn this mighty lesson as we move through adult life, invited by the events of our days to give up one by one our adolescent images of omnipotence. An illusory sense of the degree to which we can control our own destinies may have once served us well, energizing us to move beyond indecision and enter the complex world of adult responsibility. But maturity modifies both our sense of power and our sense of control. We are both stronger and weaker than we had known. Our promises are fragile, but they still have force. It is on this vulnerable strength of human commitment that we base our hope. And it is through our commitments that we engage the future.

The commitments of marriage are the promises we make — to ourselves, to one another, to the world beyond — to do "whatever is necessary" so that the love that we experience may endure; even more, that it may flourish. Our own relationship of love is, we know, similar to that which other couples share. But it is in many ways special, unique to who we are, peculiar to the strengths and needs and history we have. Our commitments, then, will reflect features in common with most marriages as well as the demands and possibilities that are particularly our own.

Two of the commitments that have been seen to be at the core of marriage are sexual exclusivity and permanence. The social meaning of these commitments has fluctuated across time. Stress on the importance of the woman's virginity at marriage and her sexual availability only to her husband after marriage is particularly strong in cultures where property and social status are transferred according to the male line of descent. It is important here that there be no confusion about paternity. And strict regulation of the woman's sexual experience is one way to keep the facts of paternity clear.

There are other instances where the stress on sexual exclusivity is intended to regulate the wife's behavior but not, or not to the same degree, the husband's. This double standard of sexual morality, which looks with some leniency on a married man's "fooling around" while it castigates a married woman as a wanton or an adulteress, has been tied closely with those understandings of marriage that see the wife as, in some ways, the property or possession of her husband.

In many current marriages the commitment to sexual exclusivity has expanded toward an expectation that neither spouse shall have any emotional involvement outside the marriage itself. By conscious decision or simply by circumstances, the couple or the small family unit depend exclusively upon one another for emotional sustenance. They have become an emotional island, apart. Neither wife nor husband has any other substantive adult friendship; their network of social acquaintances is shifting and somewhat superficial. Each may also feel that to need or seek support from someone other than the spouse is itself a kind of "infidelity." Sometimes this caution in exploring wider friendship is rooted in a fear of the "inevitable" sexual overtones of relationships between women and men. "Better not to start anything than to find this friendship slipping into an affair." Sometimes it responds to real insecurity or jealousy in one or both spouses. Sometimes, however, this insistent emotional exclusivity is more an expression of what couples judge to be "expected" of marriage. Emotions and needs, personal values and concerns — these are of the substance of my "private life." Family is the unit of private life in our society. It is to my family, especially to my spouse, that I retreat from the arbitrary and impersonal "public world." Increasingly, colleagues at work, people in the neighborhood, fellow citizens are all seen as part of the "public world." My relations with them are limited, objective and often hostile. There is little opportunity and less ability to share with them any meaningful part of life. It is in marriage that I expect that my subjectivity will be nourished. Here, and possibly here alone, "who I am" is more important than "what I can do." As the polarization of the subjective and the objective worlds, the realms of the private and the public, increases, so do the pressures for emotional exclusivity in marriage.

Many judge that the pressures of the emotionally exclusive marriage ultimately work against its development and permanence. Permanence is the second of the commitments that have generally described marriage. Here, too, the promise has been experienced differently at different times. Seldom has this expectation been absolute. Cultures and legal systems, while stressing the significance of permanence to the interpersonal experience and the legal contract of marriage, have also stipulated a variety of circumstances under which this commitment can be set aside. Sometimes childlessness was justification, frequently adultery has been sufficient cause. Religious conversion, desertion, physical abuse, psychological immaturity, emotional illness

— each has been seen as of sufficient weight to justify the dissolution of marriage, whether through annulment or divorce.

The commitment of permanence has also had different psychological meaning. As recently as a century ago "marriage for a lifetime" often did not last very long. The woman's death in childbirth ended many marriages. An average life expectancy of some fifty years meant that many marriages ended in mid-life. In 1870, for example, a married woman could expect that her husband would die before her youngest child would leave home. Today, increasingly, couples can anticipate some twenty or more years together, alone, after the children have left the family household and are on their own. Movement into this time of "post-parental intimacy" is hard on some marriages. Couples may be surprised to find that, without their shared concern for parenting, they have little left of mutuality. They face the challenge of developing anew a life in common, one that is adequate to the reality of each partner now and to the possibilities that are present in their relationship. Other couples have been aware of a deteriorating relationship and yet have chosen to remain together through the years of their most active family responsibilities. These past, they judge there is no further bond to hold them together.

The strains on permanence can be experienced earlier in marriage as well. The accelerated pace of social change today is reflected in the experience of personal change. As we approach marriage we judge — to some degree correctly, to some degree in error — that we "fit" together, that we shall be able to offer each other the resources of love and support and challenge that will enable us to find and to give life. And then we change, sometimes each of us and in ways that enrich our mutual commitment. Sometimes, though, there is not such synchrony. One of us changes in ways that are threatening or seem unfair to the other. Each of us develops — perhaps gradually, perhaps suddenly — in directions that lead us apart and leave us without a clear sense of how we can be together now. Are there ways we might stay better in touch over the course of change so that we are not so taken by surprise? Or must the loss of our relationship be the price we pay for growth?

There are those who suggest that the prevalence of divorce among us today has dissolved our expectations of permanence in marriage. Young people approaching marriage, it seems, do not expect it to last. And, so the argument goes, married people today consider divorce a ready option, one which they anticipate that they, too, will use. There are, obviously, people of whom this characterization is true. But the effect of the increasing incidence of divorce on the expectations of permanence in marriage is more complex than these attitudes suggest. Permanence is no longer a guarantee of marriage even when it is promised. This awareness permeates our consciousness today. This may lead us to question whether, or under what circumstances, permanence is possible. But it seldom leads us, whether we are beginning a relationship of marriage or ending one, to judge that permanence is not to be preferred. Permanence is not to be preferred to everything, so that under no circumstances will I consider the end of my own marriage. But permanence is to be preferred as the goal and intention of our life together. And it is to be preferred, if it is in any way possible, to the pain of divorce.

Most people want marriage to last. It is in the hope of an enduring relationship that we take the emotional and the practical, legal steps that lead us into marriage. Our standards are high for what constitutes the kind of relationship that we want to endure, and sometimes these criteria are not always clear or compatible. (We may want to be the central figure in each other's life and also want each to be open to continuing growth in new relationships. We may want to start our family now and yet to have each of us pursue the development of our own career without serious interruption.) Each of our goals for marriage, taken alone, may be worthy. But taken together they may place considerable strain on our resourcefulness. While no one of our goals may be incompatible with our marriage flourishing over a lifetime, the combination of goals and priorities that we establish may carry heavy costs. We may find, in living out these patterns that define our marriage, that the strain is taxing. This realization invites us to reconsider — to reexamine what it is we want together, to reassess the strengths and needs we bring to the relationship, to recommit ourselves to its development and continuation.

We may find, especially if it is through a period of pain or deprivation that we come to a sense of the costs of sustaining this relationship, that the price is too high. Our own goals are no longer fulfilled, our resources are spent, our trust is broken. The movement through legal divorce will seem the only reasonable option to terminate a relationship that has already died.

But for many people the prevalence of divorce set against their own hope of an enduring relationship in marriage leads not to taking marriage lightly but to approaching it with greater seriousness, even caution. The expectation of permanence, sometimes experienced as an all too fragile hope, remains. The concern becomes how we shall safeguard and make robust this fragile conviction of our love.

Each marriage today must come to terms with these two dimensions of commitment: our expectations of exclusivity (What is the meaning of the priority in which we hold each other in love? How is this priority expressed?) and our expectations of permanence (What is the significance of our hope that our love shall flourish for our lifetime? How does this hope influence our lives now?).

The Lifestyle of Marriage

Marriage is love, marriage is commitment, marriage is also a lifestyle — not one lifestyle experienced universally but the many particular lifestyles through which married couples express their love and live out the promises that hold them in mutual care. The lifestyle of marriage is the design or pattern of our life together that emerges in the choices we make. Many people do not experience the patterns of their daily life as open to personal choice. By the time of marriage, and from long before, factors of poverty or class or personality have narrowed the range of those parts of my life over which I have much say. I live out life, but I do not see myself as influencing its design in many important ways. Things happen to me, to my marriage, to my family — and I make the best of them. But I have little conviction that I can initiate changes or take responsibility on my own.

But for most Americans today there is a heightened consciousness of choice. We are aware that there are different ways in which the possibilities of life and of marriage may be lived out. And while our choices are always limited, we are aware that we not only can but must choose among these options for ourselves. The lifestyle of our marriage thus results from both our choices and our circumstances.

The choices that construct the lifestyle of our marriage include the decisions we make about the practical details of living — the routine of our daily activities, how we allocate the recurrent tasks of family and household care. But more basic decisions are involved — the values we hold important, the goals we have for our life together, the ways we choose to invest ourselves in the world.

At the heart of our decision about lifestyle is the question: What is our marriage for? Are we married only for ourselves? Does our life together exist chiefly as a place of personal security and a source of mutual satisfaction? Or is our marriage also about more than just the two of us? Is it a way for us to engage ourselves — together — in a world that is bigger than ourselves?

In previous decades the expectable presence of children in marriage answered this question in part. One of the things our marriage is for is our children. A child is so concrete an expression of the love that exists between us and so insistent an invitation that this love now go beyond itself in care. In parenting we experience the scope of our love widening to include our children. Often this broadening of concern continues, expanding to include more of the world and even the future, in which "our children's children" shall have to find their own way. Married people have always been generously engaged in the world in ways other than as parents, as well. But the central connection between being married and having children has been so clear and so prevalent for centuries that it has been a defining characteristic of the lifestyle of marriage.

Today there is more choice involved in the link between marriage and parenthood. Couples come to the decision to have a child with more consideration given to how many children there shall be in the family, how the births of these children shall be spaced, when in the marriage the commitments of family life shall begin. Some couples who have been unable to have children of their own seek other ways to expand their life together as a family — through adoption or foster care or through the assistance of recent developments in the biological sciences and medical practice. Other couples decide not to have a family and, instead, to express their love beyond themselves in other forms of creativity and care.

A comparable challenge accompanies each of these options — to develop a way of being together in marriage that takes seriously the demands of mutuality in our own relationship as it takes seriously the challenge that we look beyond ourselves in genuine contribution and care. Thus a central choice in marriage concerns our progeny — how shall we give and nurture life beyond ourselves: in our own children? in our friendships and other relationships? in our creative work? in our generous concern for the world? And the decisions that we come to here do much to determine the design of our daily life together.

Beyond this central choice concerning the focus of our creative love, there are other decisions of lifestyle. How shall we use the resources we possess? How, especially, do we allocate our money and our time? Here, again, the questions can be stated simply: What is our money for? What has priority in our time? We can respond to these questions at the practical level, offering the balance sheet of the family budget and our calendar of weekly events. But as an issue in lifestyle the question is more to the core: How are our own deepest values expressed or obscured in how we spend our money and our time?

Most American families today experience both money and time as scarce. There is not enough of either to go around. There seem to be always more possibilities, more demands for each than we feel we can meet. We have little "discretionary" income and even less "free" time. But among the demands that seem both genuine and inevitable there are others that seem to squander us uselessly, leaving us no time to be together or to be at peace and leaving us few resources to use for any purpose beyond ourselves. This sense of overextension characterizes the lifestyle of many marriages. Its prevalence invites us to reflect on our own patterns of money and time, not looking to praise or blame but trying to come to a better sense of the motives and pressures that move us and, in that way, define our lives. How much does our use of money and time revolve around "us," somewhat narrowly conceived — as a couple or a family over against "others"? What are the ways in which our decisions about time and money are more reflective of what our society expects of us than of the values and activities and possessions that make sense to us? Couples and families will differ in their responses to these questions, as they will differ on other issues of value and lifestyle. But the reflective process can lead to a greater congruence between the goals we have for our life together in marriage and the ways that this life is lived on a day-to-day basis.

Establishing our lifestyle in marriage is not done once and for all, but is itself an ongoing process. The lifestyle of our marriage must respond to the movements of development and change in each of us, in our relationship and in our responsibilities.

Marriage for a lifetime, then, is constituted by the interaction of our relationship, our commitments and our lifestyle. Our mutual love is at the core of our marriage. But in marriage we experience our relationship as more than just our love here and now. Marriage is focused by the promises to which we hold ourselves. It is the commitments that we made to one another that ground our love and give it duration. These commitments give us courage to undertake the risks of creative and procreative activity together. It is these commitments that are expressed in the choices and behavior and attitudes that make up the patterns of our lifestyle. And it is, in turn, an important goal of the commitments of our marriage and the lifestyle to which these commitments give shape, to sustain and deepen and mature the relationship of love between us.

It is important to note, as we begin our consideration of marriage for a lifetime, that the relationship and commitment and lifestyle of marriage do not exist in a vacuum. For each of us our experience of marriage is influenced by legal and historical and cultural understandings of what marriage is.

The Person You Are / The Person You Marry

3.1 The Extrovert-Introvert Marriage
Kenneth J. Eppes

AFTER A FEW YEARS OF MARRIAGE, THE TRAITS THAT ORIGINALLY ATTRACTED us became irritants. Valerie was the life of the party; I didn't even want to attend. When I needed time alone, she felt left out. Her need to talk was idle chatter to me, and she craved the compliments that were so difficult for me to give. In little ways — and some big ones — we got on each other's nerves. We found ourselves drifting apart.

There was a simple explanation for our problem. Valerie was an extrovert and I was an introvert. Our opposite personality types gave us entirely different approaches to life. Learning to understand each other's unique needs, we were able to smooth the rough spots in our marriage. We actually came to see our differences as assets that could enhance us as a couple.

No one knows why people are extroverts or introverts. "Though commonly used, the terms 'introvert' and 'extrovert' are often misunderstood," says Dr. Marshall Voris, a Dallas marriage and family therapist who has counseled hundreds of extrovert-introvert couples. They are basic personality types that affect many areas of our lives and the way we relate to others.

During courtship, opposite types help enkindle infatuation because each finds the other's traits desirable. The introvert hopes the extrovert will

48

help him or her become more outgoing, while the extrovert is enamored with the other's interior life. After marriage, different ways of doing things often breed tension.

What are extrovert-introvert couples like? How can people so different have a harmonious marriage?

Different worlds

Extroverts are at home in the concrete world of people and things. They like to be around others and interact naturally with them. Their minds search for knowledge and facts. Introverts live with ideas and look for the deeper meaning of things. To them, facts are only incidental.

Living in the everyday world comes naturally to extroverts. Valerie deals easily with store clerks, bureaucracies, and doctors. She can hold her own in a rapid-fire discussion where I am completely left out. At a social function, words flow for her while I'm groping for something to say after "hello."

Introverts quickly become overwhelmed with stimulus from the outside world because they tend to ruminate on each idea that comes to mind. As an introverted friend says, "I wish I could stop the world long enough to get caught up." I would rather have an intense discussion with one person than make small talk with everyone at a party.

People are extroverted or introverted in varying degrees. Their behavior isn't always consistent. A person may show extroverted characteristics in one situation and introverted traits in another. However, one of the personality types usually dominates.

There are other pairs of personality types — sensing-intuition, thinking-feeling, and perceiving-judging — that affect the way a couple relates. Individual backgrounds also play a part. Shirley Good, marriage and family therapist at Delos Clinic in Dallas, says that among all these factors, introversion and extroversion are key. They determine how a person sees the world and the behaviors they engender are obvious. She is not surprised that the clash between extrovert and introvert personalities causes so much friction in marriages.

Points of Tension

My inner world, which Valerie referred to as a "reflective pool" when we were engaged, became a problem in itself. Dr. Voris says there is a part of the introvert that can never be fully communicated to the extrovert. At first, the extrovert may find this intriguing but as time goes on, the extrovert frequently sees the other person as emotionally absent and often imagines he or she is up to no good.

Communication is another area where extroverts and introverts clash. We were no exception.

New York psychologist Mary D'Arcy prepares married couples for service as overseas missionaries. She explains that before expressing feelings, the introvert needs to work through them internally. The extrovert wants to bounce them off someone and get a response.

When the feeling is anger, the extrovert's raw emotions can bowl over the introvert. Valerie's expressions of anger devastated me until I realized her emotions were no more intense than mine, only louder.

Even small talk causes friction in the marriage since extroverts love to chat and introverts hate it. One introverted husband said his extroverted wife "can lie in bed for twenty minutes talking about how tired she is. If she's so tired, why doesn't she shut up and go to sleep?"

Although I was grateful Valerie could guide me through situations that would otherwise be painfully awkward for me, our social life became one more point of conflict. Valerie couldn't understand why I didn't share her enthusiasm for entertaining. "Introverts have a need for privacy and to set boundaries on their space, while extroverts want to throw the doors open to everyone," say Ms. D'Arcy. It wasn't that I didn't like her family and friends. Too much contact with people simply left me emotionally drained.

Our biggest clashes came over spending time together. A typical extrovert, Valerie needs to be around people and she expects me to be with her when we're at home. If I spend too much time in my study or workshop, she becomes upset. When I don't get enough time alone, I get uncomfortable and irritable.

Head Off Trouble

Although there is equal likelihood of either spouse being an extrovert or an introvert, Dr. Voris has found that problems more frequently arise when the husband is the introvert and the wife the extrovert. Because of traditional gender stereotypes, extroverted husbands and introverted wives meet their own and society's expectations. "Even so," says Dr. Voris, "sparks can fly in any extrovert-introvert marriage, and couples should know how to handle them."

When Valerie and I sought help in dealing with our differences, a psychologist gave us the Myers-Briggs Type Indicator test which revealed our personality types. Understanding the cause of our conflicts helped us make our differences work for us.

Build on the Differences

We found we could each assume roles that complement the strengths and weaknesses of the other. Valerie became our marriage's interface with the outside world. She planned our social life and broke the ice for us when we were in a group. I helped Valerie become more reflective and attentive to interior needs. My penchant for deliberation balanced her tendency to act first, think later.

Although she will never understand it, Valerie tries to trust my inner world. I've learned to let her in on what I'm thinking and doing to help her feel connected to me.

In many areas, we had to yield to the other's needs. For example, Valerie lets me have time alone, and I go out of my way to spend time with her. We have regular dates.

Most important of all, we learned to accept each other's style as perfectly valid. God made each of us as we are. It's okay to be an extrovert — chatting and making friends everywhere. It's okay to be an introvert — quiet and reflective. Not only does God love us the way we are, he gave us our complementary types to be helpmates to each other.

The traits that attracted us to each other when we first met can still put vitality in our marriage if we allow them to. "Remember, the Golden Rule doesn't apply here," says Dr. Voris. Treating my spouse as I want to be treated doesn't work for an extrovert-introvert couple. We each have to respect the other's special needs.

Through the experience of many mistakes and often having to ask forgiveness, we learned some guidelines that can help an extrovert-introvert couple make their opposing personality types work to their advantage.

- Respect each other's point of view, realizing that you and your spouse will look differently at any situation. There is no right or wrong here; both viewpoints are legitimate.

- Evaluate your individual strengths and weaknesses to see what strong points you bring to the marriage and how your spouse balances your weaknesses.

- Never assume you know what's going on with your spouse.

- Seek ways of doing things together (working, recreating, praying, etc.) that are comfortable for both.

- Take an interest in each other's topics of conversation and also respect silence.

- Celebrate the tension that differing viewpoints cause. That tension can enhance your creativity as a couple, giving you alternatives you never knew you had.

- When any issue arises, the extrovert should give the introvert time to think about it. The introvert should commit to discussing it at some point.

- Keep talking. Discussion of any matter should continue until you are each sure you know what the other is talking about and how important it is.

- Together, discover ways of living to give the introvert the needed time to be alone and to take care of the extrovert's need to relate to others.

3.2 Scapegoating: The Phony Equalizer in Marriage

Alexander H. Smith, Jr.

ONE OF THE ELABORATE FANTASIES ABOUT MARRIAGE IS THAT THE RELATIONship is perpetually good, nurturing, and loving. Most couples acknowledge their hopes that they will fulfill each other in unique and highly personal ways. Unfortunately, the feeling of "being in" a good or bad marriage often hinges upon how closely these expectations measure up to what the couple perceives their reality to be. They often will struggle to get more from their marriage by seeking to get more from their spouses.

The Tyranny of the Ideal Marriage

Most of us know the experience of driving home from a party with our spouses when the conversation turns to couple talk. This usually includes favorable and unfavorable observations about other couples at the party. "Bill and Jane appear to be happy but actually they're having trouble. Tom and Alice are getting counseling. Barbara constantly tries to think up new recipes, but Art never notices her efforts. And did you see how flirtatious Anne was with Joe?"

Friendly chatter between wife and husband?

Possibly not. These statements may actually reflect tension between the couple. They are comparisons about themselves: how they measure up, how closely they approximate their individual and collective ideals. A close look often reveals that the very issues they notice in others reflect their own problems. They may need counseling; they may be struggling with flirtatious behavior. These comparisons project unwanted qualities, fears, and feelings from the couple and place them on others. The couple driving home avoids an inner exploration of their own feelings in these areas. They ignore the unfinished business in their relationship; they do not think of cleaning up their own backyard.

The Couple's Image of Themselves

Early in the relationship, a couple begins to formulate a sense of who they are as a couple; the couple forms a "we" notion about themselves, an identity of being part of a twosome. Naturally, most couples select the more favorable aspects of themselves as a "we" and leave the unwanted qualities to the other couple. From time to time we all do this projecting of unwanted aspects of ourselves onto others. It becomes problematic, however, when our projections erode at our primary relationship. We begin to pressure our spouses to fulfill us, to perform, to measure up.

Couples handle the problem of "we" and "they" in different ways. Some develop their own couple persona, communicated through speech and action. "We always go to Cape Cod for the summer" (because we're financially successful). "Our oldest will be attending Yale next year" (since we all have unusually high IQs). "Oh, Honey, it's fine with me if you want to go out with the guys" (after all, being the passionate lovers we are, there's no jealousy or resentment between us). These attitudes feed into an unrealistic ideal and set the stage for disappointment and mutual blame.

Some couples go the other direction, presenting themselves as losers. They cling to the negative "we" and project the positive onto others. "Our house is too small" (because we can't make a decent living). "We're sorry we're late again" (but what do you expect from such scatterbrains). "If the Johnsons really cared about us they would have sent a card" (so let's just sit here in the dark and stew in our misery together).

Both of these patterns of projection reflect a split within the couple's system. The good qualities are heaped on one side of the scale; the negative or undesirable ones are placed on the other side. Newlyweds often do this type of juggling in an effort to help stabilize the relationship. When couples continue to equalize their disappointments and shortcomings with artificial weights, they create obstacles to maintaining a healthy system in which the individuals can differentiate out of their "coupleness."

Shame and the Origins of Scapegoating

Shame compels couples to nuance their perceptions of themselves and others. Shame-based attitudes govern couples' interactions in destructive ways. When a couple's ideals exceed their emotional capabilities, they feel deep-searing shame. Their fears about failing or falling short in the eyes of others affect practical family matters: overspending to keep up with the Joneses, failing to set limits with children, pursuing burdensome career expectations, pressuring children to excel athletically or academically. Some couples become crisis-oriented in this balancing act, bouncing from one inflammatory episode to the next by baiting each other.

Shame is the nuclear ingredient in scapegoating; it is the motive for shifting the onus of undesirability onto others. Sylvia Perera. a Jungian analyst, describes this process in her book, *The Scapegoat Complex: Toward a Mythology of Shadow and Guilt.* She details the inner dynamic process of accuser and scapegoat in the family as one in which the scapegoater has a profound fear of direct emotional contact and of the realities of life.

Emotional messages from spouse to spouse and from parent to child are misread as concrete demands with practical consequences. The fear of shame drives couples to misread each other; seemingly simple requests to take out the garbage are shorn of the emotional content and empathic possibility. Instead of allowing each other to be human beings who are tired, needy, or having a bad day, they interpret each communication as a personal blow.

Keep in mind that shame is not synonymous with guilt. Developmentally, shame seems to be internalized at an earlier age than guilt. Guilt is a different emotional experience which carries the sense of having harmed someone and the accompanying wish to make reparation. In shame there is no reparation, only the miserable gut feelings of helplessness and self-loathing. Emotional havoc results.

Why scapegoating?

Couples scapegoat each other in a misguided attempt to remain connected to their innermost being, to cope with shame. Both accuser and victim play out their respective roles that expel unwanted qualities or willingly accept blame as an offering of martyrdom. These are patterns of behavior by which the individual seeks to remove any chance of falling from grace. In its deepest meaning, scapegoating in marriage is driven by a fear that God's wholeness and unconditional love cannot contain our imperfections.

There is promise in realizing this fear, however; the scale of wholesome goodness is given an opportunity to be balanced by reality. In this experience, it dawns on us that we are limited. We do not have any assurance that our lives mean anything, that our work is important, or that the children will be grateful to us when they grow up. We experience a kind of gnawing despair that, despite our accomplishments, the dread of shame continues. We see marriage as a failing fantasy and feel angry and betrayed. When we turn to God with the prayer, "Oh God, please do not look away from me because of my imperfections," we are moving toward surrender.

Resolution Through Surrender

It's often shocking to realize just how much life we've squeezed out of each other by appointing ourselves the almighty bestowers of grace — instead of surrendering that privilege to God. We are ready to surrender our scapegoating tactics to take on healthier means of maintaining balance and harmony. We become aware of our neurotic hopes about our marriage and, with discernment, give them up. Those familiar with Twelve Step programs for Alcoholics Anonymous or related programs for family members have a decided advantage here. The surrender to a Higher Power is real; it roots life in its Source. In surrendering, we place all our drives, wants, and disappointments at the disposal of God; we are completely God's. This action of the mind is different from submission. It is like allowing Someone to jump-start our batteries in subzero weather. Such surrender affords us the initial opportunity to heal — and it relieves our spouses of a tremendous burden.

Those not associated with a Twelve Step program must find other means. The essential purpose is to cease projecting and scapegoating in the marriage and turn toward reliable experiences of wholeness.

This kind of surrender does not mean that our spouse will suddenly become more considerate or that we will realize sexual, financial, or social fulfillment. If we seek these fringe benefits, we're bargaining with God. Surrender is surrender; it is completely disowning our need to control. It is saying, "OK, I'm giving up the expectation of perfection in myself and in others. Here I am; no deals, no con jobs, no false advertising. I am yours, God, and you are mine. Direct me from here."

We help our relationship enormously when we reach this point. Even if this kind of surrender occurs only once, the marriage benefits greatly. For that moment, the relationship holds the two in balanced union; it has a ripe opportunity to take its natural course, to grow as God designed. An authentic and wholesome equilibrium is given a chance to take hold.

3.3   Identity: Vocation and Marriage
Evelyn Eaton Whitehead and James D. Whitehead

IN MARRIAGE I CHOOSE TO SHARE MYSELF WITH ANOTHER PERSON FOR A lifetime. Who is this "self" that I want to share and how is this self-giving a part of my larger sense of what my life is about? Success in sharing myself in marriage depends on my growing awareness of, and confidence in, who this self is. The maturity that comes from such clarity and flexibility about myself is rooted in the psychological strength of identity and in the religious sense of a vocation.

Identity and Vocation

In our late teens and early twenties we are especially busy exploring who we are. Information about who I am comes to me from many sources during this time: my own ambitions, the dreams and hopes that arise from within, the expectations of my parents and others who are important to me. We learn much about ourself from other people's responses to us. Am I competent or clumsy? Am I lovable or unattractive? Can I trust myself or not? It is from what other people say to me and how they behave toward me that I develop my first (and often, enduring) sense of these "truths" about myself. The process of maturing involves my coming to a sense of balance between inner and outer information about who I am and who I should become. What can emerge in this process is the psychological strength of identity, a personal resource that will contribute to, and be further tested in, my marriage.

Clarity about who I am can be expected to grow only gradually as I mature. My sense of myself in adolescence is marked by the perplexities of puberty, the expectations of my parents and peers, the identifications I establish with my heroes, whether teachers, athletes or celebrities. Some of this confusion is likely to continue into early adulthood. Daniel Levinson's research, reported in *The Seasons of a Man's Life,* points to the years of one's twenties as an extended period of testing, exploring and clarifying both "who I am" and "what I can do." It may be that as life expectancy lengthens, with more and more of us living into our seventies and beyond, more time is needed at the beginning of adult life to deal with these questions of identity.

A young person today may need considerable time and a range of experience to come to a sense of personal identity and vocation. It is only as such confidence develops that I can determine how, and if, marriage is to be a part of my life. Yet expectations to marry earlier may abound. My parents want me to "get married and settle down"; my friends are marrying; other pressures on the inside and on the outside push me into this important commitment. This is not to suggest that early marriages are doomed; many, we know, flourish. But when marriage (at whatever age) begins more as an effort to prove myself than to give myself, it can be considered "premature."

Falling in love in adolescence and early adult life is often part of an attempt to have another person help me discover my own identity. In the mirror of the person brought close in affection I hope to have revealed to me a clearer sense of who I am. Marriage in adolescence often has more to do with these issues of identity than with questions of intimacy. If I marry with little sense of who I am or what I *am for,* I may bring to our relationship the additional demand that *you* supply these answers for me. In every marriage, of course, the partners continue to learn from each other about their own identities and potential. But a marriage entered when the partners have little clarity about themselves is a marriage in which personal identity is not a resource to rely on but a task yet to be achieved. The many challenges of an intimately shared life are better met when each person has attained some clarity and confidence about "who I am."

This identity question — "who am I?" — is also intimately related to the question "what am I worth?" Confused about my identity and unsure of my worth, I may be attracted to the "worthy" roles of marriage. To be a wife or a husband, to be a parent — people see these as important. Married persons are treated as adults; parents are seen as responsible agents. I may want to marry hoping that these roles will signal to me and to others that I have achieved independent adulthood, that I am of value. But marrying to prove who I am or what I am worth adds considerable burdens to an already challenging enterprise.

Elements of Identity

The strength of personal identity is not a rigidly clear and non-negotiable picture of who I am. Rather it is a matter of consistency — between my present and my past, and between my inner experience of myself and the expectations that others have of me. As a psychological resource, identity refers to my ability to maintain this consistent sense of myself. The strength of identity, which guides and supports all my adult choices, includes continuity, congruence and self-esteem.

Continuity. As I mature into a clearer sense of my identity I come to feel more connected with my past. I am aware of ways in which my past, with all its peculiarity, is a part of who I am today. Who I was in junior high school and who I was when I graduated — these "selves" survive and contribute to who I am now. I do not need to deny or apologize for my past — its ethnic peculiarities or personal limitations or whatever. My past and my present form an increasingly satisfying continuity.

Congruence. As I mature there develops in me a better "fit" between what I know about myself and how I am known by others, especially people who are important to me. It may be easier to recognize this aspect of identity by focusing on its absence, those times when I am aware of a discrepancy between how I see myself and how I am seen by others. My parents urge me to join the family business while my own dream is to be a journalist. My spouse sees me as a full-time homemaker while I am interested in going back to school now and getting a job in a year or so. There can even be a discomforting discrepancy in regard to my expectations of myself. I have always thought of myself as emotionally strong and unaffected by personal doubts; I am embarrassed as I find myself wishing there were someone to whom I could turn now for acceptance and support. It is upon my resources of identity that I draw as I attempt to evaluate the expectations that are placed on me by myself and others. Some of these I sense as appropriate for me, confirming who I am or calling me forth toward the best of what I can be. Others I experience as inappropriate: they are not congruent with what I know about myself; they do not fit my own best hopes or dreams.

Self-esteem. Maturing in my sense of personal identity also includes a greater tolerance for, and love of, who I am. I come to recognize and appreciate the strengths and limits that are really me; I can tolerate the ambiguity that remains as my sense of who I am develops and undergoes change.

As a psychological resource, then, identity is a gradually developing sense of the abilities and limits, the ambitions and apprehensions that make up my uniqueness. These strengths and ambitions describe me to myself and suggest ways I might live my life. The psychological strength of identity develops in a growing awareness that gives me some clarity about who I am and some enthusiasm for sharing myself with others. Clarity evolves as I can better recognize my own talents and limits, and can distinguish these from what others expect of me. If the expectations of others overwhelm me, if my fears about my own uniqueness are too great, I may not be able to come to a sense of clarity about myself and my vocation. I am also likely to be unsure of what I am bringing to my marriage.

But identity needs not only clarity; it requires flexibility as well. Marriage requires that I be able to risk myself in close contact with another — in love, in sex, in cooperation, in conflict. For most of us it takes time to learn how to be "up close." In friendships, in collaboration at work, in taking responsibility for my life, I learn important lessons about myself and about how I am tested and changed in contact with others. These experiences in young adulthood can contribute to the flexibility that I will need in marriage.

It is this flexibility in my sense of who I am that saves my growing self-knowledge from becoming rigid and brittle. Being strong in my identity does not mean being well defended and unchangeable. It means I am confident that being close to others will not destroy me. The development of such a clear and yet flexible sense of self is, of course, a lifelong project. But the initial movements of this strength in early adult life are the foundation upon which my capacity for commitment depends.

Vocation — Who Am I Called to Be?

For Christians, this process of growing into a confident knowledge of who I am is personalized in a vocation. We are not just evolving into our own identities; we are called, each of us, by a loving God to be someone and to do something of significance. The psychological strength of identity can thus develop into the religious strength of a personal vocation. A vocation is both an invitation from God and our response to this call. It is an invitation to live a certain kind of life, one shaped by two powerful influences: the values of Christian faith and the gifts that we find in ourselves. The Christian story, as told in the gospel and retold in our communal history, suggests directions for our life. And when we examine carefully the shape of our own abilities and limits, our hopes and fears, we begin to clarify who we are and what we might do. A vocation is, then, an invitation into my own identity as a Christian. It is an invitation that takes shape both in my deepest hopes and dreams and in the challenges offered me by the significant people in my life. It is the particular way I find myself called to love, to care for the world and to witness to Christian faith. A vocation is not an authoritative decree visited upon me from the outside. It is rather *who I am,* trying to happen.

In recent Catholic history an unfortunately narrow translation of vocation has caused some confusion. In Catholic piety a "vocation" came to refer to the special calling of the vowed religious or priest. On Vocation Sunday, for example, Catholics were urged to pray "for vocations." A proper inference from this practice was that only sisters or brothers or priests had genuine religious vocations. The rest of us, and so all married persons, had to muddle along with no special religious identity or sense of calling. A more adequate theology of Baptism today insists that every adult Christian has a vocation — a personal invitation to live one's life transformed by grace. Grounded in the gifts and inclinations that I find in myself, my vocation calls me to spend myself in a particular way. As I mature in this sense of who I am called to be, this clarity and confidence become resources I can depend on; my vocation becomes a virtue — a resident religious strength that helps me live gracefully. Such a vocation, like a personal identity, often seems hidden to us in our youth. It can be buried beneath the expectations we inherit from our family or our society. It can be obscured by our fears or concealed by the sheer complexity of our inner lives. But its shape is suggested to us in our deepest ambitions and the personal strengths that emerge to give these hopes practical expression.

An attitude of listening is crucial to the maturing of both my identity and my vocation. I must listen to, and sort out, my dreams, apprehensions and expectations, attentive to the information these provide about who I am, how I am gifted, how I might express myself in the world. This discovery of my vocation is not achieved once and for all. It is what I continue to be about — in my marriage and in my work and leisure. A Christian vocation is a lifelong revelation of me to myself. Yet my vocation, as that initial sense of what I am called to be, to which I know I must respond, has special importance in young adulthood. It is at the foundation of the critical choices I make at this time, choices that begin to define me as an adult. As this psychological strength and Christian virtue grow in me, I come to a more confident sense of how I might commit myself in personal relationships and in a career. To marry before I have come into some initial strength of my own vocation, to marry when I have little confidence in who I am or awareness of what I am to do with my life, is to marry prematurely.

Christian Vocation and Our Dream

Our identities and vocations, the first inklings of our careers and life work, take shape as dreams. These are not (usually) sleeping dreams; they are pictures or images or hints that emerge in us of what we might do with our life. A dream, as explored by Daniel Levinson in *The Seasons of a Man's Life* and in our *Christian Life Patterns,* is a life ambition. It is my best hopes and deepest ambition for my life. It is what I most want to be "when I grow up."

A dream is thus an image, vague or clear, both of who I am and of what I might do. The first hints of a dream appear in childhood: in our toys and games and coloring books, we begin to devise and explore our own dreams. In these early experiences the very possibility of our dreaming begins to be shaped: our parents and others surround us with their dreams (thinly disguised in toys, clothes and manners), suggesting avenues for our own dreaming. The richness or poverty of these inherited dreams profoundly influences our ability to imagine our own futures.

In late adolescence ambitions and dreams emerge with great vigor. As we leave the dependency of adolescence, we are excited by the possibilities of adult life; with enthusiasm and optimism we begin to try out our powers in this exciting world. From the outside our parents are expecting us to find a job or select a career; school counselors talk about "majors," often an early test of a future direction for our dream. In or out of school we sense it is time to decide, to choose what to do with our life.

In very early adulthood we may find ourself with a dream that is quite general. I may have a powerful but indistinct dream of helping others: I want to give my energy to caring for the poor and disadvantaged — but how to do this? Should I become a social worker, a doctor, a minister? Given such a dream, my challenge is to test it out both against the world and against my own developing abilities. How will society support or foster such an ambition? Is there any encouragement out there for this fragile dream? And how does this dream correspond to the abilities emerging in me? Do I have the stuff to realize such an ambition?

Other young adults may have quite specific dreams: to be a biology teacher, a lawyer, a carpenter. With such a specific dream, they still must explore how their abilities fit these dreams — am I, as a matter of fact, very promising as a worker with wood? The necessarily gradual exploring of a specific dream might include reflection on the motivation for such a career: to what extent do I hope to please my father by becoming a lawyer, or win the respect of others by becoming a teacher? How are these motivations balanced by a conviction that such a dream is genuinely *mine* — expressing my own best hopes for my life? Levinson's observation that a dream always represents *one part* of myself is important here. As I begin to pursue a dream in earnest it is helpful to be aware of those parts of myself that will be lost or sacrificed in this pursuit. Unable to be "all things," I benefit by knowing what I am choosing and what I am putting aside. Such knowledge includes both an awareness that this dream is mine and some realization of its cost.

There are two important characteristics of the dream as it unfolds in early adult life: it is necessarily idealistic and its development takes considerable time. Dreams are by nature idealistic; they are properly bigger than life, beyond our talents. This "bigness" of a dream contributes to the optimism of youth. All things are possible; many paths lie open to us. The idealistic character of the dream (the fantasy of myself as a famous novelist, benevolent millionaire or dramatically successful nurse) gives us energy; this energy propels us into adult life, launches us boldly into a very complex world. An asceticism built into adult life and vocation will hone this bigger-than-life dream until it fits us better, expressing our identity in more limited but personalized ways.

The dream, then, is how our adult identity begins to seek expression in a career and lifestyle. For Christians the dream is not just a psychological concept that must be "baptized." Our own religious heritage is rich in dreams; Jews and Christians have traditionally met their God in dreams. Sometimes in sleeping dreams, sometimes in waking insights, they have envisioned God's invitations and commands. Abraham's ambition to journey to a new land and begin a new people was a dream and a vocation — the first of all Jewish and Christian dreams. Israel itself began as a dream: a vision of a promised land to be pursued. This dream, begun in individuals, grew into a collective vocation — an invitation from God to a whole nation to be a special people and to live according to special values and beliefs. This collective dream, inherited from Israel, was reshaped by Jesus Christ into the Christian dream of the Kingdom of God: an energizing vision of a world community where justice and love shape life and action, a place where the blind see and the lame walk and the poor hear the good news of their salvation. This dream can be twisted, as every dream can be, into an escapist fantasy of another world, an illusion used for consolation in the midst of a confusing and futile life. But the Christian dream, like an individual dream, is meant to energize and move us to action. It invites us to become just and loving persons and to transform our community and society in the direction of such an unlikely but compelling vision.

A Christian vocation is a personal dream, an invitation we find developing in ourselves. Although it is an invitation *to me* personally, it is always linked to the collective dream of the Kingdom. It is the way in which I hope to live out my Christian values and convictions through my own particular self-investment in the world.

A vocation is like a dream in a number of ways. Both a dream and a vocation *appear* within us. We are often surprised to see them and wonder about their source; they seem to come from someone or something beyond ourselves. Both are also, by nature, ambiguous. These images of exciting possibilities are rarely resolved into clear or unambiguous goals. Our dream, our vocation, can bring us into conflict with other plans, other invitations and responsibilities. Most often we follow a dream or vocation in the hope that we are doing the right thing; we find ourself unsure, yet trusting our instincts concerning this ambiguous call. Adult maturity can be described by the confidence, growing within and confirmed by others who are significant to me, that "I am doing what I should be doing"

The Failure of a Dream and a Vocation

A dream and a vocation have been described in the ideal: arising with much excitement, these impel me to give myself to a certain career and life-style. But such a development can, of course, fail. The failure of a dream is the frustration of a vocation.

The first way a vocation may be frustrated is in a dream's failure to be born. Children and adolescents may be barred from dreaming. Taught to think little of themselves, they do not expect dreams; they have no ambitions. As they move into adult life, they may join themselves to other persons — a parent or spouse, usually — and take on that person's dream. Sometimes personal choice is involved in the frustration of a dream. A young person aborts a dream that is trying to be born because it is too confusing or frightening. The heroine of Mary Gordon's novel *Final Payments,* traumatized by an event at nineteen, buries her personal dreams and ambitions in favor of the safety, the "sanctuary" of caring for her father.

> I had won sanctuary by giving up my portion, by accepting as my share far less than my share. I had bought sanctuary by giving up youth and freedom, sex and life (p. 239).

> Here I had built myself a sanctuary, covered over with approval, safe from chance (p. 272).

Whatever the choice or guilt involved, a dream and a Christian vocation can fail by never being born.

A second way a dream fails is in never being tested. A young adult may harbor the exciting dream of being a musician or scientist but never allow this dream to be tested in the external world. Perhaps feeling the dream to be too fragile, the person fosters this possibility within but cannot expose it to the tests and potential rejection of others. Such a dream and possible vocation, kept inside me, turns gradually to illusion and fantasy. In the privacy of my mind I am very good at this career; I savor my imagined success while refusing to let the world shape and tarnish this dream. Distance increases between how I see myself (in fantasy and daydream) and who others know me to be (in the everyday interaction of life). When such a Walter Mitty approach to adult life and vocation becomes predominant, the dream and vocation are frustrated.

A third way a dream fails is by becoming tyrannical. A life ambition can attract us with compulsive force: "I'm going to succeed at this no matter what it takes!" When we give our dream this power over us we may achieve it but at a very high price. My dream is an expression of only part of me, the realization of some particular aspect of myself. In the pursuit of my dream the challenge remains to find its place in the whole of my life. How does my marriage, for instance, fit in with my dream? Has our love flourished along with my ambition or has it been sacrificed to my dream? A tyrannical dream will likely lead to the neglect of my marriage and it may be only at mid-life that I realize this tyranny. At that point survival of my marriage may well require overcoming this tyranny and exploring other, neglected parts of my life and vocation.

The Dream and Marriage

The dream responds most directly to the questions of who I am and what I might do. But these questions necessarily include the question of how I will be with others. Marriage and our choices about it are profoundly intertwined with the pursuit of our dream.

Marrying can be a means of avoiding a dream. Marriage can represent a haven where I belong to others. It may appear, at least as I approach it, to be a stable place with clear roles and rewards. In such a milieu who needs dreams? Supporting my spouse's and fostering my children's dreams should be enough. Only, of course, with any luck we learn it is not.

Marriage is, as well, the milieu in which dreams are fostered. The love we receive in marriage can turn us into more confident dreamers. Marriage is a place of multiple dreams. This can present a challenge that is both exciting and complex. We are invited to support our partner's dreaming while continuing to dream ourselves. As our children begin to dream we need the discipline to distinguish our dreams from theirs. It is most often in the context of marriage that we may discover a dream too long deferred or confront the tyranny of a dream we have pursued compulsively. If these cannot be healed, the anger and guilt released here can destroy a marriage. The reconciliation demanded at such a time begins in the recognition of what is really happening. Because we continue to grow throughout adult life, continue to be revealed to ourselves, our dreams necessarily grow and change. This can be unsettling for us personally and disruptive for our marriage. It can also induce significant change, conversion and forgiveness — of myself and of my partner.

Marriage is not only the milieu of dreams. We bring to it a dream *of* marriage — a hope and ambition for what our marriage might be. This dream, idealistic as all dreams, is refined and purified in the living. Sometimes our experience of marriage breaks this dream. Marriage turns out to be very different from what I had hoped; my hope seems illusory and unrealizable. But when our dream of marriage survives, despite all the changes and compromises, something of significance has happened. It is this lived dream of marriage among Christians that can be transmitted to the next generation of believers.

This transmission of the dream of Christian marriage bears some reflection. We begin as inheritors of dreams, especially the dreams of our parents. Among these received dreams is our parents' lived dream of Christian marriage. If we are fortunate we approach Christian marriage with a sense of what it is about because we have seen it lived in our own families and communities.

As we struggle to live our own dream of marriage we likely experience, as our parents and others before us have done, how inadequate to it we are. This is, in part, because this dream is bigger than life and we are not. As we, despite our limits and failings, mature in our marriage and our Christian faith, we begin to hand on the dream of Christian marriage. We give this ideal, now in lived form, to the next generation. It is, in fact, only through us and our generation of believers that this dream can reach the future. Although it is remembered in the gospel and Christian history, it is in our own lives that the dream of Christian marriage is, practically, handed on. When no one believes in Christian marriage — no longer is excited by the dream of marriage according to the hopes of our religious tradition — Christian marriage dies. Conversely, it lives and survives in our lives. Married Christians not only bear new Christians; they cause the vision of Christian marriage to be reborn again. This may be as holy a gift to the community as their children.

Careers, Identity and Marriage

How does marriage as a life choice relate to a person's vocation? Is there such a thing as a specific calling *to* marriage? Is not marriage just the normal context of adult life? If almost everyone marries, how can it be a specific calling or vocation?

A vocation develops in response to my awareness of who I am and what I can do. The complementary awareness — how I will be with others — has, perhaps, been too little considered in discussions of vocation and identity.

Who I am is expressed not only in what I shall do but also in whom I am with. A vocation to the life of a vowed religious (as, for example, a Dominican brother or a Franciscan sister) is a calling that includes a style of intimacy and community; though it excludes marriage, it includes a commitment to a certain style of life together. Such a lifestyle commitment must fit a person's sense of self and her or his capacity for relationships.

Other Christians find themselves called to careers (foreign service, research, social advocacy) that, *for them,* exclude marriage. As their own identity seeks expression in a certain work they find marriage does not fit this particular life and vocation. Fidelity to their own vocation excludes, they find, the enduring relationship and commitment of marriage. The conscious choice of such a future requires a strong sense of identity since there is so much social pressure for every adult to marry.

Such variation in adult choice and vocation reminds us that marriage is to be a *chosen* way of life. It should match both who I find myself to be and what I feel called to do with my life. Marriage is not just "what everyone does when they grow up," nor is it a way to prove myself. It is not the best or only place to find myself, nor a means to escape loneliness. Marriage is a complex way of living that should fit, not substitute for, my identity. It is a demanding commitment that should be compatible with the career I am pursuing. As marriage becomes less a biological demand for the survival of the race, the Church might be expected to assist its members to more consciously decide if this lifestyle and commitment really fit their identity and vocation.

If marriage is a most significant aspect of a personal vocation, it is less and less an *exclusive* vocation for anyone. The historical factors which led many women to give their full energy over a lifetime to child rearing and family have changed. With a smaller portion of their lives taken up with the active tasks of raising small children, many women today judge that marriage and family are not their total vocation. Other parts of themselves, a wider range of their abilities, call for expression. The change in consciousness signals an important vocational shift. Increasingly, women recognize that child rearing and a family, an important part of the vocation of most women, is just that — a part. As a result of this realization, the questions of identity, vocation and marriage may be especially important for women today.

Woman's Identity and Marriage

The question "who am I?" is asked by both women and men. But often they look in different places for the evidence that moves them toward an answer. Men, in adult life, have characteristically understood themselves in terms of occupational roles and accomplishments, as worker or warrior or leader. Traditionally, women have answered this question — who am I? — in terms of their interpersonal relationships: I am daughter, wife, mother. Thus the interpersonal relationship of marriage came to figure very prominently in the identity of women. Marriage and especially motherhood were, it seemed, what women *were for*. To have children, to nurture life, to care for others — this is what it has meant to be a woman. These have been her highest privileges and weightiest responsibilities. Not to be married, not to have children has been to be "unfulfilled." Some spinsters or "barren" women (and note the negative feel of these words) might sublimate this frustration of their nature through roles of "spiritual motherhood" — as teachers or nurses or advocates of the needy. But not to be "mother" was, so it seemed, at the deepest level not to be fully woman.

This personal identity as "mother" has been accompanied by a social identity centered in the private sphere. "A woman's place is in the home." A man's involvement in the public world is direct, as wage earner and citizen and decision maker. A woman acts directly in the world of "private life." She supports her husband's goals, she guides her son's ambition, she prepares her daughters to be, in their turn, supportive wives and mothers. Woman participates in the public world only indirectly — as consumer, homemaker, hostess, companion. Woman's absence from the world of paid employment and career has reinforced her lack of a public or social identity.

Work in the world is one of the characteristic ways in which the adolescent-becoming-an-adult begins to establish a social identity. This vehicle of identity formation is often lacking for young women. In past decades many women married just after completing their education (in high school or college) and thus had no young adult involvement in the world of work or career. Many of those women who did work in their late teens or twenties saw this as a period of "waiting to be married" more than as a period of investment of self in a project that had a meaning of its own. Thus work was not a part of "who I am" but rather what I do until I find "who I am" in a relationship with a man in marriage.

Today there are both pragmatic and psychological reasons that urge young women to delay marriage until they have tested themselves in the world of work. The pragmatic reasons are visible in a look at the current scene, the contemporary experience of women. In 1980 over half the adult women in the United States were working. In almost half of American families both wife and husband work outside the home. In most of these families, especially in the face of rising inflation, these two paychecks are needed to maintain the standard of living. Every year thousands of women who are divorced or widowed find themselves suddenly responsible for their own economic well-being and, often, that of their children as well. Of the nearly five million single-parent families in our country, 90 percent are headed by women. Pragmatically, then, it seems useful for a young woman today to obtain not only the education but the subsequent work experience that will enable her to support herself and, quite possibly, others as well.

But an even deeper reason moves many young women to engage in work. Work in the world is a vehicle of self-expression and self-transcendence. It is one of the central ways I find out who I am. An experience of financial independence and work autonomy before marriage can be crucial to the psychological development of young women, many of whom are still socialized to evaluate themselves primarily in terms of their relationships — who they are with and who wants to be with them. For both men and women work involvement through the twenties is likely to bring them to the marriage commitment with greater self-awareness and self-assurance. And perhaps especially for women, facing the multiple demands of the changing roles of women in marriage and beyond, this critical experience of self-exploration and growing self-confidence needs to be safeguarded.

Fidelity — To Marriage and Vocation

When we think of the virtues of marriage, the first to come to mind is likely that of fidelity. Marriage is a commitment of fidelity, of faithfulness to each other. The importance of fidelity is seen in the destructiveness of its opposite, infidelity. Sexual infidelity is for most of us the most dramatic instance of a failed commitment, but our faithfulness to each other is likely to be tested in our marriage in many other ways.

How do we develop the strength and virtue of fidelity? Why do some people seem able to be faithful while for others it is such a struggle? Where is this strength of fidelity rooted in us? In *Insight and Responsibility,* Erik Erikson suggests that fidelity arises out of our sense of identity: "Fidelity is the ability to sustain loyalties freely pledged. . . . It is the cornerstone of identity" (p. 125). My ability to be faithful to my commitments in life depends on a clear and resilient sense of who I am. Faithfulness does not begin in marriage — though it is for most of us thoroughly tested and developed here — but in fidelity to who I am called to be, in faithfulness to my vocation.

For the Christian this is a faithfulness not just to my own desires and goals; it is fidelity to what God would have me become. Beneath and beyond all my social roles and identities — as spouse, as parent, as worker — I am invited into a unique and God-given identity. Although I learn about this identity and personal vocation in relationships and in my work, it is ultimately *my* identity — that particular and peculiar path that I am to follow in life. Such a vocation demands fidelity, a faithfulness to the continuing invitation of God in my life.

Without the strength of a (somewhat) clear sense of who I am, my choices and commitments in life will be responses to external pressures. My actions leading to marriage and a career will be efforts of conformity rather than of fidelity. I will be trying to match others' expectations and ideals because I lack a stable, enduring sense of who God would have me be. Fidelity to another person is grounded in the ability to be faithful to myself. Often we speak of this as integrity or authenticity, but we may also use the word fidelity to describe this faithfulness to my vocation that, in turn, prepares me to be faithful to a marriage commitment.

Fidelity, as a virtue of relationships, includes congruence, confidence and conscience. Fidelity is — like identity — a question of congruence, of "fit" between who I am and what I do. It depends on my knowing and trusting myself sufficiently to be able to commit this self to certain actions and life choices. A vocation refers both to an identity (who I am) and to an expression of this (what I am to do). Acting in a way that is faithful to who I am is an act of fidelity; with this virtue we become able to *do* who we *are*.

Fidelity is also related to confidence — having faith in myself. As I arrive gradually at a clearer sense of myself and my vocation, what I can and should do with my life, I learn to trust myself. This confidence and trust in myself allow me to trust myself with someone else. Entrusting myself to my marriage partner, I give a self that I am familiar with and know I can trust. Trusting myself and believing in the direction of my life, I gain the confidence to meet the surprises and changes that marriage has in store for me.

Self-confidence, as an important part of the strength of identity and the virtue of fidelity, is also related to conscience. Conscience — the ability to discern and decide what is right for me to do — is grounded in my sense of who I am and what I am for. My youthful identity matures as I select and internalize values from my religious faith and culture. As these values become personally mine, adult conscience and responsibility become fully possible. Conscience, then, is the strength and virtue of being able to rely on inner criteria for my actions. A well-developed conscience allows me to trust myself and my decisions; I know my actions and commitments are right and good because they fit, they are faithful to who I am as *this Christian* adult.

Conscience allows me to choose what I should do, not out of a compulsive "should," nor mainly to please others, but because this action is faithful to who I am as *this* Christian, with this set of commitments and gifts. Individual conscience has always been a frightening concept for religious institutions because it can suggest a self-reliance and independence which threaten control and conformity. In fact, as we have noted before, Erik Erikson defines conscience as that independence that makes a person dependable. Both religious and psychological maturity demand this movement beyond conformity to external norms and rules into a confident trust in oneself. As Christians we believe it is God who invites each of us into our particular vocations. And these invitations lead, we believe, not to individualistic self-expression and self-defense, but to a common pursuit of gospel ideals: we are all called to follow the same Lord and to live the same values of love and justice. But we may each do this differently. Christian maturity includes the ability to trust both our own vocation and those of other Christians.

That fidelity is both a virtue necessary for marriage and more generally a virtue required of every adult, can be seen in two important examples. A Christian who divorces must survive a failure of faithfulness. Whatever its causes, a divorce acknowledges a break in the fidelity of a relationship and commitment. If a person's identity and fidelity are understood almost exclusively in terms of *this* relationship, how can the person survive divorce? Indeed, the horror of divorce is that it suggests the inability to be faithful; if this relationship fails, what does not? How can I trust myself or someone else again? Surviving a divorce begins when people are invited, in this

strange silence which follows years of a marriage relationship, to reinvesti-
gate their own personal identity and vocation. With the fidelity of this marriage ended, how am I now called to be faithful to who I am? How shall I be
faithful to a personal vocation and relationship with God that continues
through this break? If my vocation has been exclusively identified with my
marriage, survival will be most difficult: nothing of worth seems to remain.
A central challenge in marriage is fidelity to our mutual commitment. A
central challenge in divorce is fidelity to my own vocation. (This will include my fidelity, as a parent, to the children who themselves must be helped
to survive this break.) When a divorce is unavoidable I must find how my
vocation and identity continue and how I am to be faithful to these. The
movement toward divorce can be precipitated by the realization that our marriage is irreparably broken and that fidelity to myself — to my sense of
self-worth, to my own religious beliefs — demands a formal end to this
relationship. Fidelity, then, is a virtue that belongs to marriage, but a virtue
grounded more radically in a recognition of who I am and a commitment to,
and trust in, this vocation.

A second instance in which fidelity is seen as a virtue apart from marriage concerns the person whose vocation does not point to marriage. In a
culture which celebrates marriage as *the* way to live, some Christians will
find that fidelity to their own vocation, to who they are finding themselves
to be, does not include marriage. Thus a young woman in her late twenties
begins to suspect that marriage will not be a part of her life. This can be
disappointing and confusing: I may be tempted to marry anyway, going
against my best judgment. Motivations are scrutinized minutely: Am I just
selfish? Am I afraid of others, of such a commitment? The challenge here is
to discern and then to trust this developing sense of who I am and what I
should do with my life. This is essentially a challenge of fidelity: to be faithful to *my* calling as best I see it. Such a decision not to marry, out of fidelity
to my vocation, may accompany the move into a formally celibate lifestyle
or, less formally, to the Christian vocation of a single adult. It may also be
an important part of the maturing of a gay Christian. Pressures from within
and without may push a gay Christian to enter a heterosexual marriage.
Against such pressures, the gay Christian tries to discern his or her own
vocation and identity: what kind of intimacy and lifestyle fit who I am and
how God has gifted me? For the gay as for the straight Christian, the challenge of fidelity begins in the invitation to come to know, and then to love
and trust, who I am. My ability to be faithful to who I am (as this identity
continues to be revealed to me all my life) grounds my fidelity to others and
to my work.

Two final observations about the virtue of fidelity and marriage may be
useful. The experience and exploration required for the development of this
virtue means it will rarely be fully available to seventeen-year-olds; it is
much more likely to be a strength of the twenty-seven-year-old. This is not

to suggest that we should legislate an older minimum age for marriage. It simply reminds us that just as marriage makes demands that mature us further, it also requires considerable maturity to undertake. Fidelity, as we have defined it here, is a strength best brought to marriage rather than sought only within marriage. Put another way, it is healthier to find out who we are (and come to trust this) before marriage rather than by means of marriage. However we are to deal with the desire of very young Christians to marry, if we believe that Christian marriage is for a lifetime, we had best delay this commitment to interpersonal fidelity until fidelity to one's own vocation has begun to develop.

Secondly, the virtue of fidelity — whether to myself or to my marriage — is a faithfulness not to a finished but to a moving reality. Just as a person's adult identity does not crystallize clearly and finally at age twenty-one, neither is a Christian vocation revealed to us in so finished a fashion. A vocation is a lifelong conversation (rather than a single cosmic command) in which we may expect to hear new invitations throughout our life. This means my fidelity must be to this growing and changing sense of myself. Fidelity is possible because in the midst of significant change, my identity — my vocation — endures. Were my identity totally changeable, there would be no enduring person (myself or my marriage partner) to whom to be faithful. Because we are neither totally changeable nor totally finished, we must learn the difficult virtue of fidelity to growing and changing persons — ourselves and others. In marriage I am called to be faithful not only to the person I married, but to the person I am now married to. As I change and grow, my partner can be expected to do the same. Fidelity is not a virtue which allows me to hold doggedly to a remembered commitment; it is a virtue which provides resilience in responding to a continuing commitment. This strength allows me to be faithful both to my commitments and to where these commitments lead me. Without a confident sense of who I am and what I am for, I cannot be faithful to this self; in turn, it will be most difficult to sustain fidelity to another person in marriage.

Church Tradition

4.1 Marriage in the Old Testament
Thomas M. Martin

CHRISTIANS CONSIDER THE SCRIPTURES NORMATIVE FOR THEIR SENSE OF reality. True, the Old Testament and the New Testament comprise a body of literature that represents a very limited understanding of the earth, of the makeup of physical reality in general, and of certain dimensions of human nature. But it is also a literature that represents the conscious reflections of a people with a unique experience of God.

The Jews before Jesus and those who had the Jesus experience reflected on their lives in light of their experience of God. Christians feel that this God experience and its implications for human life are so profound that it is normative for their community. True, the vision must be weighed against what has been learned through the centuries, but it cannot be dismissed.

Many people, of course, reflect on their experience of God, and through this effort they gain valuable insight into human efforts and destiny. Vatican Council II in its "Declaration on the Relationship of the Church to Non-Christian Religions" states that the church must respect the truth of other religions:

> She looks with sincere respect upon those ways of conduct and of life, those rules and teachings which, though differing in many particulars from what she holds and sets forth, nevertheless often reflect a ray of that Truth which enlightens all men.[1]

Given this respect that most Christians feel for the activity of God in other religions, in creation, and in the activities of human events, Christians

---

1. "Declaration on the Relationship of the Church to Non-Christian Religions," section 2, in *The Documents of Vatican II*. Walter Abbott, ed. (New York: America Press, 1966) p. 662.

still give an honored position to scripture. They feel that God was uniquely active in human affairs during the formative years of the Bible. In particular they see the Jesus event as so fundamental to any realization of life that subsequent religious reflection must weigh itself against what was brought to light by Jesus' words and actions and the experiences of those who had immediate contact with Jesus or his disciples.

Any reflection on Christian marriage, then, must start with an appreciation of what is said about marriage and family in scripture. At first that task may sound easy enough. However, there are significant complications simply because the experience of family life is so culturally conditioned. Family deals with the very fabric of a people. It is going to be steeped in the practices and the sense of reality of the day.

Many of the practices of the early Jews are simply scandalous when measured by what is acceptable today. In the Old Testament the conflicts within the most important families, the treatment of women, and the way the individuals drew their identities from the group are quite baffling to a person living in present western culture. Similarly, in the New Testament the apparent dismissal of domestic life takes many readers' breath away.

From the very beginning, then, a distinction must be made between the cultural practices of the day and the theological reflections that the people made on their experience. The two are not unrelated, of course, but they cannot be assumed into one. The theological reflection is clearly influenced by the practices of the day. Likewise, the practices of the day can be seen to change ever so subtly as the people reflect on their experience of God. Nevertheless, there is a tension that exists between the style of life that the religious sense of reality called forth and what in fact was the practice of the people.

Likewise, there must be a distinction between the immediate theological conclusions that are drawn by a people and those which stand the test of time. In the Old Testament, for example, many times the Israelites justified their savage treatment against their enemies by appealing to the revenge of God. In the New Testament, on the other hand, the early Christians were taken up with an apocalyptic vision in which they expected the risen Jesus to return to the earth within their lifetime to establish a radical new order. The modern reader of the Bible cannot make sense out of either of these theological underpinnings.

The Christian, then, listens to the Bible, but it must be critical listening. There must be an appreciation of how the Israelites and the early Christians were transformed by their experience of God. There must also be an awareness of how their own peculiarities caused these people to formulate their response according to the dictates of their own culture.

The Old Testament covers a considerable expanse of time. Some significant figures and their approximate dates as set by modern scholarship indicate just how wide a scope of time the Old Testament encompasses:

Abraham — 1600 BC
Moses — 1275 BC
Joshua — 1225 BC
Samuel — 1025 BC
David — His reign lasted from 1005 to 965 BC
Solomon — His reign extended from 965 to 926 BC
Northern Kingdom — Lasted from 926 to 722 BC
Southern Kingdom — Lasted from 926 to 587 BC

This chapter is obviously limited in what it can say about the origin and nature of the Old Testament. However, some sense of its scope is necessary to appreciate the primitive ways of family life reported in most of the books as well as the changes in life seen throughout its development.

What must be realized is that for most of the history of the Israelites nothing was written down. They were an oral people. The different tribes that came to identify with the Israelite nation had their own versions of the founding covenant which they passed down from generation to generation. None of the material was written down until about 950 BC. Actually the process was a complex one in which different oral versions were consolidated into different written versions. In turn numerous written versions were woven into consolidated forms.

The process was finalized in the middle of the sixth century of that era with modern scholars identifying four main traditions in the first five books — the Pentateuch — of the Old Testament. These earliest books are important for understanding the remaining books of the Old Testament. They capture the founding traditions against which later developments are measured.

The four traditions of the Pentateuch are called the Yahwist tradition, the Elohist tradition, the Priestly tradition, and the Deuteronomic tradition. These traditions present the earliest reflections of the Israelites on their family lifestyle. As they think about their family in light of their experience of God, the Old Testament people undergo a long, tortuous journey. Any change that takes place is not a question of a dramatic breakthrough in which God laid down the laws and practices that were to govern how a husband and wife were to deal with each other. There were no simple handbooks on how to raise children.

A. Marriage and Family in the Culture

One who has grown up in a culture where family is seen primarily as a community of intimacy simply finds life in the Old Testament rather raw and shocking. Perhaps the family reality that most experience is far from ideal. However, the ideal that is expressed in television stories featuring families such as the Huxtables *(The Cosby Show)* and the Keatons *(Family Ties)* shows what we would like our families to be. In a sense they indicate what many in our society measure their experience of family life against. The shows may be recognized in part as unrealistic; however, they are not simply dismissed by their faithful audiences. The repeated experience of the close and warm families raises a good number of sighs and secret longings in those who watch. Somehow the shows touch on what could be. Perhaps they call to mind what is — at least in imperfect form — in the present family lives of the viewers.

Even the harsher television stories with the Ewings *(Dallas)* and the Carringtons *(Dynasty)* do not measure against the gritty reality of family life in the Old Testament. Perhaps a few case studies will bring the point home more dramatically. The following are examples of some of the family situations found in the Old Testament. They are presented in a "Dear Abby" format. Read the case and think about your response before moving on to how Solomon unravels the drama according to life in the Old Testament.

Case One

Dear Solomon:

My wife has not been able to get pregnant. I have done everything I can. We desperately want children since without them we are nothing. What should we do?

Signed,
Abe

Dear Abe:

Since your wife is obviously being punished by God and will probably never become pregnant, your only course of action is to take a concubine and have children by her. I would suggest you talk your wife into the idea and have her pick one of her maidservants. That will ease the potential jealousies that are bound to develop.

Signed,
Solomon

Case Two

Dear Solomon:

I was given to the master of the household to have children for the family. When my time comes, I am supposed to sit upon the lap of the wife, Sara, and allow the child to pass through her legs so she can claim the child as her own.

I am willing to be used this way; otherwise, I may never have children and my life will be for nought. However, I cannot tolerate the abuse that the wife heaps upon me. She is driven by a blind jealousy at my good fortune. She hates me because God has looked upon me with the favor of a child. I am about ready to run away even though I have little hope for sustaining myself or my child. I just cannot bear her continual cruelty to me.

Signed,
Hagar

Dear Hagar:

First, realize that part of the problem may stem from you. Do not act in a haughty way, flaunting your fertility and blessing in front of your mistress. Life is difficult enough for her since God has seen fit to punish her by depriving her of children.

Second, do not run from your master and mistress. Tolerate your suffering and God will bless you. You will have so many kids you will not be able to count them all.

Signed,
Solomon

Case Three

Dear Solomon:

My family has been disgraced. Last week in the town square in Sodom I met two men who were travelers. I offered them the hospitality of my house for the night. They accepted.

As you know, our city is not known for its morals. All the men of the city, both old and young, came to my door demanding that I cast the visitors out so that they could have their sexual pleasure with them. I had offered these visitors the mantle of my hospitality. My family honor was at stake. I would have done anything to avoid such a shame being brought on the name of my family. What could I have done?

Signed,
Lot

Dear Lot:

You should have thrown your two virgin daughters out to the crowd. That might have contented the mob and saved the honor of your family. It would at least have been worth the try.

Signed,
Solomon

Case Four

Dear Solomon:

We have had a difficult life. We lived in that cesspool of human debauchery, Sodom. Life there was difficult enough. People were such animals. One night our father, on the advice of some screwball seer, even tried to throw us out the door to a mob of lustful idiots. He tried to explain how we must be willing to sacrifice ourselves to the good of the family and its honor.

Our situation is desperate now. Sodom was destroyed by a firestorm. Our mother was turned into a pillar of salt because she looked back with fond memories at what was in Sodom. As a result we are now living in a cave with our father. There is no hope of our getting married and having children. Who would want us in our impoverished, filthy condition?

Please help us. We cannot face the prospect of virtually having no identity. Without a family one is nothing.

Signed,
Daughters of Lot

Dear Daughters:

It sounds as though you have a Lot on your mind. The only solution I can think of would be to get him drunk and sleep with him so that you might become pregnant. It would not improve your immediate situation. It will give you some brighter hope for the future.

Signed,
Solomon

Case Five

Dear Solomon:

My husband, Er, displeased the Lord and was slain. My father-in-law, Judah, realized that he had the sacred obligation to provide one of his other sons to fulfill the levirate obligation to carry on Er's name. Accordingly he sent his second son Onan to have intercourse with me so that the children could be considered as the offspring of Er and carry on his name.

Onan did not want his own children to be deprived of some of the inheritance. Therefore, he wasted his seed upon the ground before we would have relations; and I was not able to have children by him. God saw the injustice and slew Onan.

At this point Judah got rather nervous. He had already lost two sons. He blamed me in some way. He was not about to send me his third son, Shelah. His excuse was, at first, that Shelah was simply too young. He promised to have him fulfill the sacred levirate obligation once he achieved sufficient physical maturity. Meanwhile, I was sent back to my family of origin where I am considered little more than a lowly servant. I have no husband. I have no children. I have no hope.

What should I do?

Signed,
Tamar

Dear Tamar:

I would suggest that your only course of action lies in seducing or tricking either of the two remaining males of your husband's family. From what you have told me, I see little hope of an honest seduction. They do not look upon you kindly. However, they have a duty toward the memory of Er. Some trickery might be in order.

Try disguising yourself as a prostitute and see if you can win one of the men to your bed. At your age, you'd better concentrate on the father. When you begin to show with child, you'd better be prepared for the floodgates of fury. However, if you can prove that you were impregnated by your father-in-law, I believe he will be shamed enough at neglecting the levirate obligation that he will leave you be in peace and not stone you to death.

Signed,
Solomon

Case Six

Dear Solomon:

I am getting desperate. When we first got married, God blessed me with children. He kept my husband's other wife barren as a punishment, for Jacob loved her and not me.

Life was fine. Even though my husband did not love me, I was able to get respect because I was the only one bearing children. Rachel, however, was not content to abide by God's will. She gave her maidservant to our husband. The maidservant started to bear children. Then for some strange reason God permitted Rachel to bear children. I am losing my position of honor in the family. What should I do?

Signed,
Leah

Dear Leah:

If you find yourself temporarily unable to bear children and you are losing your place of honor to the other wife, I think it is time for some action. Go to your husband and demand that he take one of your maidservants to bed so that you also may claim a child through your maidservant.

Signed,
Solomon

These examples are drawn from the first book of the Old Testament, Genesis, and give a good flavor of the Semitic life upon which the Old Testament sense of family was based. The Abraham and Sarah story is taken from the sixteenth chapter of this book. It illustrates how important family was to these people. They would do literally anything in order to have family. They had no developed notion of an afterlife. This life was the only dance they had to do. Family therefore fulfilled many functions.

Family as a Source of Material Goods

As God's chosen, the Israelites expected to be blessed if they obeyed the will of God, but this life was the only one in which to receive blessings.

They therefore thought of material goods. They wanted large herds, many tents, and other signs of material prosperity. In that sense they were enthusiastic materialists. The key to understanding their emphasis on family is to realize that family was pivotal to all other blessings. It supplied the workers and the fighters that in turn provided prosperity and security.

Family as a Source of Immortality

There were other functions of family. Besides the material benefits of a large family, particularly a large family of males, there were the more existential benefits. In the absence of any viable afterlife, family was the only source of immortality. With children, the bloodline could in some way continue to exist. The father and mother would also be assured that some people would tell their stories. The memory of the parents would live on.

Living on in the memory of your offspring may not sound like an exciting sense of immortality. If it is the only game in town, however, one must participate or face the reality of extinction. One's family tree will come to an end without children. There were in their sense of reality no other alternatives to the family if one wanted any continued existence.

Most people today find the idea of dying without leaving any children a difficult reality to face. Yet many choose not to have children, and others simply are not able to have any. While a childless life is not without its trials and difficult decisions, the trauma is muted to some extent because we are such strong individualists. Family is important, but the basic unit of identity for people today is the individual.

There is a fluidity to the modern setting that allows people to become oriented in a variety of human experiences. The sense of the natural has been blunted in a technological world. Products are made to meet immediate demands. Similarly, human relationships or communities can be built to meet the demands for belonging and roots. Besides, the majority of the population has either a vague or a developed notion of personal immortality in which their spirit will live independent of the body. With such an alternative there is not as desperate a need for a continued presence in this physical life.

Family as a Source of Identity

The Old Testament did not have any developed notion of the spiritual immortality of the individual. Toward the latter part of the Old Testament period, around the second century BC, there was some sense of continued physical life after death centered around the resurrection of the body. However, belief in the immortality of the soul, so common in society today, was inherited from the Greeks and adopted by the Christians in the first few centuries of the present era. The Israelites of the Old Testament could not think of themselves apart from belonging to the earth and belonging to a people. Throughout most of the Old Testament era, family was needed not only for some sort of immortality but also for a sense of identity in their earthly life.

This concept of a family, a clan, a tribe, a nation is not all that easy to unpack for the modern mind. There were a number of realities that overlapped. There was the *beth 'ab* or "house of one's father," the *go'el* or sense of family solidarity, the *mishpahah* or motive of the clan, and the *shebet* or tribe. The nuclear family was obviously not isolated from the larger association of relatives. In fact the lines were not always that easy to distinguish. But the nuclear family was the basic unit. It was the foundation.

Abraham and Sarah's actions indicate that one must try different avenues to have children. Their days saw the practice of modified monogamy. There was only one wife; but at least when the wife was barren, concubines could be employed. In a ritual in which the pregnant woman sat on the knees of the man's wife, the child was claimed to be the offspring of the main couple.

Women and the Need for Family

The story also intimates the dire position of women who faced a life of barrenness. The more children a woman had, the greater her prestige. This social reality is what motivated Hagar to flaunt her belly in front of her barren mistress. It also gave her the energy to face the cruel punishments thrown her way by the enraged Sarah. The prestige that comes with children also explains the motivation behind some of the other stories.

The competition between Rachel and Leah (Gen 30) is an intense battle for more and more children in which they employ the efforts of their maidservants Bilhah and Zilpah. Their peculiar form of rivalry makes sense only to the extent that one understands the importance of children in the lives of these women. Similarly, Lot's seduction by his daughters is completely incomprehensible unless the reader makes an effort to enter their world. Women faced a life without identity if they could not find some way of getting children.

When a woman was left in a family without husband and without offspring, as was the case with Tamar (Gen 38), she was left with nothing. When a later book of the Old Testament, the book of Ruth, tried to preach a sense of undying loyalty to a kin, one got a glimpse of just how dire was the life of an unwed woman without offspring. Ruth refused to abandon her mother-in-law even though her own husband and her father-in-law were deceased. There were no immediate males to offer the two any hope. Ruth was forced to glean grains from the field. In other words she had to go out and pick up the droppings after the harvest in an attempt to keep herself and Naomi, her mother-in-law, from starving. Only after a distant male cousin consented to take the women under his protection was there any hope that life might take a more positive turn. The book is clearly trying to teach that those who live a life of sacrificing love will be rewarded by God. However, within the context of the day, God had to work through the good intentions of a male to show how Ruth was rewarded for her efforts.

Perhaps no story depicts the dire position of women better than the story of Lot and his concern with the honor of the family's name. Just before the destruction of Sodom and Gomorrah (Gen 19) the messengers from God come to the town to warn Lot and his family. He does not recognize them as coming from God, but he does offer them the graces of his home. Once the blanket of hospitality was extended, the family was responsible for the well-being of its guests. If somehow the guests were mistreated, the family was disgraced. Likewise, if the family was disgraced, all in the family were disgraced.

Family identity explains part of Lot's actions in the story. By itself it does not account for Lot's willingness to cast his daughters to the crowd. He probably would not have been willing to throw out his sons, if he had had any, to the mob's pleasures. No, one must appreciate the lowly position of women to understand Lot's behavior.

A woman was always under the control of a man — her father, her brother, her husband. From the point of view of the marital relationship the husband was called the "master" or *ba'al* of his wife (Ex 21:3; 22:2; 2 Sam 11:26; Prov 12:4), and in places the married woman is called the possession of her master (Gen 20:3; Dt 22:22). The control of the male was so extensive that the husband could nullify vows made by his wife (Num 30:10-14).

Styles of Marriage in the Old Testament

The marriages of the Old Testament run the gamut from modified monogamy, seen in the Abraham and Sarah story in which concubines were permitted, to polygamy and practical monogamy. Obviously with Jacob, Rachel, and Leah, the Israelites practiced polygamy. Polygamy was recognized as a legal reality in Deuteronomy (Dt 21:15) and later in the Talmud which limited the king to eighteen wives and the commoner to four. A survey of such books as Proverbs, Ecclesiastes, Song of Songs, Wisdom and Sirach, however, would seem to indicate that the monogamous marriage is presumed.

The movement toward monogamy may be the result of simple practical considerations. Large families were an important asset when one lived a nomadic lifestyle. They were an economic liability for one who was a craftsman living a settled life in a small town or village. The other force moving the people to the practice of monogamy may have been the growing sense of what marriage is in light of their experience of God. The impact of the God experience on marriage practices will be addressed more thoroughly later in this chapter.

At any rate, the woman was, by modern standards, at the will of her husband. While there were few restrictions on his sexual behavior, there was no question of her fidelity. It was through her that the purity of the line was guaranteed. The women were strictly watched and controlled in their dealings with men outside the family.

The laws governing extramarital relations and rape are helpful in realizing the importance put upon the woman's fidelity. If a married woman was found to have had relations with another man willingly, she was to be put to death. When Judah found out Tamar was pregnant, he fully intended to put her to death until she proved that she had relations with him in an attempt to have offspring. When a rape of a married woman or one betrothed took place within the city walls, both the woman and the man committing the crime were to be stoned. The man's fault was that he did not respect the rights of another family. The woman's fault was that she did not resist with her very being when there was a possibility that the attack could have been overheard and stopped (Dt 22:22-24). If, however, the rape took place in the country, only the man would be executed since there was little hope that the woman in her distress could be heard by others.

On the other hand, the laws governing the sexual relations of a single woman show a concern for protecting the woman as well as the rights of the family. Originally the law (Ex 22:15-17) stated that in the case of sexual relations with an unmarried woman, the man was forced to pay the value of the daughter to the father. The father then had the option of forcing the man to marry the daughter or not. The reform in Deuteronomy 22:25-27 stated that once the fifty shekels were paid to the father, there was no choice. The man had to marry the woman and was not permitted to divorce her.

It is not easy for people today to see how the provisions of Deuteronomy are a reform in an effort to give some protection to the woman. The woman was given no choice. Conceivably she could be forced to marry a man who had raped her. What woman would want to marry such an individual? Secondly, why tie the hands of the father who would want to seek a better marriage for his daughter?

These questions simply show how foreign the cultural practices of the Israelites really are to the modern experience. Certainly today a woman would not want to marry someone who raped her. Marriage today is for personal reasons. We marry for love. We marry to form a community of intimacy. Besides, a woman who is raped has a good deal of trauma to face, but she does not become an anathema to other men.

By contrast, the Israelite woman lost any prospects of a decent marriage once she was raped. She was used, and usually only desperate men would even consider such a woman for a wife. As for taking the decision out of the father's hand, one can get a clue as to why the reformers would do so from Lot's treatment of his daughters just prior to the destruction of Sodom. There were probably fathers who loved their daughters deeply and considered them daddy's little girl. In the culture, however, this deep parental love was not the norm. Women were a point of bargaining for a family. Their relationship with their father was not primarily one of personal intimacy. Conceivably what the reformers were trying to avoid were the many fathers who would take the initial money from the men guilty of the rape and then try to strike whatever bargain they could elsewhere with little or no regard for the well-being of the daughter.

In short, from the woman's perspective, any marriage was preferable to a life where one remained single and without offspring. Secondly, as the story of Leah shows, marriage to someone who loved you was preferable, but intimacy was not the primary reason for family life. If a woman could find some marriage that would bring her an element of prestige, she took it.

Conflict and Divorce in the Family

Once married, of course, the woman was not all that secure. She could easily be divorced. The governing text for divorce is the opening verse for Deuteronomy 24. A man may divorce his wife if "he finds in her something indecent."

The passage is rather vague and clearly leaves itself open to a variety of interpretations. Lawyers today would have a field day with a term as open as "something indecent," and in fact the Old Testament period saw its range of interpretations. In the rabbinical age of later years there were two main schools. The followers of Shammai admitted divorce only for "adultery and misconduct." The followers of Hillel "would accept any reason, however trivial, such as the charge that a wife had cooked a dish badly, or merely that the husband preferred another woman."[2]

With the possibility of the husband resorting to such trivial cases as those proposed by the school of Hillel, one can appreciate just how tenuous a woman's position was in married life. The only way to find some security beside the obvious luck of being given to a compassionate man was to have children. Motherhood cemented her bond to the family. It raised her esteem in the community. It increased her worth to her husband.

The emphasis on the value of children to the mother, so evident in the Rachel and Leah competition, should not conjure up scenes of a woman tenderly caring for her offspring and in turn being nurtured in her old age by those who addressed her every wish. Undoubtedly such realities existed at least in muted forms. But again the modern person must stretch the imagination to try to get into the reality of family life as experienced in the culture of Israel. Family was primarily an economic and social unit for the Israelites.

The general tone of family life reported throughout the Old Testament is one of conflict, jealousy, and struggles — I against my brother, my

---

2.   Roland de Vaux, O.P., *Ancient Israel* (New York: McGraw-Hill, 1961) p. 34.

brother and I against our cousins, my brother, my cousins, and I against the world. That sequence would be one way of capturing the underlying attitude of Jewish family life. The books are filled with sibling rivalry. Cain slays Abel (Gen 4:8); Jacob blackmails Esau as the older brother is at the point of starvation (Gen 25:31); Joseph is sold by his brothers into slavery (Gen 37:25-28); Amnon rapes his sister Tamar (2 Sam 13:14). Similarly, relations between parents and offspring are often at odds. The classic story is found in Rebecca favoring Jacob over Esau. She ruthlessly plots with her favorite to trick Isaac in his old age. she wants Jacob to gain the blessing of the first-born (Gen 27).

Most of the stories of parent and sibling hostilities single out the father-child conflict. The father was, after all, the dominant parent, and the conflicts would naturally focus on him. Similarly, the celebration of children was often done in terms of the joy they brought to the father (Ps 127; 128).

The bottom line is, however, that there is ample evidence of how important children were for women in adding stability and honor to their lives.

B. The Old Testament Theology of Marriage

The previous section investigated what the overall practice of family life was in the cultural setting. As explained in the beginning of this chapter, that is only one consideration. A specific look at how the Israelites reflected on their experience of God is important. More to the point of this study, it is important to consider how the reflection in light of their God experience, how this theology, caused them to ever so subtly change their ways of behavior. At the very least it should have changed their ideals of behavior.

There is no doubt that the Israelites were conscious of God active in their lives. The stories related in the first section spoke readily of God choosing who would be fertile and who would not be. Modern explanations, obviously, would look to other causes. For the Israelites, God was directly responsible for everything. He certainly was responsible for the most important reality in their lives — their families.

The Theology of the Creation Accounts

One place where the influence of their religious experience is evident is in the beginning of the Old Testament. Chapter 1 of Genesis gives the creation account as presented by the priestly tradition. Chapter 2 presents the Yahwist tradition's version of how the world was created.

The priestly account was probably written in the sixth century of that era by the priests of the southern kingdom. It reflects the theological position that benefited from centuries of experience and growth in their appreciation of God's calling. From the point of view of marriage, the important verses are Genesis 1:27-28.

In the first of these two verses there is a play on words. Translation
from the original texts to English is not easy; however, most interpretations
agree that somehow the play on words is designed to capture the complementarity of the male and the female. The New American Bible translation
presents the verse:

> God created man in his image;
> in the divine image he created him;
> male and female he created them.

This particular translation shifts from the singular masculine pronoun
in the second line to the plural in the third line. It captures how the species
is one, but the one species is not complete without both the male and the
female. There is no attempt at this point to establish any hierarchy.

By implication, therefore, this sense of complementarity and equity is
the way that God intended the relationship to be from the beginning. This is
the ideal. There is no hint that the two are not equal in the original design.
The harsh reality that was in fact the life of the Israelite women was not the
way things were intended.

Some may argue that the sense of equity in the text is not that evident.
They may insist that at best it is implied. However, if this and the second
creation account are interpreted in light of the curse after the fall, it becomes
evident that the author of this creation account is indeed presenting the two
species as equal. The story of the fall, which will be discussed in the next
section, clearly shows that the inequality of the sexes in the life of the Israelites was a punishment that resulted from the fall and was not intended by
God from the very beginning.

Verse 28 of the first chapter continues by addressing the marital relationship more directly:

> God blessed them, saying: "Be fertile
> and multiply; fill the earth and subdue it.
> Have dominion over the fish of the sea,
> the birds of the air, and all the living
> things that move on the earth."

Obviously, marriage is presented as God's plan to increase the human
race. Since the human is made in the image of God, as verse 26 asserts, then
it is logical that the human is meant to be the dominant creature on the earth.
The human is called upon to take charge of creation.

Such a charge may cause people steeped in the modern experience to
cringe. They have seen humans gobble up huge portions of the earth to the
point where other life forms are threatened. It is quite possible that before
the end of the century there will not be any wild elephants, tigers, lions, or
pandas left on the earth. And these are just the more dramatic examples of
how other life forms are threatened by human presence.

If the creation account were written today, it might well urge humans to live in harmony with the ecosystem. But just as many of the experiences of the Israelites are difficult if not impossible for us to comprehend today, so this modern reality could not have been foreseen by the writers of the first creation account. They were dealing with a people struggling to make their presence felt in a world that was quite overwhelming. The modern experience is not the Jewish experience of the sixth century BC.

Turning attention to the second chapter of Genesis, the creation account from the Yahwist tradition is of much older origins. The God here is a more simple, homey type. Where the God of the Priestly tradition goes around and gives commands only to see cosmic powers come into being and take their ordered places, the God of the second creation account must go about his task on a much simpler scale. When he wants to make man, he must work with a hunk of clay. He formed the figure of a man and then breathed into the nostrils. The clay sat up and looked around.

What followed is not without its touching humor as the story pictures a man who after the initial excitement of creation becomes lonely. God in an attempt to relieve this loneliness begins forming all types of wild creatures, presents them to the man, and allows the man to name them.

This naming process concurs with the first creation account which commanded that humans were to have dominion over the earth. Those who had the power to name had the power to control. God, in allowing the man to name the products of his creation, was giving the human creature the power to rule over other creatures.

The humor of the second creation account is caught in the unsuccessful attempts. God had intended to relieve the man's loneliness. His attempts were in vain. The most he was able to cull from the man was a mild interest as the creature would pass on a weak compliment and a name when the hard-working God would show the results of his latest effort. Finally God got an idea. He would try to stimulate his lethargic prize of creation by making a creature similar to the man but with important differences. Man's reactions verify that finally God got it right. Verse 23 reports:

"This one, at last, is bone of my bones
and flesh of my flesh;
This one shall be called 'woman,'
for out of 'her man' this one has been taken."

The following verse then goes on to address the passage that has the most direct application to marriage. It is the passage that will be quoted in the New Testament. It is the passage that forcefully shows how the two must form a close unity:

That is why a man leaves his father
and mother and clings to his wife, and
the two of them become one body.

The sense of complementarity, the sense of bonding, the sense of unity is stronger here than in the first account of creation. Some commentary from conservative groups will stress that since man came first, he is the prototype and is meant to have the place of honor. Some liberal commentators, on the other hand, have argued that since the woman was made last, she is the perfection of man. Both cases seem to be arguing their causes rather than taking the passage as presented.

As found in the text, there is a clear presentation that the two in the marriage become one in some fundamental way. There is a bonding that goes beyond simple social custom, personal intentions, or practical design. There is a unity that grows out of the very nature of human existence. The couple must think of themselves in unison and not simply as two individuals who have entered into a contract.

Both creation accounts, therefore, present a strong message about the dignity of male and female. Both stress the unique relationship of husband and wife.

This, then, is the explicit theology of the two creation accounts. The key message is the same. The expression does vary to some extent. But there is another important theological point made in the creation accounts which may not be too evident to the modern reader. It is a central point, however, and a sore spot in the continued history of the Israelites.

Although marriage is seen as involving a special bonding which calls upon the spouses to think and live as though they are one, it is not pictured as in any way opening the doors to special epiphanies. It is not an avenue for tapping into the sacred powers of the divine as so many of the fertility cults would insist. On the contrary, creation itself was holy. Creation itself was a part of God's handiwork, and marriage was placed in the context of creation taken as a whole.

Israel was frequently tempted to imitate the practices of the people who surrounded them and turn the sexual experience itself into a special religious ritual. Humans experienced such a powerful expression of life in the sexual act that they felt they were breaking into sacred time and space. But the Old Testament continually calls its people to place the end and goal of marriage within the universal call of creation. In a sense one could say that sexuality and marriage were secularized.

The Theology of the Fall

With such a beginning, then, how did the realities of Israelite life come into being? How could women be treated so lowly? How could the marriage bond be treated so lightly with polygamous marriages and with the ease of divorce? What happened between the creation accounts and the practice of family life in the remaining parts of the Genesis account?

In a sense the clash between the ideal presented in the creation accounts and the realities of Israelite life cannot be understood unless one realizes that the creation accounts represent the considered religious reflection of a people who have had many centuries to mature. In a sense, the creation accounts are saying: This is what marriage should be. This is what the relationship of male and female should be. This is what was intended by God from the very beginning, from the moment of creation.

As a text, the Bible links this ideal intended by God from the very beginning to the realities of Semitic life by reporting the fall from the ideal. In other words sin comes into the picture. Humans do not live up to the ideal. Adam and Eve disobey God and are in turn punished by him in proportion to their guilt.

The tradition generally sees the story of the fall presenting the woman as having the greater guilt since she is pictured as leading the man into the sin. When the punishments are meted out, it is not surprising, therefore, that the woman receives the greater sentence.

Eve receives a threefold punishment. She is now to bring forth children with intense pain. She is still going to lust after her husband only to find herself with child again. Finally, the male will be her master. In other words the ideal set up by God has been disrupted.

Such a typography is not surprising given the patriarchal structure of the society. In a sense the mandate that the literature had was twofold. It had to justify the given practices of the society. That is a function that myths and the sacred stories of a people fulfill. Secondly, myths and the founding stories of a people are supposed to stretch them toward an ideal.

The theologians working with the creation accounts could not simply condemn the traditional way of life of its audience. They did, however, want to challenge the practices of the day. Their solution was to present the ideal as the original order and to present the fall as the alternative order. The effect of this strategy, in all probability, was to strengthen a growing sensitivity among the people for the need to treat each other with love and respect.

Other Theological Themes

Against the reality of Semitic family life, one finds celebrations of marriage that capture in some degree the ideal presented in the creation accounts. In other words, despite the effects of sin, there developed a sense that marriage was a moving, unique bond. The language and the images used clearly indicate that there was a more powerful force active in marriage than was recognized by the legal realities of Israelite life.

One finds in the Song of Songs a sensual celebration of passionate love that pushes aside the legalities of divorce and the conflicts that dominate the families found in the Genesis account. Here the unity of the couple is captured through the sensuous bonding of the love.

The bride sings out to her beloved:

Let him kiss me with kisses of his mouth.
More delightful is your love than wine!
Your name spoken is a spreading perfume.
That is why the maidens love you.
Draw me! (1:1-4)

Later in the first chapter, one of the responses of the groom is to praise the beauty of his spouse:

To the steeds of Pharaoh's chariots would I liken you, my beloved:
Your cheeks lovely in pendants, your neck in jewels.
We will make pendants of gold for you, and silver ornaments. (1:9-11)

There may not be, in truth, many girls today who would be swept off their feet as their loved one compares them to a horse. Every culture has its images that excite them. But such language exchanged by men and women capture in some way how on a sensual level, at least, Israel senses how taken a man and a woman can be with each other.

On another level one finds the marriage bond being given the utmost compliment by comparing the relationship of marriage to the bond between God and Israel. The experience of God and Israel was not an easy one, but it was an enduring one because no momentary unfaithfulness can undo the bond between them:

The Lord calls you back, like a wife forsaken and grieved in spirit,
A wife married in youth and then cast off, says your God.
For a brief moment I abandoned you, but with great tenderness I will
take you back.
In an outburst of wrath, for a moment I hid my face from you;
But with enduring love I take pity on you, says the Lord, your redeemer.
(Is 54:6-7)

The context of the statement is Israel's constant unfaithfulness. There are times when God becomes angered and turns his back, but the love is an enduring one which cannot be broken by the infidelity of the partner. God always relents and accepts his bride back into the good graces of his love.

The implications for the marital bond is obvious. It is a relationship that should not be taken lightly. Perhaps marriage can never live up to the ideal offered by the faithfulness of God. Still, the challenge of the ideal should serve marriage well.

Similar passages that compare the marital relationship and the domestic life to the love Yahweh has for Israel can be found in other parts of the Old Testament. Jeremiah 2:2-32, Ezekiel 16, Ezekiel 23, and Hosea 1-3 are some examples.

In fact these comparisons were probably introduced to draw upon daily life to emphasize just how good and faithful God was. The practical effect of the comparison was not simply to impress upon the people how dependable God was. In reality the comparison served to raise the Israelite appreciation of the beauty of marriage. The contrast is dramatic between the following quotes taken from both ends of the Israelite tradition.

In the laws of marriage taken from the book of Deuteronomy the twenty fourth chapter reads:

> When a man, after marrying a woman and having relations with her, is later displeased with her because he finds in her something indecent, and therefore he writes out a bill of divorce and hands it to her, thus dismissing her from his house: if on leaving his house she goes and becomes the wife of another man, and the second husband, too, comes to dislike her and dismisses her from his house by handing her a written bill of divorce . . . then her former husband, who dismissed her, may not again take her as his wife after she has become defiled (Dt 24: 1-4).

By contrast one reads in the prophet Malachi the following passage which shows a significant change in the sense of commitment in marriage:

> Did he not make one being, with flesh and spirit:
>   and what does that one require but godly offspring?
> You must then safeguard life that is your own,
>   and not break faith with the wife of your youth.
> For I hate divorce, says the Lord, the God of Israel,
> And covering one's garment with injustice, says the Lord of hosts;
> You must then safeguard life that is your own, and not break faith.
> (Mal 2:15-16)

There are many experiences which cause this significant shift. Somewhere in the measure of events, the comparison of marriage to the bond existing between Yahweh and Israel must be measured.

Actually the honored comparison for marriage must be placed in a larger picture. In the last line of the quote from Malachi, one reads the phrase, "and not break faith." Throughout the Old Testament an important theme is the sense of covenant.

There are several covenants or agreements mentioned in the Jewish scriptures. They signify an agreement or a bonding that exists between God and his people. A covenant is not like a modern contract in which people confront each other with different sets of obligations. In the contract, if one of the parties fails, then the contract is voided. By contrast, the covenant between Israel and Yahweh was a generous bonding initiated by Yahweh. He accepted Israel despite its continued unfaithfulness. This is the sense of commitment which had its impact on the thinking of marriage in the Old Testament. It will also have its impact on the thinking in the Christian era.

4.2   Marriage in the New Testament
Thomas M. Martin

THE PREVIOUS SECTION ON THE OLD TESTAMENT TRIED TO SHOW HOW THE experience of God stimulated a very gradual change in the family life of the Israelites. The sense of sacredness in life that their experience of Yahweh created could not help but have an impact on their sense of how husband and wife were to treat and to consider each other.

The New Testament inherited this tradition of the Old Testament. However, the translation was not an easy one. In the Old Testament the experience of God was persistent, but it did not match the dramatic, all-absorbing experience of God in the Jesus event. The sense of God's pending activity was so intense among the earliest Christians that everything in daily life paled in its light.

The New Testament spans only a few decades. It does not show the gradual change in family and marriage. In fact, most of its books do not focus in any direct way on marriage and family. Where there is reference to marriage and family, the passages usually are attempting to drive home the all-important message of preparing for the kingdom of God which the early Christians expected to be established within their lifetime.

It would make little sense then to try to glean what were the customs of marriage and family during the times of Jesus. He did not spend time trying to reform the practices of the day. His presentation for the most part bypassed the practices of daily life and challenged his listeners to a radical conversion.

This present section, therefore, will be organized differently than the previous one. Where the treatment of the Old Testament looked at the customs of the Semitic people and then examined how the experience of God caused gradual but important changes, this section will go more directly to the theological reflections. Comments will be made on the customs of the day where these provide an appropriate context for understanding the nature of the New Testament challenge.

A. The New Testament Theology of Marriage

Perhaps the best way of understanding how the early Christians incorporated the heritage of the Old Testament into their thinking about marriage is to look at a passage from Ephesians 5:

> Wives should be submissive to their husbands as if to the Lord because the husband is head of his wife just as Christ is head of his body the church, as well as its savior. As the church submits to Christ, so wives should submit to their husbands in everything.
> Husbands, love your wives, as Christ loved the church. He gave himself

up for her to make her holy, purifying her in the bath of water by the power of the word, to present to himself a glorious church, holy and immaculate, without stain or wrinkle or anything of that sort. Husbands should love their wives as they do their own bodies. He who loves his wife loves himself. Observe that no one ever hates his own flesh; no, he nourishes it and takes care of it as Christ cares for the church for we are members of his body.

For this reason a man shall leave his father and mother,
and shall cling to his wife,
and the two shall be made into one.

This is a great foreshadowing; I mean that it refers to Christ and the church. In any case, each one should love his wife as he loves himself, the wife for her part showing respect for her husband (Eph 5:22-33).

It is difficult for readers today to appreciate the endearing relationship that is pictured here. The elevated position given to men is obvious and offensive to those whose daily life is a struggle for an appreciation of their true worth as women. However, if one can understand the patriarchal structure of the society, the passage can then be appreciated for how it moves the relationship of husband and wife to a new level because of the Jesus event.

In the previous section the covenant theme was seen as playing a central role. God conferred his help, or he graced the world with his presence and commitment. Jesus was seen as the final covenant by the Christians. He was seen as the final graceful presence that would permanently transform the world.

Where the Old Testament compared the marriage bond to that of the covenant that existed between God and Israel, this quote compares the marital bond to the relationship that exists between Christ and the church. If the wife is to submit to the husband, it is not business as usual for a patriarchal society. The model used is Christ. The husband is therefore expected to respond in kind. They are exhorted to "love your wives, as Christ loved the church."

Probably the passage has limited pastoral use today because of how serious the patriarchal issues are for marital relations. In the future, if the community grows sufficiently, perhaps it can more easily appreciate how this comparison called Christians far beyond the normal practices of the day. The relationships are transformed as they are moved to the level of relationship experienced in Jesus.

Theologically, the passage has been important. Marriage is placed at the heart of the mystery of God relating to the world. After quoting the second creation account in verse 31, the text goes on to explain that this bonding of husband and wife is the foreshadowing of the bond between Christ and the church. The New American Bible translation quoted here uses the word "foreshadowing" in verse 32. Other translations use the term "mystery" while earlier Catholic editions would follow the Vulgate edition and use "sacrament." At any rate marriage is seen as in some way symbolizing or capturing the essence of God's activity in the world as fulfilled in Jesus' relationship with the church.

In strong contrast to the passage from Ephesians, one finds a startling statement about Christian marriage in the first letter to the Corinthians. In chapter seven of this epistle, St. Paul presents a jolting passage. It flies in the face of the Old Testament thinking and shocks the sensibilities of many present day Christians. The passage reads:

> A man is better off having no relations with a woman. But to avoid immorality, every man should have his own wife and every woman her own husband. The husband should fulfill his conjugal obligations toward his wife, the wife hers toward her husband. A wife does not belong to herself but to her husband; equally, a husband does not belong to himself but to his wife. Do not deprive one another, unless perhaps by mutual consent for a time, to devote yourselves to prayer. Then return to one another, that Satan may not tempt you through your lack of self-control. I say this by way of concession, not as a command. Given my preference, I should like you to be as I am (1 Cor 7:1-6).

Not only is this difficult for modern day Christians, but it was equally difficult for the Jews of the day. It serves clear notice that one faces in the Christian message a call for a radical change in life. Everything lost its importance in the presence of God's impending action.

In the first sentence, the advice that a man is better not having any sexual relations is almost incomprehensible in light of the Jewish tradition. The previous section showed how everything revolved around the family. The Jews considered themselves as God's chosen people. They expected to give obedience to God, and in return they expected to be blessed. However, this life was the only one for which they could gather much enthusiasm. Therefore, they expected to be blessed in this life, but family was the key to all other blessings. It was the source of immortality, prosperity, security, and identity.

The previous section showed how desperate both men and women were if they could not have a family with an appropriate number of offspring. To the people who identified with the main line of Jewish tradition, Paul's opening words of advice would be all but incomprehensible.

True, there were Jewish groups around the first century of this era who reflected the mystical influence of other religions. Greek religious traditions in particular with their dualistic sense of life had some impact on small groups in Palestine. The dualistic view of human life saw two parts in conflict — the spiritual part and the physical part. The spiritual part was the important one and had to be nurtured over the physical part.

But the overall Christian message certainly did not fit into a dualistic pattern. It does not present the physical and spiritual dimensions of human life as in conflict. In fact the largest portion of the New Testament remains thoroughly Jewish in that it could not conceive of human beings in anything but physical terms. When it presented a sense of an afterlife, it spoke of the resurrection of the body and not the immortality of the soul.

There were other Jewish fringe groups which had picked up on what is called an apocalyptic vision. Such a view of life sees the present order coming to an end and a new time being established in which life will be changed in ways so radical as to virtually defy human imagination. The Christian message has more in common with these religious movements.

The Christians were expecting Jesus to come in glory within their lifetime. He was to establish a radical new order that was described by Matthew in the following passage:

> Immediately after the stress of that period, the sun will be darkened, the moon will not shed her light, the stars will fall from the sky, and the hosts of heaven will be shaken loose. Then the sign of the Son of Man will appear in the sky, and "all the clans of earth will strike their breasts" as they see "the Son of Man coming on the clouds of heaven" with power and great glory. He will dispatch his angels "with a mighty trumpet blast, and they will assemble his chosen from the four winds, from one end of the heavens to the other" (Mt 24:29-31).

Christianity did share its call for a radical lifestyle with other groups that had Jewish roots. But the Christian message was primarily intended for the mainstream Jewish audience. For these Jews the message would not be easy to take or to understand. For these people, marriage and family were so deeply ingrained in their life that every male was legally charged to marry by a certain age.

Paul's opening sentence is indeed startling when placed within the mainstream Jewish culture of the day. His passage does not dismiss marriage and family as bad. This is clear in his second sentence. In fact he counsels most Christians that they should marry. But his presentation of marriage as almost a concession to the weakness of the average person fails to celebrate the Jewish enthusiasm for the family.

Paul's vision of marriage is not dripping with idealism. The purpose of marriage, in rather blunt terms, is to avoid immorality. Paul speaks of the "conjugal obligation." It is a rather curious term for today's audience which has such an appreciation for the beauty and the value of physical love. Did you do your "conjugal obligation" today? What a strange mentality. And in truth the New Testament attitude about marriage and family is strange for modern readers be they Christian or the curious.

Given Paul's situation, however, it did make sense. He was writing his letter advising a community of Christians who were anxiously awaiting the return of Jesus. They were living in the North African city of Corinth that had simply an atrocious reputation for its moral life in a declining Roman empire not noted for its high standards of human behavior. Prostitutes in many sections of the empire were often referred to as Corinthian girls. In other words, if other Romans thought that Corinth was a bad place, it must have been really bad.

One does not have to be a dualist to recognize that passions and appetites can cause one to act in life-destroying ways. This Christian community was living in the midst of moral chaos. Paul had enough insight into human nature to realize that the community of believers would not go unaffected by the larger society. He appreciated the difficulty that the Christians in this community had in living a life of responsible commitment.

Paul was not a modern person whose environment encouraged him to appreciate the positive qualities of passions, appetites and emotions. He lived in a society that was struggling for a basic order and sense of human respect. His view of marriage as a way for the Corinthians to control their urges is understandable then if seen in this light. However, for those who go to the New Testament without any background and are simply looking for inspiration for daily life, the message of 1 Corinthians 7 is indeed difficult.

There are a number of reasons why Paul's counsel strikes a strange chord with the modern Christian. The crux of the problem, however, can be seen in verse 5. The religious imagery of this passage sees daily life as a distraction from God. Those involved with the cares of a spouse or of children are taken from concentrating solely and completely on God. Today, by contrast, most see the search for God and daily life as being harmonious. One contributes to the other. They are not at odds.

Paul advises the married couple not to separate unless "by mutual consent for a time, to devote yourselves to prayer." In other words the relationship between the spouses is seen as a hindrance in their attempt to reach God. This tension is made clear by other passages not quoted in the opening verses. For example, verses 32-33 of the same chapter explicitly state:

> I should like you to be free of all worries. The unmarried man is busy with the Lord's affairs, concerned with pleasing the Lord; but the married man is busy with this world's demands and occupied with pleasing his wife. This means he is divided.

The following diagram captures the way Paul presents the husband and wife relationship as it interferes with the search for God. The spouses who wish to find God can do so most effectively as they separate from each other and look for God in their private or communal prayer. The benefits of withdrawing from the domestic life of the family is clearly stated. The spouses can find God better if they can escape from the demands of daily life, because there is no direct connection between household chores and the search for God. With time so short, the individual would be well advised to do the work of the Lord.

By contrast to the above way of thinking, most modern Christians are more comfortable seeing daily life and the search for the holy on a continuum. One discovers God in the true depths of the other, the true depths of the self, or the true depths of creation. In other words, this is God's creation, and God is the ground of all that exists. True, one can be distracted by the pursuit of material goods. True, one can be corrupted by misusing the goods and people of this world. True, one can frantically pursue the self and its needs and land in a wallow of aimlessness and isolation. However, if one probes the mystery of the world and others by treating them with respect and reverence, then one finds the sacred that lies at the mysterious depths of everything.

Put in these terms, the marriage relationship is often seen today as a way of discovering God and not a hindrance in one's journey to God. There is no need to withdraw from the daily chores and rhythms of life. God is found at the heart of all creation. Everything, especially a loving spouse, can be the source of discovering God. The diagram below would capture how this way of thinking sees the relationship of marriage and the search for God.

The contrast between the two mentalities, then, is telling. Paul presents his Christian ideal in the final sentence of the passage quoted. He tells his readers, "Given my preference, I should like you to be as I am."

What did Paul mean by this challenge? Obviously he was calling those who could hear his message to the celibate life. In all probability he was married at one time. After he became a Christian, his wife either died, left him because of his conversion, or he left her because she would not live in peace with his Christian calling. His present vocation, however, was to remain unmarried. He gave his complete effort to serving the Lord. He worked

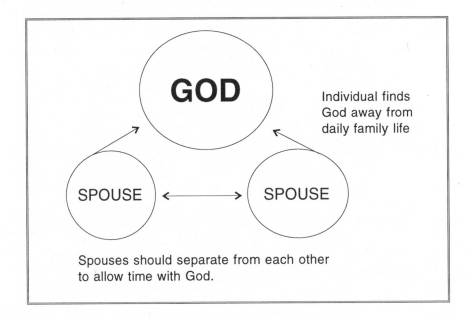

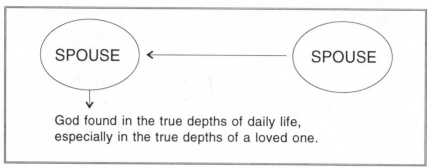

tirelessly in spreading the word and was intent on supporting himself in his own trade so that he would not be a burden on any of the local communities.

Paul finishes the chapter by exhorting his listeners on items that are consistent with his opening verses. He encourages both widows and virgins to remain unmarried if possible. He is clear that they commit no wrong if they decide to marry. By grouping virgins and widows together, he clearly shows that he is not working within the dynamics of a dualistic worldview. Sexuality is not the issue. The cares of this world, even the self-sacrificing of the mother caring for her children, are simply distracting in the search for God.

His advice to those already married is to remain together. They have made a commitment and should honor it. He does admit that those who converted after their marriage may face particularly difficult situations. Often the spouse may not have any respect for the Christian calling. Still, Paul urges the Christian to remain with the unbeliever if possible. The one who has found the faith may be the source of conversion for the spouse. If everything fails in an attempt to win peace with the unbelieving spouse and he or she wishes to leave, then one should let such a spouse go.

Paul's treatment of marriage in his letter to the Corinthians is the most direct and forceful statement of the theology of marriage in the New Testament. But it cannot be understood without Ephesians 5. The two passages balance each other and foreshadow the constant struggle the tradition will have in giving marriage its due while still accounting for how overwhelming the personal call of God can be.

God's activity in marriage captures the heart of the redemptive initiative in the world. Still, Christians who experience the intensity of a personal calling from God have a difficult time focusing on the concerns of daily family living.

Some of the passages in the Corinthian text reflect the peculiar quirks Paul faced in dealing with a Christian community known for its radical behavior in a city that had its own struggles with chaos. However, the main thrust of the passage urges Christians to put the preparation for the kingdom above everything else. While not the final or complete word of the New Testament, this message does capture the main thrust of the early Christian teaching. The Christians were a people who were obsessed with the expected coming of Jesus to establish a new order.

The theology of marriage is in fact never treated in an extended way outside the epistles. It simply was not central to the concerns of the earliest Christians. They were taken with preparing for the kingdom. They presumed the message spelled out in Paul's letter.

Marriage and family, of course, could not be ignored in the other books of the New Testament. To the first century Jews who were the original audience of Jesus and who were for the most part the intended audience for the New Testament, family was as central as the study of the Old Testament would suggest. If Jesus were to be an effective teacher, therefore, he would have to draw heavily upon the family images that were so dear to the hearts of his listeners.

B. The Family Image in the New Testament

Family images are certainly used in the New Testament. The images were used, however, to teach a lesson about the central theme that runs throughout the New Testament — prepare for the kingdom for it will come in its fullness shortly.

Each treatment of the family usually brings out a slightly different message. Each however is clearly related to the kingdom.

The Family of Jesus

Combing the volumes of pious literature today, the reader can uncover long treatises on the domestic life of the holy family. Volumes have been written about Joseph. Dramas have been developed about the domestic skills of Mary. The fact is, however, that the New Testament was not interested in the domestic virtues found in the common life of Jesus, Mary, and Joseph. It was intent on simply keeping the focus on the kingdom.

The gospel accounts did not address whether Joseph was a good carpenter or not. They did not mention whether he taught Jesus how to make doorstops. They did not even concern themselves with how Mary and Joseph got along in daily life. On the contrary, whenever the family of Jesus is mentioned, the writers of the gospels simply used the incident to teach about the kingdom.

We know virtually nothing about Joseph except that he was fairly kind to Mary. When he found her with child, he was going to put her away quietly rather than hold her up to public punishment. However, that point is incidental to the main lesson. Joseph was at the complete disposal of God's will. The gospel writers wanted to drive home the central message that Joseph lived to do the will of God. They wanted to show this obedience as the governing principle of his life.

When he finds that Mary is with child by God's design, he takes her as his wife. When he receives instruction that the family is in danger, he immediately obeys God and removes the family to Egypt. When instruction comes that it is safe to return to Palestine, Joseph picks up and returns to his homeland.

Whatever the facts of the situation may have been, it is obvious that the gospel writers are crafting a lesson for their readers. They continually insist that those who wish to enter the kingdom must be like Joseph. They must do the will of God. They must exist to do the will of God.

Similarly, the message is basically the same with the treatment of Mary. She is mentioned a little more frequently than Joseph. The point made time after time, however, can be summarized in the canticle assigned her when she learns that she has been chosen the mother of God. The passage reads:

> My being proclaims the greatness of the Lord,
>   my spirit finds joy in God my savior,
> For he has looked upon his servant in her lowliness;
>   all ages to come shall call me blessed.
> God who is mighty has done great things for me,
>   holy is his name. . . .
> (Lk 1:46-49)

As with Joseph, the main point is that Mary's person, her life, her being, honors God. She calls others to an awareness of God by her willingness to do anything that pleases God or that forwards his designs for the world. This is what the disciples of Jesus must strive to achieve in their personal lives if they want to enter the kingdom.

The message of the gospel writers was persistent. It did not slacken even when treating the interaction of the son and parents. In the one scene mentioned where Jesus and both his parents deal directly with each other, there is little domestic tranquility. Jesus is returning from a visit to the temple with his parents. After a day's travel they discover that he is missing. They return to Jerusalem in search of him.

When they find Jesus in the temple on the third day after he was missing, he is mildly reprimanded by his mother, "Son, why have you done this to us? You see that your father and I have been searching for you in sorrow" (Lk 2:48). In response, Jesus does not say that he is sorry that his parents worried so much. The gospel accounts present him as oblivious to the worry and concern of his parents. In fact he replies, "Why did you search for me? Did you not know I had to be in my Father's house?" (Lk 2:49).

In many ways the scene is insensitive to any of the domestic concerns one might try to bring forth. Readers sometimes react to the report that it took Joseph and Mary a full day to realize that Jesus was missing. However, what the story implies is probably a rather fluid extended family unit that traveled together. More to the point, however, the gospel writers blunt any interchange between a loving son and his concerned parents. The family reactions are short-circuited by the assertion that God's work takes precedence over anything. The parents of Jesus should recognize this reality. The problem is theirs.

Put in easier terms, the gospel writers were trying to assert that domestic life must give way for the kingdom and its preparation. There simply was no interest in the virtues of home life. Were it not for the expectations of the impending events — what is called in the tradition the eschatological expectations — the gospel writers no doubt would have given more attention to the family setting. Indeed, when the second coming did not materialize, the Christian community was flooded with apocryphal literature which included among its major themes the domestic life of the family of Jesus. In other words, many writings appeared and tried to pass themselves off as written in the time of Jesus or at least taken from sources that originated during the time of Jesus. These writings clearly show how the hunger for domestic details rushes to the forefront with the retreat of the eschatological expectations.

Finally, there is one more scene which perhaps rounds out the treatment of the domestic life of Jesus. In the second chapter of John's gospel he reports that Jesus and his mother attended a wedding feast together. Nothing is said of Joseph. As might be expected in accounts which give such little stock to the domestic setting, if Joseph had died by the time Jesus reached his public life in his late twenties, the gospels did not see fit to report it.

The scene at Cana is meant to depict the dramatic way that Jesus proclaims his mission to the world. He performs his first public miracle. He does it at the request of his mother before he is prepared to give public witness. His time had not yet come.

St. John's gospel has a number of different ways of trying to emphasize the importance of Mary. This is one of them. But even given his desire to place Mary into a position of prominence, John does not dwell on a warm interchange of feeling between mother and son. The mother simply informs the son that the hosts have run out of wine. The son replies, "Woman, how does this concern of yours involve me? My hour has not yet come" (Jn 2:4). The mother responds by simply telling the servants: "Do whatever he tells you" (Jn 2:5).

Obviously, John is attempting to honor the mother. But even granted that the term "woman" was one of honor in its day, the writer was obviously not interested in honoring her in her capacity of domestic mother. Family is once again pushed aside, and Mary is honored in some formal way as she initiates the work of the kingdom.

Readers who approach the New Testament, then, must realize that its books are designed around a central message for a given audience. The message was not that family life is the way to God. The message proclaimed quite loudly that everything of this world, including the family, must be put aside. They are but of passing importance.

The Prodigal Son

A slightly different message about the kingdom is developed in the story of the prodigal son. Where the treatment of Mary and Joseph taught what qualities were necessary to enter the kingdom, this parable drives home the point that it is never too late to prepare for the kingdom no matter what type of life one has led. No matter how bad one has been, no matter how serious the offense, all will be forgiven by God the loving Father.

The use of the family in this passage is significant in many ways. First, the image of God is that of a loving Father. This is the dominant image of God throughout the New Testament. It shows that the experience of a loving father made sense to the experience of the people in that day. Perhaps the family was not primarily a unit of intimacy as it is today. Certainly, though, the experience of a loving family must have been common enough to the first century Jews; otherwise, the image of a loving father would not make sense.

Second, the choice of sin is significant. Nothing could be harder for the people of the time to understand than a father who would give of the family's property to a son who wanted to go on his own. To divide the property before the death of the father was almost an unthinkable act of love given the values of the day. Even more incomprehensible was a son who would be so unappreciative as to waste these precious goods in loose, irresponsible living.

To bring the tale one step further and picture a father who would open his arms in welcome to such a son would definitely challenge the imagination of Jesus' audience. If this is the way God would act, then truly it is never too late to repent no matter what the hour, no matter what the fault.

Rejecting the Family

To some extent, the story of the prodigal son may not be as shocking today as it was to the audience of Jesus. We have many examples of indulging our children. We also have many examples of ungrateful children. Many readers can, then, resonate with the story of the prodigal son. Few on the other hand can easily work with the passages in which Jesus apparently challenges family loyalties and ties.

At the end of one of his teaching sessions, Jesus is informed: "Your mother and brothers and sisters are outside asking for you." His response is fairly abrupt: "Who are my mother and my brothers?" Looking around at his audience he concludes, "Whoever does the will of God is brother and sister and mother to me" (Mk 3:32-35).

This challenge dismisses what was of first importance for these people. Their lives revolved around their families. Jesus is proclaiming that God and the fellowship that existed among those who lived in the spirit of God took precedence over the family.

It was indeed a hard saying, but there is a harder saying yet. Luke's gospel has its own challenge to the family in which Jesus proclaims, "If anyone comes to me without turning his back on his father and mother, his wife and children, his brothers and sisters, indeed his very self, he cannot be my follower" (Lk 14:26).

Frequently, Jesus challenged his audience in a jolting way. This is obviously what is being done in these passages. Was it the intention of either passage to attack the family? No, in the sense that family was not the issue. Rather, the intent was to emphasize that the work of God must take precedence over everything in life including something as important as family.

Actually there are two points to such passages. There is the ideal presented to these people that God must be the center of their lives. There is also the very practical challenge. Many of the early Christians embraced the faith only after direct opposition from their families. They in fact had to be ready to renounce their family if they wished to embrace the message of Jesus.

Anyone who is converted to a radical religious calling often comes into conflict with other members of the family who are intensely religious in a different way, are only casually religious, or are not religious at all. The values and concerns that govern the converted member of the family are significantly different from those which guide other members. Such differences do not have to lead to a break in the family, but where there are significant differences, there can be pronounced tensions if not a break-up of the family.

In cases where the religion is counter-cultural, there is almost sure to be a rift in the family. The convert is drawn to a value system that radically challenges the norms governing the lives of other members of the family. In our own culture one can simply appreciate the difficulties families have with their members who join the Moonies or the Hare Krishnas. Putting aside their methods of conversion, these religions challenge in a fundamental way many of the presuppositions that serve as the fabric of a given family's lifestyle.

The Martha and Mary Story

The radical character of Jesus' call is developed in perhaps a gentler way in the account in which he visits the house of Martha. While the message is presented in a gentler fashion, it is no less persistent.

During his travels, Jesus stops at the house of a woman called Martha. He begins to teach. Eventually he is confronted by the owner who is busy caring for the needs of the guests. She insists that her sister Mary, who has been listening to the teachings of Jesus, should help her with the chores so necessary to please such a large gathering. She wants Jesus to reprimand her sister.

Jesus' response to the complaint is direct: "Martha, Martha, you are anxious and upset about many things. One thing only is required" (Lk 10:38-41).

To those familiar with the context of the saying, the "one thing" is very obvious. Nothing should take precedence over the preparation for the kingdom of God. Mary was listening to the teachings about the kingdom. This was far more important than the domestic concerns of the household which were absorbing Martha.

The message of the text is consistent with the previous ones. It is interesting from a number of different angles. First, we learn that Martha welcomed Jesus to "her home." A woman's position obviously had improved over the days of the Old Testament. Second, the passage is indicative of the unique treatment of women in Jesus' ministry. Women were allowed to travel with Jesus' entourage and listen to his message. This was indeed unusual in the first century Jewish religious setting.

Most scholars argue that Jesus' treatment of women shows that he made a concentrated attempt to uplift their position. And in fact during the early years of the community there is evidence of women taking unique positions of leadership. What is important for the present concern of family life is what this challenge to the male-dominated culture must have meant for the family life of the first Christians. It must have presented some challenge to them in the daily flow of the husband and wife relationship.

In the long run the challenge seemed to be more than the community was able to meet. The patriarchal lifestyle was so deeply ingrained in the fabric of the culture that the male dominance was almost bound to rise to the surface. In fact one can see the struggle in the New Testament itself. The earlier passages seem to resonate with the improved position of women. The later writings, composed in the last decade of the first century or later, by contrast present positions on women that seem almost irreconcilable with the original teachings of Jesus. Thus, in 1 Timothy 2:12-15 one finds the following passage:

> I do not permit a woman to act as a teacher, or in any way to have authority over a man; she must be quiet. For Adam was created first, Eve afterward; moreover, it was not Adam who was deceived but the woman. It was she who was led astray and fell into sin. She will be saved through childbearing, provided she continues in faith and love and holiness — her chastity, of course, being taken for granted.

Again, the woman question is not the central concern to the present text. What is of present concern is what the New Testament writings suggest about the fabric of family life among the early Christians. The struggles must have been difficult. One can get some hint of the dilemma that the early Christians faced when one examines the vacillation of St. Paul on this question.

In passages such as 1 Corinthians 11:8-10, Colossians 3:18, and Ephesians 5:22-24, there is a general submission of women to men. The Corinthian text maintains: "A man, on the other hand, ought not to cover his head, because he is the image of God and the reflection of his glory. Woman, in turn, is the reflection of his glory." In Ephesians wives are told to "be submissive to their husbands." The letter goes on to compare the marriage bond to the bond between Christ and the church. The comparison parallels Christ to the husband and the wife to the church.

Looking at these passages, then, one could easily conclude that Paul had no doubt about the status of women. They were to be in a secondary position to men in all things. Whether one is addressing the church or the domestic scene, women are subject to men. But that is not the whole of Paul. Even where the language is one of inequality, the passages stress the deep reverence and respect that should exist between the spouses. Paul offers little doubt as to the call that the husband has to honor, love, and respect his wife as he would respect himself or as he would have Christ respect members of the church.

Paul goes even further, though, in his positioning of women. There is a part of Paul that simply wants to challenge any inequality. In 1 Corinthians 11:11-12 one finds Paul saying, "Yet, in the Lord, woman is not independent of man, nor man independent of woman. In the same way that woman was made from man, so man is born of woman; and all is from God." One also finds Paul stating in Galatians 3:27-28 the following:

> All of you who have been baptized into Christ have clothed yourselves with him. There does not exist among you Jew or Greek, slave or freeman, male or female. All are one in Christ Jesus.

There seems to be a real struggle in Paul. Facing the call of radical unity and love in the Lord, all distinctions seem to evaporate. Faced with the practical decisions of daily life as he tries to advise the communities struggling with the thorny issues of their lives, he falls back into the prejudices of his culture.

In all probability this tension existed in the lives of the earliest Christian families as they struggled with the message of Jesus which called all to be brothers and sisters in Christ. All the evidence seems to indicate that for the most part, the male prejudice won out over the Christian message in the ensuing centuries. Many of the statements about women by the early leaders of the church, the fathers of the church, would clearly shock the modern audience.

C. The New Testament Teaching on Divorce

The only time that the gospels address the nature of marriage is when Jesus is responding to a question about divorce. When confronted by a direct question as to whether divorce was permitted, Jesus quotes the second creation account: "Have you not read that at the beginning the Creator made them male and female and declared, 'For this reason a man shall leave his father and mother and cling to his wife, and the two shall become as one'?" (Mt 19:4-5).

With that as a background, Jesus lays out a strong condemnation of divorce. The passage is similar in Matthew, Mark, and Luke which are known as the synoptic gospels because they have many passages in common, with slight adjustments to meet the peculiar needs of the intended audiences.

Mark and Luke are fairly straightforward in their condemnation of divorce. Matthew, however, does have, for many modern Christians, a troubling exception. After addressing the prohibition of divorce, Matthew has Jesus say "except for *porneia.*" The term could be translated as fornication, immorality, or incest. A number of important scholars make a good case for arguing that the exception is addressing marriage within the forbidden limits of blood relationship as stated in Leviticus 18:6-18. The issue, however, cannot easily be put to rest.

If there is any doubt about how culturally shocking Jesus' message was to his audience, Matthew leaves little doubt. His disciples state in disbelief, "If that is the case between man and wife, it is better not to marry" (Mt 19:10). Jesus simply responds, "Let him accept this teaching who can" (Mt 19:12).

Other passages dealing with divorce can be found in the fifth chapter of Matthew, the tenth chapter of Mark, the sixteenth chapter of Luke, and in Paul's letter to the Corinthians. They do not add anything very different to Matthew's treatment except to acknowledge the possibility of the woman also divorcing the man. In condemning that practice as well, these passages were probably reflecting their audiences who were dispersed throughout the Roman empire and were familiar with the Roman law allowing women to divorce their husbands, a practice unknown to Jewish law.

The New Testament writers clearly showed that they were rejecting the ways of the Old Testament. They have the Pharisees challenging Jesus by arguing that Moses allowed divorce in the Old Testament. Jesus counters by charging that Moses permitted this simply because of the hardness of their hearts. He knew, in other words, that the Israelites could not live up to the ideal. Jesus, though, insists that to be his follower one must live up to the ideal set forth in the creation account.

D. The New Testament Teachings About Children

Needless to say, with such a limited emphasis on the family, there is very limited attention given to children in any of the books of the New Testament. Despite the many pious paintings and pictures depicting Jesus taken with angelic young ones, the writers of the early Christian literature were not drawn to focus on children.

One passage that stands out despite its brevity is a scene in which Jesus blesses the children who are brought to him. The disciples who see the people pressing upon Jesus rebuke the people to leave the Lord alone. Jesus will have none of it, however. He responds, "Let the little children come to me. Do not shut them off" (Lk 18:16). The next verse puts the incident into perspective. Jesus continues to state, "The reign of God belongs to such as these" (Lk 18:16).

Just as all the other domestic passages were designed to teach a lesson about preparing for the kingdom, this passage is no exception. Those who wish to participate in the new order must realize that "whoever does not accept the kingdom of God as a child will not enter into it" (Lk 18:17).

The passage is interesting for the way children are offered as the norm for behavior. In a sense Jesus reverses the normal roles. Children for the most part were considered imperfect adults. Evidence does not suggest they were placed in any special privileged position as in many sectors of our culture. Nevertheless, Jesus offers the simple, trusting faith of the child as the norm for his disciples.

There are not any other substantial texts dealing with children aside from the few domestic counsels offered in the letters to local communities. In Colossians 3:18 and Ephesians 6:1-4, for example, we find essentially the same message. Children are urged to honor and obey their parents. Certainly this is a message that fits in well with the Jewish family customs of the day. He also goes on in both passages to warn the father not to be harsh with the children lest they lose heart. Paul urges his fellow Christians to instruct their children in the spirit of the Lord.

Such a loving counsel is interesting in view of some of the harsher Christian attitudes toward raising children that will develop in succeeding centuries. When Christianity becomes immersed in a sense of original sin, a dualistic worldview, and a hierarchical society, its main caution is often the need to break the rebellious will of the child.

Conclusion

The ideal of New Testament community is pictured in the passage from the Acts of the Apostles in which the early Christians are depicted as living in a community where goods were freely shared according to the legitimate needs of each member. The passage reads:

They devoted themselves to the apostles' instruction and the communal life, to the breaking of bread and the prayers. A reverent fear overtook them all, for many wonders and signs were performed by the apostles. Those who believed shared all things in common; they would sell their property and goods, dividing everything on the basis of each one's need. They went to the temple area together every day, while in their homes they broke bread. With exultant and sincere hearts they took their meals in common, praising God and winning the approval of all the people (Acts 2:42-47).

The ideal for the Old Testament can be captured to some extent in Psalms 127 and 128. The first reads in part:

Behold sons are a gift from the Lord; the fruit of the womb is a reward.
Like arrows in the hand of a warrior are the sons of one's youth.
Happy the man whose quiver is filled with them. . . .
(Ps 127:3-5)

The second psalm reads in part:

Your wife shall be like a fruitful vine in the recesses of your home;
Your children like olive plants around your table.
Behold, thus is the man blessed who fears the Lord.
(Ps 128:3-4)

The question these quite different views of life offer to the Christian of the present time is challenging. If scripture is to be taken as a norm, what does it possibly have to say to someone seeking guidance for family life today? Indeed the domestic life is so culturally conditioned that every Christian community at different points in history does in fact present its own peculiar versions of family. There are even radical shifts within relatively short time periods. No change could be more dramatic than what was witnessed within the scriptures themselves.

The reality is that scripture is not a handbook of family living. It is a challenging journey by a people who reflect on their experience of God, the Jesus event. What these people have to say to succeeding generations is not easily translated. It requires one to listen carefully to the message. David Tracy suggests the best way to appreciate the challenge of scripture is to accept it as the religious classic for the Christian community.[1]

A classic delves so deeply and intensely into the fabric of life in a given period that it has a universal significance. It captures something that is so basic to the life of an age that the underlying reality is a ground found in the life of any age. Applied to the Christian scriptures, the writings of the Old and the New Testaments capture in such a fundamental way the experience and meaning of God in human life that every age must listen to the witness of these people.

Obviously, the translation for something as peculiar as family life will not be easy. For the sake of the present study, certain points will be articulated as hopefully helpful in appreciating the New Testament challenge. No simple list of a few points is adequate, of course. Nevertheless, they may stimulate discussion.

What must be avoided is a triumphant Christianity. Christianity does not simply challenge, it learns from the insights of each culture. It should expect to learn from these cultures. Human societies are formed in response to the movements of creation, a creation that is grounded in God.

The first key point by which later Christian communities must be measured is whether they adequately appreciate the special value of each individual. Both testaments insist that each person has a unique relationship with God. If God cares so much as to continually pursue and forgive his people they must be something of great worth.

Following that position, Christians should insist on the depth of mystery contained in each marital relationship. Where two people who are special to God promise a lifelong relationship, there can be no trivial promises. There must be a bonding that reaches to the depths of the couple's life.

Paradoxically, a third point that the scriptures insist upon is that people are going to fail. Furthermore, they are going to fail in significant ways. All the main characters of the Old Testament have major failures — Abraham, Sarah, Isaac, Rebecca, Jacob, Moses, David. All the disciples of Christ likewise have their embarrassing failures — Peter, James, John, Thomas. There were not simply dramatic failures. Frequently there were petty failures such as the mother of James and John urging that her sons be placed at the right hand of Jesus.

Such a view clearly challenges the prevalent sense of romantic love. The couple might walk off into the sunset. The sun, however, moves faster than anyone can walk. Soon darkness will fall. Hopefully the light of day will be equally present as the relationship continues. There will be dark moments.

A fourth challenge that the scriptures offer future generations of Christians is that they sense the call to pass on life. The world is seen as a place of importance and meaning. Humans are seen as having a pivotal role in bringing that destiny or meaning to fruition. This contribution to life is certainly not limited to making babies. There is an awareness that discipleship, parenthood, or mentorship is a challenge that taxes the full range of one's talents. Contributing to new physical life is but one way of giving to the reaching for life. In marriage, however, children would naturally be a primary way of passing on life to future generations.

These then will be the four points that will continually emerge in the Christian response to a given culture. Others may likewise emerge given the peculiar quirks of a particular culture. These, however, will be recurrent themes.

Note

1. David Tracy, "The Particularity and Universality of Christian Revelation," *Revelation and Experience* (New York: Seabury Press, 1979) p. 112.

Love, Intimacy and Sexual Intimacy in Marriage

5.1 Can We Get Real About Sex?

Lisa Sowle Cahill

DURING MY YEARS AS COLLEGE PROFESSOR (SINCE 1976), LECTURER, WRITER, and mother I have learned that the task of trying to make sense of Catholic teaching on sexuality has to be geared to different audiences with different life experiences. Each generation has its own questions. Those of us who were teen-agers before Vatican II still carry on a struggle of "liberation" from a negative and restrictive picture of sexual dangers. But most younger adults and virtually all teens today face a different battle: to carve out some sense of sexual direction in a peer and media culture which presents sex as a sophisticated recreational activity for which the only moral criterion is mutual consent. I have finally learned that my invitations to appreciate the goodness and pervasiveness of sexuality sound not only redundant but even naive to audiences hungry for a solid answer to shallow or cynical versions of precisely that same message.

Currents of ethical and theological thought within the church manifest similar differences in perspective. Controversies over sexual morality are shaped by at least four constituencies, having different and perhaps incompatible agendas. Though this is to simplify, we may think of them as the traditionalists, the revisionists, the skeptics, and the alienated. These groups

109

represent different responses to the exciting but tumultuous changes which beset the church as well as the culture in the 1960s. The traditionalists put conformity to magisterial teaching high on the list of Catholic identity markers. They stand behind the idea that Vatican positions on matters like premarital sex, birth control, abortion, homosexuality, and divorce can brook no "dissent." Holding a united front on these questions is perceived as essential to the continued strength of church authority. Traditionalists try to connect past teaching with the modern world by arguing that those who *experience* sexual intimacy and honestly examine it will agree that the relationship is a form of "mutual self-gift" (in a phrase of John Paul II), which intrinsically requires heterosexuality, commitment, permanency, exclusivity, and procreation.

A second group, the "revisionists," mostly grew to maturity before Vatican II, and remember vividly the revitalization the council brought. These Catholics, some parents of adolescents and young adults, see the church as their religio-cultural home, even as "mother" and "teacher," but they disagree that sexual and marital experience necessarily confirm all current church teaching. At least since the sixties, they have had serious doubts about whether the positions on contraception and divorce can really hold water. They continue to struggle within the church to find room and a voice for moderate reformulations of and possibly a few exceptions to the Catholic view that sex belongs in indissoluble marriage and leads to parenthood.

A third group might be called the "skeptics." Many, but not all, of them are younger adults who are less willing to take church credibility for granted. They tend to look on in disbelief as the church of their parents promotes teachings on sex which appear oblivious to the realities of human relationships, at least in the U.S. They observe the same phenomena as do the "revisionists" — the widespread acceptance of contraception, "living together," homosexuality, abortion, the threats of AIDS and marital breakdown. But although the skeptics still consider themselves "Catholic," they differ from the "revisionists." They openly assert that church teaching on sex as formulated primarily by celibate male clergy should be declared irrelevant to modern needs. Ready to relegate the traditionalists to the lunatic fringe, they smile at the earnest and rather dogged reinterpretive efforts of the revisionists, wondering when they will realize the impossibility of making headway toward change within present structures.

The fourth group, the "alienated," no longer feel any special tie to the Catholic church or any necessity to justify, struggle with, or refute its teachings. Roman Catholicism is not a resource to which they turn (at least not consciously) for guidance on sex or any other issue. Church sexual teachings, when considered at all, are written off as obsolete, oppressive, and outrageous. Even though "alienated" Catholics are in a sense no longer a "constituency" for church teaching, it is significant that that teaching evokes so negative a response in a group whose size is far from negligible.

This author would be best identified as a member of constituency two attempting to convince constituency three that there is something worthwhile about sex still to be mined in Catholic teaching — though I would have to concur in the quite legitimate impression that its practical value is not always easy to discover.

The Catholic tradition on sexuality has always defined its moral parameters in terms of *marriage.* More than a union of two individuals, marriage is set in the context of *family,* and especially of *procreation.* Augustine and Aquinas saw procreation in marriage as the only reason fully justifying sexual intercourse, and saw both procreation and marriage as especially important insofar as they contribute to the species, the society, and the kinship network or extended family. Although companionship and friendship of spouses were ideals, premodern authors, like the society around them, were unable to recognize the later ideal of "interpersonal union" both because they lacked our sense of the importance of individuals, and because women were considered inferior and subordinate to their male partners. Procreation as the primary purpose of sex was maintained as late as 1930 (in Pius XI's encyclical *Casti connubii).* A breakthrough occurred in Vatican II's *Gaudium et spes* (1965) and in the encyclical *Humanae vitae* (1968), when love and procreation were ranked equally as the purposes of marriage. This shift raising love to a level with procreation represented the influence of philosophical "personalism," and the emergent awareness of women's equality. Yet official church teaching continues to tie respect for these values very much to the physical act of sexual intercourse, not to the overall or long-range relationship of the couple. Today it teaches that both purposes must be present in "each and every act." That is, every act must be part of a permanently committed, heterosexual, love relationship; and every single act must be procreative, *in the sense that* the outcome of procreation must not be artificially prevented.

Contemporary experience and thought raise challenges to this specific presentation of the teaching that should not be underestimated. "Sexuality" is now recognized as a basic dimension of the personality, and covers far more than genital acts designed for reproduction. The affective and interpersonal dimensions of sex, along with the occasions it offers for intimacy and reciprocal pleasure, have become far more important. The wrongness and harm of defining all or most nonprocreative sexual pleasure as "sinful" is evident. The feminist movement has sharply critiqued the distorted forms with which patriarchy has shaped both marriage and family, and has begun to reshape sexuality with a new appreciation of women's experiences of sex, spousehood, and motherhood. Delayed marriage for many young adults who pursue educational and vocational goals also means a longer period of sexual maturity and potential relationships before marriage. The responsibility of the marriageable to choose their own partners rather than relying on parental negotiations or social and religious similarity, along with the high incidence of divorce, has led to premarital sex and "trial marriages," which many see as prudent exploratory arrangements. And there are many single adult Catholics who may not have the opportunity or desire for marriage, but who yearn for intimacy and sexual expression, for which they may find occasions outside marriage. Many lesbian and gay persons see their sexuality as a gift to be valued both for personal identity and in relationships. They call for church support of their efforts to live as faithful Christians and to gain protection of their civil rights. All of these considerations pose challenges to church teaching which, it must be admitted, the church has not adequately met. They also raise questions which I cannot pursue here, though I have advocated modifications (a group-two goal!) of church teaching on many of these points. Indeed, it sometimes seems that both "conservatives" and "liberals" (terms that in practice refer to the traditionalists and the revisionists, since neither the skeptics nor the alienated see the relevant intra-ecclesial debates as worth the investment) become unduly distracted from more fundamental issues by battles over the morality of sexual acts: premarital, contraceptive, homosexual, etc. If we could transcend the limits of such discussions, we might recover the essential message about sexuality which Roman Catholicism transmits.

What is that message? What is a credible, convincing, and helpful expression of Christian sexual values today? I think that message pertains to three dimensions of sexuality: 1) sex as a physical drive for pleasure; 2) sex as intimacy or love; 3) sex as procreative. It is the value of the third that is the most necessary and the most difficult to communicate to today's young adults.

Sex as a physical drive. In the past, there has been in Christianity (in Augustine, for instance) a deep suspicion of sexual drives or sexual desire. This suspicion was no doubt based on sex's undeniable tendency to break social and moral restraints, and to seek fulfillment in self-centered, manipulative, and even violent ways. Today this attitude might be revised into the recognition that the sexual drive has real limits as a guide to sexual relationships. The dominant "cultural message" — that sex is natural, enjoyable, good, and even recreational — has an obvious legitimacy in itself, and exponents of a Catholic Christian approach to sexuality should not appear grudging in their acceptance of the "joy of sex." But the message is incomplete and inadequate. Using sexual acts and relationships as an outlet for our physical drives or as a means of access to physical enjoyment is not *bad,* but it is *limited.* Media images aside, I doubt that many people really disagree with this point, however much some may be tempted to rationalize indiscriminate sexual behavior. Physical desire and enjoyment taken alone as motives for sex make sex unfulfilling, lonely, and perhaps ultimately boring. Although women seem to understand better than men that sexual intimacy naturally entails psychological intimacy, I doubt this difference is innate. Rather it is a matter of women being socialized or socially encouraged to take intimacy more seriously. Intimacy adds to the fulfillment of both men's and women's sexuality. This leads to sex's second dimension.

Sex as love. Seeing sex as an expression of love seems to verge on the romantic, yet it is not all that foreign to most of our experiences and personal goals. Our culture is prone to cynicism about the trustworthiness of human relationships. But sexual intimacy can express and augment psychological intimacy, affection, reciprocal understanding and encouragement, partnership, companionship, compassion, and even commitment. One Catholic Christian value of sexuality is permanence: the love relationship established sexually between a woman and a man should be long-term and not transient. Sex with little or no commitment shortchanges sex's potential for intimacy. Unlike other animal species, humans have a deep capacity for friendship and interpersonal reciprocity, which, when expressed sexually, constitutes the most intense of human relationships. The appropriate moral context for complete sexual union is a commensurate level of interpersonal commitment. Unequal commitment between partners leads to manipulation, disappointment, and pain. Sex without commitment is unfaithful to the human potential of sexuality.

The psychological and personal aspects of sexual union are complemented by the relation of the sexual couple to the family and society. Our sexuality is not simply an individualistic capacity but binds us with others in families, that is, in some of the most rewarding and most demanding of human relationships. A man and woman bring to their union links with and commitments to other persons, including their respective families and friends and, eventually, the children their union may produce. Although not all sexual couples give birth to children, the procreative potential of sex is always a part of that relationship. The prospect of pregnancy and parenthood is not always intentional and dominant in the relationship, but it is nonetheless a latent and morally important possibility. Obviously a faithful commitment between parents is the best context for the nurture of children.

Like many group-two Catholics, I have often considered the common practice of "living together" with some misgivings along with the feeling that there might be in it something to be learned about the nature of sexual commitment. Some of my intuitions came together upon hearing a Ugandan bishop observe that, in his culture, marriage was a *progressive* reality, which did not come into being in an instant during a single ceremony, but which developed through a process of negotiation, visiting, and gift-giving among bride, groom, and their families. Although at some time during the process the couple might have sexual relations and even bear children, there was actually no one "point" before which a marriage did not exist and after which it did. Perhaps many couples in our culture are making a similar statement about their growing trust in and love for each other. However, the shortcoming of "progressive marriage" as we see it in the U.S. is the isolation of the unmarried sexual couple from the social support and account-ability that accompanies formal marriage. In Uganda, the whole family has an investment in the growing relationship and expects the couple to make it work, persuading, admonishing, and supporting them as need be. This system also has clear understandings about how children will be cared for within the families if the couple subsequently parts. In other words, the African form of gradual marriage carries with it at every stage an increasing level of per-sonal, familial, and social weight and responsibility. One thinks also of an-cient Israelite betrothal and marriage, reflected in Matthew's and Luke's stories of the premarital pregnancy of Mary. The sexual relations permitted before marriage occurred in a context of religiously and socially specified conditions. Though the provisional sexual relationships common in our cul-ture may represent a valid insight about the development of commitment, they still lack the social forms which would make them accountable to the genuine personal and communal significances of sex. One of these is parent-hood, which leads us to the next point.

Sex as procreation. In modern Western cultures, the value of procreative sex may be harder to "sell" than pleasurable sex and loving sex. We are in an era in which procreation has been reduced to an incidental meaning of sex, usu-ally to be avoided, and certainly to be accepted only if freely chosen. The deep associations and mutual reinforcements of sex, love, and parenthood are missing — partly because the church's teaching authority itself has narrowed their reciprocity to an experientially unintelligible focus on reproductive genital acts taken as separate events. But it is the unity of sex, love, and parenthood in this broader sense that is probably the major message Roman Catholicism has to offer today's young adults, who more easily see that sex expresses love than that sexual love leads to permanent commitment, parent-hood, and family.

A better expression of this link, one we should aim to attain, lies in contemporary thought's repudiation of dualism, and its insistence that the body and the spirit or psyche form an integrated reality, not two uneasily aligned "components." We no longer tolerate a sexual ethics that sees the body as "bad," and to be repressed, while only our spiritual side is "holy." But a non-dualistic view of sex requires that we premise a sexual morality on the goodness of sexual acts and sexual pleasure. It also requires that we look at these acts and their reproductive potential as an integrated whole or process. This is not to say that it is always wrong to interfere with concep-tion as an outcome; but that moral analysis starts with a presumption in favor of the conduciveness of sex to shared parenthood. In other words, physical satisfaction or pleasure, interpersonal intimacy, and parenthood are not three separate "variables," or *possible* meanings of sex which we are morally free to combine or omit in different ways. Sex and love as fully *embodied* realities have an intrinsic moral connection to procreativity and to the shared creation and nurturing of new lives and new loves.

A more flexible and experientially adequate way to express this unity is not in terms of acts, but of *relationships.* Certain basic human relationships come together through our sexuality and link us not only to our partners but to the wider community, through the social relationships of marriage and family. These basic relationships are the woman-man and the parent-child relationships. Spousehood and parenthood are linked in the long-term commitment of the couple, sexually expressed. Both are not only intersubjective, but also embodied relationships. *Spousehood* is embodied through the shared material conditions of economic and domestic life, and through sexuality, which can give rise to a shared physical relation to the child. *Parenthood* is embodied through the shared material conditions of family life, again through the genetic link, and through the fact that the physical relation of spousehood is that which gives rise to parenthood.

To recapitulate, the Catholic tradition yields a set of moral attitudes toward sexuality, even before the point of dealing with concrete moral dilemmas or moral norms and prohibitions. The tradition can encourage respect and appreciation for sexuality as mutual physical pleasure, as intimacy, and as parenthood (or at least receptivity to it). These three relationships come together in the ongoing relationship of a couple. In all its dimensions, sex is both a psychospiritual experience and an embodied one, and both aspects contribute to its moral character.

Having said this, however, one also realizes that human circumstances sometimes arise in which not all three values (sex itself, commitment or love, and parenthood) can be realized simultaneously. In their sexual lives, as elsewhere, human beings are often confronted with moral conflicts, in which no choice is free of ambiguity. Of the three values, it is certainly love which is the *sine qua non,* the primary value in the triad. Since personhood is the most distinctive quality of the human being, it is the most personal aspect of sexuality which is *most* morally important. In unusual or difficult circumstances, the other two (sexual intercourse and procreation) can be subordinated to the love relationship of the couple as long as they are still given significant practical recognition. For example, in the use of contraception, procreation is temporarily set aside, but it still can be realized in the total relationship of the couple. In some infertility therapies, sex itself is set aside as the means to conception, but certainly the relationship of the couple which is both loving and procreative is otherwise given sexual expression. On the other hand, couples who are absolutely intolerant of the prospect of parenthood, perhaps resorting even to abortion as a means of birth control, do not give adequate moral recognition to the relation of sex, love, and procreation. Similarly, couples so desperate to conceive that they are willing to set aside the unity of their spousal-sexual-parental bond by using donor sperm or a surrogate mother to create a reproductive union between one spouse and a third party are also less than faithful to the values which sexuality represents. Although marriages as human realities sometimes fail, a tragedy that church teaching on "indissolubility" may not have met satisfactorily, the asset of the tradition is that it holds up an ideal of permanency. The meaning of "love" in the sexual triad goes far beyond romantic affections. It means a commitment to build a mutually satisfying sexual relationship, to mutual respect, to understanding and support. It entails persistence, repentance, and forgiveness. However justified divorce may sometimes be, the very high incidence of divorce seems to be due to cultural forgetfulness that the commitment to marital partnership requires both ongoing personal dedication and strong social supports.

Since at least the 1960s, interpersonal values have moved to center stage in the Catholic picture of sex, just as more attention has been paid to the experience of actual sexual relationships. At the same time, the inclusion of love and commitment as central along with parenthood has been sidetracked by acrimonious exchanges over contraception and other issues. Such debates have drained energies from the real task of reappropriating the essentials of Catholic teaching for the next generation. What our culture most needs to hear is an effective critique of individualist, materialist, and transient sexual relationships — not lists of specific transgressions which are "against church teaching." The Catholic "message" is that the interdependence of sex's pleasurable, intimate, and parental aspects can anchor our sexuality in some of the most enduring and rewarding human relationships. That message will be heard only if it is addressed honestly to the real sexual experiences of young adult Catholics, and only if the messengers can listen to and even learn from their audience's response.

5.2 Sexual Intimacy
Challon O'Hearn Roberts and William P. Roberts

THE EXPRESSION OF LOVE IN SEXUAL INTERCOURSE IS AN INTEGRAL PART OF marital intimacy. Intercourse, however, has many meanings. It can comfort or sadden, unite or alienate, enrich or devastate.

How can sexuality be approached in marriage, so as to build a unique relationship between the couple, rather than be a block to their growth in personal intimacy? In addressing this question we first explore the meaning of sexuality and sexual intimacy. We then reflect on some aspects of the sexual relationship in marriage. Finally, we consider the topic of premarital sexual preparation.

Human Sexuality

The young man sat in the counseling room, discouraged and down on himself. "Here I am, only twenty-nine and I have been through two marriages, two divorces and eleven affairs, yet I have nothing to show for it. I am alone, and have no one. I have found plenty of sex, but have never discovered love."

The experience of this man underscores the fact that sex and love are not necessarily intertwined. Humans must make free choices about their sex life. Sex is not something that just happens to them. Through our free choices we determine the meaning that sex has in regard to our personal growth and the development of personal relationships.

It is this freedom of choice that distinguishes human sexuality from sexuality in the rest of the animal kingdom. Humans are not driven by blind instinct. They are not victims of uncontrollable sexual urges. They must choose what they wish to do with their sexuality and what meaning sexual experience will have for them.

In general, we have three major options regarding how we choose to engage in the genital expression of sex: indulge in sex merely as a means of recreation; use sex in ways that exploit other people; channel our sexual energies and drives toward a committed, loving, lasting relationship with one person.

The casual use of sex in many circles today underscores the allurement that sex for recreation has. "Sex is fun," the student observed. "What's wrong with having a little fun, as long as both people agree?" The problem is that such a choice is made at the price of foregoing personal commitment, fidelity and love.

Exploitative sex is another option open to us. Sexual exploitation is using someone sexually for one's own self-centered purposes, regardless of what destructive effect this might have on the other. Prostitution, rape and sexual abuse, pornography, and much advertising are clear examples of such exploitation. Sexual exploitation is dropping someone after you have gotten what you want sexually. It is using a person as a sexual object.

What is unique to us as humans is our ability to know, to love, and to enter into bonding and lasting relationships. Sexuality is expressed in a human way to the degree in which we know and love the other, and are committed to an enduring relationship. To the degree these qualities are lacking, sexuality is less than human.

In a good marriage sexual expression takes on its fullest meaning. There are many aspects to the significance that sexual intercourse can have in an intimate marriage. Here we reflect on eight of them.

1. In intercourse the couple present themselves to each other in their physical *nakedness*. They reveal themselves as they are. Nothing external is hidden. This physical nakedness before one another is symbolic

of the desire they have to reveal to each other their inner selves, in all of their spiritual "nakedness."

2. There is no way for a couple to achieve any greater physical *closeness* than in sexual intercourse. Through this physical closeness, they enter into emotional, psychological, and spiritual closeness. This sexual intimacy celebrates and nurtures the intimacy of their whole married life.

3. The couple give of themselves in sexual intercourse for the *enjoyment* of one another. The enjoyment they experience in intercourse catches up the other moments of joy in their marriage, and intensifies those moments.

4. In sexual intercourse the couple not only give and do for one another, they *are for one another*. They bask in the intimacy of each other's presence. The experience of being for one another in intercourse makes the couple more sensitive to the beauty and transforming power of personal presence. This experience can color how they relate to one another in the rest of their marriage. They learn to slow down and take time to be with one another. They discover that it is not necessary to be always doing something for one another.

5. The married couple in sexual intercourse show their *appreciation* for each other. They are "saying" through their sexual intimacy: "I find you attractive." "I like being with you." "You are the most important human in my life." This celebration of their mutual appreciation in intercourse leads them to show appreciation for one another in the other aspects of their married life.

6. The exclusive giving of oneself to one's spouse in sexual intercourse is an act of *faith* and *trust*. They express their belief in one another and in each other's love. There is belief that "I mean as much to you as you mean to me." There is faith that "you will be there for me tomorrow, as you are today."

7. Marital intercourse expresses the couple's acceptance of each other as *equals* who relate "on equal ground." In intercourse the couple meet one another in the depth of their basic humanness, in their human commonality. This presupposes that they have already acknowledged one another as equals in their relationship. The experience of commonality in intercourse will deepen their awareness and acknowledgment of equality and oneness in all of the dimensions of their marriage.

8. Sexual intercourse is an expression of *reconciliation* and the serious intent to grow in personal unity. Even the best of marriages has its stresses and strains. In sexual intercourse the couple express their desire not to allow the failings to create a barrier to their growing intimacy. They express sorrow and forgiveness. They show their deter-

mination to work beyond the hurts, and to continue to grow toward oneness.

Dispelling the Misconceptions

The misconceptions about sexuality that some people bring to a marriage can block sexual intimacy. The following five exemplify some of the more common misconceptions.

1. *Sex, if not "dirty," is at least tainted.* This impression has been burned deeply into the consciousness of many. Two quite opposing groups have specially fostered, even if unwittingly, the perception of sex as tainted: the pornography industry, and the Church.

The pornography industry portrays sex as violent, lustful, insensitive and abusive of women and children. The correct response to pornography is revulsion and disgust.

Coming from an entirely opposite direction, the Catholic Church has also been a powerful influence in shaping negative views about sex. It has done so, first, through an excessive preoccupation with sexual sins. While Jesus' teaching concentrated on love for all humans, and compassionate concern for the needy, the focus of the Church's most rigid moral teaching has been on sexual sins. According to this teaching, one could commit "venial sins" in matters of lying, stealing and the physical abuse of others, but the slightest deliberate indulgence in sexual pleasure "outside of marriage" was a "mortal sin."

The Church has also fostered negative attitudes toward sexuality and marriage by its bias in favor of celibacy. This bias is seen, for example, in the exaltation of Mary more for being "ever Virgin" than for being a married woman of faith. The long litany of women saints is dominated by "virgins." The relatively few married women among the saints made the list as "widows." This bias against marriage has obscured many of the beautiful and positive things the Church has had to say during the past twenty-five years in regard to married life.

Against this background of negativity, it is understandable that many experience difficulty feeling good about their sexuality and freely enjoying the sexual pleasures of marital intercourse. However, through their open communication with each other and their experience of the personal growth that comes from tender and loving sexual experiences, the couple can gradually learn to put aside negative impressions and feelings about sex.

2. *Men are supposed to be sexually aggressive, while women are to be passive.* This misconception has been fed by cultural stereotypes. According to the stereotypes, the male is "macho-man," who, almost beside himself with sexual passion, is on the prowl to conquer his "female prey." The female's

role, in the stereotype, is to submit passively to "her man's passions." Her enjoyment is "to give him pleasure." The stereotype even perceives her as "enjoying it" when he is violent and rapes her.

One can easily perceive how dangerous these misconceived stereotypes are. They can have a number of damaging effects on the efforts to establish sexual intimacy in marriage. They warp one's perspective in regard to the opposite sex and to the nature of heterosexual relationships. They block one from discovering a partner as a unique other and instead lead one to see the partner through the prism of the stereotype.

The stereotype of husband as initiator and wife as passive submitter puts unnecessary pressure on the husband "to perform," and places unjust pressure on the wife to submit and endure all sorts of possible abuses that are intolerable in a marital relationship. The stereotype is also blind to the sexual drives, energies and "assertiveness" of the woman. Finally, it obstructs mutual initiative and enjoyment, and prevents the partners from experiencing each other as persons who are equal in human dignity and deserving of the same respect and treatment.

3. *Good sex will make a good marriage.* There are at least two ways in which this misconception can operate. It can lead a couple before marriage to believe that because they have an intense sexual involvement, they are in love, and united in mind and heart. Blinded by their sexual infatuation, they may not think it necessary to step back and take a good look at each other and reflect on the element of compatibility in their total relationship. They may not realize that an enduring, satisfying sex life flows from personal intimacy. Knowing and loving the other and getting along well in married life do not necessarily flow from "good" sexual encounters.

This misconception can also lead to the illusion that a good sex life will automatically solve problems. Instead of confronting a drinking problem, or facing together the issue that caused a serious dispute, the couple may be led to bury the difficulty, or to "drown" the pain by sexual intercourse. It is true that marital intercourse can play a very important role in the process whereby a couple work through a difficulty, and become reconciled after hurt and pain. But in order for intercourse to have this healing effect, it must take place within the framework of the broader process of consciously and honestly facing the problem and working it out. Sexual intercourse provides no easy escape from that task.

4. *Sex is always a "super" experience.* Despite this common misconception that somehow sex is always going to be an extraordinary, almost ecstatic experience, sexual intercourse shares in the plight of all human experiences. They are limited, dependent on mood, and on a variety of changing conditions and circumstances. To expect every sexual encounter "to reach the heights" is obviously an illusion, and is bound to lead to disappointment.

Relatively few sexual experiences will be "five star." Some will be "one star," and most will fall somewhere in between the two.

5. *Married people are always "ready for sex."* This misconception may be due in part to what is experienced in the courtship situation. When a couple who are serious about each other date, they often experience an almost irresistible sexual attraction for one another. If they have decided not to engage in premarital intercourse, they realize what a struggle this can entail. From this experience a person might come to think that married couples are always in the mood for a sexual encounter. Courtship, however, is different from marriage. In the dating situation the couple see each other at choice times: they usually look their best, are exhilarated to be together again, and are unencumbered from other demands and distractions. In marriage the couple journey together through all the diverse moments, good and bad, that make up married life. They see each other at their best and at their worst. They struggle to find time for each other in the midst of the demands of supporting the family, maintaining a household, and caring for the children. While, indeed, in a loving marriage a couple grow in sexual intimacy, this takes place within the rhythm of the entire marital reality.

Creating Sexual Intimacy

Taking seriously the true meaning of human sexuality, and correcting any misconceptions one might have, will serve as an important foundation for a healthy sex life in marriage. Beyond that, a couple can work at ensuring the presence of several elements in their sexual encounters that will make a significant contribution toward creating sexual intimacy.

Communication. Perhaps one of the most difficult topics for a couple to talk about is their sex life. Because the topic is so personal, some are embarrassed to discuss it. And since it is such a sensitive issue, spouses may be very reluctant to criticize one another and make suggestions that might improve their sexual experience. Hence, it is very tempting to bury the topic and endure the status quo.

One woman explained her silence this way: "He goes into a long pout if I even criticize his table manners. You can just imagine how he would react if I criticized how he acts in bed." One husband observed: "It's stupid to talk about how you make love. You just do it. Who needs all those discussions and books?"

While it may be difficult, it is also crucial for a couple to discuss honestly how they are experiencing their sexual encounters. They need to be able to express how they feel, what they like and what they don't like, what is bringing satisfaction and what is causing dissatisfaction or hurt. They need to be able to guide and direct each other. They ought to create an atmosphere in which both are free to communicate these feelings before, during and after intercourse.

Mutual Respect and Regard. A couple's respect for the dignity and uniqueness of each other reflects itself in sexual matters. They respect each other's conscience about the moral aspects of sexual behavior and have regard for what each finds tasteful or distasteful. They are sensitive to one another's moods and physical states. They refrain from exerting undue pressure on one another, and come to decisions about sexual matters through mutual agreement.

Variety. Like everything else in life, marital intercourse could become routine and mechanical. The most basic way to keep marital intercourse alive, new and exciting, is to instill continually into the relationship new life and excitement. In order for romance to be preserved in marital intercourse, it must be kept in the entirety of the marriage.

More specifically, variety can also be achieved by changing, at least occasionally, the immediate environment in which lovemaking takes place. Diversifying the time, location, or technique from time to time can help prevent routine. Variety can also be enhanced by candlelight, flowers, music or a night away.

Another way of bringing variety into lovemaking is to enter into the different moods of each other at the time of lovemaking. Entering fully into the distinctive spirit of the other, be it playfulness and joy or discouragement or grief, gives a very particular and memorable tone to individual encounters. Such variety prevents routine and boredom and provides a rich and meaningful diversity to the couple's sex life.

Sense of Humor. There is a human tendency to take ourselves too seriously. Sometimes we become over-sensitive to criticism and too touchy. One place where this tendency could easily manifest itself is in sexual intercourse. One of the remedies to all of this is to lighten up and enjoy. Couples need to be able to laugh at themselves and see that we humans really are sort of funny creatures. They need to be able to view in a lighter vein some of their foibles and shortcomings, and to see the humorous dimensions in human lovemaking.

Going Beyond the Biological. The difficulty with many "how to" manuals on sexual intercourse is that they concentrate heavily, if not exclusively, on physical "techniques" and the biological aspects of the act. Obviously, the physical aspects cannot be overlooked, and some "techniques" can be helpful. However, complete mastery of these alone will never bring lasting satisfaction. Unless attention is also given to the psychological and spiritual aspects of sexual intercourse, sexual encounters will ultimately leave the couple emotionally and spiritually starved.

Sexual yearnings are an expression of our far deeper yearnings for love and for personal union. The best way for a couple to enhance their sex life is to become intimate lovers in all of the dimensions of the ordinary realities that comprise married life. As this happens, a couple become increasingly capable of sensing and responding in intercourse to each other's emotional and spiritual yearnings, as well as to their physical desires. Sensitivity, gentleness, caring, and the willingness to reveal to each other our deeper selves are qualities that, if present in the marriage and in sexual intercourse, will greatly enhance the sexual experience. These qualities will enable the couple to touch, through the physical contact of intercourse, the profounder dimensions of one another's being.

Sensitivity Toward Difficulties

Creating sexual intimacy will not be without at least some occasional difficulties. In some marriages the problems may be of a sufficiently serious nature that expert counseling or therapy may be required. In most marital relationships the occasional sexual difficulties are average enough that they can usually be worked out by the couple themselves, if the total picture of their marriage is a healthy one, and if the couple are able to discuss frankly the matter with sensitivity and encouragement. We include here just a few examples of the kind of moderate difficulties that could occur, at least occasionally, in the course of just about any marriage.

Frequency. During various periods of the marriage one partner may experience notably more intense sexual desire than the other. Accordingly one may wish to make love much more frequently than one's partner. Such a difference could become a real battleground if one starts engaging in name-calling, or begins making accusations ("You don't love me anymore." "Are you seeing someone else?"). The situation is also aggravated by trying to put one's partner on a guilt trip ("After all I do for you, this is the least you can do for me"), or by making authoritarian demands ("This is my right, and your duty!"). On the other hand, a mutually satisfactory compromise could be reached if there is calm discussion in which both partners try, in a nonjudgmental way, to understand and appreciate where each other is in this regard.

Premature Male Orgasm. Foreplay is an integral and indispensable part of lovemaking. It helps situate sexual intercourse in an environment of tenderness, fun and mutual excitement. It prepares both partners psychologically and physically. It also involves the art of timing. Both partners try somehow to synchronize the pace and rhythm of their sexual excitement. Achieving a mutually satisfactory tempo does not come automatically. So, it is very possible, especially in the beginning of a relationship that the male may reach climax before he has penetrated. This can be frustrating for the female partner and perhaps embarrassing for the male. Disappointment could easily lead to anger. If both partners, however, are sensitive to one another, they can work this difficulty out in a constructive way. The husband ought to be concerned about his wife achieving some kind of satisfaction. The couple can then discuss ways of better synchronizing in the future.

Temporary Impotency. It is within the realm of "normal" experience for a male, either on a given occasion or for a period of time, to be unable to have an erection or to maintain one in the course of lovemaking. The environment of the marital relationship has a great deal to do with how well a couple can work through a situation of temporary impotency. Negative reactions on the part of one's spouse can only increase anxiety over the matter. The anxiety, in turn, aggravates the impotency. On the other hand, understanding, support, and patience, along with honest dialogue, are often all that is needed to deal successfully with this problem.

Temporary Frigidity. This term refers to the inability of a woman to achieve orgasm over a limited time period. There can be a number of reasons for this. It can be due to psychological or physical conditions. Is enough foreplay taking place for both to be adequately prepared for intercourse? Are there difficulties in the marriage that might be interfering with the woman's experience of lovemaking?

Again, as in the case of other sexual difficulties, understanding, sensitivity and communication are the first keys for addressing this problem. Sometimes the couple can work through the difficulty themselves. At other times counseling might prove helpful. Certainly, frigidity ought not be ignored and allowed to persist indefinitely.

Planning Conception

Though the emphasis so far in this chapter has been on the relational dimensions of sexuality, obviously sexual intercourse is also intrinsically linked by its nature to the conception of new human life. Responsible sexual intimacy must have regard and concern for this aspect of sexual intercourse and assume responsibility for it. Decisions in this regard must be made jointly by the couple. In doing so, a couple must dialogue honestly and openly about where each stands in regard to the main issues involved: desire for children, moral, aesthetical and risk aspects of various methods of family planning, and the question of who will be responsible

Desire for Children. Even before marriage, it is imperative that a couple discuss at some length how they feel about having children. They may need to face some serious questions. Do they want to have children in their marriage? If so, how many, and according to what time frame? Both partners need to satisfy themselves that their views on these questions are compatible. The impossibility of reaching some mutually agreeable compromise on these issues ought to forewarn the couple that they have not yet found a suitable partner. The earlier this is discovered in the premarital relationship, the better for all concerned.

Moral Aspects. It can no longer be assumed that two people belonging to the same religious denomination hold similar views regarding what is moral or immoral in the matter of family planning. Sociological surveys have shown, for example, that approximately seventy-five percent of Catholics disagree with the official Roman Catholic position on birth control. Hence, even if both partners are of the same religious persuasion, it is necessary for them to discuss their moral perspectives on a variety of questions: Is natural family planning the only permissible form of contraception? Are all forms of artificial birth control acceptable, including abortifacients? Are sterilizations ever permissible? What about the morality of abortion?

Divergences in a couple's convictions in regard to these issues need to be addressed. Both partners have to respect the conscience of one another.

Aesthetical Aspects. Every method of contraception, "natural" or "artificial," involves some inconvenience, and often interferes to some degree with spontaneity. In choosing a means of contraception, a couple need to discuss which method both of them find least unaesthetical.

Risk Aspects. Some methods of contraception carry with them a risk factor. These ought to be carefully weighed. It ought also be noted that many of the greatest risks are connected with contraceptives used by women.

The Responsibility Factor. In our male dominated society, it has too frequently been assumed that contraception is the woman's responsibility. "It's her fault that she got pregnant. She should have done something to prevent it." The couple need, in fairness, to be co-responsible for family planning. It is unjust to let the burden fall on the woman because the male doesn't want to be bothered.

Premarital Sexuality

Preparing for sexual intimacy in marriage does not begin on the wedding day, but in the developmental years prior to marriage. What one does with one's sexuality in these years has implications for one's marriage. Hence, before we conclude this chapter we wish to take up the topic of premarital sexuality.

High school and college religion teachers are used to being besieged with the question, "Do you think it's all right to engage in premarital sex?" There are two serious problems with the way this question is asked. First, the term "premarital sex" is too broad. It is essential to clarify what the person using the words has in mind. Second, the questioner usually wants an answer in terms of whether or not "it is a mortal sin." Addressing the question merely in this way often overlooks many of the other important aspects of the issue.

We are concerned in our treatment of premarital sexuality in this book with the effects the various forms of premarital sexuality can have on the person involved and on a future marriage. Hence, we will address the topic by dealing individually with several forms of premarital sex.

Joe was sixteen when he had his first encounter with a prostitute. During his last two years of college his visits averaged twice a month. He wondered what effect this might have on his future marriage.

While no one can predict the answer to that question, a couple of concerns come to mind that go beyond the obvious one of possible disease. The first concern is about the attitude toward sex and toward women that is manifested in males hiring prostitutes for sexual services. In the dynamic of prostitution the male purchases the sexual use and service of a woman for a price. The prostitute is subservient to the demands and wishes of the male. Authentic love, sensitivity, and consideration have no place in the package. Male concern for what is and will happen to the prostitute is almost non-existent.

Is a person like Joe going to be able to abandon easily the attitude toward sex and toward women that is imbedded in his past practice? Or will these attitudes be brought into the marriage and tinge the way he relates to his wife? Will the habit of divorcing sex from love affect his marital sexual encounters and be an obstacle in achieving true sexual intimacy with his spouse?

The second concern has to do with the addictive element in lust (i.e., sex without love). In his sexual purchases, Joe has had genital entanglement with many different kinds of women. He has also had available to him all sorts of "kinky" behavior that are not part of most marital relationships. Will the appetite that Joe has built up reappear after the "first excitement" of marriage has died down? This question takes on deeper significance in light of studies and media interviews with certain prostitutes that reveal that a high percentage of the men engaging the services of prostitutes are married!

Another form of premarital sexual experience is the "one night stand." "Why pay for it?" Walt commented. "There are enough people out there willing to go to bed. All you have to do is look for them." While "one night stands" do not share in all of the evil attached to prostitution, this practice bodes poorly for a future marriage. It involves using people sexually, and then dropping them. It can also whet the appetite for a variety of partners, thus making marital fidelity a more difficult goal to achieve. It is a serious mistake to think that all these attractions will automatically disappear after marriage. "I'll have my fun now and settle down after marriage" may be much easier said than done.

Rachel had always rejected "one night stands." Her story exemplifies another form of premarital sex. She would only go to bed with someone for whom she "cared" and for whom she "had some feeling." This led her, during her late teens and early twenties, through four affairs, each ranging from three months to a year. What she discovered was: "Two of the men never really loved me. All they were doing was using me. The remaining two, on the other hand, did care. It just didn't work out."

Rachel's story reflects two very distinct kinds of experiences of premarital affairs. In two of the affairs, Rachel believed her partner shared the same feelings for her that she had for him. When she discovered otherwise, she felt used and abused. There is an evil of sexual exploitation in this kind of experience that is missing from her other two affairs, where both she and her lovers did have some care and feeling for each other. While this distinction does not make the second kind of affair morally right, it does make it morally different. Further, one who has sexually exploited others is certainly less prepared for marriage than one who has not.

A final major category of premarital sex is the sexual involvement of two persons who are engaged to one another. They are in love, are committed to each other, and have set a date for the wedding. "We are all but married, except for the piece of paper. Waiting has become almost impossible. What is wrong with having sexual intercourse in these circumstances?"

The authors of this book are traditional enough to continue to maintain that the most meaningful and, hence, ideal context for sexual intercourse is marriage. However, the reality is that a growing number of people do not share this view. Is there any guidance that can be given to an engaged couple who are determined in their consciences that for them "premarital sexual intercourse is all right"? Does one just say flatly, "I disagree"? or does one help them at least to face certain questions that might clarify for them their situation? The latter seems the more helpful approach.

Here are some of the questions an engaged couple who have decided to have sexual intercourse before marriage would do well to consider: If we already "feel married," why don't we get married now? Do the reasons we give for delaying marriage outweigh the reasons for marrying now? Do we both feel the same way about postponing the marriage? If so, do we both have the same reasons? Does sexual intercourse have similar meaning for both of us in terms of our love and our exclusive permanent commitment toward each other? Have we discussed and agreed upon a course of action in the event of premarital pregnancy? Are we economically independent, or is one person pretty much financially supporting the other at this point in time? Have we achieved a degree of good communication and intimacy in the other areas of our relationship that is commensurate with the physical intimacy expressed in bed?

Honestly addressing such questions together enables the couple to see where each is coming from in regard to their decision. It protects against the possibility of one person taking advantage of the other.

Whatever one wants to say about the morality of an engaged couple having premarital intercourse, this issue needs to be kept separate from other forms of premarital sex. It is very unhelpful and unrealistic to put all the diverse forms of sexual activity just described under the one heading "premarital sex" and then to treat them on equal moral footing. It is much more useful to help people see the specific characteristics that are at work in their sexual involvement, and to assess what effect this involvement is having on them, their partner, and their future marriage.

Summary

The sexual expression of love finds its most meaningful context in marriage. Sexual intimacy, however, does not happen automatically. The quality of marital intercourse is related to the degree of intimacy achieved in all the other areas of the couple's relationship.

Sexual intercourse has many meanings and a variety of moods. By exploring these meanings, being open to these diverse moods, and bringing the total gift of themselves to their lovemaking, a couple can experience the richness of marital intercourse and achieve true sexual intimacy. In light of a positive understanding and experience of sexuality, misconceptions regarding sex can be corrected and problem areas can be constructively addressed.

5.3   Of Apples, Serpents, and Sex
David M. Thomas

SOMETIMES A STORY CAN BE TOLD SO OFTEN THAT IT BECOMES STALE. IT NO longer impresses. It loses its ability to stimulate new thinking. But if it is a really good story, told in a creative way, it has the power to excite no matter how often it gains a hearing.

Many of the stories in the Bible are like that, although they, too, can become "old hat" if they are told without enthusiasm. Haven't you found yourself almost bored to tears while listening to the story of the Prodigal Son for the umpteenth time? I have.

Yet, boredom may not be simply a matter of content. In fact, it is probably more a matter of personal disposition or space at the time of the telling. That personal disposition is closely related to expectations, understandings of the material, and even related, as some would suggest, to biorhythms (whatever that is), sunspots, or the alignment of the planets.

Let's tell a story. Once upon a time there was a garden filled with ripe, plump fruits and vegetables. It was the most beautiful garden ever grown. It had huge, ripe watermelons and sweet corn, green beans, and turnips. The trees were bent with gigantic apples, peaches, pears, and my favorite, red bing cherries. In an open clearing where the wind blew ever so softly through the knee-deep grass, a wonderful chance encounter took place one day between a guy and a gal. Their names were not important because it was neither their past nor their future which was central to that moment. At that time, all their space was filled with the momentous present.

Quite spontaneously and simultaneously, they addressed each other, "Who are *you*?" They laughed. Both felt a bit awkward but also quite relaxed. Here standing before each one was almost their mirror image, another "me." The impression created perhaps the most glorious sense of curiosity ever experienced in that garden — or anywhere else.

Of course, it took only an instant for each to notice the differences, too. As they looked across each other's unclothed bodies, they were not embarrassed or bothered. In fact, a pleasant sense of delight filled their senses. Their wordless exchange expressed a simple yet profound sentiment: "You are indeed beautiful."

Possessing an innate capacity for these matters, they also thought of the Maker. "What have you given to me here?" was their prayer. A moment like this was a once-and-forever event. New in creation was the forming of a special space most sacred. Within that space flowed a sense of wonder and appreciation. Most of all, there developed between them an awareness of commonality and kinship. "I am of you and you are of me. Together we stand as does the hardness of bone through whatever assails us. Joined we cling in the softness of flesh against whatever life may bring."

Until that moment of encounter, each had an uncomfortable feeling of being alone. There were many wonderful things in the garden. The various animals often provided exciting diversions. You really haven't lived until you have ridden on the back of a tiger at full speed. And a mixed salad of the best pick of the garden was a feast indeed. Yet, riding alone or eating by oneself in the shade of the most giant of sequoias still left one with a sense that more was possible.

So it was that a new sense of completeness, a joy at having discovered what may be missing, filled the minds and hearts of that first human couple. Mere eating could now be experienced as sharing food, and savoring the enchantment of the garden might now be enhanced by exciting conversation about its mysteries.

Most of all, there was a sense that all was now right. They had entered a place of discovery where an answer to the deepest question of all was beginning to appear. The answer came not in their being apart as separate individuals, pleasant as that may be. Rather, the truth of their life was present in their relatedness, in their standing before each other as they affirmed companionship. They felt a wondrous unearthing of that secret, right there from the beginning, yet demanding a ripening of the universe before it could be harvested. In their hearts, they knew in that instant they were made for each other.

Upon reflection, they liked to note that neither felt the need to elevate the other to a superior position nor the desire to stand above the other. Although they were somewhat different in body (which was obvious) and spirit (which only gradually became apparent), they basked in their equality. In that posture, they grew to know that only then would their deepest friendship be possible.

They also came to know that what held them together was not just some mystical cement created by their own inventiveness. They were joined by the power of the Maker who treasured them as the most important inhabitants of the greatest garden ever. The Maker smiled on their embrace as an indicator that not only could it all work, but, in fact, it did!

What gave the Maker full satisfaction was this: their caring for each other, despite their differences.

As woman and man, their overcoming singleness, their spanning the differences in affirming acceptance, was the very process which generated that force called life. In a word, their love gave birth to life. And it is the process which keeps the furnaces of the universe bright with light. It is the way God creates.

For this reason, when the story was put in print, the woman and man together were described as "being created in the image of God." Their accepting love of each other was full of power. This not only enriched their own experience but (as the story unfolds) became the way whereby new life was ushered into the universe.

Like all stories good and true, the garden story captured a truth applicable to all times and places. It is worth noting that given the cultural context of the ancient people who first told the Genesis story, it was remarkable that they affirmed the full equality of woman and man. The secular culture of their day (and even our own) was dominated by males who saw women as inferior. Listings of a man's possessions in those days would include farm implements, livestock, and women as if all were the same category of being. Against that cultural bias, the Genesis account of creation lives to underscore sexual equality as God's firm intent right from the beginning.

Also emphasized in fine poetic fashion is the essential goodness of human sexuality. Being comfortable with their nakedness indicated a fundamental positive acceptance of being created either woman or man. The fact of sexual distinctiveness is intended by God. It was no mistake, a part of creation which occurred when the Maker wasn't thinking about what was occurring. More positively stated, in the relationship between woman and man as intended by the Maker, a creative power was released which embodied the same creative power of God, a power capable of creating new life.

But let's get back to the story as it developed after their first meeting. They were to do more than just stand looking at each other in wonder and admiration. And this makes sense because soon after they ask the question, "Who are we?" there follows another question. "What are we going to do?"

As it was told, their range of possible activities was enormous. A million options were available. They could travel anywhere and do anything; they didn't even have to worry about the kids (yet). But there was one limitation. (Isn't there always?) It had to do with a tree and its tantalizing fruit. So it was and so it remains today: you cannot have everything and live.

With the abundant possibilities for good choices, why is it that there is a peculiar attraction to what is known as an evil choice? That is not easy to determine. Maybe it's a desire to replace the Maker with ourselves. Maybe we reject any limitation of choice. Maybe we want to live as if we are alone. Maybe there's a rebellious streak in us. We're an unruly bunch. And maybe it's a bit of all these factors.

We also know the rest of the story. A wily serpent suggests the obvious: "If you are willing to be restricted in any way, you are not number one. Number ones get everything they want. They operate without checks. They move with full wind at their back on the open road. If you think you are number one, go for it!"

The woman engages in a clarifying conversation with the tempter before she decides to break away. The man just does the forbidden. (Is the storyteller of the view that women are more critical and superior in moral intelligence because here the woman at least wonders a bit while the man simply acts?) They both eat the forbidden fruit; they both sin.

You have to be impressed by the human perceptiveness and profundity of the story. Evil is described as the result of a free decision on the part of both parties; their sinning is socially elicited, and it affects virtually everything significant about their relationship and their life thereafter. The stage is clearly set for the need for some kind of improvement. Much later, this will be called the need for redemption.

It's not so much that the man and woman are punished for their failure to live out the available good. More precisely, they are left to experience the consequences of their decision to attempt to become number one. Their own relationship lost its pure joy (they could no longer be freely naked); their proper work (childbearing and tilling the soil) was experienced as pain and labor.

What was intended by the Maker was seemingly lost through an exercise of choosing which was not originally intended. Yet, the Maker is not finished with the couple nor their descendants. The power of the Maker is immense, and more will be added to the story in due time. But remember this: the Maker's mind was not changed concerning the possibilities of life in the garden. The story is not simply to be told as a means to explain why things got rotten. It is a story of hope and the desire of the Maker for human happiness.

Each subsequent married couple will have their garden, their "tree of the knowledge of good and evil," and their choices about what to do. The Genesis story suggests that making the right decision will not be easy — that which is forbidden will appear mighty attractive. There will be others who will advocate its value. We live in a society which argues that any limitation is a sign of weakness. Being number one is the ideal. Choices based on that philosophy can reap a negative harvest for even those relationships we, at least in word, say are very important.

The story of the first couple was not recorded simply out of historical interest. Like medieval morality plays, the story was told to create a new understanding and awareness in the community of its hearers. The primary elements which make up the story are timeless in their capacity to reveal the deeper events of life. And though the story about the garden is quite ancient, it has a power to ask us whether our marriages are helped or hindered by that which grows on some quite interesting trees in our own garden plots. Overeating was certainly their downfall. Might it also be for us?

Sacramental Marriage

6.1 I Knew My Marriage Was a Sacrament When . . .

Five people describe the moments of grace that were turning points in their marriages.
Anna C. Erhart, Nancy Forest-Flier, John Garvey, Jo McCowan, and Linus Mundy

Strength in Numbers
Anna C. Erhart

It was a dark winter afternoon 12 years ago and my husband, David, was sitting on the edge of our bed staring into space. All at once he burst into tears and said, "I just don't think I could do it. If James dies, I just couldn't bear to wait around watching this one die, too. It's too hard to watch kids suffer."

His outburst brought back vivid memories of years before when our oldest son, James, had just come out of ten hours of experimental reconstructive surgery. When we were finally allowed into Intensive Care to see him, James' skinny, little 5-year-old body was strapped to the bed with tubes running out of his nose, mouth, arm, and leg; drains in his abdomen and penis; and sensors taped to his chest. David had taken one look at James twisting and moaning and groaned that it wasn't right for such little ones to hurt — why couldn't it be him instead?

On that winter afternoon 12 years ago, the two of us had just returned from Children's Hospital, where we had visited a 2-year-old up for adoption. We had decided that we would look into adopting again, a girl this time. We had adopted James, our 11-year-old, and also had a 5-year-old son, Peter. We wanted a girl, since we thought this would be our last child.

Because our oldest son's chronic medical problems were so serious, we had decided we needed to ask for a healthy child this time, though we thought we could handle a child with some motor handicap. Neither of us was really interested in a brand new baby, and we knew it would be easier to obtain a child no longer an infant.

Our pastor had heard of our plans and suggested that we think about an interracial adoption since we lived in a well-integrated neighborhood and attended a well-integrated parish. We had been a little surprised at that suggestion initially. We had moved to the Midwest from New York, where there was strong black opposition to whites adopting black children. But here in the Midwest, the lines did not seem to be drawn so clearly, and we knew there were many black and mixed race children who had no chance of homes without white placements. In the end we asked for a relatively healthy 2-to-3-year-old biracial girl.

The city's department of human services had told us that the process could be hastened if we signed a permission for them to obtain a copy of the home study done on us during the earlier adoption in New York. We agreed.

When the city received the papers, the social workers were thrilled because they discovered that James had been born with the same syndrome as one of their kids up for adoption: a 2-year-old biracial child named Anthony. Of course, he wasn't healthy, and he wasn't a girl. But to their minds, a family who wanted a 2-year-old biracial child and already had a child with the same condition was heaven-sent. They invited us to meet Anthony at the hospital, where he had lived since birth.

Anthony was a tiny little monkey with ears that dwarfed the rest of him. Although he was 2, he was about the same size as our Peter had been at 6 months. Anthony did not speak, walk, or even crawl. He sat wherever he was put and looked out at the world with blank eyes. He did not respond to speech, not even to his own name. We also heard tales of how ornery he was, but it was a touching orneriness.

The medical resident in charge of his care told us how Anthony had put on two hunger strikes, the first when he was only 8 months old. He refused to eat, or even to be fed. When the staff managed to get food into him, he learned to spit it out or gag to get it up. The first time they were reduced to tubal feeding with restraints before the resident decided that the strike might be a protest against the lack of continuity in Anthony's care. He decided to appoint the same three or four nurses to care for Anthony, with two of them doing the majority of his feedings.

On the sixth day of this new regime, Anthony gave up the strike. It was only when nursing transfers broke up the continuity in his care ten months later that he reinstituted the hunger strike. This time it was settled more quickly. The resident told us he thought Anthony was desperate for a family and would respond quickly to love and concern.

But we also learned that he was far from normal. Two severe bouts with pneumonia had required restarting his heart and lungs, and brain damage was likely. This was in addition to the medical problems from his congenital syndrome that we already knew of from James, which included frequent infections, failing kidney function, abnormal ureter and bladder, and eventual kidney transplant.

Now we had to decide whether or not to take this child as ours. David was not alone in fearing that taking on Anthony was more than we could handle. After all, we both agreed that we had been horribly naive when we had adopted James. We had known at the time that he was considered medically terminal and given only two to five years to-live. But we had been young — both of us 25, and six years married — and felt invincible.

Despite our early marriage, we had both gone on to complete our undergraduate degrees on time while supporting ourselves and paying our own tuition. Later while putting ourselves through law school and a doctoral program, we adopted James and had Peter. We had been so sure of ourselves, sure we could give James a loving home in the years before he died and still be strong enough ourselves to survive his death.

Now, years later, we had come to see that earlier decision as naive and arrogant after living through the surgeries, hospitalizations, and breakthroughs in kidney treatment and transplantation. Now we knew how devastating the fear for one's child's life was. The thought of voluntarily taking on another such burden was overwhelming for me as well as David.

At the sight of his tears I was undone, for David never cried. I pulled him down on the bed and held him. Neither of us said a word. We didn't need to; we knew we shared the same fears. As always, holding each other slowly developed into lovemaking, a slow, deliberate, pleasuring of the other designed to distract us from the decision to be made and to reaffirm the love that allowed us to even consider such a decision.

Later we went downstairs to start dinner for the boys. We didn't talk much over dinner preparation, and what we did discuss was news about our workdays earlier, not thoughts about the decision.

But my mind had never left the issue. I had been trying to decide exactly where David was on the decision. The real problem was that the social worker had shown us the paperwork. The hospital wanted Anthony moved because he no longer required full-time medical care, and the city had no place to put him — no foster home would accept him, no adoptive home was in sight, and the city no longer had orphanages, only short-term homes for kids in transition.

The social worker said that if they did not find a placement within the week, he would be moved to a publicly owned nursing home for the elderly. For us, one dimension of the problem was guilt: could either of us live with ourselves if our refusal left the child in a nursing home with geriatric patients?

I didn't at the time think about the nature of marriage, about its sacramentality, or anything more than trying to weigh the risks of overestimating our emotional resources against the risks of underestimating them. What was likely if we took him, what would it cost us, and at what cost would we say no? There seemed no compromise. That's where I was as we sat down to eat.

James asked us why Dad had come home early, and Peter asked why we had been upstairs. James, showing his extra years, elbowed Peter and winked; he had already caught on that when our door was locked before bedtime we were making love. David told them we had been to the hospital to see a prospective addition to the family.

Their first interest was the child's sex. Both of them were enthusiastic about another boy; neither was too interested in girls. But when we explained all the problems and that we thought that our responsibilities to the two of them made it impossible to take Anthony, they balked.

Peter insisted that Anthony didn't have a mother and father and needed us. He said that he would help out taking care of the baby. It was James' response, however, that punched us in the gut: "But, Mom and Dad, he's just like me! Are you sorry you took me?"

We had asked the social worker to give us a couple of days to think about our decision. The next day I mentioned our dilemma to one of the people I worked with, a Jesuit. The gist of his response was that I was crazy to consider it. I already had responsibilities to two children, one of them a high-needs child. I remember replying that there were two of us, that I wasn't parenting by myself. Being more than a bit sexist, he replied that I was the mother and mothers raised children while fathers paid the bills (regardless of the fact that my association with him was based on our working together full time!).

But this priest's response did set me to thinking. It suddenly hit me that I would never have considered adopting either James or Anthony alone. It wasn't a question of money, time, even general disapproval of single mothers. I would never have considered myself strong enough to bear either the pain or the responsibility for getting through what needed to be done.

Apart from David, I was not strong. If our first adoption had been naive, it had nevertheless been based on our feeling strong as a couple. Perhaps — even probably — we were not as strong as we had thought. We *had* been naive about what we were getting into. But we had evidently not been so naive about our ability to deal with it, for we *had* successfully come through a lot of pain and hardship already with James.

All of a sudden I began to consider the many ways in which we had each changed in our marriage, and it occurred to me that there was a connecting thread. In many different areas of our lives we were each stronger, surer of ourselves, who we were, and what we wanted. And there was no area where that greater strength was more evident that in our planning for and dealing with James' handicaps.

When I came home that evening, I waited till the dishes were done and then pulled David into the study and started to tell him what I'd been thinking. Before I could even get started he said that he'd been thinking a great deal about Anthony, and it had occurred to him that we had been doing okay with James.

He said, "I've been thinking that we have a lot. Anthony has many of the same problems as James, and we've dealt with all of them. We have even shown the doctors and therapists that kids with this syndrome can do things they didn't think they ever would. Remember when they told us James might never walk well and certainly would never have the balance or coordination to run? Now he rides a bike, plays Little League, and swims like a fish.

"We have a house with plenty of room, a very comfortable income, a mixed neighborhood and social circle that would both welcome and support a biracial child. If we can't do this, then who can? Who's in better shape than us to take this on?" He went on, "I guess we would be letting ourselves in for a lot of grief. And I'll probably cry again, but then you cry at movies on TV, so that's not so bad. What do you think?"

Looking back on that decision of ours 12 years ago, I am clear that it was not only the beginning of our career as Anthony's parents but the beginning of our recognition of the sacramentality of our marriage. We had been taught, as Catholics are, that marriage is a sacrament because it is a sign instituted by Christ to give grace. But neither of us ever had a good sense of what grace was until this decision.

This decision, and a number of events since, have convinced us that grace is not nebulous and abstract, discernible only to God, who sees our souls with X-ray eyes. At least sometimes grace is concrete, clearly present to us, and felt as it grows in us. Grace is experienced as the strength to love and commit oneself to another person even when you know that commitment will bring pain.

In marriage, for those of us who work hard at it and are incredibly lucky, the grace that each spouse brings to the marriage is multiplied and bestowed on the spouses in the form of strength — strength to love not only each other but together love others as well. We knew how important intimacy was to us and had come to realize that, for us, sexual sharing of pleasure helped create the bond in intimacy that kept us together. But we had not, until then, realized that the power and strength — the grace — that marriage gives is also, and not necessarily secondarily, oriented to activity outside the marital relationship itself, to the way we as a couple interact with the world.

In the years since, it has occurred to us many times that marriage is not best understood as something that preoccupies us and distracts us from the pastoral work of constructing the Kingdom — as most of us have been

taught — but instead marriage can be a tremendous resource for the Kingdom's construction.

Mercy First
Nancy Forest-Flier

If failed marriage and divorce can be said to have anything positive to offer,
it's respect for human frailty (mostly your own) and gratefulness for the
little, significant gestures of love. When Jim and I were married eight years
ago, we each had behind us the charred remains of unsuccessful attempts at
permanent relationships. The scars we both bore had only recently begun to
lose their awful sting. The baggage we carried included fear of failing again,
insecurity about our ability to sustain love for the long haul, and an enormous need to be understood and appreciated.

One vow we each had made separately and secretly before getting married
again — probably the greatest lesson that marital failure had taught us — was
that the next time we'd choose someone with whom we could pray and with
whom we could travel on what, up to that point, had been solitary spiritual
pilgrimages.

For many reasons my first marriage had not been sacramental. Aside
from the most obvious (I was still a Protestant at the time), the marriage was
characterized by an adolescent need to keep score, a ruthless insistence that
nothing — no personal purchase, no task, no gesture — should tip the scale
in favor of one of the partners.

The book *Open Marriage* had just been published, and most likely our
unfortunate arrangement had something to do with these new ideas about
marriage that were being trumpeted. When the relationship died of a predictable lack of care many years later, I had become accustomed to this ultra-in-
dividualistic, scorecard approach to life together.

Jim and I had been friends for many years and had been witness to
each other's sad failures. When the idea of marriage finally came up, we
knew that this one had to contain that thing that had been lacking before.
Our moment of grace occurred when we realized that something was there,
germinal but unmistakable; and if I try to recall a single event, it must be the
day my daughter got sick.

Jim was living in Holland at the time, and I was still in New York. He
had come to visit for a couple of weeks and was spending each day at a local
peace-movement office while I put in my full-day's work as a type editor at
a graphics studio. My work was high-pressure, exacting, and very exciting
with barely enough time for lunch; but I loved the drama of it.

In the midst of a particularly important job, I got a phone call from the
day-care center. My 5-year-old daughter had suddenly broken out in a rash,
and they wanted me to come pick her up. Struggling with the dual anxiety
over my daughter (Is it chicken pox?) and my work (Is there anybody here

who can take over for me?), I called Jim to let him know I'd be at my apartment in case he wanted to call me for any reason.

"Why?" he asked. "Don't you feel well?"

"It's not me," I explained. "It's Cait. She's got a rash, and I've got to take her home."

"Well, I can do that," he said. "I can borrow a car and pick her up. Don't worry about it. We'll see you later."

I was stunned. I was overcome. I remember getting the attention of all the other women in the typesetting room when I exclaimed, "What planet are you from!" He laughed and told me to go back to work.

It turned out fine. When I got home, Cait, with rash gone, excitedly told me of how Jim had picked her up. Then they had to climb into the apartment through a window because they didn't have a key, and finally they made cookies together.

What was the vital ingredient that became so apparent that day? It was mercy; an utterly gratuitous gesture made out of love. That, I knew, was where the sacramentality of marriage begins: with the promise to love the way God loves, without keeping score and without waiting for payment.

The Mystery Unfolds
John Garvey

One old definition of *sacrament* (or *mysterion* in Greek) is "an outward sign of inward grace." It is a sign that makes possible what it signifies. That works well on paper. So do a lot of the other definitions of sacrament. All the definitions are lacking, but I'll stick with that first one. Sometimes the outward and the inward rush together with the force of railroad trains colliding and you understand that the mystery, the sacrament, is not some simple rite of passage or any moment arranged by family and priest, bride and bridegroom.

Like most people, I married without knowing this mysterious other as well as I thought I did, and so I stepped into the dark. Regina did, too. There was the usual attempt to overcome ego, to live well with the other. Then just when you think you may have this difficult dance almost mastered, after many falls (it's an illusion, the idea that you ever finally get the hang of it), along comes a child to change the equation.

Or, more accurately, along comes the pregnancy that precedes the child. It wasn't an easy one, and ended two months before we thought it would. Maria was born at 7 months and weighed three pounds, four ounces; she later fell under three pounds. We were told that she had a chance of brain damage. When I noticed irregular breathing (the hospital staff hadn't), she was wired to an alarm that stimulated her breathing when it went off, which it did, periodically.

Maria was in the hospital for six weeks. During that time she almost died. It all ended well, and she came home when she hit five pounds and has been well from then on. What I will never forget, though, is the fierce love I felt looking at her through two panes of glass in a hospital corridor — looking at this tiny human being with her face clenched against the glare of our world, struggling, wired up with an alarm to tell nurses when her breathing faltered — and thinking with every nerve end in my body that I would die to keep her alive.

It became clear to me in that moment that this is what marriage, and love, and the idea that God loves us, all come down to: this fierce thing, this love that rough circumstance sometimes has to pull out of us unwilling human beings, is pervasive throughout creation.

The love I couldn't help at that moment was only a pale reflection of the love by which God drew the fullness of reality from nothingness. It was a participation in divine love. And that is what sacraments are: invitations to participate in divine life, in the death and resurrection of Jesus.

Having committed myself to our marriage more than a year before, I walked through the wedding ceremony like a sleepwalker, doing what was expected, nervous about all the people watching. I tried to bring, with what low wattage I possessed, a good Christian attitude toward being married. But it was not until I experienced, before a helpless baby struggling to be alive, an absolutely helpless love, that I understood how limitless love might be, and how merciful — and at the same time how searing — is our participation in the reality of an unlimited love.

The sacraments are our participation in the life, death, and resurrection of Jesus; they allow us to stand before God as Jesus did. That's the definition we need most. The idea of an "outward sign of inward grace" had always seemed so calm, a way of uniting something elemental like water with a prayer about water. But water can drown as well as wash (it presents a threat of death as well as a way of cleaning, and this ambiguity is part of what it means in Baptism).

The sacraments that unite us to Christ's life may be glorious, but are never meant to leave us settled. It was a surprise to me to encounter the first fruits of the sacrament of Matrimony in a little child's struggle not to die, and in my fullest hope and prayer that she would not. It was a revelation that God's love for us is, in a way, as helpless as mine for my daughter — God cannot *not* love us — and that as fierce as my love was, God's is infinitely fiercer.

Grammar Lessons
Jo McGowan

When I married my husband at the age of 21, I believe I was living right in the middle of the cloud of unknowing. He is from India, a country I had never seen but was reasonably sure I wouldn't like, and he wanted to settle there permanently. I agreed to this; and about two years after our wedding we went there to live.

It was almost exactly as I had feared. Bombay, where we landed, was hot, dirty, crowded, and unimaginably foreign. As we traveled around the country, I could feel myself freezing into an attitude of dislike. "What had I done? How on earth had I promised to live here?" I kept asking myself.

Although Ravi was willing to return to the United States if I were absolutely miserable, it was clear to me that doing so would in turn make him pretty unhappy. And since learning to adjust to India seemed a more worthwhile project than learning to adjust to the United States (how hard is it to adjust to ice cream parlors, fancy cars, air-conditioning, and VCRs), I made myself believe that I should be the one to change.

This exercise was purely intellectual, however; and during that first year I was full of repressed rage at what seemed a totally unfair situation. The unfairness seemed most acute when everyone was speaking Hindi. As often as not, those people could just as easily have spoken English; and their pointed preference for their own language felt to me like a conscious rejection, a deliberate attempt to leave me out.

It didn't occur to me until much later that by refusing to learn Hindi, I was the one doing the rejecting, not only of India but, in some fundamental way, of Ravi as well.

On my first trip back to the United States (after a year in India), the one thing everyone was sure to ask was whether I had learned the language yet. Over the course of my visit my excuses came to sound more and more feeble until I was finally forced to confront myself: Why hadn't I learned Hindi?

I don't know whether I was too young or too afraid, but I was not prepared for the snake pit that this question threw me into. Did I not want to live in India? Didn't I love Ravi? Was it really possible, anyway, to leave all the people I cherished and the only life I knew for a man I'd only met two years earlier? And, by the way, what about all my feminist principles?

During the 1970s, when "personal growth" was the rage and people were finding themselves by looking deeply into their pasts, their motivations, and their true feelings, my mother commented that if you dig up a plant too often to check for root rot, you end up killing it. Too much soul-searching may not be such a good thing.

I thought about that, and I thought about the promises Ravi and I had made on our wedding day. I asked myself what my mother would do in such a situation. My mother, who is a very practical woman, would probably enroll in a Hindi class.

And that's what I did. I returned to India and went to the mountain town of Mussoorie, where I became a full-time student in an intensive, total-immersion language school. I stopped thinking about my fears and doubts and concentrated instead on the dative and subjunctive cases.

I discovered the truth of an old adage: if you act as if something is, it becomes so. Studying Hindi for eight hours a day made me appear as if I were very serious about making it in India.

As the weeks went on and my fluency increased, I found that, in fact, I was becoming serious about it. As people's perceptions of me changed, their responses became warmer and more positive. My slightest attempts at communication evoked such delight wherever I went that it was impossible not to feel welcome. I began to relax, to see India as an adventure rather than an endurance test.

By making the effort to learn Hindi, I was admitting, at last, that I lived in India; but more than that, I was admitting that my husband was Indian; his outlook, his culture, and his background were all Indian; and I accepted him. I don't think I really understood this fact when we were married, but I also don't think it matters. The discipline of a permanent commitment allows for all kinds of changes and discoveries. What I keep learning is that if you concentrate on the grammar, the poetry takes care of itself.

To Know Her Is to Love Her
Linus Mundy

A writer by the name of Belleruth Naparstek tells about her marriage in a recent issue of the magazine *Common Boundary:* "The reasons we are still together," Naparstek says of her husband and herself, "have something to do with our having been in five or six different marriages with each other."

I sort of feel the same way. It's our many "different marriages" — all to each other — that have kept Michaelene ("Mikie") and me together. Further, I would go so far as to say that what has kept us together is knowing that each of these "different marriages" was and is in itself a sacrament.

Through the good times and the bad, we have come to see sooner or later the overriding and abiding signs of love in our marriage. That doesn't mean that in some of the toughest times we could sit back and say, "Gee, we're glad our marriage is a sacrament; therefore, things are going to work out just great!" Rather, in these toughest of times we relied on the fruits of our sacrament to save us: the love that was there. It was and is always the love that works, if anything at all can work.

"Signs of love," that's the phrase that writer Leonard Foley and other popular theologians have aptly used to describe the essence of sacrament. Signs of love. We are speaking of God's love here, of course, which "comes down" and blends with our human love and makes it the most powerful force on earth.

But how does this love happen? How does any love happen? A deeply satisfying answer has recently come to me: love happens through knowledge, through knowing. Let me explain my not so original but, to me, very convincing conclusion:

My loving wife encourages me to get away from our noisy, five-person (three of us are under the age of 11) household once or twice a year to visit my favorite thinking ground, the Abbey of Gethsemani at Trappist, Kentucky.

While there on my most recent visit, I was asking myself the deepest of questions, as I always try to do there. (It's that kind of place.) My Radical Question Number One was: What does God really *want* out of me/us anyway?

"God wants us to love," came the clear reply from somewhere there on those holy grounds. (I think I was missing my wife a lot by then.) "God wants us to love God and to love one another," came the gospel elaboration.

Simple enough, I thought. But how can one really come to love a God one doesn't know — or a neighbor or "another" one doesn't know, for that matter? It was then that I came to remember the astonishing thing 17 years earlier that made me come to love my future wife despite all my efforts to keep this love from happening. (I was holding out for someone richer, prettier, wittier, more suave and urbane like me at the time, if I recall correctly.) How did I come to love her? *I got to know her!*

After that, it was not only easy to love her; I couldn't *not* love her anymore. That has been — and will continue to be — the story of our marriage(s) together, the story of this great sacrament we share. But even more, we hope it can be the bigger story of our Christian lives together: coming to love — and coming to Love — through getting to know.

6.2   Spirituality of the Difficult Marriage
Thomas Fitzpatrick

I CALLED DAVID AT HOME BUT DARLENE'S FLAT RECORDED VOICE LEFT ME with a touch of anxiety. "I can't come to the phone right now, but leave a message and I'll call you back as soon as possible." Her return call confirmed my fear, "David can be reached at this number. . . ."

I hesitate to ask an acquaintance how their spouse is lately because too often I learn there is no longer a spouse. My wife keeps tab of these split couples and the list now tops fifty. As the list of broken marriages grows, there is diminishing community encouragement for couples struggling to improve their marriages. We especially feel this since we have a difficult marriage.

Ours is a difficult marriage, not a bad one. We are ill-suited in temperament. Brenda is reserved, proper, and deliberate. I am impulsive, sloppy, creative, and have few inhibitions. She packs her suitcase three days before we take a trip. That's about the time I make a plane reservation. When we were first married, I teased Brenda that her primary emotion was embarrassment. She needs to have things planned and secure; I thrive on chaos. We disagree, too, on child-rearing methods.

Most marriage articles center on happy marriages or they propose workable solutions to problems. I was recently excited about an article on marital communication. With the subtlety of an ambulance, I suggested that we try this. Brenda communicated right back. "I'm so sick of communication. If I see another article about communication, I'll throw up!" Articles often feature the happy couple that triumphs over adversity through God's grace. I hope we will some day be that couple. Today we are not. We have had repeated sessions with at least five counselors as well as three hours at a Marriage Encounter. Our marriage is not growing; it is not dying; it's just not moving much.

Ours is not a healthy relationship that is in a temporary lull or a passing crisis. Neither is there impossible neglect or abuse. Brenda and I love each other, but our life together can be extremely frustrating. When I become exasperated, I forget that in our twelve years together we have grown in individual maturity. Brenda has become a Christian, and I have begun to deal with my alcoholic upbringing. While our sex life is in hibernation, we want to love each other passionately. We are beginning to master the art of resolving disagreements without emotional bloodletting. Revealing these embarrassing truths and sharing the slow growth we enjoy, it is my hope that others will take heart.

As a man, it is particularly difficult for me to share my feelings with friends. In our culture, I can joke, make improbable boasts, and complain, but to reveal myself as vulnerable, angry, confused, and desirous of love is nearly impossible. No one seems to know the answers to my questions even if I had the courage to ask.

At times, even the scriptures seem to abandon me. Scripture presents the ideal marriage. "Your wife like a fruitful vine in the heart of your house, your children like shoots of the olive around your table" (Ps 127:3). It treats the ruined marriage. "You are right to say you have no husband; for although you have had five, the one you have now is not your husband" (Jn 4:18). But there is little that specifically addresses the struggling couple. Some of my loneliest, unhappiest hours have come late at night after an unresolved fight. Unable to sleep, I search the Scriptures fruitlessly for some specific comfort. I understand that as we become more mature Christian individuals, our marriage is bound to grow. Here Scripture helps. But there are few passages written directly for the unhappy couple, unable to resolve their chronic marital problems. The *Song of Songs is* sometimes painful to read.

Those without faith must be even more at a loss. Articles in the popular press do not discuss the loving but difficult marriage. Several friends who are counselors confirm the fact that professional journals do not treat the subject. There are few role models for those of us who want to bring to life a marriage long unhappy but never quite in crisis. The models seem to be happily ever after or splitsville.

I am not writing this article to complain or to blame Brenda. I am just as difficult to live with as she is. Rather, I want to affirm the value of a marriage that is not much to brag about.

What models are there for my marriage? First is the metaphor of the cross. This marriage is good for us because through suffering we complete the sacrifice of our Lord on the cross. I reject this as an incomplete and damaging concept of marriage. Yes, we have our Good Fridays and there is value in suffering; but we also enjoy each other's company. Taken alone, the cross is a warped model for an already wounded relationship. The cross, then, can have value when it describes some of our time together or some of the aspects of our life together but never our entire marriage.

Are we living in the second half of "for better or worse"? When I blissfully said the vow, I scarcely imagined that "worse" would ever come or that "worse" could last so long that it dulled the hope for "better." However, a relationship cannot make strides toward recovery if a mentality of endurance dominates it. If I am committed to sticking this thing out come hell or high water, then hell and high water will probably come. I need to be receptive to the small miracles of our life that are opening to happiness.

Perhaps it is good to think of our marriage as a desert or a furnace, uncomfortable places where we can meet God and be made more pleasing to him. This is a healthier metaphor. We do not deny our pain, but we transform it into an opportunity for growth.

We are stripped of the unimportant in the desert, emptied to meet afresh each other and God. I do petty things that annoy Brenda. I have a truly obnoxious habit of trying to run the lives of my wife and our daughter. In the furnace these are burned away, as they must be burned away since they are a second skin that I am loathe to gingerly peel away. But as in the *Book of Daniel,* another person was walking amid the flames with the three faithful Jews. So, too, Christ walks with us.

In the desert, we can be unaware of God though he is very near. Similarly, while Brenda and I know that our love is deep and real, we are often unable to feel it or to express it. If God is present to the degree that we need him, he must be very near to us. Sometimes I spend an entire week foregoing the deep urge to criticize, correct, and direct Brenda's life. Brenda becomes free to be herself, the woman I love. We begin to enjoy each other's company, a novel sensation. The desert begins to bloom. At present, these interludes do not last long, but they nourish hope and remind us of the life that can grow here. Sometimes the week is frustrating. Either I slip into old patterns or Brenda does not respond.

I have prayed that God would make Brenda more loving and have sought counseling to maneuver Brenda into changing. This was similar to a ruse my father-in-law once performed. He feigned a heart attack to prevent his wife from leaving him. My efforts were more sophisticated but no less manipulative than his "coronary." If God made Brenda free, how could he force her to love me? I began to wrestle with the uncomfortable mysteries surrounding love and free will. Only love freely given will truly satisfy my heart and I must risk rejection to gain the genuine article.

Brenda can be affectionate. Often, though, she recoils from me, from past wounds that have yet to heal. She reminds me of a vulnerable, brown-eyed wren — a beautiful bird that must protect herself with a nest of barbed wire. I long for us to grow beyond this, but at times the only avenue open is individual growth.

A godsend has been the movement for the Adult Children of Alcoholics. I was raised by loving parents who were children of alcoholics and who, eventually, became alcoholics themselves. The unhealthy behaviors I learned in my first home have contributed to the unhappiness in my home today. Now I work the Twelve Steps to become healthier. I am learning to be responsible for my own actions and to let go of Brenda's choices. As I drop my critical attitude and accentuate the good in our lives, I find there is more and more I should be grateful for. My hope is that it will become easier to be married to a happier me.

Just as our marriage could grow, it could also be dying. Ours probably resembles many marriages now dead. I am not privy to pain, frustration, or danger that motivated others to choose divorce. I am humbled. Our marriage is too close to the edge, too risky, and too fragile for me to judge others. We are vulnerable. Now we need to learn to be gentle and to shelter each other in a home that is a safe place.

My focus has been on the unhappy side of our life. But we laugh together, work together, and we are even slowly growing together. I suggest that in a difficult but loving relationship there is strong hope, perhaps because there needs to be.

What are the specific things that make staying together worthwhile? First, I see the solution of divorce as an illusion. We've seen too many friends and their children suffer and struggle. I cannot believe divorce is a speedy route to relief. It does seem, though, to be a quick way to work and worry away the pounds. Although adult children of alcoholics tend to be excessively loyal, I have decided never to leave Brenda. I take our vows seriously. We offered ourselves to each other for as long as we lived, and it is good to remain faithful to this promise. Perhaps this is especially valuable in a relationship that is not particularly rewarding. My personal, immediate pleasure is not the most important thing in the world. Our families and our culture would be stronger, perhaps even happier, if people waited patiently upon love.

People who endure physical disabilities are encouraged to see themselves in light of those things they can do rather than those things they cannot do. So, too, our marriage has its own strengths. We remain faithful to each other. We invest time and caring into raising our wonderful daughter. I love Brenda's honesty, her sensitivity, her love of nature and social justice. Though our life together is not easy, we really do love each other.

What, then, are my hopes? I look forward to a stronger faith and a more adult emotional relationship with Brenda. After a long wait, we see this beginning to grow and I hope our child will be blessed to see our broken lives healed. May our weak marriage become good for us and serve as a witness to others. There is value in loving another who cannot now meet my needs. This is how God loves. God has no needs. He loves each of us more than his very life.

Twelve years ago we married out-of-doors on a lawn soggy after a week of relentless rain. But the sun was brilliant on our day. Following communion, a hawk flew directly over the grassy aisle and beyond the altar. That sight has often consoled me. After years of rain, the sun is beginning to re-emerge slowly, and I believe that the Spirit is returning to our life together.

6.3   The Sacrament of Marriage
Leonardo Boff[1]

THERE IS A WELL-DEFINED THEOLOGICAL DOCTRINE ON THE SACRAMENTAL nature of marriage. This, this doctrine states, is properly and truly a sacrament of the evangelical rule (DS 1801). Like all sacraments, it is a sign that contains in itself and brings about that which it signifies. The sign is the realization of marriage itself on the level of a union of two wills and two bodies *(matrimonium ratum et consumatum)*. This sign produces what it signifies: the indissoluble union of the two partners. This union is in turn a sign of a deeper union between Christ and the Church. Marriage is thus an image of the marriage between God and humanity, or between Christ and the Church; this forms the *res et sacramentum* of matrimony. Finally, both the exterior sign *(sacramentum)* and the interior sign *(res et sacramentum)* produce the grace specific to the sacrament *(res sacramenti):* the grace proper to the married state, which enables the partners to live their sacramental union in such a way that it mirrors the mystical union between Christ and his Church. This grace furthermore assists them in the tasks, temptations and vicissitudes of married life. Such is the set of assertions that forms the kernel

---

1.   Translated by Paul Burns.

of classical theology of the sacrament of matrimony. Despite its undeniable virtues, it is difficult today to see how this doctrine applies the concept of sacrament to the fact of marriage. The task of theology is not to elaborate or defend doctrines with ever-increasing refinements of argument, but essentially to reflect radically on the religious reality from which all doctrines must spring. Marriage is such a profound human reality that it cannot be grasped adequately through the doctrinal co-ordinates of one system of thought. It is a "great mystery" (Eph. 5. 32), and theology, if it is to grasp its mysterious nature, must always be questing beyond the realms of doctrine. It is on the level of mystery that marriage takes on its sacramental character, and also in this dimension that it can be seen as a matter of grace and salvation.

From this, a number of questions immediately follow. Does the mysterious character of marriage, for example, only apply when it is celebrated as a sacrament, in the marriage of two baptized persons? Is, in other words, only the marriage of two baptized persons a sacrament? Or is the sacramental character inherent in marriage by virtue of its human reality alone? Can the sacramental reality be held to be always one and the same thing, or can it exist on different levels of perfection and in different degrees of wholeness? What is specific to Christian sacramentality in its fullest form?

These questions do not arise merely from an ecumenical interest, as subjects for discussion among the Churches, but stem from the very reality of marriage as an important anthropological fact, as we shall see later.

I. What Is a Sacrament?

Perhaps a deeper look at what a sacrament is will bring us closer to the sacramental reality of all marriages. We have become used to the classical definition of a sacrament: "an outward sign of inward grace," or St. Augustine's *"Sacramentum est sacrae rei signum"* (Epist. 138. 1), or Trent's "A sacrament is the visible sign of invisible grace, to which is given the power of making holy" (DS 1639). Behind all these rigid formulations stands a whole thought system, a whole manner of approaching reality. It is a primitive and savage way of thinking, as Claude Lévi-Strauss has pointed out; primitive not only because it belongs chronologically to the early stages of man's development, but also because it is closest to the origins of our modes of thought and speech. Technological man, thinking in scientific formulae and planning with computers, is still *sauvage et primitif*. This way of thinking involves signs, symbols and sacraments: G. van der Leeuw has called it simply sacramental thinking. In it, things are not thought of as things in themselves, nor the world simply as the world, but everything has to be a sign, symbol, or image of a higher reality. Reality is not only transcendent and immanent, but also transparent: one has to look through it to something beyond.

Now, this way of thinking is specific to mythical and theological thought, in which everything is seen from the starting-point of God. Then everything becomes transparent and changes into a sacrament of God. In the words of St. Irenaeus: "in God there is no emptiness, but everything is a sign" (*Adv. Haer.* 4. 21). This habit of thought extends into the personal domain: the basic realities of life, such as spirit, freedom, love, friendship, encounter, etc., can only be expressed adequately through signs and images. These make the realities they signify present, but also refer back beyond them. Everything that touches man deeply becomes surrounded with rites and ceremonies that reveal both its mystery and its links with a deeper reality.

There are, for example, certain nodal points in human life that are truly sacraments, and these are endowed with rites that enhance their importance and emphasize their transcendence: birth, marriage, sickness, death, eating and drinking. . . . In these situations, which belong in the physical, not the spiritual sphere, man feels his insertion into the mystery of life. He feels that there is a power that transcends him and on which he always depends; he realizes that he does not create his own being, but receives it continually from the world from food and drink, from other people who make up his life and without whom he would lose the basis of his existence. These situations are charged with a sacramental content: eating is not just eating; it is also a sign that makes present and communicates a power that is greater than the action of eating and cannot be manipulated by it. So eating becomes a sacrament of the divine and eternal God who sustains all and penetrates and confers meaning on existence. The basic life situations — birth, marriage, death, eating, etc. — form the basic sacraments of creation. These essential life situations are sublimated, "a sublimation because in the sacrament, these vital situations are seen from the standpoint of their ultimate basis, the point where they meet with the divine." In these basic sacraments, situated at the points where man realizes the potential of his biological nature, he experiences his links with God. This is why he surrounds them with marks of respect, sacralizes them.

The sacraments, then, express a symbolic understanding of the world. This is not to deny the consistency of material things in themselves, but to discover in them a dimension that transcends analysis of their physical-chemical components and that makes present in the world the reality of the transcendent and the eternal. Man is called to grasp the divine message that calls to him from all reality. He is not only a worker in and fashioner of the world; he is also the one being who can see through the transparency of the world to its ultimate ground: God.

II. Marriage: A Natural Sacrament

Marriage is undoubtedly one of the nodal points referred to. As the well-known phenomenologist of religion G. van der Leeuw wrote: "The old primitive world knew marriage as a sacrament in the literal sense of the word. This implies that in some ways the end of marriage is not mutual comfort or procreation, but the salvation to be found through it." In fact, marriage seen on its own is already a sacramental sign of the love of two lives. Through it, the meeting and flowering in love of an I and a Thou are expressed on the personal and social levels. Human love, therefore, seen in its totality, possesses a transcendent need and dimension. In love, man experiences fullness, the generosity of living for another, and the encounter that makes two one. Nevertheless, he also knows that love can be threatened by infidelity, by separation and by death; he can also find that the other is not the full and exhaustive answer to the longings of his heart. Man sighs for a deep and lasting love. What he loves is not in fact just another person, but the mystery of personality, revealed and made flesh in the loved one, but also veiled and withdrawn. In marriage, both husband and wife feel called to transcend themselves and to unite in the deeper reality that lies above them, the answer to their latent quest and the principle of union between them. Religions have seen God as the supreme and ineffable mystery that penetrates everything and encompasses everything, in which everything is revealed and kept. So the real Thou to whom man is radically open is not a human Thou but a divine Thou, and, ultimately, man is married by and to God. The other person is the sacrament of God: the personal vehicle for the communication of the divine love in history. One person becomes the sacrament for another when God is seen to be near because he is felt in the excellence of their love, and also felt to be distant, because he is veiled under the sacrament.

Human love, we can see, is always supported and surrounded by divine love; it is never a merely human love, since its link with the transcendent gives it a saving aspect. In other words, whenever a marriage contains genuine love, there will also *de facto* be the grace of God within the human love, making it possible, keeping it open in its transcendence and ensuring that, through the love of one person for another, God's saving action is brought about.

This reality is brought about even when God is not explicitly or systematically involved in the human love. The structure of marriage itself, when it is lived with sincerity, naturally embodies permanent reference to and inclusion of God.

This transcendent dimension of marriage is already contained in the priestly account of creation, in which God gives the man and the woman the commandment to grow, multiply and fill the earth, in the image and likeness of God (Gen. 1. 27-8). The human reality of marriage is sacramental by its nature; it refers back to the mystery of God. In the prophets the idea of the alliance between God and his people is expressed in terms of marriage. Yahweh is the faithful husband establishing a community of love and faithfulness with Israel. The latter is unfaithful and breaks the bond (Hos. 2-3; Jer. 3; Ez. 16-23; Isa. 54). Yahweh still professes his faithfulness in tender terms that overcome human faithlessness: "I have loved you with an everlasting love; therefore I have continued my faithfulness to you. Again I will build you, and you shall be built, O virgin Israel" (Jer. 31. 22). The eschatological dimension of the wife's eternal faithfulness is also expressed in terms of prophetic desire: "For the Lord has created a new thing on the earth: a woman protects a man" (Jer. 31. 22).

In conclusion, we can state: marriage as a human order possesses a sacramental character; it does not merely express the loving union of a man and a woman, but also the loving and gracious union of God with mankind, as the prophets clearly saw. It is theologically accurate to say that it is the love of God for men that makes possible true love between man and woman. For this reason, marriage, in the final analysis, is part of God's alliance with his people and so becomes, of itself, a permanent sacrament, which makes present and communicates the love, grace and salvation that come to us from God.

III. Marriage as a Christian Sacrament

If every marriage is a sacrament *per se,* what is specifically sacramental in marriage between Christians?

The Council of Trent taught that marriage was instituted by God and not invented by men (DS 1801). But it did not indicate what such a statement might mean. The New Testament gives no indication of any words of Jesus that might be taken as instituting this sacrament, any more than it does about other sacraments of the Church. Modern sacramental theology holds that formal institution is not necessary for a sacrament to be considered as having been instituted by Christ. Christ left the Church as the primordial sacrament of his saving, victorious presence in the world. All its actions possess a sacramental character, particularly the seven principal rites through which it actualizes the saving power of Christ in the basic situations of human existence. Christ and the Church took up the natural human sacraments that already implied a reference to God and placed them in a context of special relationship to the Christian mystery. The institution of a sacrament by Jesus Christ should be understood in this way.

Such an understanding fits better with Jesus' attitude to Jewish marriage. He breaks with the casuistry ruling at the time, which distorted the human order, and appealed to the divine origin of matrimony. He did not institute anything new, but restored the ancient form in its original theocentricity, recalling the words of Gen. 2. 24: "A man shall leave father and mother and be joined to his wife, and the two shall be one flesh; so they are no longer two, but one flesh. What therefore God has joined together, let no man put asunder (Mt. 19. 5; Mk. 10. 1-11; Lk. 16. 18).

This *parti pris* of Christ's against the legislation of his time should not be seen as an attempt to impose new legislation in his turn; it is of a prophetic, not a legalistic nature. Indissolubility as a sign and a precept is an ethical requirement — man *should* not put asunder — rather than a statement of fact man *cannot* put asunder. Voluntary separation is said to be a sin, re-marriage no longer permitted, but this is not an immutable law. Man does not have the right to separate what God has united, but this does not exclude the possibility of what God has united being separated, whether by unfaithfulness, death, or the causes contained in I Cor. 7. 11. The absolute character of Christ's precept is as an ethical demand to which man must always pay attention, and not a juridical law of absolute validity.

So in what specifically does the Christian sacrament reside? We have seen that Christ did not institute a sacramental sign proper to matrimony, but built on marriage as it existed, restoring its original human dimension. Christ did not come to build a new cultural pattern and new forms of interrelationship between men. He left the world as he found it, displaying a notable indifference to the social, political and economic structures of his time. And yet he introduced a new spirit and a new ethic with which to confront all things. So Paul can write that the Christian slave is the freed man of the Lord, and the free Christian is the slave of Christ (cf. I Cor. 7. 22). What Christ introduced was a new spirit of brotherly love towards all men and a new capacity for transforming human relationships from the master-slave pattern to the brotherly pattern.

Likewise with marriage: Christian marriage is like other marriages in its structure and pattern of organization. But it is lived in a new spirit: marrying, Paul says, is marrying in the Lord (I Cor. 7. 39), and if one can understand this, one will understand what is special to Christian marriage.

In the Epistle to the Ephesians (5. 21-33) Paul explains the underlying meaning of marriage: "He who loves his wife loves himself. For no man hates his own flesh, but nourishes it and cherishes it, as Christ does the Church, because we are members of his body. For this reason a man shall leave his father and mother and be joined to his wife, and the two shall become one. This is a great mystery and I take it to mean Christ and the Church" (28-32). *Mystery* here is based on the Hebrew word *sôdh*, and means the latent divine plan that gradually manifests itself in history. Marriage, as the intimate joining together of two loves, shows its true meaning in the light of Christ and his Church, Paul says; it does not only signify the union of God with mankind, as the priestly account of creation states in Gen. 1. 27, nor is it just a figure of the alliance between God and Israel, but it has a deeper meaning, revealed with the Christ event: it prefigures the unity between Christ and his Church in one mystical body (flesh). The words of Gen. 2. 24 — "they shall be one flesh" — take on a more radical meaning referring to the unity of one body with Christ. "In this vision," as Schillebeeckx has observed, "Creation, the covenant and redemption are intermingled.. Christ is the bridegroom whose bride is the Church. Christ, the one who loves, redeems and cares for the Church, is presented as a model for the husband in his married relationship with his wife."

Marriage as a human reality gains its final dimension in the light of Christ. It was ordained to Jesus Christ. Grace exists in nature, and nature in grace. Nature was created by and for Christ (Col. 1. 16). He is the first-born of creation and the mediator of all creation (Col. 1. 15; Jn. 1. 3). Wherever Christians marry, they should see it from this christological viewpoint, as orientated and penetrated by the reality of Christ and his Church.

The sacrament is not, therefore, something added to marriage; it is marriage itself seen from the standpoint of Christian faith. The more it is seen from this point of view, the more it emerges as a sacrament; faith detects and reveals a dimension that was already present in human marriage (Gen. 2. 24; Eph. 5. 31-2); now, with Christ, it declares itself and becomes clear. In other words, marriage does not become a saving action only where it is seen and identified as a sacrament by Christian faith; it is a sacrament whenever it is lived in the true human order of two in one flesh. In this case its sacramentality may not be obvious (though it tends of its nature towards this aspect that the Christian faith defines), but this does not make it any the less the means and the place for God's saving communication of his love for men and union with them. Certainly it was only in Christianity that this sacrament reached its full revelation, but wherever it is lived in a right order it achieves what the full and complete sacrament in the bosom of the Church achieves: the grace and communication of God.

What belongs specifically to Christian marriage is the full revelation, in Christ and the Church, of the ultimate meaning of love in the created order between husband and wife: the love of Christ and his saving covenant with mankind, particularly with the believing section of mankind, the Church. The sacrament reaches its fullness when it is brought about in the bosom of the Church-Sacrament of the Lord. The sacrament of marriage is a moment and a particular means of realizing the primordial sacrament that is the Church. Then the sacramental sign, through its participation in the Church, confers *ex opere operato* the grace of God that is always and indefectibly present in the Church.

IV. Sexuality, Eros and Agape as Components of the Sacrament of Marriage

If the sacrament of marriage is marriage itself in its human state, then the human components of married love are also taken up into the sacrament. *Eros,* as the Song of Songs vigorously proclaims, is a natural force by which man is drawn to woman and vice versa. They are called to form one flesh not only in the bodily sense, but also in the fusion of two wills, two minds, two lives. *Eros* reveals man's transcendence over himself and his openness to another. This openness is a sacrament of even greater transcendence when man aspires to the absolute and the divine. *Eros* reveals the riches and the poverty of human life: the riches of being able to give oneself in the happy joy of a meeting of two hearts and two loves; the poverty of longing to be completed and to accept joyously the gift of the other. Living the erotic dimension, in the giving and receiving of love, allows man to glimpse the meaning of God's grace. It is a gift to be able to give and receive: it is not in our power to win love or ensure a meeting; we live in the gratuitousness of the gift.

Sexuality, which is always more than genital sexuality, expresses the fundamental fact that human beings live as male or as female, relating to each other not as two incomplete beings that only become complete when they unite, but complementing each other. Each exemplifies *humanitas* in a particular way, and reveals different facets of the mystery of humanity, to their mutual enrichment. Genital exercise of sex, in God's plan, is always within the context of marriage, crowning the deep closeness and union of the two partners at all levels of their lives, and now in their corporeality too.

Agape should not be seen as a reality extrinsic to marriage in contradistinction to *eros*. *Agape,* as a being "in the Lord" (I Cor. 7. 39), means being able to live the conjugal union in its final essence, as an expression of Christ's love for men: "Husbands, love your wives, as Christ loved the Church and gave himself up for her" (Eph. 5. 25). Christ makes his presence felt in the married state and in marital relations. These can be practised according to the pattern laid down by prevailing social norms, but through *agape,* being "in the Lord," they are transformed in their inner nature: this again is a form of grace in the world. "As the covenant without creation would be empty, so *agape* without *eros* is inhuman."

Marriage as a sacramental earthly reality shares in the ambiguity common to every condition of fallen humanity. It is love, but also domination; it is self-sacrifice, but also a power structure; it is giving, but egoism at the same time. Married love, in fact, is lived with the psychological burden inherited from earliest childhood, with the frustrations and personal failings that hinder or obstruct our purity of vision and experience of this great mystery. Because of this, marriage, more than the other sacraments, is lived under the aegis of the cross of Christ. So the *agape* expressed in married life takes on the nature of a medicine for the wounds humanity inflicts on the sacrament, and of a revitalizing force for the underlying meaning of marriage as a sacrament of union between Christ and humanity. By virtue of this, love between man and woman should always and continually be in a process of purification from egoism and every hint of the will to power. The sacrament of matrimony is truly a sacrament that lasts throughout the life of the partners, and not a moment that marks the start of married life.

V. Conclusion: Marriage as a "Domestic Church"

One thing should be clear from these reflections: when two baptized persons validly contract matrimony, they receive the sacrament *ipso facto.* The love that unites them is not just a symbol of the love of Christ for the Church. They make this love visible and actual; then, as baptized Christians, take part in the building up of the Church. In one way they form what *Lumen Gentium,* n. 11, calls a "domestic Church"; in another, they are manifestations of the Church, which accommodates them in its bosom. The Church is present in the sacrament of marriage, not through its sacred ministry, but through the contracting partners themselves. The sacred ministry completes the sacrament in the sense that it provides the liturgical rite through which the implicit sign of marriage is made explicit on the level of profession of faith, and the juridical-canonical form in which the partners express their consent. The juridical-canonical form belongs to the *full* sacrament, in the sense that marriage is never merely a private affair or one of love between an I and a Thou, but always includes a social dimension and is naturally subject to the order and rules of society.

Just as the universal sacrament of the Church knows various degrees of actualization and explicitness, from the atheists in good faith *(Lumen Gentium,* n. 16) to Catholic Christians in a state of sanctifying grace, so marriage likewise expresses its sacramental character in various ways, from the imperfect but real forms of the world's various civilizations and other religions, to its perfect and complete form within the Church.

This perspective forces us to look with the eyes of faith not only at Christian marriage, but at all validly contracted marriages. All marriage is a sign of the transcendent and an incomplete realization of the mystery of Christ and the Church, moving towards an ever greater explicitation of its religious entelechy and inner Christianity.

6.4   Marriage as a Sacramental Passage
Evelyn Eaton Whitehead and James D. Whitehead

WE HAVE BEEN DISCUSSING MARRIAGE AS A COMPLEX PASSAGE OF SOME duration. In the sacramental theology of our recent past, however, Matrimony was understood as a more abrupt entry into a state in life. A different theology of sacraments will be necessary to support the view of marriage as both a sacrament and a passage.

Catholic liturgists and theologians have been reluctant to compare Christian sacraments and life passages. There are important differences between the two symbol systems: Baptism does not belong to biological infancy, but to a person's entry into Christian faith and community, *whenever* it occurs; Confirmation is not a religious puberty rite. Yet despite these and many other differences, marriage does appear as both a life passage and Christian sacrament. A reflection on marriage as a passage may help us recognize the ongoing quality of this and other sacraments.

Such a reflection begins with the now common insight that marriage is not a state that we suddenly enter on our wedding day. The sacrament of marriage cannot be understood in terms of a single ritual which magically transforms us from two into one forever. The sacramental celebration of marriage in the rites and ceremonies of the Christian Church must be the celebration of a process already well under way and of a process which has still some considerable way to go. We will try, then, to rescue the meaning of sacrament from a narrow "rite only" interpretation and explore how the *process* of approaching and beginning marriage is part of the sacrament of Matrimony.

This effort to understand a sacrament as more than a ritual — as, in fact, a combination of ritual celebration and gradual induction ("leading into") — is not restricted to the transition of marriage. The sacrament of Baptism clearly includes this combination of ritual and process. In the sacramental ritual of Baptism, Christians celebrate the entry of (most often) a child into the Christian community. In this sacramental celebration the Church and the family welcome the child into Christian life: we invoke God's blessing on the long journey just beginning; we hope for the child all the goodness and holiness that such a life can mean; and we ritually celebrate the child's passage from an unnamed infant to a named member of this faith community. But this celebration, effected in a brief ritual on a single day, must be complemented by the process, years long, of actually bringing the child into Christian living. The ritual celebration of Baptism depends on this process of love and care and example which will show this child what Christian living means in practice. The importance of this *process* of being practically introduced into Christian life is such that we may think of it as part of the sacrament.

Changing practices in Christian missions today point to this broader understanding of the sacrament. Missionaries no longer baptize every child possible, believing that this ritual *of itself* will transform the child into a Christian. Without the support of a believing community — a group that can show the child what Christian loving trusting and caring actually look like — a child is not properly baptized. A fascination with the sacramental ritual itself has in the past distracted us from the importance of the *process* of the sacraments. To baptize a child and not provide a community which, over time, can practically effect this introduction into Christian life, is a magical and false application of the sacrament.

The parallels between the sacraments of Baptism and Matrimony are easy to see. The sacrament of Matrimony combines a ritual celebration and a process or passage. In the ritual celebration the couple publicly express their life commitment and formally begin their life together. In this public and Christian commitment, the couple are empowered (receive the grace of this sacrament) to pursue the fidelity and fruitfulness of a Christian marriage. But the celebration of a single *ritual* must be complemented by a Christian sacramental *process*. This process, like that of Baptism, can be expected to have a significant duration. As with Baptism, we often do see the sacrament of Matrimony celebrated without any supporting process. A couple who have little or no practical commitment to Christian living are married in the Church. (The parents may insist on it, or the couple think it is more appealing than a ceremony before the justice of the peace.) A narrow focus on the sacrament as effected in a single ritual leads to the impression that this is Matrimony — the beginning of an explicitly Christian marriage. But, as in Baptism, this ritual celebration does not enjoy the magical power to effect a way of life to which the couple are not otherwise practically committed.

The narrow focus on Matrimony as a single ritual celebration has been aided by a restricted view of Christian responsibility and ministry. As ministry in the Catholic tradition became increasingly understood as the exclusive domain of the clergy, the laity became more and more passive. The sacraments were administered by the clergy; the laity received the sacraments; the faith community became the almost neutral site where this ministry transpired.

Today we are recovering a view of Christian ministry that more powerfully involves all adult believers. Regarding Matrimony, we are recalling that the couple are themselves the celebrants of their marriage; the priest does not marry them but witnesses in the name of the Church their performing of this sacrament. And our recovery of marriage as an ongoing passage further reminds us of the active role of the believing community. Just as the individuals marrying do not passively receive this sacrament, the faith community has an active contribution to make to this and every sacrament. Our changed vocabulary signals this shift: the priest does not "say Mass"; the faith community "celebrates the Eucharist."

If the priest is not the minister of Matrimony, neither can the couple be its sole and independent celebrants. The community's support, expressed in wedding gifts and congratulations, must also find a more sustained and explicitly religious expression. Sacramental theology since Vatican II has stressed again the role of the Church as itself a sacrament. Practically, this means that a particular Christian community is called to witness, to couples approaching and those already living marriage, to what Christian marriage really looks like. Further, this sacramental role of the community necessitates more than a general witness. A faith community concretely participates in the ongoing celebration of Christian marriage by structuring educational opportunities for those approaching and living marriage. These will include specific programs in the parish or elsewhere that allow a couple, engaged or married, to explore their relationship and deal with its questions and challenges. These opportunities should not be understood as merely psychological or secular events, however helpful. When structured skillfully and with a specifically religious intent, these programs are an integral part of the sacrament of Matrimony. In this assistance a community itself becomes a sacrament in more than rhetoric and gracefully contributes to the sacramental passage of its members into Christian marriage.

This sacramental response of a community to couples entering and pursuing married life can more broadly be understood in terms of rites of passage. In a variety of ways, over an extended period, we are called to provide practical means of caring for those entering marriage. This is a challenge not just for a pastor but for the community itself. And the community will structure effective means of support and challenge as it better understands the different stages of this transition into marriage.

Divorce and Remarriage

7.1 What Makes Love Last?

Alan Atkisson

MY OLD FRIENDS KAREN AND BILL, MARRIED SINCE 1955, RECENTLY CELEBRATED another anniversary. "I wore the same nightgown I wore on our wedding night," confessed Karen to me over the phone. "Just as I have every anniversary for thirty-nine years."

"I wore pajamas on our wedding night," offered Bill. "But last night I didn't wear nothin'." They laughed, and even over three thousand miles of telephone wire I felt the strength of their love for one another.

Long-lasting marriages like Bill's and Karen's are becoming increasingly rare. Not only do more than 50 percent of all first marriages in the United States end in divorce (make that 60 percent for repeat attempts), but fewer people are even bothering to tie the slippery knot in the first place. One fourth of Americans eighteen or older — about 41 million people — have never married at all. In 1970, that figure was only one sixth.

But even while millions of couples march down the aisle only to pass through the therapist's office and into divorce court, a quiet revolution is taking place when it comes to understanding how long-term love really works. Inside the laboratories of the Family Formation Project at the University of Washington in Seattle — affectionately dubbed the Love Lab — research psychologists are putting our most cherished relationship theories under the scientific microscope. What they're discovering is that much of what we regard as conventional wisdom is simply wrong.

"Almost none of our theory and practice [in marital therapy] is founded on empirical scientific research," contends the Love Lab's head, John Gottman, an award-winning research psychologist trained both as a therapist and a mathematician. Indeed, it is this lack of solid research, Gottman be-

159

lieves, that contributes to a discouraging statistic: for 50 percent of married couples who enter therapy, divorce is still the end result.

Gottman believes that, although relationship counseling has helped many people, much of it just doesn't work. Not satisfied with warm and fuzzy ideas about how to "get the love you want," Gottman is scouting for numbers, data, *proof* — and he's finding it.

For the past twenty years, in a laboratory equipped with video cameras, EKG's, and an array of custom-designed instruments, Gottman and his colleagues have been intensely observing what happens when couples interact. He watches them talk. He watches them fight. He watches them hash out problems and reaffirm their love. He records facial expressions and self-reported emotions, heart rhythms and blood chemistry. He tests urine, memories, and couples' ability to interpret each other's emotional cues. Then he pours his data, like so many puzzle pieces, into a computer. The resulting picture, he says, is so clear and detailed it's like "a CAT scan of a living relationship." [See "Putting Love to the Test," below.]

What Gottman and his colleagues have discovered — and summarized for popular audiences in a new book, *Why Marriages Succeed or Fail* (Simon & Schuster) — is mind-boggling in its very simplicity. His conclusion: Couples who stay together are . . . well . . . *nice* to each other more often than not. "[S]atisfied couples," claims Gottman, "maintained a five-to-one ratio of positive to negative moments" in their relationship. Couples heading for divorce, on the other hand, allow that ratio to slip below one-to-one.

If it ended there, Gottman's research might remain just an interesting footnote. But for him and his colleagues, this discovery is just the beginning. In fact, Gottman's novel and methodical approach to marriage research is threatening to turn much of current relationship therapy on its head. He contends that many aspects of wedded life often considered critical to long-term success — how intensely people fight; whether they face conflict or avoid it; how well they solve problems; how compatible they are socially, financially, even sexually — are less important than people (including therapists) tend to think. In fact, Gottman believes, none of these things matter to a marriage's longevity as much as maintaining that crucial ratio of five to one.

If it's hard to believe that the longevity of your relationship depends primarily on your being five times as nice as you are nasty to each other, some of Gottman's other conclusions may be even more surprising. For example:

- Wildly explosive relationships that vacillate between heated arguments and passionate reconciliations can be as happy and long-lasting as those that seem more emotionally stable. They may even be more exciting and intimate.

- Emotionally inexpressive marriages, which may seem like repressed volcanoes destined to explode, are actually very successful — so long as the couple maintains that five-to-one ratio in what they do express to each other. In fact, too much emotional catharsis among such couples can "scare the hell out of them," says Gottman.

- Couples who start out complaining about each other have some of the most stable marriages over time, while those who don't fight early on are more likely to hit the rocky shoals of divorce.

- Fighting, whether rare or frequent, is sometimes the healthiest thing a couple can do for their relationship. In fact, blunt anger, appropriately expressed, "seems to immunize marriages against deterioration."

- In happy marriages, there are no discernible gender differences in terms of the quantity and quality of emotional expression. In fact, men in happy marriages are more likely to reveal intimate personal information about themselves than women. (When conflict erupts, however, profound gender differences emerge.)

- Men who do housework are likely to have happier marriages, greater physical health, even better sex lives than men who don't. (This piece of news alone could cause a run on aprons.)

- Women are made physically sick by a relentlessly unresponsive or emotionally contemptuous husband. Gottman's researchers can even tell just how sick: They can predict the number of infectious diseases women in such marriages will suffer over a four-year period.

- How warmly you remember the story of your relationship foretells your chances for staying together. In one study that involved taking oral histories from couples about the unfolding of their relationship, psychologists were able to predict with an astonishing 94 percent accuracy which couples would be divorced within three years.

◆

Putting Love to the Test
How the "Love Lab" researchers decode blood, sweat, and tears.

The studio apartment is tiny, but it affords a great view of Seattle's Portage Bay. The ambiance is that of a dorm room tastefully furnished in late-'80s Sears, Roebuck. A cute kitchen table invites you to the window. A Monet print graces one wall. Oh, and three video cameras — suspended from the ceiling like single-eyed bats — follow your every move.

Welcome to the "Love Lab," wherein Professor John Gottman and a revolving crew of students and researchers monitor the emotions, behaviors, and hormones of married couples. Today, lab coordinator Jim Coan — a calm, clear-eyed, pony-tailed young man in Birkenstocks who started out as a student volunteer three years ago — is giving me the tour.

The Love Lab is actually two labs. I have entered through the "Apartment Lab," whose weekly routine Coan describes: A volunteer couple arrives on a Sunday morning, prepared to spend the day being intensely observed (for which they are modestly compensated). Special microphones record every sound they make; videotape captures every subtle gesture. The only true privacy is found in the bathroom, but even there science has a presence: A cooler by the toilet has two little urine collection bottles, today marked "Bill" and "Jeannie."

At the end of a relaxed day doing whatever they like (and being watched doing it), the couple welcomes a house guest — a psychologist who listens to the story of how they met, fell in love, and began building a life together. This "oral history," which most people greatly enjoy telling, will later be closely scrutinized: Gottman and company have learned that how fondly a couple remembers this story can predict whether they will stay together or divorce.

Then, after a sleep-over on the Lab's hide-a-bed (cameras and microphones off) and a blood sample, a technician takes the pair out for breakfast, gives them their check, and sends them on their way. The videotapes will later be analyzed in voluminous detail. Every affectionate gesture, sarcastic jab, or angry dispute will be recorded and categorized using Gottman's "specific affect" emotional coding system (the lab folks call it SPAFF for short). At the same time, the couple's blood and urine will be sent to another lab and tested for stress hormone levels. Finally, in four years or so (depending on the study), the lab will follow up with the couple to see if they're still together — and take another look at the data they gathered to see if a predictable pattern can be discerned.

Other couples who visit the Family Formation Project, as the "Love Lab" is more formally known, merely pass the pleasant apartment on their way to a less coy destination: the "Fixed Lab." Here they are seated ("fixed") in plain wooden chairs and hooked up with a dizzying array of instruments — EKG electrodes, finger-pulse detectors, and skin galvanometers ("a fancy word for sweat detectors," says Coan). A thick black spring stretched across their chests registers breathing. Their chair itself is a "jiggleometer," recording every fidget and tremor.

A "facilitator" first interviews the pair about what issues cause conflict in their marriage, then gets them talking about the most contentious ones. Video cameras focus on the couple's faces and chests. Computers track the complex streams of data coming in through the sensors and displays them on a color monitor in a rainbow of blips and graphs.

After fifteen minutes of surprisingly "normal" and often emotional conversation, the couple are stopped by the facilitator, who plays back the videotape for them. While watching, each partner rates his or her own emotional state at every moment during the conversation, using a big black dial with a scale running from "extremely negative" through "neutral" to "extremely positive." Then the pair watch the tape again, this time in an attempt to similarly judge their partner's emotional state (with widely varying levels of success).

Later, students trained by Coan will review the tape using a specially designed dial and the SPAFF coding system, to chart the feelings being displayed. It's eerie to see the range of human emotional expression represented on a high-tech instrument panel: disgust, contempt, belligerence, domination, criticism, anger, tension, tense humor ("very popular, that one," Coan tells me), defensiveness, whining, sadness, stonewalling, interest, validation, affection, humor, joy, and positive or negative surprise (students made Gottman aware of the two different kinds). In the middle is a neutral setting for when couples are merely exchanging information without noticeable emotion.

Back in the apartment lab, Coan shows me videos of couples who have agreed to be involved with the media. Two young parents from Houston discuss the stress around caring for their new baby, and Coan gives me the play-by-play: "He's being very defensive here" or "See that deep sigh? She's feeling sad now" or "Now that was a nice validation."

Coan says that most people seem to enjoy the lab experience and even get some benefit from it (though it's not meant to be therapeutic). Amazingly, even with sensors attached to their ears and fingers and chests, the couples seem to forget that they're being watched. They giggle and cry and manage to create a genuine closeness while fixed under a physiological microscope.

"It's a real privilege to work here," Coan says thoughtfully. Even in a short visit, I feel it too. The observation of intimacy, both its joy and its pain, is more than just scientific video voyeurism. It's as though the love these couples are trying so devotedly to share with each other seeps out of the box, a gift to the watchers.

◆

The Three Varieties of Marriage

In person, Gottman is a fast-talking, restless intellect, clearly in love with his work. Now in his late forties and seven years into a second marriage (to clinical psychologist Julie Schwartz), he seems very satisfied. Yet, in his book, he sheds the mantle of guru in the first sentence: "My personal life has not been a trail of great wisdom in understanding relationships," he says. "My expertise is in the scientific observation of couples."

Gottman began developing this expertise some twenty years ago, when a troubled couple who came to him for help didn't respond well to conventional therapy. In frustration, Gottman suggested that they try videotaping the sessions. "Both the couple and I were astonished by the vividness and clarity on the tape of the pattern of criticism, contempt, and defensiveness they repeatedly fell into," he recalls. "It shocked them into working harder . . . [and] it gave me my life's work."

Struck by the power of impartial observation, Gottman became fascinated with research. His goal: to systematically describe the differences between happy and unhappy couples, and from those observations develop a scientific theory capable of predicting marital success. This seemed a daunting task, both because "marriage is so subjective" and because "personality theory, in psychology, has been a failure at predicting anything."

The result of Gottman's passion is a veritable mountain of data: tens of thousands of observations involving thousands of couples, gathered by the Love Lab's researchers and stored in its computer data-bases. The geography of that mountain reveals a surprising pattern: Successful marriages come in not one but three different varieties, largely determined by how a couple handles their inevitable disagreements. Gottman calls these three types of stable marriages *validating, volatile,* and *conflict-avoiding.*

Validating couples are what most people (including most therapists) have in mind when they think of a "good marriage." Even when these couples don't agree, they still let their partner know that they consider his or her opinions and emotions valid. They compromise often and calmly work out their problems to mutual satisfaction as they arise. And when they fight, they know how to listen, acknowledge their differences, and negotiate agreement without screaming at each other. "These couples," Gottman notes, "look and sound a lot like two psychotherapists engaging in a dialogue."

But where modern therapy often goes wrong, says Gottman, is in assuming that this is the only way a marriage can work — and trying to force all couples into the validating mold. While viewing this style of marriage as the ideal has simplified the careers of marital therapists, it hasn't necessarily helped their clients, he says, who may fall into the other two types of stable pattern.

Volatile couples, in contrast to validating ones, thrive on unfiltered emotional intensity. Their relationships are full of angry growls and passionate sighs, sudden ruptures and romantic reconciliations. They may fight bitterly (and even unfairly), and they may seem destined for divorce to anyone watching them squabble. But Gottman's data indicate that this pessimism is often misplaced: These couples will stay together if "for every nasty swipe, there are five caresses." In fact, "the passion and relish with which they fight seems to fuel their positive interactions even more." Such couples are more romantic and affectionate than most but they are also more vulnerable to a decay in that all-important five-to-one ratio (and at their worst, to violence). Trying to change the style of their relationship not only isn't necessary, Gottman says, it probably won't work.

Nor will conflict-avoiding couples, the third type of stable marriage, necessarily benefit from an increase in their emotional expression, he says. Gottman likens such unions to "the placid waters of a summer lake," where neither partner wants to make waves. They keep the peace and minimize argument by constantly agreeing to disagree. "In these relationships, solving a problem usually means ignoring the difference, one partner agreeing to act more like the other . . . or most often just letting time take its course." The universal five-to-one ratio must still be present for the couple to stay together, but it gets translated into a much smaller number of swipes and caresses (which are also less intensely expressed). This restrained style may seem stifling to some, but the couple themselves can experience it as a peaceful contentment.

Things get more complicated when the marriage is "mixed" — when, say, a volatile person marries someone who prefers to minimize conflict. But Gottman suggests that, even in these cases, "it may be possible to borrow from each marital style and create a viable mixed style." The most difficult hurdle faced by couples with incompatible fighting styles lies in confronting that core difference and negotiating which style (or combination of styles) they will use. If they can't resolve that primary conflict, it may be impossible to tip the overall balance of their relational life in the direction of five-to-one.

The important thing here is to find a compatible fighting style — not to stop fighting altogether. Gottman is convinced that the "one" in that ratio is just as important as the "five": "What may lead to temporary misery in a marriage disagreement and anger may be healthy for it in the long run." Negativity acts as the predator in the ecosystem of marriage, says Gottman. It's the lion that feeds on the weakest antelopes and makes the herd stronger. Couples who never disagree at all may start out happier than others, but without some conflict to resolve their differences, their marriages may soon veer toward divorce because their "ecosystem" is out of balance.

◆

Four Keys to a Happy Relationship

Despite all his sophisticated analysis of how relationships work (and don't work), researcher John Gottman's advice to the lovelorn and fight-torn is really quite simple.

Learn to calm down. This will cut down on the flooding response that makes further communication so difficult. "The most brilliant and philosophically subtle therapy in the world will have no impact on a couple not grounded in their own bodies to hear it," he says. Once couples are calm enough, suggests Gottman, they can work on three other basic "keys" to improving their relationship.

Learn to speak and listen nondefensively. This is tough, Gottman admits, but defensiveness is a very dangerous response, and it needs to be interrupted. One of the most powerful things you can do — in addition to working toward the ideal of listening with empathy and speaking without blame — is to "reintroduce praise and admiration into your relationship." A little appreciation goes a long way toward changing the chemistry between people.

Validate your partner. Validation involves "putting yourself in your partner's shoes and imagining his or her emotional state." Let your partner know that you understand how he or she feels, and why, even if you don't agree. You can also show validation by acknowledging your partner's point of view, accepting appropriate responsibility, and apologizing when you're clearly wrong. If this still seems too much of a stretch, at least let your partner know that you're trying to understand, even if you're finding it hard.

Practice, practice, practice. Gottman calls this "overlearning," doing something so many times that it becomes second nature. The goal is to be able to calm yourself down, communicate nondefensively, and validate your partner automatically — even in the heat of an argument.

◆

The Four Horsemen of the Apocalypse

Even the most stable marriages of any style can fall apart, and Gottman and company have observed an all-too-predictable pattern in their decline and fall. He likens the process to a cascade — a tumble down the rapids — that starts with the arrival of a dangerous quartet of behaviors. So destructive is their effect on marital happiness, in fact, that he calls these behaviors "The Four Horsemen of the Apocalypse."

The first horseman is criticism: "attacking someone's personality or character" rather than making some specific complaint about his or her behavior. The difference between saying, say, "I wish you had taken care of that bill" (a healthy and specific complaint) and "You never get the bills paid on time!" (a generalizing and blaming attack) is very significant to the listener. Criticism often engenders criticism in return and sets the stage for the second horseman: contempt.

"What separates contempt from criticism," explains Gottman, "is the intention to insult and psychologically abuse your partner." Negative thoughts about the other come out in subtle put-downs, hostile jokes, mocking facial expressions, and name-calling ("You are such an idiot around money"). By now the positive qualities that attracted you to this person seem long ago and far away, and instead of trying to build intimacy, you're ushering in the third horseman.

Defensiveness comes on the heels of contempt as a seemingly reasonable response to attack — but it only makes things worse. By denying responsibility, making excuses, whining, tossing back counter-attacks, and other strategies ("How come I'm the one who always pays the bills?!"), you just accelerate your speed down river. Gottman also warns that it's possible to skip straight to the third horseman by being oversensitive about legitimate complaints.

Once stonewalling (the fourth horseman) shows up, things are looking bleak. Stonewallers simply stop communicating, refusing to respond even in self-defense. Of course, all these "horsemen" drop in on couples once in a while. But when a partner habitually shuts down and withdraws, the final rapids of negativity (what Gottman calls the "Distance and Isolation Cascade") can quickly propel the marriage through whirlpools of hopelessness, isolation, and loneliness over the waterfall of divorce. With the arrival of the fourth horseman, one or both partners is thinking negative thoughts about his or her counterpart most of the time, and the couple's minds — as well as their bodies — are in a perpetual state of defensive red alert.

The stress of conflict eventually sends blood pressure, heart rate, and adrenaline into the red zone — a phenomenon Gottman calls *flooding*. "The body of someone who feels flooded," he writes, "is a confused jumble of signals. It may be hard to breathe . . . . Muscles tense up and stay tensed. The heart beats fast, and it may seem to beat harder." Emotionally, the flooded person may feel a range of emotions, from fear to anger to confusion.

The bottom line is that flooding is physically uncomfortable, and stonewalling becomes an attempt to escape that discomfort. When flooding becomes chronic, stonewalling can become chronic, too. Eighty-five percent of the time the stonewaller (among heterosexual couples) is the man. The reason for this gender discrepancy is one of many physiological phenomena that Gottman sees as critical to understanding why marriages go sour, and what people can do to fix them.

Though flooding happens to both men and women, it affects men more quickly, more intensely, and for a longer period of time. "Men tend to have shorter fuses and longer-lasting explosions than women," says Gottman. Numerous observations in the laboratory have shown that it often takes mere criticism to set men off, whereas women require something at least on the level of contempt. The reasons for this are left to speculation. "Probably this difference in wiring had evolutionary survival benefits," Gottman conjectures. An added sensitivity to threats may have kept males alert and ready to repel attacks on their families, he suggests, while women calmed down more quickly so they could soothe the children.

Whatever its origin, this ancient biological difference creates havoc in contemporary male-female relationships, because men are also "more tuned in to the internal physiological environment than women," Gottman reports. (For example, men are better at tapping along with their heartbeat.) Men's bodily sensitivity translates into greater physical discomfort during conflict. In short, arguing hurts. The result: "Men are more likely to withdraw emotionally when their bodies are telling them they're upset." Meanwhile, "when men withdraw, women get upset, and they pursue [the issue]" — which gets men more upset.

Here is where physiology meets sociology. Men, says Gottman, need to rely on physiological cues to know how they're feeling. Women, in contrast, rely on social cues, such as what's happening in the conversation.

In addition, men are trained since early childhood not to build intimacy with others, while women "are given intense schooling on the subject" from an equally early age. Socially, the genders are almost totally segregated (in terms of their own choices of friendships and playmates) from age seven until early adulthood. Indeed, it would seem that cross-gender relationships are set up to fail. "In fact," Gottman writes, "our upbringing couldn't be a worse training ground for a successful marriage."

Yet the challenge is far from insurmountable, as millions of marriages prove. In fact, Gottman's research reveals that "by and large, in happy marriages there are *no* gender differences in emotional expression!" In these marriages, men are just as likely to share intimate emotions as their partners (indeed they may be more likely to reveal personal information about themselves). However, in unhappy marriages, "all the gender differences we've been talking about emerge" — feeding a vicious cycle that, once established, is hard to break.

Married couples who routinely let the Four Horsemen ransack their living rooms face enormous physical and psychological consequences. Gottman's studies show that chronic flooding and negativity not only make such couples more likely to get sick, they also make it very difficult for couples to change how they relate. When your heart is beating rapidly and your veins are constricting in your arms and legs (another evolutionary stress response), it's hard to think fresh, clear thoughts about how you're communicating. Nor can the brain process new information very well. Instead, a flooded person relies on "overlearned responses" — old relationship habits that probably just fan the flames.

All this physiological data has enormous implications for relationship therapists as well as their clients. Gottman believes that "most of what you see currently in marital therapy — not all of it, but most of it — is completely misguided."

For example, he thinks it's an exercise in futility when "the therapist says 'Calm down, Bertha. Calm down, Max. Let's take a look at this and analyze it.

Let's remember the way we were with our mothers.' Bertha and Max can do it in the office because he's doing it for them. But once they get home, and their heart rates get above 100 beats per minute, whew, forget about it."

Teaching psychological skills such as interpreting nonverbal behavior also misses the mark. "We have evidence that husbands in unhappy marriages are terrible at reading their wives' nonverbal behavior. But they're great at reading other people's nonverbal behavior. In other words, they have the social skills, but they aren't using them." The problem isn't a lack of skill; it's the overwhelming feelings experienced in the cycle of negativity. Chronic flooding short-circuits a couple's basic listening and empathy skills, and it undermines the one thing that can turn back the Four Horsemen: the repair attempt.

Heading Off Disaster

Repair attempts are a kind of "metacommunication" — a way of talking about how you're communicating with each other. "Can we please stay on the subject?" "That was a rude thing to say." "We're not talking about your father!" "I don't think you're listening to me." Such statements, even when delivered in a grouchy or complaining tone, are efforts to interrupt the cycle of criticism, contempt, defensiveness, and stonewalling and to bring the conversation back on track.

"In stable relationships," explains Gottman, "the other person will respond favorably: 'All right, all right. Finish.' The agreement isn't made very nicely. But it does stop the person. They listen, they accept the repair attempt, and they actually change" the way they're relating.

Repair attempts are "really critical," says Gottman, because "everybody screws up. Everybody gets irritated, defensive, contemptuous. People insult one another," especially their spouses. Repair attempts are a way of saying "we've got to fix this before it slides any deeper into the morass." Even people in bad marriages make repair attempts; the problem is, they get ignored.

Training people to receive repair attempts favorably — even in the middle of a heated argument — is one of the new frontiers in relationship therapy. According to Gottman, "Even when things are going badly, you've got to focus not on the negativity but on the repair attempt. That's what couples do in happy marriages." He's convinced that such skills can be taught: One colleague has even devised a set of flash cards with a variety of repair attempts on them, ranging from "I know I've been a terrible jerk, but can we take this from the top?" to "I'm really too upset to listen right now." [See Upfront, July/August 1993.] Even in mid-tempest, couples can use the cards to practice giving, and receiving, messages about how they're communicating.

Breaking the Four Horsemen cycle is critical, says Gottman, because "the more time [couples] spend in that negative perceptual state, the more likely they are to start making long-lasting attributions about this marriage as being negative." Such couples begin rewriting the story of how they met, fell in love, made commitments. Warm memories about how "we were so crazy about each other" get replaced with "I was *crazy* to marry him/her." And once the story of the marriage has been infected with negativity, the motivation to work on its repair declines. Divorce becomes much more likely (and predictable — consider that 94 percent accuracy rate in the oral history study).

Of course, not all relationships can, or should, be saved. Some couples are trapped in violent relationships, which "are in a class by themselves." Others may suffer a fundamental difference in their preferred style — validating, volatile, or conflict-avoidant — that leaves them stuck in chronic flooding. With hard work, some of these marriages can be saved; trying to save others, however, may do more harm than good.

In the end, the hope for repairing even a broken marriage is to be found, as usual, in the courage and effort people are willing to invest in their own growth and change. "The hardest thing to do," says Gottman, "is to get back to the fundamentals that really make you happy." Couples who fail to do this allow the Four Horsemen to carry them far from the fundamentals of affection, humor, appreciation, and respect. Couples who succeed, cultivate these qualities like gardeners. They also cultivate an affirming story of their lives together, understanding that that is the soil from which everything else grows.

The work may be a continuous challenge, but the harvest, as my long-married friends Bill and Karen would say, is an enormous blessing: the joy in being truly known and loved, and in knowing how to love.

7.2   Canon Law and Broken Marriages
Peter Huizing[1]

THE APPARENTLY SO FIRMLY ESTABLISHED PRINCIPLES OF CANON LAW WITH regard to the dissolution and annulment of marriages and the possibility of re-marriage have become the centre of discussion especially since the Second Vatican Council. A very full critical review of recent opinions was published in 1969 and since its appearance not only canonists, but also dogmatic and pastoral theologians, exegetes, Church historians and sociologists have contributed to the debate. Changes in church practice have also taken place in many countries, though seldom openly. It will be clear from what is said in

---

1.   Translated by David Smith.

this article how the Church's law has been subjected throughout history to frequent discussion and how this is still the case today.

I. The History of Canon Law Regarding Dissolution and Re-marriage
1. The Pauline Privilege

In answer to the question as to what action should be taken if someone became a Christian and his or her unbelieving partner wished to separate, Paul said: "let it be so; in such a case the brother or sister is not bound. For God has called us to peace" (I Cor. 7. 15). For centuries, hardly anything was heard about this privilege and it would seem that re-marriage was not permitted in the practice of the early Church. Augustine believed that a believer could leave his unbelieving partner, but could not re-marry. Theodore of Canterbury († 690) thought that the marriage should be dissolved if the unbelieving partner was not converted. According to a definition of the Council of Toledo (633), Jews who were married to Christians had to become Christians on pain of divorce, since believers could not remain married to unbelievers. Some twelfth-century theologians were of the opinion that a believer could always terminate marriage with an unbeliever, whereas others believed that this was only possible if the unbelieving partner separated. The first pope to express his opinion about this question was Clement III († 1191), who declared that converts from Judaism and Islam might keep their unbelieving spouses, but should not be compelled to do so — as long as the unbeliever was prepared to live in peace with the Christian, the latter should not re-marry. Innocent III († 1216) decided that a convert might re-marry if his unbelieving partner did not want to cohabit with him, which was later extended to "could not" cohabit with him, without his committing mortal sin or defaming God's name. The Roman curia also followed the opinion expressed by many theologians, namely that dissolution and re-marriage were permitted if the unbelieving partner would not be converted. The unbelieving partner had in every case to be questioned about this, in order to gain some certain knowledge of his or her intentions. Various dispensations were introduced under certain conditions, so that divorce and re-marriage became possible without the interference of the unbaptized partner. All these extensions were based on the Pauline privilege.

2. Unconsummated Marriage

In the early Middle Ages, there was a widespread belief that a marriage was dissolved if one of the partners — usually the woman — entered a monastery or convent. Alexander III († 1181) was the first pope to make a decision in such a case. A nobleman had sworn an oath to marry a girl, but then expressed a desire to enter a monastery. Alexander believed that it would be safer for him to fulfill his oath and afterwards enter the monastery on condition that coitus had not taken place, since the commandment not to put asunder what God had joined together only applied to a marriage that had been consummated by coitus, which made husband and wife "one flesh." In 1298, Boniface VIII declared that unconsummated marriage could only be dissolved by the solemn profession of monastic vows, a declaration that was confirmed in 1563 by the Council of Trent.

Alexander had on several occasions permitted unconsummated marriages to be dissolved without any entry into a religious community, but his successors would not accept this principle for more than two centuries after his pontificate. Martin V († 1431) was the first to accept it again. A man wanted to divorce his wife because, although he had not had intercourse with her, she had borne another man's child. The pope advised the bishop to ask both to enter the religious life — if they did not wish to, the bishop could dissolve the marriage on condition that the wife did not oppose the dissolution. A deacon was given the same power in a similar case and on one occasion a papal notary.

Nonetheless, most theologians believed that the pope did not possess this power, although most canonists thought that he did. From the seventeenth century onwards, if proof had to be provided of the absence of coitus and the existence of a reason for dissolution, the proceedings had to take place before the Congregation of the Council. If the proofs were accepted as satisfactory, the pope, acting on the Council's advice, would grant a dissolution. In 1741, Benedict XIV was also to state that this particular papal power was no longer open to doubt.

3. The Marriages of "Indians" and Slaves

In the sixteenth century, the popes were confronted by new problems caused by the missions in the new Spanish and Portuguese colonies, the "Indies." Numerous converts were married to several wives, sometimes at the same time, sometimes consecutively. In 1537, Paul III decided that a convert could marry one of these women according to his choice, on condition that he could not remember which wife was the first; otherwise, he had to remain with the first. Later, Pius V was informed that many "Indian" converts were permitted to remain with the wife who had been baptized with them even though she was often not the first wife and in 1571 he declared that such marriages were valid and would be regarded as such in the future.

With the slave trade, thousands of marriages were broken, husbands and wives losing all contact with each other and often not knowing each other's whereabouts. In 1585, Gregory XIII empowered the bishops, priests and Jesuit fathers in the "Indies" to grant dispensations to enable new marriages to be solemnized in cases where the first partner could not be reached or had not replied within a fixed period of time. A new marriage of this kind remained valid even if it appeared later that the first partner had not been able to reply or even if that partner had already been baptized. The marriages of unbaptized persons were regarded as real marriages, but they were not so confirmed *(rata)* that they could not be dissolved in cases of necessity.

It is clear that these popes were at least four hundred years ahead of their time.

4. The Roman Practice

These three papal decisions were not published officially and only applied to certain persons in certain places. Rome preserved an attitude of extreme reserve. In 1631, for instance, a missionary in Latin America sought the power to allow his "Indian" converts to marry one of their wives according to their choice. The Congregation for the Propagation of the Faith at first refused permission, then, in 1637, granted it on condition that the first lawful wife had refused to be converted. In the so-called Florentine case of 1680, a Jewess became a Catholic and was divorced by her husband, who re-married. Later, he and his second wife became Catholics and the first wife insisted that he should return to her. The Congregation of the Council advised the pope to concede to her demand. Another example is to be found in the Far East, where more women than men were at this time being converted, so that Rome granted them numerous dispensations to marry non-Christian men, who later frequently divorced their wives and re-married. From 1708 until 1874, Rome maintained that the Catholic wife could not re-marry, claiming that "marriage, even if it is contracted in unbelief, is of its very nature indissoluble; the bond can only be broken by virtue of the privilege of faith granted by Christ the Lord and proclaimed by the Apostle Paul."

Roman theologians and canonists insisted that the only possible exception to the divine law of indissolubility could be a divine exception, namely the Pauline privilege, to which even the sixteenth-century papal decisions were, by means of subtle legal artifices, traced back.

5. The Vicarious Power

In 1891, Pietro Gasparri, who was to be responsible for the Codex of 1918, returned to a doctrine that had already been suggested by several earlier canonists, namely that the sixteenth-century decisions had not been an application of the Pauline privilege, but that the popes, as vicars of Christ, had dissolved marriages by virtue of their own power. The fact that they had dissolved these marriages showed that they had the power to do so and this power was included within the power conferred on Peter by Christ of binding and loosing.

In canon 1125 of Gasparri's Codex, the decisions of Paul III, Pius V and Gregory XIII were applied to all parts of the world where such circumstances prevailed and, in practice, everywhere to people in such circumstances. Gasparri's doctrine was also to have further consequences.

6. Dissolution "in favour of faith"

In 1924, during the pontificate of Pius XI, there were three hitherto unknown cases of dissolution of marriages of non-Catholics, one baptized and the other not. These marriages ended in divorce, but afterwards one of the divorced persons wanted to become a Catholic and marry a Catholic. The pope granted dissolution and ten years later the Holy Office sent the bishops a secret instruction, "Norms for the dissolution of a marriage in favour of faith by the highest authority of the pope."

A Catholic man had married an unbaptized woman in church with a dispensation; after divorcing her, she became a Catholic and wanted to marry a Catholic. According to the Code of Canon Law, the Pauline privilege could not be applied to marriage between a Catholic and an unbaptized person concluded with a dispensation (canon 1120, §2). None the less, the marriage was dissolved by Pius XII in 1947.

This dissolution "in favour of faith" was originally granted in favour of the faith of the divorced non-Catholic who wanted to become a Catholic and marry a Catholic. Dispensations have, however, been regularly granted during the pontificates of Pius XII, John XXIII and Paul VI in favour of the faith of Catholics who wanted to marry a divorced non-Catholic who had no intention of becoming a Catholic, the condition being that in the first, non-Catholic marriage at least one of the partners was not baptized. This practice was ended suddenly in 1970, the Congregation for the Doctrine of Faith apparently regarding it as lacking sufficient theological justification.

7. The Contemporary Principle of Dissolution

Only a "sacramental" marriage, that is, marriage between two baptized partners, is, after "consummation," that is, sexual intercourse between the two baptized partners, absolutely indissoluble. All other marriages are, subject to certain conditions, canonically dissoluble. It is clear from this historical outline that this principle has become established only after a long and painful process.

8. The History of the Annulment of Marriages

In his recent book, J. Noonan has given a very instructive account of this history, which is too complicated even to summarize here. I can only note that, since the introduction of the Codex in 1918, there has been a great increase in the number of cases of annulment and the grounds for annulment have also been much more widely interpreted. Since the Second Vatican Council especially, the will to bring about a lasting personal relationship in marriage and the ability to preserve this marital relationship have come to play a far greater part in assessing the validity of marriages. In practice, this means that a second chance of church marriage may be offered to victims of broken marriages who, in the past, would never have had this opportunity.

II. The Present Situation

In this section, I can do no more than simply discuss briefly some points of central importance raised in recent publications. In the first place, several authors have examined the biblical arguments on which the canonical system claims to be based. The indissolubility of marriage as an abstract aspect of marriage in the abstract — and ultimately this is how it is regarded in canon law — does not, however, occur at all in Scripture. In the legal discussion in Matt. 19:1-9 about the reasons for a man putting away his wife, Christ referred to the Yahwistic account of how God created man and woman to be joined to each other and become one flesh and thereby lifted the whole debate above the level of laws and exceptions to the law. He did not speak about a law imposed from without, but about human life itself and its inner development as demanded by human nature. In this quotation from Genesis, the term "one flesh" means far more than simply the first coitus. What should happen if marital fidelity is disturbed by human limitations and even sinfulness cannot be deduced simply and solely from what the Bible has to say about marriage. The Pauline view that the brother or sister is not bound if the unbelieving partner wants to separate "for God has called us to peace" does not necessarily point to any power to dissolve marriage. It is rather a judgment expressed concerning a situation in which remaining bound apparently cannot be reconciled with living in the peace of God. The Bible does not define the legal conditions for a possible dissolution of marriage.

Dogmatic theologians have also drawn attention to the fact that the theology of marriage is based on the norms that have been maintained in canon law and because the Church has always maintained certain norms, those norms have come to be regarded as the only ones that can be justified theologically. This has given rise to various problems which can only be dealt with by renewed theological thinking.

According to canon law, every canonically valid marriage between two baptized persons is a sacrament, even if those persons are in no way influenced in their lives by their baptism, or do not know that they are baptized or attach no religious value at all to their marriage. It is not so much a question as to whether or not they call their marriage a sacrament — many Protestants do not, but still regard marriage as essentially related to Christian faith. But if there is no faith, how can we then speak of a sacrament? Should marriage not be consciously accepted in faith if it is to be a sacrament or sign of an encounter with Christ? It is possible to say, on the basis of a legal presumption, that baptized persons are acting sacramentally especially if they want to be married in church, but to identify a canonically valid marriage between baptized persons and the sacrament of marriage is problematical.

Another problem that has been widely discussed recently is that of the decisive value that has been attributed to the first coitus in connection with the indissolubility of marriage. The symbolic value that has been attached to sacramental and consummated marriage as the most perfect image of the union between Christ and his Church can only be a subsequent explanation, which could only arise if, for different reasons, the first coitus played a *real* part in bringing about marriage. This was certainly possible in Germanic society, where the only contracts that were recognized were "real" and those based on a consensus were not. In contemporary society, however, the first coitus no longer plays such a decisive part. Certainly, popes have declared, on the basis of this theological symbol, that they have no power to dissolve consummated marriages between Christians, but is it perhaps not possible that such theological symbols may be meaningful in certain social relationships and meaningless in others? We have, after all, seen that a very long evolution has taken place in the papal views concerning the indissolubility of marriage.

In recent years, many conflicting opinions have been expressed about the papal power to dissolve marriages. Some authors believe that, in principle, the pope also has the power to dissolve sacramental and consummated marriages if this is in the best interest of all concerned. Others, however, insist that the construction of this special power has no basis in tradition and that it has only come about in recent centuries. It is, they claim, only an aspect of the universal, hierarchical power of the Church to govern.

Different views have been expressed also with regard to the nature of this power. It has, for example, been suggested that marriages can neither be concluded nor dissolved by the Church Unless the pope wishes to reserve it for himself, the bishops, these authors think, have the authority to declare as binding on the Christian community that it is no longer necessary for married partners to remain bound to each other in certain cases, if the state of being bound leads to a loss of "peace with God."

The contemporary emphasis on the personal relationship between the husband and wife in marriage has also given rise to many questions concerning the meaning of canonical "indissolubility." Is it, for instance, possible to speak of marriage if the personal relationship is completely and permanently broken? Is it possible for a marriage to consist simply of a prohibition against entering a second marriage? It is in any case clear that this is not what Christ had in mind when he said: "What God has joined together . . . ." It is not my intention to take up a particular attitude in this whole debate, but I am convinced that it is absolutely necessary for the whole theological problem to be studied by experts before the Church's law regarding marriage is definitively revised.

7.3 Divorced and Remarried Catholics: Come to Communion

Father Paul Jacobs

IF YOU'RE DIVORCED AND REMARRIED, PLEASE COME TO THE EUCHARIST.

I know what you'll tell me. You'll say, "Don't toy with my emotions. I want to receive Communion more than you can imagine, but I can't. The church says that it's wrong."

The church does teach that you aren't free to receive the Eucharist if you remarry after a divorce without first receiving an annulment. But there are many other truths the church holds dear, truths that justify my inviting you to Communion. And there are many truths the church has yet to learn, truths you may already grasp intuitively.

I don't know what happened to your first marriage or why it ended in divorce.

Some marriages had doom written all over them from the start, while others began with love and fond hopes and every appearance of success. Some withered slowly under the dry heat of routine and indifference, while others were killed by a moment of betrayal. And a great many simply ended, seemingly for no reason at all, and left everyone confused and hurt. Anytime love dies and for whatever reason, it's a tragedy. Divorce wreaks havoc on everyone involved — the individuals themselves, their children and extended family, friends — and its consequences can be devastating and long-lasting. However your marriage came to an end, I hope that before remarrying you gave yourself time to sift through your memories and to salvage from them some understanding of what happened. You don't need to justify yourself to me or to anyone else, but gaining insight into your previous marriage and its ending is an important part of the healing process and will strengthen your current marriage.

I don't know why some of you remarried without the church's blessing.

If you were previously married in the church, you need to receive an annulment before you can have your current marriage recognized. The church has high ideals about what makes up a true marriage. The couple must enter it with maturity, freedom, and knowledge. They must be capable of establishing a lifelong, faithful relationship that is open to children. If a marriage, even one that lasted many years and produced children, ends in divorce, the church is willing to examine it to see if it was indeed a true marriage in the full sense of the word. If you apply for an annulment, you will be asked to submit your reflections about your marriage to a diocesan court (called a tribunal), and it will seek evidence from others who knew the circumstances of the relationship. If it decides that something essential to the formation of a true marriage was lacking, it will grant an annulment and state that you are free to remarry in the church. If you want more information about annulments, your pastor or a parish support group for divorced Catholics should be able to help you.

Annulments give a great deal of peace to some people. One woman told me, "When I married the first time, I thought we were the perfect couple. But what did I know? I was only 19, and he was the first man I ever dated. I was naive enough to think love could overcome every problem, including his drinking and violent temper. Going through an annulment helped me understand what went wrong and my role in it without condemning myself. I'm glad I have the chance to start over again." But many people are sickened by the thought of applying for an annulment. As one man put it, "Don't tell me I wasn't really married. I have good memories, three children, and scars to prove it."

In some dioceses the annulment process is unnecessarily complicated and drawn-out. People may be discouraged from filing for an annulment by priests who don't themselves understand the process or by the prospect of digging up a painful past. And even those who go through the whole process aren't guaranteed a positive decision by the court.

There are many reasons why Catholics remarry without first receiving an annulment; and while I don't know your reasons, I assume that you acted in good faith.

I don't have to know about your previous marriage, how it ended in divorce, or why you remarried to invite you to the Eucharist. It's not that I don't care about those things (I do), it's just that I'm convinced that receiving Communion has nothing to do with self-justification and everything to do with need.

When I was growing up and learning my Baltimore Catechism, I thought of Communion as the *Good Housekeeping* Seal of Approval. Good Catholics went to Confession on Saturday and tried to keep themselves pure overnight so they could worthily receive Communion the next day. I thought of it as spiritual housecleaning before the arrival of an honored guest.

Such an approach to Penance and Communion has a lot to teach us about reverence for Christ, who comes to us in Communion; but it doesn't do full justice to Christ or the Eucharist.

Christ came to call not the self-righteous but sinners, and in the Eucharist he feeds those who hunger for mercy.

Jesus was a scandal in his day because he associated with all the wrong sorts of people; and the gravest charge leveled against him was "he eats and drinks with sinners." The sinners he dined with were Jews who had abandoned their faith and betrayed their people by cooperating with the Romans, the oppressors who occupied Palestine at that time. Tax collectors (who took up the taxes that impoverished the countryside and paid the Roman soldiers) and prostitutes (who had sex with the soldiers) were two main categories of sinners. The good people shunned those who collaborated with the Romans and were appalled that Jesus reached out to those he called "the lost sheep of the house of Israel."

The good people of Jesus' day were shocked when he invited Matthew to be his follower. Matthew had not repented of his sins or changed his way of life; on the contrary, he was sitting at his toll booth when Jesus called him. When Matthew threw a dinner party for Jesus and invited his friends, the good people asked Jesus' disciples, "Why does your teacher eat with tax collectors and sinners?" Associating with them was bad enough, but eating with them was intolerable.

According to Jewish custom, each meal was a holy event and began and ended with a blessing. To eat together was to sit at table with God; it was a declaration of mutual acceptance and alliance. Jesus responded, "Those who are well do not need a physician, but the sick do. Go and learn the meaning of the words 'I desire mercy, not sacrifice.' I did not come to call the righteous but sinners." Staying away from the Eucharist when your life is in disarray or conflict or when you are struggling to pick up the pieces and fit them together with integrity is like staying away from the doctor when you are sick. one early Christian writer called the Eucharist the "medicine of immortality."

No one deserves the Eucharist or earns its grace and forgiveness or merits the balm of God's healing mercy. No one can stand before the altar of God and claim, "I have lived a good and holy life. Because I have kept myself free from sin, I am worthy to receive Communion." It's a paradox; to be worthy to approach the Lord's table, all we need do is admit that we aren't worthy. Perhaps that's why the last thing we say before receiving Communion is, "Lord, I am not worthy to receive you, but only say the word and I shall be healed."

In the Eucharist, Christ invites those who are weary and burdened by life to come to him. It's as if he says, "You look thin and pale. Sit down and eat what I set before you. Let your spirit grow stout on my love."

Receiving Communion even though you haven't lived up to the church's expectations isn't an excuse for complacency. You may well need to change (who doesn't?). You may need to mend relationships, let go of bitterness and fear, forgive those who have wounded you and seek forgiveness from those you have hurt, and fulfill obligations (especially to your children) from your previous marriage. But you'll never be able to do all those things without the grace of the Eucharist. Communion isn't a sign of God's approval, an endorsement of all you have done or are doing. It's a sign of God's acceptance, a loving and compassionate embrace. When you accept God's acceptance of you (which you'll have to do many times before it sinks in), you can give up the urge to prove yourself to God and everyone else. Then you can grow in self-acceptance, healing, holiness, and compassion.

Won't you come to the Eucharist?

You undoubtedly know others who are hurting or who fall short of their Christian calling or who are weighed down by their failings. Won't you invite them to the Eucharist?

7.4 Annulment: The Process and Its Meaning
Patrick R. Lagges, JCD

FOR SOME, IT IS A SOURCE OF HEALING; FOR OTHERS, A SOURCE OF SCANDAL. For most, it remains a dark, murky process that is heard about only through rumor and gossip.

The subject of declarations of nullity in the Roman Catholic Church has been a source of misunderstanding for many Catholics, especially those who grew up in the Church prior to the Second Vatican Council. For many people with a traditional Catholic education, annulments were rarely, if ever, obtained, and then only for the most serious reasons. Marriages which produced children or lasted for any length of time were believed to be incapable of being declared null. Much of that had to do with the Church's teaching about the nature of marriage. With the advent of the Second Vatican Council, however, that teaching was reexamined and formulated in a different way.

An Unfortunate Choice of Terms

To say that the Church annuls a marriage is not quite correct — for several reasons. First, the term "annulment" implies that the Church is doing something to a marriage. In reality, by granting an annulment, the Church is simply declaring something about a marriage. It says that some key element was missing from the very beginning which rendered the marriage invalid.

Second, the term "annulment" implies that a relationship is being denied or done away with. This is the source of most people's question: "How can you deny that our marriage ever existed?" Once again, declaration of nullity does not mean this. The Church, or anyone else, could never deny that a relationship existed. At the very least, there is a civil document and a Church document that state that these two people joined themselves together on a certain date and in a certain place. However, in declaring marriage null, the Church states that something was there in the beginning which prevented a true marriage in the first place. Although the relationship resembled a marriage and may have produced children (who, according to Church law, are considered legitimate), there was some key element missing that prevented a real marriage from taking place.

What is a "True Marriage"?

The Church's description of a "true marriage" has changed in the wake of the Second Vatican Council. Prior to the Council, the Church described marriage as an exchange of rights. Both parties were to bind themselves to the right of their partner to sexual intercourse, to the procreation and education of children, to the permanence and indissolubility of the union, and to fidelity to their spouse. A marriage could be declared null only if something impeded that exchange of rights: if the person excluded the right to sexual acts proper to the procreation of children or the right to permanence or fidelity. Marriages could be declared null if one of the parties entered into the union placing some sort of condition on their consent, was forced into the marriage, or was in error about the person they were marrying. In addition, marriages could be dissolved if they had not been consummated or if one or both of the parties had not been baptized.

In the Second Vatican Council, however, the Church's description of marriage changed. Instead of considering marriage as an exchange of rights, it was talked about as an exchange of persons. In Christian marriage, the parties give and accept each other in a permanent, faithful, fruitful union which is to mirror Christ's relationship to the Church.

Thus, the Council spoke of marriage as an "intimate partnership of life and love," and referred to the marriage covenant rather than the marriage contract. It described marriage as " . . . a means by which a man and a woman render mutual help and service to each other through an intimate union of their persons and of their actions; by which they experience the meaning of their oneness and attain to it with perfection day by day"; and by which "they increasingly advance their own perfection, as well as their mutual sanctification and hence contribute jointly to the glory of God." (These quotations are from paragraph 48 of the *Pastoral Constitution on the Church in the Modern World, Gaudium et spes.*)

In speaking of marriage in this way, the Church acknowledges that marriage is a far more complex reality than had been described previously. It was far more encompassing than two people merely exchanging certain rights and far more personally demanding than we had seen before. It now involves the whole person and is described in terms of the faithful, fruitful love of Yahweh toward the people Israel, and the total self-giving love of Jesus for his people, the Church.

This teaching about marriage forms the whole basis for any discussion about annulments in the Church. It is impossible to understand the concept of annulment unless at the same time you understand the Church's teaching on marriage. This may account for the fact that many people today are confused about the high number of annulments that are granted. The Church's teaching on marriage has changed and unless we understand what the Church teaches about marriage, our understanding of annulments will always be cloudy.

In declaring a marriage null, the Church states that there was some key element missing at the time the two people exchanged their consent.

At times, it was the canonical form of marriage that was missing. For Latin-rite Catholics, that means exchanging their consent before a properly delegated priest, deacon, or lay person and two witnesses. For members of the Eastern Orthodox Churches, it means receiving the blessing of the priest within the marriage liturgy. However, these laws apply only to Catholics and to the Eastern Orthodox. The Church recognizes all other marriages as valid, regardless of where they take place. For example, when two non-Catholic Christians marry before a judge or a justice of the peace, the Church looks upon that marriage as a valid, sacramental union. To state otherwise would be to imply that marriages of non-Catholics were of less significance than marriages of Catholics. It would also deny the fact that marriage is first and foremost a human reality which, in the presence of the Lord, becomes the sign of a divine reality.

Sometimes, though, the person's freedom to marry is lacking. This would include people who are bound to a previous valid marriage, those who were not of a certain age, those who were related in certain ways or who had professed permanent vows in a religious community, or received the sacrament of orders. These facts, as well as several others called impediments, restrict a person's freedom to marry within the Church. Some of these impediments, such as a previous bond of marriage, are considered to be of divine law and hence bind all people. Others, like age, are merely Church laws and do not affect those who are not marrying in the Catholic Church.

At still other times, it is the person's actual consent that is called into question. These are the cases that are usually lumped together when people speak of annulments. They are handled by a judicial process which usually takes place over a period of time and requires certain legal procedures.

When Consent is Impaired

The overwhelming majority of cases before Marriage Tribunals in the United States involve some form of defect of consent. Father William Woestman, O.M.I., of Saint Paul University, Ottawa, Ontario, writing in *Studia canonica*, noted that this is a world-wide phenomenon. His statistics indicate the percentages of cases decided in 1987 on the grounds of defect of consent: Australia, Great Britain, and the Republic of South Africa, 100 percent; Canada, the Federal Republic of Germany, Ireland, and the Netherlands, 99 percent; France and the United States, 98 percent; Italy, 96 percent; Poland and Spain, 91 percent. These cases deal with a person's ability to understand and choose marriage — an actual understanding of the commitment and what it is they are choosing. If marriage involves the pledge of two people to commit themselves to each other in an intimate union of life and love, then certain things are necessary. Both parties have to have an adequate understanding of themselves before they give themselves to each other. They have to have an adequate understanding of each other so that they know the person they are accepting as their marriage partner. They have to have a basic capacity for intimacy since this forms the essence of marriage. If either of the parties is seriously lacking in one of these areas, the marriage could be declared null.

Tribunals generally state these reasons as the "grounds" for the case. What follows is a brief explanation of what those grounds might be.

Grounds for an Annulment

According to canon law, a person is incapable of entering into marriage if he or she suffers from a "grave lack of discretion of judgment concerning essential matrimonial rights and duties which are to be mutually given and accepted" (Canon 1095.3). Cases heard under these grounds usually deal with a person's maturity, motivation, and understanding of marriage.

Because the commitment to marriage is so all-encompassing, a person has to have a maturity that is proportionate to the decision he or she is making. In a normal developmental process, a child gains the ability to make more and more complex choices based on an ability to understand the consequences of one's actions. Thus, there's usually a certain point when a parent allows the child to cross the street alone or go to the grocery store. Another point is reached when the adolescent is allowed to date or use the family car. Society, too, recognizes this development process when it states certain ages before a person can vote or purchase alcoholic beverages.

A far greater maturity is needed for marriage because the decision to marry has far greater consequences than some of the other choices that people make. It involves a person's whole life and is a commitment to the future as well as to the present. Until a person is able to understand that and is mature enough to make that commitment, he or she is not capable of entering into a valid marriage.

In other cases, though, the person's motivation comes into question. Canon 1057.2 states that the parties mutually give and accept each other "in order to establish marriage." This means that when a person exchanges consent with their partner, it must be motivated by the desire to enter into marriage and not for some other reason. At times, though, people have a different idea in mind. Some people view marriage as a "rite of passage" in society. It's something you do when you're too old to live at home or need to do before you start on a career. Other people marry for the purpose of escaping from a dysfunctional home environment. They suffer the physical or sexual abuse of one of their family members, they've been thrown out of their home, or they can no longer live with the unpredictability of alcoholism or other drug abuse. This consent is not "in order to establish marriage," but "in order to escape from home." Hence, they have not entered into a valid union.

In still other cases, a person fails to understand the implications of their commitment. They see part of the picture and mistake it for the whole thing. A person may see marriage as freedom but fail to see the responsibilities that go along with that. Another person may look to the good times they share with their partner but never realize they must share the struggles as well. They see the good aspects of their partner but overlook the fact that he drinks too much, has been violent on occasion, or has been unable to follow through on his commitments to school or to work. They may see the bad aspects of their partner but believe that marriage changes people and makes them into something they are not. In these cases, too, the person is gravely lacking in discretion of judgment about essential marital rights and duties. They have not formed a correct judgment about those rights and duties, and hence enter into marriage invalidly.

Incapacity to assume the obligations: A second category of cases is heard under the grounds of one of the parties being "not capable of assuming the essential obligations of matrimony due to causes of a psychic nature" (Canon 1095.3). Some tribunals refer to this as a "lack of due competence" or "lack of canonical competence."

There is some psychological ability needed to enter into Christian marriage. In some cases, the person does not have the psychological ability to enter into Christian marriage. There is some psychological factor in their personality which makes them incapable of establishing a life of intimacy with their partner or of committing themselves to a permanent union or to one that essentially involves fidelity to one's spouse, or to the generation of new life.

For the most part, this includes people who suffer from personality disorders which produce characteristics directly opposed to the nature of marriage. For example, someone suffering from a narcissistic personality would not be capable of entering a relationship which is essentially directed toward the good of another. A person with an anti-social personality would not be capable of forming a relationship which essentially involves permanence, fidelity, and responsibility. And people with a paranoid personality or a schizoid personality would not be capable of the trust or the intimacy essential for a valid marriage. These people, along with those suffering from some of the other personality disorders, would be judged incapable of assuming the essential obligations of marriage. Also included in this category would be those psychosexual disorders or dispositions which would make a normal, heterosexual relationship impossible.

It's important to realize, though, that these must be serious psychological problems. All people have certain quirks and idiosyncrasies. All of us have isolated characteristics associated with certain personality disorders. It's only when those characteristics describe a person's major mode of acting, though, that it can be said that the person is incapable of assuming the essential obligations of marriage. In these cases, the tribunal relies heavily on psychological experts for their understanding of the human personality.

Lack of intention: Tribunals in the United States use less frequently the grounds that involve the intention of the parties when entering into marriage. These are some of the more traditional grounds used in the past. They include an intention against forming a union that can be dissolved only by the death of one's spouse, an intention against remaining faithful to one's partner, an intention against allowing the marriage to be fruitful or against fulfilling the responsibilities of parenthood, or an intention against working for the mutual good of each other. This also includes an intention against marriage altogether; for example, those who marry to regularize their immigration status, or to get their child baptized or enrolled in a Catholic school. Such people lack the proper intention for marriage since they exclude something essential from the marital commitment.

Other factors: Other factors can also influence a person's consent. These include such things as placing a condition on one's consent, entering marriage because of force or fear, entering marriage deceived by fraud, or being in error about the person you are marrying. These factors, however, are difficult to establish. Tribunals use these less frequently, especially when other grounds are clearly evident.

The Process

One of the unfortunate parts of the 1983 Code of Canon Law is the fact that marriage nullity cases are still treated as contentious cases, even though it's not entirely clear about who the contending parties are. Treating these as contentious trials, the law presumes there are opposing parties. This is not true in most instances. In the majority of the cases before marriage tribunals, both parties agree that the marriage was null from the beginning. This produces the anomaly of having a contentious case with no contending parties. However, since these are the procedures that must be followed at the present time, most tribunals seek to apply these laws as pastorally and as sensitively as possible in order to find just and equitable solutions to the pain of marital breakdown.

The nullity process usually begins within the local parish. This is always going to be the key contact for the person seeking to have a marriage declared null. While at one time, divorced people were excluded from participation in the life of the Church, this is no longer true today. Pope John Paul II, in his *Apostolic Exhortation on the Christian Family in the Life of the World*, has stated: "I earnestly call upon pastors and the whole community of the faithful to help the divorced and with solicitous care to make sure that they do not consider themselves as separated from the Church, for as baptized persons they can, and indeed must, share in her life" (n. 84). Therefore, those who are divorced have a right to be part of their local community of faith. It is for this reason that most tribunals start the nullity process on that level. It helps pastoral ministers become more aware of the needs of their people and helps people become more integrated into their parish community. In many parishes, support groups allow those who have gone through the experience of divorce to come together to share those experiences and to support one another. These groups also assist people in the nullity process. Through sharing their experience of marriage and divorce, people gain a greater understanding of the factors that entered into their decision to marry in the first place.

Once the initial contact is made, tribunals differ on procedure. In some, the person contacts the tribunal directly for an interview; in others, much of the preliminary work is done through a written questionnaire. In either case, the main goal of the tribunal is to have the person tell the story of their relationship with their former spouse from beginning to end, to tell their own life story, and what they know of their former spouse's family history. Through this process, the tribunal gets a better understanding of these two people who entered into marriage: the families, their early life experiences, when and how their relationship began to develop, the factors that entered into their decision to marry, the ways they lived out their marital commitment to each other, and the factors which caused the breakdown of the union.

This is usually the most difficult part of the procedure since it requires the person to reflect upon the events of the past and to see how those events influenced the choices they made. At times, this involves reliving painful experiences of marriage or family life and gives the person the opportunity to gain greater personal insight, understanding, and appreciation for the complexity of Christian marriage. It also gives the Christian community the opportunity to support the person who is going through this process. The sensitive questioning of an interviewer or the discussions in support groups help to share burdens and so fulfill the command of the Lord.

The names of witnesses are also required. Like the term "annulment," the term "witness" is not exactly correct. Unlike the witness in a civil trial who generally testifies for one person and against another, the witnesses in a marriage nullity case are asked to describe the marriage as they saw it. Often, the witnesses can give the tribunal greater insight about the parties in the marriage and into the dynamics of that relationship as they lived it out. Witnesses are usually family members, but they can be nearly anyone who know the parties during the course of their marriage. Since the tribunal focuses on the parties at the time of their marriage, however, it is essential that the witnesses have some knowledge of the marriage from its inception. Tribunals differ in the way they obtain witness testimony. Some require the witnesses to be interviewed in person while others send out written questionnaires. Some tribunals seek the witness testimony before they begin the formal procedure; others wait until the case is actually accepted.

To begin a case, the person presents a formal petition to a tribunal which has jurisdiction over the marriage case. The case is then assigned to a judge, who accepts or rejects the petition. If he accepts it, he must also determine the grounds under which the case will be heard.

At this point, the judge informs both parties that a case has begun. Since there is a presumption in law that the marriage is valid, and since the other party (usually called the respondent or the defendant) has the right to uphold the validity of that union, it is absolutely essential that he or she be contacted and given an opportunity to participate. Failure to do so results in the whole process being null. At times, petitioners have requested that respondents not be contacted because of previous violence or harassment and the fear of a respondent's reaction when informed of the proceedings. This may seem reasonable but the fact is that respondents will generally hear about these proceedings from other sources in addition to the tribunal. Children of the marriage or relatives of one of the parties usually talk about the case long before the tribunal accepts it. Keeping it a secret is not an option that is open to the petitioner. The respondent has a right to know about the proceedings and to participate in them.

In some cases, though, the respondent has disappeared. This is especially true of a marriage which ended a number of years before. The petitioner has no knowledge of the respondent's whereabouts and has made every effort to find a current address. In these cases, the tribunals can proceed with the case but usually appoint an advocate to protect the rights of the respondent.

The judge may also need additional information from the petitioner and will request an additional interview for a psychological evaluation. In addition, he may ask the person to sign a release form so that he has psychological records available. Since many cases today involve psychological grounds, the judge may ask the psychologist specific questions about the maturity of the parties and their ability to enter into marriage.

Once the judge has all this testimony, the case is presented to the advocates (if there are any) and to the defender of the bond, who presents arguments upholding the validity of the marriage. After that, the judge writes his decision and states his reasons for declaring the marriage null or upholding its validity. An affirmative decision is automatically appealed, however, and must pass through a review process where the decision is either confirmed or the case is opened to a new process. If the appeal court confirms the affirmative decision or reaches an affirmative decision on its own, the case is concluded and the parties are free to marry in the Church. If the appeal court overturns the affirmative decision, the case can be appealed to Rome for a third hearing.

The length of time that this takes varies from tribunal to tribunal, based upon available personnel. Some tribunals can conclude cases within eight months while others take several years. Lack of cooperation on the part of the petitioner or the witnesses can also impede the progress of a case. A lack of cooperation on the part of a respondent should not impede the progress of a case. Although the respondent has a right to participate, no one can be forced to exercise a right. Furthermore, the petitioner has a right to have the case heard, and to have it concluded in a timely fashion.

The fees that tribunals request also vary widely. Some tribunals are subsidized through the diocesan tax on parishes or through a special collection for diocesan needs. Other tribunals have a fee based on the petitioner's income, while still others ask the petitioner to determine how much he or she can contribute toward the total cost of the case. Most tribunals have liberal policies for the reduction or total waiver of the fee.

Conclusion

It is no secret that more declarations of nullity are being granted today than in the past. Twenty years ago, tribunals heard slightly more than fifteen thousand marriage nullity cases throughout the world. In the present year, the number of affirmative decisions will approach sixty thousand. There are many reasons for this including better staffing of marriage tribunals throughout the world and a greater number of dioceses with functional tribunals. But, in large part, it is due to a greater understanding of the nature of Christian marriage and a greater appreciation of the commitment that couples make to each other when they marry "in the Lord."

Definitions

Canon Law: The laws by which the pastoral activity of the Church is coordinated, organized, and directed. The Code of Canon Law was most recently revised in 1983 so that it conforms to the teaching of the Second Vatican Council. (Codes of law have been around in the Church almost from the beginning. At various times, they have been gathered together; but the first attempt at a systematic codification of the laws of the Church was in 1917. At the time he convoked the Second Vatican Council, Pope John XXIII also called for a new codification of law. This revision process took almost twenty-five years to complete.)

Canonical form of marriage: Catholics are normally required to marry before a priest, deacon, or designated lay person, and two witnesses. The Orthodox are required to marry in the Orthodox Church and receive the blessing of the priest. All other people — Christians or non-Christians, baptized or non-baptized — can marry in whatever way they choose. The Catholic Church recognizes the marriage as valid.

Covenant: An agreement between two parties that implies a mutual relationship between them. It is distinguished from a contract, which merely sets out certain rights or duties, regardless of a relationship. While in times past, marriage was spoken of as a contract, the Second Vatican Council restored the term "covenant" to the church's teaching on the nature of marriage.

Defect of consent: Consent to marriage must be made freely and totally by two people who are capable of giving that consent. If a person is forced into giving consent, withholds something from their consent, does not have the ability to make such an important decision or the capacity to carry it out, their consent is called "defective."

Impediments: Impediments are obstacles to a valid marriage. Some impediments can be dispensed, however, since they are merely Church law. For example, a dispensation can be given to allow a Catholic to marry in a non-Catholic church. Other impediments, though, cannot be dispensed since they are based on natural law or divine law. Thus, a person who was in a previous valid marriage cannot receive a dispensation to marry again; the previous marriage must be declared null or dissolved through the Pauline or Petrine Privilege before a second marriage can take place.

When the Church declares a marriage null: it states that at the time two people exchanged consent there was either something present (for example, an impediment, a personality disorder, etc.) or something missing (such as the required maturity, the necessary freedom or the proper intention), which prevented the parties from entering into a true, valid, and binding union.

A Tribunal: is a church court usually composed of at least three judges who are assisted by various notaries, advocates, and other experts. Canon law provides that the number of judges can be reduced to one for certain cases and under certain circumstances. While Church Tribunals can become involved in a wide variety of issues, in the United States they deal almost exclusively with cases involving the nullity of marriage.

A Valid marriage: is one which is entered into with the proper form, intention, freedom, discretion, and capacity. An invalid marriage is one which is lacking in at least one of these areas.

◆

7.5 Authority in the Church: Who Makes the Final Call?

When Jesus exercised authority, he made it a point not to act like a lord. Since then Catholics have struggled to find the best way to carry out his reign.
Robert J. McClory

Percentage of Catholics who think the church should permit couples to make their own decisions about forms of birth control: 87%.

Percentage of Catholics who think Pope John Paul II is doing a good job leading the church: 84%.

THE FIGURES DEFY EASY EXPLANATION. ACCORDING TO THE RECENT GALLUP poll cited above, U.S. Catholics by overwhelming margins resist official church positions not only on birth control but on abortion, homosexuality, women as priests, and other issues. Yet these same Catholics, who Gallup contends represent U.S. Catholic thinking (within 4 percentage points), agree that Pope John Paul II is discharging his duties in an admirable manner.

What does it mean? Have Catholics lost their minds? Don't they see the inconsistency in rejecting a leader's clear position on critical matters while commending his performance?

Some will say the poll results are inaccurate, that the sample of people was not representative, that the questions were skewed or misleading, that it is flawed because it was funded by liberal groups. But there is no evidence to support such conclusions.

Gallup is a respected organization that uses accepted sociological methods in conducting and evaluating polls.

Moreover, the findings are consistent with the results of similar polls and surveys over the past 25 years; they show Catholics increasingly at odds with official church positions yet still respectful of the pope and bishops. Others will declare that if the poll is accurate, it follows that millions of U.S. Catholics have lost their faith, if not their minds. But most of the Catholics in those surveys, according to the pollsters, attend Mass fairly regularly, receive the sacraments, pray, and consider themselves members of the church in every sense of the word.

Another way to view the glaring inconsistency is to say that great numbers of U.S. Catholics hold a very different concept of religious authority from that of their parents and grandparents — different too, it must be admitted, from that of some puzzled fellow Catholics.

At the very least, it seems, a new approach to authority is developing. Because its form is somewhat unclear, there is a lot of room for misunderstanding and argument. The situation is not unlike the upheaval that occurs in families when children pass through adolescence to adulthood; they experience turbulence in their relationships with parents until those relationships are (it is hoped) re-established on more solid ground.

Indeed, different approaches to authority are at the root of just about every dispute in the church today. And since authority was a dominant characteristic of the church for every Catholic born before the first atomic bomb was dropped in 1945, the disputes can become quite emotional.

Struggle for Power

To understand where we are, says University of Notre Dame historian Jay Dolan, it's necessary to see where we've been. In his book *The Catholic Experience,* Dolan notes that in the late 1700s and throughout the 1800s, the church in Europe was under siege in every way. France's Napoleon Bonaparte, Italy's Guiseppe Garibaldi, Germany's Otto von Bismarck, and other nationalist leaders wrested from the Vatican the last vestiges of its political power. Rapidly expanding technology and new philosophies threatened its moral authority by proposing entirely secular ways of viewing the world and humanity's place in it. The church took a decidedly defensive posture in this era, writes Dolan, attempting to reassert its authority "with excessive vigor."

As never before, the worldwide church was centralized in Rome; papal power was extolled and reached its zenith in the declaration of papal infallibility in 1870; national and local churches came to be viewed as mere local outlets for the one authoritative dispenser of truth.

The proper relationship between clergy and laity was spelled out by Pope Pius X: "The church is essentially an unequal society . . . comprising two categories of persons, the pastors and the flock." Since the pastors alone possess authority, "the one duty of the multitude is to allow themselves to be led and, like a docile flock, to follow the pastors."

A whole battery of church laws was set in place to aid the faithful; some universal, such as weekly Mass attendance; some national, such as prohibiting membership in the Oddfellows organization; some purely local, such as requiring definite minimum donations to establish official membership in certain parishes. Yet, as older Catholics will recall, almost all obligations tended to be wrapped in and stamped with full church authority. Thus, something as seemingly trivial as eating meat on Friday was presented as a mortal sin and merited eternal hellfire because it represented (or at least implied) contempt for the divinely established lawgiver.

Nowhere in the world was church authority taken more seriously than in the United States. Officials in the Vatican were much concerned about this nation of immigrants that put such store on principles of freedom and democracy. To counteract excessive independent thinking, U.S. bishops were urged to imbue in people an unshakable sense of loyalty.

Says Dolan, "Catholicism was clearly a religion of authority, and people learned not only to pray but also to obey. Being Catholic meant to submit to the authority of God as mediated through the church — its pope, bishops, and pastors. In such a culture, the rights of the individual conscience were de-emphasized, as each person was conditioned to submit to the external authority."

The effort, he notes, was not totally successful: "Trustee conflicts, parish wars, and church schisms were a fact of life in immigrant Catholicism. Yet as the authoritarian culture of devotional Catholicism strengthened its grip on people, obedience, rather than rebellion, became the standard." Church was seen as essentially a vertical creature with the truth coming down from above: from God to the pope, pope to bishops, bishops to pastors, and pastors to laity. In the United States, Pope Pius X's definition of church came close to realization.

There are those who maintain that is the way Christ intended the church always to be governed; they lament the passing (or at least the weakening) of that simpler arrangement; and they work and pray for its full restoration. Others (and it would seem great numbers of Catholics in the United States) prefer a less rigid structure; they believe such a structure is more consistent today with the message of the gospel; and they pray for a reformed church.

Several factors account for the shift in Catholic thinking about authority: historical and scriptural awareness, a clearer sense of church, the birth-control watershed, and disillusionment with authority.

Did Jesus Set the Rules?

Historical and Scriptural Awareness. When he imparted to the 12 apostles the commission of passing on the Good News and feeding his sheep, Jesus did not explain in detail how their authority was to be exercised. However, he did say in no uncertain terms that their use of authority was to be radically different. This is how he puts it in Luke's gospel (chapter 22, verses 25-26): "Among pagans it is kings who lord it over them, and those who have authority over them are given the title Benefactor. This must not happen to you. Rather let the greatest among you be as the youngest, and the leader as the one who serves."

"This must not happen to you." Jesus' words here can hardly be taken as a pious recommendation. Leaders in his community are to function in a way diametrically opposed to the accepted styles of secular leadership.

In John's gospel, after Jesus has washed the feet of the disciples, he says: "Do you understand what I have done to you? You call me 'master' and 'lord,' and rightly; so I am. If I, then, master and lord, have washed your feet, you should wash each other's feet. I have given you an example so that you may copy what I have done to you" (John 13:12-15).

To describe what he means, Jesus returns often to words such as *servant, slave,* and *lackey.* It has been pointed out by scripture scholars that this is not due to deficiencies in the language he spoke. Notes Jesuit Father John L. McKenzie in his book *Authority in the Church,* "If Jesus had wished to say that those in authority should rule with justice and kindness, there are a dozen ways in which this could have been said. But such words as 'rule' are exactly the words that he did not use. The sayings reveal a new conception of society and authority, which must be formed not on the model of secular government but on the mission of Jesus himself."

When questioned by what authority he issues radical edicts like this, Jesus appeals exclusively to the will of the Father. He does not argue from accepted biblical principles or historical precedent, nor does he spell out in detail how this new conception is to operate in the practical order.

The terms Jesus uses regarding authority are metaphors, which, by their very nature, do not answer all questions; in fact, they seem to raise more than they settle. But as McKenzie notes, "One does not preserve the metaphor by removing from it exactly those features which make it distinctive. Jesus himself refused to describe his own mission in terms of rule over others; and the Church which carries on his mission must make his disclaimer her own."

In its early days the church attempted to follow Jesus' injunction and model a special style of leadership: the successor to Judas' apostleship was not appointed but chosen by the 11 apostles from two names selected by the whole community; the Apostle James presided over the Council of Jerusalem and carried out its decisions; Paul felt free to differ with Peter publicly over the religious responsibilities of converts.

The most visible characteristic of this early community was gritty, day-to-day service, especially to the poor. Yet the poor were not to be regarded as mere recipients of Christian charity. The church saw itself as one body in Christ, with the Holy Spirit operative not merely in the apostles but in all the members. Therefore, the designated leaders had to be respectful and sensitive to the action of the Spirit wherever it showed itself — whether in the highest or the lowest.

Says McKenzie, "In a secular society authority is conceived as the central motive function which directs and moves subordinate functions. In the Church direction and motivation is from the Spirit to all the functions of the body; authority is not and cannot be absolute, for authority too has its interdependence."

As the church grew and moved out from its humble Mediterranean nursery into the vast reaches of the Roman Empire, it became difficult to maintain this unique relationship between leaders and members. And after the Roman Emperor Constantine approved Christianity as the state religion in the 4th century, the concept of the church as a Spirit-filled body was put to a real test.

A tension developed (which continues to this day) between those who see church and state as highly compatible twins, each working in very similar ways within its own jurisdiction, and those who view the church as operating by radically different standards. The former view most often predominated, so church authority and operations were frequently modeled on existing forms and structures in civil society.

Writing in *America* magazine, Jesuit Father George Wilson, an ecclesiologist, notes, "Depending on the political ethos of the era, the church has modeled its governance on a variety of political systems. It has imitated not-so-holy Roman emperors, Byzantine suzerains, feudal lords, mystical charismatics, and medieval monarchs."

Bishops, for example, have been elected by the clergy of the area, imposed by rulers, or called forth by popular acclamation. Clear moral teachings have been altered or abrogated with time. Usury, the practice of taking interest on loans, was firmly condemned by popes and councils for centuries until the ban was lifted in the 1500s (partly due to the public's refusal to abide by the ban). Similarly, slavery was accepted by the church as a morally permissible institution almost until the end of the 19th century, when Pope Leo XIII corrected this blatantly erroneous position,

The question that must be wrestled with, says Wilson, is not, What has God ordained for all time?, but rather, What can human wisdom tell us about the best methods to nurture the Christian community in this culture and in this age? The church is for all time, Catholics of all stripes agree; but there is a growing awareness that a lot more about it may be relative (and changeable) than they once thought.

The Pope Is No CEO

A Clearer Sense of Church. Perhaps the most important factor in altering Catholic self-understanding was the emphasis placed by the Second Vatican Council on the local church. The worldwide church, said the Council, is not (as some Catholics still believe) a very large, single parish with a single pastor, the pope, who, because of the sheer size of his congregation, needs bishops and priests to assist him in carrying out his duties. Nor is the church a huge corporation with one chief executive officer and a vast team of division managers heading all the local outlets and answerable primarily to the boss. Clearly, the Council Fathers were trying to express in modern terms the old sense of church as a unique, Spirit-filled body.

They said, "The Church of Christ is truly present in all legitimate congregations of the faithful, which, united with their pastors, are themselves called churches in the New Testament." Bishops, said the Council Fathers, are not to be regarded as "vicars of the Roman Pontiff for they exercise an authority which is proper to them . . . Their power, therefore, is not destroyed" by papal power; "on the contrary, it is affirmed, strengthened and vindicated thereby."

Furthermore, "the Holy Spirit is present in the faithful of every rank." And even the much discussed and debated gift of infallibility is shared: "The body of the faithful as a whole . . . cannot err in matters of belief. Thanks to a supernatural sense of faith which characterizes the People as a whole, it manifests unerring quality when . . . it shows universal agreement in matters of faith and morals." The council acknowledged the ancient "sense of the faithful" *(senses fidelium)* as an important instrument in determining correct teaching and interpretation.

The church in its totality is described as the "People of God," a kind of community of communities, each of which exists in its own right. None of this denies the unique position of the pope as the unifying center of this college of churches, nor does it spell out just how the churches are to act in a collegial way, especially in their relations with the Vatican. What the Council's teaching does is point up the dignity and power of the local church and the responsibility of its members to take initiative to be the People of God.

Many older lay Catholics have come to see membership in the church in this light, and younger Catholics, educated in a Vatican II era, have never seen it in any other light. Without ridiculing the prerogatives of pope, bishop, or pastor, they earnestly believe their insights and concerns may come from the Holy Spirit present in the whole body. Pressure for active parish councils, for collaboration in the planning and carrying out of projects, even for consultation with the whole church community in selecting bishops and in formulating church law are initiatives justified under a broad understanding of collegiality.

By now, everyone realizes the collegial principle makes for a more hectic, more messy Christianity. The potential for excessive and irresponsible enthusiasm is ever present and exacerbates current conflicts. And a protracted effort continues by the current pope and high Vatican officials to get the genie back in the bottle, to place strict limits on collegiality, and to emphasize papal authority and the virtue of obedience in disputed questions. But then Jesus never promised that the Holy Spirit would create a tidy church.

A Bitter Pill

The Birth Control Watershed. Long before Vatican II, artificial contraception had been a disputed point among theologians and moralists. The official position of the church was clear; it had been enunciated by Pope Pius XI in a definitive 1930 encyclical. Since the primary purpose of marriage is the procreation and education of children, he wrote, any marriage act that excludes the possibility of conception is by its very nature immoral.

But that hard saying did not end the discussion. Thirty years later when Pope John XXIII called the Second Vatican Council, pressure to rethink that position mounted from many sides. The development of the birth-control pill, concern about world overpopulation, a less mechanistic understanding of the purpose of marriage, these and other factors seemed related and quite threatening to the official position of the church on birth control.

At the Council, the convened bishops declined to ratify Pius XI's notion of primary purpose; they called procreation only one among marriage's many purposes and did not attempt to rank them in order of importance. They urged parents to make responsible choices about having children "in the light of the material and spiritual condition of the times."

Thus, the door appeared open for a dramatic shift on this important moral doctrine. But the Council Fathers never got through that door because Pope Paul VI pulled birth control off the agenda in 1964 and announced that a special commission would study the matter and make its recommendations to him and that he would make the final decision himself.

The creation of the commission was considered by many a good omen — an indication of the openness of the highest teacher to the insights of the larger church. The members included various theologians, historians, bishops, priests, and even three married couples (including Pat and Patty Crowley, co-founders of the Christian Family Movement). After more than three years of discussion, the commission issued its report with better than 80 percent of its members in agreement that contraception was not intrinsically evil and that the old strictures should be relaxed.

In 1968 Paul VI released the encyclical, *Humanae vitae,* which rejected the commission's work and reiterated in the strongest terms the traditional doctrine: "Any use whatsoever of marriage must retain its natural potential to create human life . . . . Excluded is any action which either before, at the moment of, or after sexual intercourse, is specifically intended to prevent procreation."

Given the expectations of change aroused by the council, the credentials of the commission members, and the signs of the times, *Humanae vitae* sent a shock wave through the Catholic world. More than 600 theologians in the United States and scores from Europe signed dissenting statements and large numbers of lay Catholics said they felt betrayed and confused. Father Karl Rahner, S.J., one of the church's most respected theologians, took vigorous exception to the teaching; he noted that opposition from all quarters was "far greater, far swifter, far more decided and far more vocal" than at any other time in the history of the papacy.

Though *Humanae vitae is* not an infallible teaching (even the Vatican acknowledged that at publication), it was presented with full papal authority and as absolutely binding on all. As such, it created a special crisis of authority for married Catholics. Many who could not accept it left the church and have not come back. Many others rethought the degree of their affiliation and slackened in their church activities. Still others sought some way to hang on to their full Catholic identity without obeying the injunction. The struggle has been difficult, and the teaching of *Humanae vitae* has been regularly defended by Pope John Paul II.

Father Andrew Greeley and a team of sociologists noted in their study "Catholic Schools in a Declining Church" that U.S. Catholics' attendance at Sunday Mass underwent a striking decline between 1963 and 1973, a far greater decline than could be accounted for by the general U.S. religious decline during those years. Their research indicated that attitude shifts on birth control and papal leadership were the major reasons.

Mass attendance has stabilized since but not because Catholics are gradually returning to the papal position. In the mid-1970s national polls showed more than 65 percent of Catholics did not consider artificial birth control intrinsically wrong. The percentage rose to 76 percent in the mid-1980s. And the most recent figure, 87 percent, suggests near unanimity on the matter. Polls of U.S. priests have indicated that fewer than 15 percent will deny absolution to a penitent who believes he or she has a valid reason to practice contraception.

Fifty years ago such dissent would have been unthinkable, and transgressors could expect quick ecclesiastical penalties. Indeed, the Vatican has curbed prominent theologians like Fathers Hans Küng and Charles Curran for presenting their contrary views in highly public ways. Such actions haven't brought most back into line, however.

A kind of veiled dissent can even be seen in the position taken by bishops' conferences in some countries after consultation with the people. Responding to the papal ban, the U.S. bishops said Catholics should conform their consciences to the church's interpretation of divine law as a general norm, yet they explicitly acknowledged that some might in good conscience reject a definitive interpretation.

They even cited Cardinal John Henry Newman's discussion of conscience as a "sovereign master." Newman held that conscience could discount official, noninfallible positions, but only after prayer, serious thought, and the use of available sources to come to a right conclusion. In this instance, the bishops saw themselves as "witnesses to a spiritual tradition which accepts enlightened conscience, even when honestly mistaken, as the arbiter of moral decision."

Much written about the birth-control encyclical in recent years has focused on the "sense of the faithful," portrayed by Vatican II as a legitimate source of information and at times as a corrective on misguided tendencies. Many people would argue that the position of Catholics on birth control today is an instance of this sense of the faithful manifesting itself in the modern world.

Theologians also speak of a "teaching that is not received," in reference to the encyclical. Since the Holy Spirit, as the Council taught, is present in the whole church, they argue, church teaching cannot be a one-way street with directives issued unilaterally from above; Jesus never promised infused knowledge to the apostles or their successors. Therefore, as the Council also taught, pope and bishops must "strive painstakingly and by the appropriate means to inquire properly" into what God has revealed "and give apt expression to its contents."

That means, according to Father Richard McBrien, former chair of the University of Notre Dame theology department, official teachers of the church must have recourse to sacred scripture and the work of biblical scholars, historians, dogmatic theologians, anthropologists, sociologists, and so on.

"A consistent effort must be made to overcome the tendency to rely exclusively on one school of theology . . . and . . . there must be a free and open exchange of views, living contact with the faith and public opinion of the whole community," he wrote in his syndicated column soon after the release of the encyclical.

"If the teaching of *Humanae vitae is* faithful to the authentic tradition of the gospel, it will eventually produce a consensus of approval throughout the whole church. If not, it will take its place with past authoritative statements," including ones on taking interest and the primary purpose of marriage.

Now 25 years later, a near consensus of disapproval exists among U.S. Catholics, and similar negative views are reported among Europeans. In his remarkably popular book *Why You Can Disagree and Remain a Faithful Catholic* Benedictine Father Philip Kaufman argues that *Humanae vitae* "was a non-collegial exercise in a matter where the broadest collegiality and extreme sensitivity to the sense of the faithful were essential for the edification of the church."

Hence, Kaufman concludes, there is strong evidence that here we have a definitive teaching that has simply "not been received." There is no good reason, argues Kaufman, why some of the better elements of the democratic political system — consultation, collaboration, negotiation — should be barred from the church's decision-making operation.

This position is certainly not the Vatican's nor the position of those who hold that anyone who dissents on a teaching automatically ceases to be Catholic. But it does appear to be the position of many married Catholics who neither argue about nor lose sleep over their practice of birth control. In fact, when questioned, they seem surprised that the subject is still being debated. Parishioners' general reaction, said the pastor of a large Chicago parish, is, "Oh, I thought that was settled long ago."

Trust No One Over 30

Disillusionment with Authority. Even if Vatican II never happened, even if there never had been a birth-control encyclical, a crisis of authority would undoubtedly still exist for U.S. Catholics. Americans have been exposed during the past 30 years to so many instances of misused authority in civil life that they have become suspicious of everyone in high position and wary of every authoritative declaration. "Question Authority" is not only a popular bumper-sticker slogan, it has become a state of mind for millions.

The civil-rights movement educated an entire generation to the fact that laws are sometimes blatantly unjust, law-enforcement officials are sometimes cruel and capricious, and justice may sometimes be best achieved through civil disobedience. Throughout the 1960s television viewers observed governors, city officials, and state troopers barring (sometimes beating) unarmed demonstrators who only wanted to get a decent education, eat at a lunch counter, or perhaps drink from a public water fountain.

Skepticism about authority reached the highest secular levels in the late 1960s and 1970s as thousands of young men refused to fight in the Vietnam War, a conflict they regarded as useless and immoral. They heard the clarion call of their country and said, "Hell no! We won't go!"

The image of all right-minded, patriotic citizens marching in obedience lockstep by their commander-in-chief was permanently tarnished. Then as a coup de grace came Watergate and the revelation that a presidential administration, which took law and order as its motto, was riddled with the sleaziest kind of hypocrisy, corruption, and deceit.

The intervening years have not dispelled the mood of cynicism. Many contend that the Iran Contra scandal, if the facts were exposed, would make Watergate look like a minor indiscretion. The 1980s, the so-called decade of greed, saw unprecedented instances of people in authority — judges, members of congress, savings and loan officials, and television evangelists — using their positions for personal gain.

Americans have been so bombarded with the misuse of authority that they almost expect politicians and other leaders to be deceitful and dishonest. They are no longer shocked at instances of secrecy, manipulation, dirty tricks, or indifference to the concerns of constituents.

One may argue that religious authority is a different kind of reality deserving of a more honored status. But the church has not been immune to charges of misused authority itself. The vigor to maintain its position, referred to by historian Dolan, showed itself earlier in this century in ill-advised documents condemning biblical scholarship, the possibility of evolution, and the U.S. notion of separation of church and state.

The machinations of authoritarianism — secrecy, threat, manipulation — are not unknown to high church officials even in the late 20th century. Scholars such as Fathers Teilhard de Chardin and John Courtney Murray were officially silenced, while others such as Fathers Bernard Häring and Edward Schillebeeckx pursued their careers in almost continuous turmoil with Vatican authorities. Most recently revelations about pedophilia among priests have attracted widespread notice, with some of the charges allegedly covered up by diocesan officials.

Given all these developments, Catholics are not so inclined to accept church authority unquestioningly, perhaps less so than at any other time in history.

Take It or Leave It

In his book *Tomorrow's Catholics, Yesterday's Church,* psychologist Eugene Kennedy says there are two kinds of U.S. Catholics: Culture One and Culture Two. Culture One adherents, says Kennedy, work to support the church as institution and protect its lines of authority. They are not apologetic about this because the church, after all, is an institution with an organized structure, a worldwide presence, a hierarchy of duties and responsibilities, and a list of rules and regulations.

Culture Two people don't ridicule this preoccupation, in Kennedy's view; they just don't find it very interesting. They view the church more as mystery, that is, as the external, visible, and sometimes flawed transmitter of traditions, teachings, stories, and insights about the deepest meanings of life and death; they see church as providing access to invisible realities, and these cannot be easily codified.

Culture Two Catholics, says Kennedy, "look to the church for support in carrying out their responsibilities to their families, and, in the work force and the professions, they expect that the church can speak to them with wisdom and encouragement about the great moral issues of the day. They expect that the church will comprehend tragedy and joy and that it will stand with them in both."

Although they don't "accept official pronouncements automatically anymore," he says, they are actually searching "for an authority that is credible to them"; and they believe it can come from unofficial as well as official sources. Put simply, they are not intimidated by church authority because they feel themselves, no less than their leaders, to be full members of the church.

Similar views have been expressed by sociologists Greeley and William McCready, who are both familiar with Catholic opinion. Young Catholics, says McCready, are sincerely concerned with religion in their lives and expect the church to enlighten and challenge them; but they don't relate well to the institution or its regulations — a situation that causes him some concern. Will Catholic identity survive into coming generations, he wonders, or will it mutate into a vague kind of spiritual consciousness?

Greeley is more optimistic. In his book *The Catholic Myth* he says that Catholics "stay in their Church because they like being Catholic, because of loyalty to the imagery of the Catholic imagination, because of pictures of a loving God present in creation, because of the spiritual vision of Catholics that they absorbed in their childhood, along with and often despite all the rules and regulations that were drummed into their heads."

Also upbeat are James Castelli and George Gallup, Jr., whose 1987 book, *The American Catholic People: Their Beliefs, Practices and Values,* offers a sociological portrait of the modern Catholic. Although Catholics differ with church positions on numerous issues, they found "neither criticisms nor disagreements have changed their sense of belonging to the Church."

In fact, Catholics were found to have more confidence in the church than in any other institution. Castelli and Gallup said Catholics "don't even necessarily want the church to change all of its teachings with which they disagree; they just want those teachings viewed as ideals that may seem impractical in the real world and from which they dissent in conscience."

Kennedy puts it in more exalted prose: Culture Two Catholics are "delighted when, as in the life and work of Pope John XXIII or Mother Teresa, it lights and warms a dark, cold world. They are proud of Pope John Paul II as he strides manfully and confidently, on pilgrimages of peace across the globe . . ."

They see prominent church leaders as symbols of important realities, not as supreme lawgivers. Culture One proponents find such a stance basically schizophrenic and cause for great distress; they deplore what appears to them as "cafeteria Catholicism," a kind of have-it-your-way religion. Culture Two is fully prepared to live with the ambiguity.

Thus we return to the contrast revealed in the most recent Gallup poll — overwhelming numbers disagreeing with the pope yet respectful of his position and performance. In light of what has had an impact on the Catholic mind in the past 30 years, the contrast is not so unintelligible. Depressing to some, exciting to others, a bit confusing to everyone. But it's here to stay. The toothpaste will not fit back in the tube.

Communication in Marriage

8.1   The Wall

Anonymous

Their wedding picture mocked them from the table,
these two whose minds no longer touched each other.
They lived with such a heavy barricade between them
that neither battering ram of words or artilleries of touch
could break it down.

Somewhere, between the oldest child's first tooth and the
youngest daughter's graduation they lost each other.
Throughout the years, each slowly unraveled
that tangled ball of string called self,
and as they tugged at stubborn knots,
each hid his searching from the other.
Sometimes she cried at night
and begged the whispering darkness
to tell her who she was.
He lay beside her, snoring like a hibernating bear,
unaware of her winter.

Once, after they had made love,
he wanted to tell her
how afraid he was of dying,
but, fearing to show his naked soul,

he spoke instead about
the beauty of her breasts.

She took a course in modern art,
trying to find herself in colors
splashed upon a canvas,
and complained to other women
about men who were insensitive.

He climbed into a tomb called the office,
wrapped his mind in a shroud of paper figures
and buried himself in customers.

Slowly, the wall between them rose,
cemented by the mortar of indifference.
One day, reaching out to touch each other,
they found a barrier they could not penetrate,
and, recoiling from the coldness of the stones,
each retreated from the struggle on the other side.

For when love dies,
it is not a moment of angry battle,
nor when fiery bodies lose their heat.
It lies, panting, exhausted . . .
expiring at the bottom of the wall
it could not scale.

8.2   Communication

Kathleen Fischer Hart and Thomas N. Hart

WHEN TONY AND SUE CAME IN FOR COUNSELING, THEY HAD BEEN MARRIED five years and had two children. But things were not going at all well. At a recent workshop for couples, the two of them had been asked to recall one or two of the peak experiences of their marriage, and Tony could not think of any. He wondered if he was just so angry that his recall of anything good was blocked. As we talked, the roots of the anger were gradually uncovered. Tony summed up the problem this way: "Sue never understands me, and so she always reacts in the wrong way. But you know, the reason she doesn't understand me is that I have never really let her know me." Sue chimed in and said: "Everything he said is true. What's worse, he doesn't understand me either. And that's my fault, because I've held back too. So you can imagine what our guessing-game interaction is like." They went on to say that it had been like this from the beginning.

This clear analysis of their problem, offered by the couple themselves, set the agenda for counseling. The task was to assist them to begin to talk to one another about what was going on deep inside, to open out their inner worlds to one another. The heart of that was to get them expressing how they felt about themselves, each other, and the myriad situations of their lives. Tony admitted that the reason he held himself in was that he did not like himself very much, and he found it much easier to remain crouched behind his wall sniping at Sue than to come out from behind it and let her see who he was. To do the latter would be to make himself vulnerable, to admit hurt, weakness, inadequacy, and need, and to put the truth in Sue's hands for her to deal with. That required a degree of courage he had long been unable to muster.

We talk in Christian terms of the gift of the self. In marriage, that is what two Christians pledge to one another. It is *the* great gift of love. Many married people stay with one another and serve each other in many ways. But this is not yet the gift of the *self,* which can only be given if one is willing to open one's heart to the other. One can do many external deeds of love and still hold back the really precious gift, the inner self. This gift can be given only through communication. It costs, like all of the better gifts. But union between two persons is hardly possible if they have not let each other into their inner worlds. This always involves the disclosure of feelings.

Some feelings are harder to communicate than others. Some people, for some reason, find it next to impossible to say "I love you." Many people, especially men, find it difficult to admit their fears, their sense of failure, or their sadness. Some find it hard to affirm others, to give positive feedback. Husbands stop telling their wives that they are beautiful, saying, "She already knows that," or "It would go to her head." We have yet to meet someone who does not need to be told the good things over and over (and even then still doubts it), or whose head is in much danger of an over-swell from too much affirmation. But there is another reason why people hold in their feelings in marriage. They care about their mates and do not want to hurt them. So they do not express dissatisfaction, irritation, or any other uncomfortable feelings.

What happens in an intimate relationship when uncomfortable feelings are held in? Terrible outbursts from time to time, when feelings reach the breaking point. A note on the kitchen table announcing the divorce. Or, in milder forms, sarcasm, silence, and various forms of subtle punishment. One thing is certain. If people cannot deal with their anger, they cannot be intimate either. You either have a relationship in which there are angry exchanges at times and warm closeness at others (often shortly after the angry exchange), or you have a relationship in which all is smooth on the surface but the psychological distance is unbridged. In these latter relationships there are several forbidden subjects and an abundance of silence.

In intimate relationships, communication is the foundational skill. There is none more basic. It is the indispensable condition of union. It is the key to resolving conflicts. It is the only way two people can continue growing together, or even living together.

The question is: How do you do it? It is an art, and it takes time to cultivate. The following are eleven hints to point the way.

1. Use "I"-statements rather than "You"-statements.

Talk about yourself rather than your mate. Don't say things like, "*You* never care about anybody but yourself," or "*You* think you know everything all the time," or "*You* never do anything around here." Say instead, "*I* often feel lonely," or "Sometimes *I* feel put down by things you say," or "*I* feel overburdened with household chores and sometimes *I* resent it because it doesn't seem fair to me." Talk about yourself, in other words, and your feelings, in response to concrete behaviors of your mate. Do that instead of making judgments about your mate ("You're always flirting"; "You're so damn sure about everything") or giving commands ("Get out of here"; "Why don't you loosen up once in a while?").

The approach we are suggesting is risky because it exposes you. But it has many distinct advantages. It does not make your mate so defensive, and so it gives you a better chance of getting a hearing and an honest response. It lets your mate in on your inner world, and so reveals important information. It does not pronounce judgment about who is wrong, but leaves the question open. For instance, if I am bothered by the way you socialize at parties, it may indeed be your fault. But it could just as well be mine. Maybe I am very insecure, and cling too much, and am very easily threatened and jealous. Maybe I misinterpret what you are doing. If I find you overly emotional, it may be that you are. But it may also be that I am emotionally repressed and uncomfortable with the expression of feelings, or simply that I feel inadequate to meeting the needs you make known to me. When I stay with my own feelings, owning them and letting you know them, I let you know me and I leave the question open about who should do what. We can work on that together. "I feel uncomfortable around your dad" is not yet a comment about your dad, still less about you. So far, it is just an informative comment about me.

Talking about your mate is legitimate to this extent: As far as possible, tie your feeling statements to your mate's concrete *behaviors*. "When you come in without saying hello, I feel unloved." "I start to feel insecure when I see you having a good time with another man." You are talking here just about concrete *behaviors*, externally observable. You are not guessing at your mate's *feelings* or *intentions*, which are hidden from view.

There are four basic "I"-statements which carry most of the weight in an intimate relationship. They are: (1) I think, (2) I feel, (3) I want, and (4) I need. All of them are positive steps in self-assertion and indicate an underlying self-respect. All of them make me vulnerable to you. They do not state what is right, nor do they make a demand. They simply tell you who I am and what is going on with me right now. If you are willing to make a similar self-revelation, we have the materials for really learning to care for one another.

2. Express Feelings Rather than Thoughts.

Not that it is bad to express thoughts. There is plenty of scope for those too. But our feelings reveal more of who we are. One can sit for an entire course before many professors, and know a good deal of their thought and almost nothing of who they are. A wife expressed this eloquently once, saying that everything her husband said to her could be said on television. He was an engineer, and lived much more in the realm of thought than of feeling. He was not untalkative, but she was always left wondering what was going on inside. It is in expressing our feelings that we give the gift of the self. That was the gift she was still waiting for.

People sometimes hide their feelings behind their thoughts. "A woman's place is in the home" is an apparent statement of principle, but it may be a man's way of saying that he feels he has failed as a provider if his wife takes a job outside the home, or that he fears he will lose her if she has much occasion to be with other men. Those are feelings. "Should" statements can also be masks. "You should enjoy sex" is probably best translated "I enjoy sex," or "I feel inadequate as a lover when you don't seem to enjoy sex, or hurt when you turn me down." In more open communication, people just talk about their feelings, not about the eternal order of things (as they see it), or the common sense truths embraced by all (but you). Most of our feelings, after all, come out of our cultural relativity.

Some people are not very aware of their feelings. You cannot communicate what you do not know. To develop a greater awareness of feelings, it is a helpful exercise to go inside yourself from time to time during the day, inquiring what you are feeling right now. Watch the variations in typical situations: talking with your child, talking with the boss, hearing the phone ring, approaching the front door at home, waking up in the morning, watching TV at night, going about your daily work, getting into bed at night. Move gradually from becoming more aware of feelings to becoming more expressive of them.

3. Listen Attentively Without Interrupting.

Good communication requires more than good talking. It demands good listening too. Listening is difficult. It requires setting other things aside, even the ruminations of the mind. It is especially hard when we do not like what we are hearing, or when we think we have heard it all before. One of the things a marriage counselor does most frequently is stop married partners from interrupting each other, suggesting instead a three-step process which can revolutionize the way they talk to each other: (a) listen without interrupting; (b) say back what you heard, and check it out; (c) respond to it.

In poor communication, the listeners are working on their responses instead of listening, and cut in to make them as soon as they are ready. In the approach suggested here, you have to listen closely or you will not be able to say back what you heard. This is how you make sure you got the message. There are often surprises here, as the original speaker makes the necessary corrections. Then you can respond. This may seem cumbersome and time-consuming. But if you really get your mate's message, and respond to it rather than to something else, you end up saving time. And your mate has the gratifying feeling of being heard, even if you end up differing. If two people are in the habit of interrupting each other as they argue back and forth, the entire time is probably being wasted. Neither is listening. Neither is open. Nothing is being produced except more bad feeling.

4. Check Out What You See and Hear.

Part of this is summarizing what you hear your mate saying and asking if that is the message. It keeps the conversation on track. But there are other parts to this checking out too. Listen for the feelings behind the words, and check those out. Listen for anger and frustration. Listen for loneliness. Listen for fear. And test what you think you hear, saying, for example, "You sound weary," or, "You sound as if this is really hard for you to tell me." This approach is especially useful with people who do not express feelings directly, but prefer to make statements of fact, pronounce judgments of good and bad, and give direct or indirect commands. You cannot get them to play by your rules. If you say, "Don't make judgments; tell me your feelings," you have given them a command instead of expressing your frustration and leaving them free. Even if they persist in their usual ways, you can listen for the feelings behind the words, and check those out.

Checking out can be useful outside of times of conversation. You come home, and seem tired, discouraged, or distant. But I am not sure. Mostly you are silent. If I want to relate to you appropriately — giving you space, encouraging you, or inviting you to unburden yourself — I have to know what you are feeling. I can ask the open question, "How are you doing?" Or I can check out my impressions: "You seem distant." Or, "You look as if you had a hard day."

Such an approach invites mates to express themselves. The ideal situation would be that they would volunteer this information, and ask for what they need. But the situation is not always ideal.

5. Avoid Mind-Reading.

Mind-reading is the attempt to reach inside the sanctuary of the other person's psyche and declare what is going on there. You tell others what they are feeling or what their motives are. "You're saying that because you're jealous." "You're just telling me what you think I want to hear." This kind of statement almost always gets an angry reaction. It deserves it. The statement is a violation of the other's privacy, and what is alleged is often inaccurate besides. We have *impressions* of other people's feelings, and *hunches* about their motives. It is legitimate to inquire. It is also all right to voice our impressions, if we do it tentatively, with recognition of our uncertainty. Mind-reading is another matter. It is a violation of the person. It shows disrespect for that person's integrity, destroys trust, and invites retaliation.

6. Make Your Needs Known.

Sometimes those needs are general: "I need about half an hour's space when I get home from work before I can face any new challenges." "I need relief from child care at least one day a week." Sometimes they are particular: "I need a hug." "I need to get away some weekend soon."

A couple came for counseling. The problem they brought was that the husband was angry much of the time. What came to light was that he expected his wife to anticipate his needs and take care of them, and when she did not, he got angry. He expected her to know when he needed space, and not to talk to him then. He expected her to know when he needed affection, and to be affectionate then. When she guessed wrong and acted unsuitably, he was angry. This is an extreme form of a common fallacy: "If you really loved me, you would know what I am feeling and what I need." Not so. All of us are unfamiliar territory, often even to ourselves, certainly to others. Our only hope of getting our needs met is to be assertive in declaring them. They will not always get met, of course, because others have their needs too and some limitations in their ability to meet ours. But if needs are declared, they can at least be negotiated.

7. Learn Your Mate's Language of Love.

All of us have a language in which we like to be told that we are loved. And one person's language differs from another's. What tells Randy that he is loved is a massage by Betty. But what tells Betty that she is loved is not a return massage by Randy, but just being held by him. What told your mother that your father was sorry was a single red rose, but what tells *your* wife you are sorry is not a rose at all but an apology and an explanation of what was going on inside you at the time of the incident. A woman might express her love by keeping a very clean house, but what would actually speak love to her husband would be her relaxing more with him.

There is usually a lot of love in the first two years of marriage, but sometimes it is spoken in your own language rather than your mate's, and so it does not have much impact. The trick is to learn your mate's language and to speak that. One very ironic situation of our acquaintance was that of a couple who differed in how they wanted to be treated when they were sick. She liked people to come into her room, freshen the air, bring her some orange juice, ask her how she was, and leave some flowers behind. He liked to be left completely alone so he could sleep. So when she was sick, he left her alone. And when he was sick, she visited him often and did all kinds of nice things for him. It took them a while to learn each other's language. It usually does. The Golden Rule here is "Do unto others as they would have you do unto them."

8. Avoid the Words "Always" and "Never."

This is an easy one to understand, but a hard one to do. "Always" and "never" are very tempting words, especially when you are angry. "You *never* listen." "You're *always* complaining." "*You never* want to do anything but watch TV." Because they are exaggerations, they provoke anger and invite a quick denial. And so the point is missed. Wouldn't "sometimes" be a better word than "always," more accurate and easier for the other person to hear? Then there is "often," and, when you really want to be emphatic, "usually." Never use "never."

9. Avoid Name-Calling.

Names usually come into the game in the heat of anger. They hurt (which is why they are used). They stick. That is the problem. The fight ends, you make up, and things are supposed to be all right again. But your mate cannot forget that name you called her. Did you really mean that? If you didn't mean it, why did you say it? You have unwittingly planted a weed, and weeds are very hard to eradicate.

A couple once agreed in marriage counseling to just two contracts with one another. They would not read each other's minds and they would not call each other names. Seventy-five percent of their wrangling dropped away.

10. Deal with Painful Situations as They Arise.

Have you had the experience of setting off an angry tirade by some simple slip-up, like being five minutes late to pick up your mate? There has probably been some gunnysacking going on, and the sack has just burst. You take it over the head not just for the present offense but for several others stretching back over weeks and months. You didn't know your mate was carrying all this around. You can't even remember the incidents they refer to.

If couples would be close, they must learn to deal with anger honestly and constructively. That means handling it by occasions, not allowing it to build. There is no point in trying not to hurt your mate with the bad news that you did not like something. You will harm your mate more in the long run if you hold these things back. You can soften the pain by telling the truth with love each time. That way you avoid the big outburst with white-hot anger, exaggerated statements, name-calling, and sometimes physical violence.

11. Make Time for Talk that Goes Beyond Practical Problems.

Most couples manage to get the day-to-day problems solved. They communicate enough to get the bills paid, the food bought, the baby taken care of, the guests entertained, the car fixed. But many couples gradually neglect talking about themselves. The very thing that made the courting period such a deeply happy time, talking about you and about me and about us, gets pushed from the center to the periphery and sometimes dies out altogether. We make love less frequently, and I notice it, but I don't say anything. We do more things separately, and talk about them less. I go to work and muse a lot on the general drift of my life, but I keep these thoughts and feelings to myself. You go off to be with your parents. We keep solving the day-to-day problems, but we do not talk about *ourselves*. And both of us notice in our interaction a growing distance and irritability.

Marriage Encounter has a simple idea to keep marriages going and growing. Each day the couple write each other a short letter, no more than ten minutes' worth, on some subject that draws out feelings. Some couples accomplish the same purpose in other ways. They keep an agreement to do something together one night a week, to be by themselves and talk about things that are important to each of them. It may be a dinner, or it may just be a walk. Other couples commit themselves to a weekend away every few months. These exercises in deliberate cultivation of the relationship are vital. Often all that is needed is to remove the obstacles, the challenges that ordinary living throws in the way of deeper communication. If we can free ourselves from these regularly, the deeper currents can keep flowing and joining. There is an amazing power of resurrection in marital relationships if they are not neglected too long. The coals may seem a little quiet at times, but don't call the fire out. Couples who make a little time and tend the embers see some amazing things happen.

Communication is the foundational skill, and the key to all the rest of the elements that build a marriage. It is learned over time. Doing some reading about it, and attending marriage enrichment events that foster it, are very helpful in making it grow. It is actually possible for two people to be open and honest with each other, to entrust each other with nothing less than the gift of the whole self, and to become increasingly one instead of increasingly two. It takes courage, but it is one of the most satisfying experiences that life offers.

8.3   The Search for Intimacy
Thomas M. Martin

EVERYONE ASSUMES THAT ALL PEOPLE WANT INTIMACY. OUR MODERN society is built on interpersonal relationships. Who does not want to be close to another person? Surprising as the answer might seem, quite a few people do not want to be intimate. At least they lack the personal qualities or personal drive to be open and trusting enough to achieve the intimacy that appears so attractive to everyone. People want the end product seen in the loving affection of a romantic picture. Intimacy, however, does not come easy. Many are incapable or unwilling to make the necessary journey.

Seldom do couples go into a marriage with a good sense of the other's personal needs. Most of the time a prospective spouse cannot discuss what the other's sense of intimacy is because few men or women are aware of their own expectations and limitations. A case in point would be in order:

> Buffy and Biff married last October. Biff has had one year of experience in a local accounting firm. Buffy was one year behind him in school and just recently graduated. She is looking for a teaching job in English. He finds her exciting. She looks great. She smells great. His spirits and his body come alive when she is around. He likes her softness, her ease in relating with people, her infectious giggle, her sense of adventure as she never settles for the apparent or the ordinary.

Buffy on the other hand loves his hardness, his strength, his security, his sense of control. He can take stock of a situation, step back and calculate, and come to a reasonable conclusion as to how the situation should be handled. If things get hairy, he can usually put the pieces back together.

When they were together before marriage, they loved each other's company. They would rather be together than with any other people. After a half dozen months of marriage, however, there is trouble in paradise.

Buffy grew up in settings where she could always share her feelings with the people around her. In her younger years there was always her mother. Later, as a teen, when her mother had to be protected from the realities of life or at least the realities of Buffy's life, she had her girl friends. Finally, in college there was always a running conversation in which others were talking about how they felt. When she looks back on the constant chatter in the sorority house, it probably centered more on feelings than on sex or school or money. She is aware of her strong mood swings. She can be very high, and she can also hit bottom At either of those extremes she has a real need to talk her way through and to share her feelings with others.

Biff on the other hand is what could be termed a man of few words. His father did not talk a lot. His uncles did not talk a lot. Robert Redford, Clint Eastwood, Burt Reynolds, his high school coach Cyril Beorokoski, Sylvester Stallone, and more recently Rob Lowe and Tom Cruise did not talk a lot. His high school friend Pete Puma, his college roommate Percy Jackson, his fraternity brothers — they did talk quite a bit. They did not spend a great deal of time talking about their emotions, however. Rather, their world of conversation was dominated by sports, girls, sex, school, religion, politics, and most certainly parties. They talked about things going on much more than their reactions to things going on or their mood swings. When feelings were expressed, they were mentioned in a direct fashion and not belabored.

Buffy and Biff were brought up in two different worlds. As they face life together, they must not only adjust to each other. They must also become aware of how they are different. They must learn to know themselves better.

Obviously, the new husband and wife have difficulty in meeting each other's needs. There are friends, and there are jobs. More often than not, however, their personal time when they can let their guards down and unwind is spent in the presence of each other. She tires him out. He infuriates her because he will not tell her what is going on inside of him.

In a sense the very thing that attracted them to each other — their differences — are now causing problems as they reach out to each other. On one level it could be argued that they have a different need for intimacy. At another, probably a more accurate level, it could be argued that they achieve intimacy in different ways. She depends heavily on talking about what is inside her. He is satisfied in sharing actions, in the camaraderie that comes with sharing a common task.

Why did Biff and Buffy fail to discuss their different ways of finding closeness with others? The most obvious answer is that they were not aware of their needs or the way they related with others. Even if they took Psychology 101 and had some sense of their ways of relating, who could discuss such heavy things as communication when they are in love?

The search for intimacy is a maddening quest. Martin Buber seemed to have given many people some helpful handles when he spoke of "I-Thou," "I-You," and "I-It" relationships.

The first phrase (I-Thou) captures the moments of intense intimacy. At such times there is a real rubbing of souls. The presence of the other is dramatic and moving. The closeness, the immediacy makes the blood run quicker in rhythm with the heart. Even the sinuses clear up, and the headache fades if the moment lasts long enough. The trouble is that such experiences of intensity are so demanding, so fatiguing, so fragile that they seldom last long. Like olfactory fatigue, the senses and the self simply cannot maintain that level of awareness. It climaxes. It fades.

The thrill of the experience remains and is enjoyed in an individual's memory and fantasy life. The quest for renewed experiences is often frustrating, however. John Cheever captures the maddening dance in one of his short stories, "The Sorrows of Gin." Amy, a fourth grader, is receiving only distracted attention from her parents who are caught in a whirlwind of social and business engagements. In her frustrations, she decides to leave home. She gets as far as the train station before the ticket master phones her father. He comes down to retrieve her. The following scene is presented:

> He saw his daughter through the station window. The girl, sitting on the bench, the rich names on her paper suitcase, touched him as it was in her power to touch him only when she seemed helpless or when she was very sick. Someone had walked over his grave! He shivered with longing, he felt his skin coarsen as when, driving home late and alone, a shower of leaves on the wind crossed the beam of his headlights, liberating him for a second at the most, from the literal symbols of his life — the buttonless shirts, the vouchers and bank statements, the order blanks, and the empty glasses. . . . Then, as it was with the leaves, the power of her figure to trouble him was ended; his gooseflesh vanished. He was himself.

Moments of intense intimacy are often that fleeting. The excitement of the other can come from a place, a book, an antique chair. Usually such moments come with another person. Ideally in the present schema of things they come — most frequently come — with one's spouse.

The reality is, of course, that a married couple does not go around "I-Thouing" each other several times a day. Twice a day would be fine, thank you. How about once a week? Would you believe once a month? A couple must nurture a positive life with each other at the "I-you" level. Spouses must treat each other with care and respect. They must place a high priority on the other's feelings, goals, intentions, and happiness. If they are successful at that level, the more intimate life will follow.

The dance of intimacy truly is maddening. On the one hand a couple must reach for the intimacy. They should help it along. It usually does not come if it is intently pursued. Its existence is too fragile to tolerate such direct action. The couple determined to celebrate their eighth wedding anniversary, the parent embarrassing the teenage son by admitting to self-doubts, the empty nest parents trying to share their interests in life — all can attest to the futility of the pursuit. However, there is a need to try. The very effort assures the other and the self that the intimacy is important.

If the life together is there, however, the moments will come. Who knows how frequently? The circumstances of each couple and of each family are so diverse. The engines which drive the couple, the fuel which feeds the mutual life are also quite diverse:

Scenario One: The Young Marrieds

The younger married couple has passion and newness and excitement urging them toward each other. They are each energized by the newness of their own individual adult person. Their personal energy compels them to look for contact and encounter. Their bodily energy, their lust, strongly urges them to seek contact with others.

They are driven in a very positive way to reach out. The young married couple lacks, however, the comfortableness, the history, the skills, the bonding of years that makes the intimacy very easy. The very energy often drives them past each other — sometimes into the arms of another. Often they do not have a time in which they can develop the skills for being husband and wife. Often children come on the scene before they break in their wedding rings. They often become mommy and daddy before they learn how to be husband and wife.

The very force of their life during this time might well lead to more moments of intimacy than at other periods in their married life. By contrast, the more volatile base of their life can also cause more violent and more frequent periods of distance.

Scenario Two: The Mid-Life Marriage

The bodily and psychological drives which were such allies in the young marrieds' dance with each other now turn to at best questionable assets. There is much going on in the life of the typical mid-life spouse. Often the dynamics can cause so much turmoil within that they have quite a difficult time reaching out toward each other. As they give up their primary roles of mommy and daddy, they must turn toward each other as husband and wife once again or perhaps for the first time or face a destruction of their marriage.

The typical woman in her late forties faces a continually changing body whose hormonal shifts and creeping wrinkles and sags cause her to struggle in a culture that worships hard bodies. A woman at this age, even if she had a career, faces the empty nest. More than likely her main identity has been as mother. Her work outside the home was often secondary to the husband's and was more job than career. With the children gone, even if there was a little glee felt as they walked out the door, the woman must develop a new focus for her life. As she turns toward a career, there is often a cultural and economic barrier between the spouses. She is putting aside the job and looking for a career. He is well up the ladder. All these changes cause self-doubt in her; and at the moment when she needs assurances, often her husband is experiencing a decline in his sexual drive which she can easily translate into a loss of interest in her. To top it all off, just as the children are leaving the nest, often the woman must face the challenge of aging parents. That challenge requires a great deal of dedication as well as quite an identity adjustment.

The man working through his fifth decade has his own crazies to face. His hormonal shifts may not be as dramatic, but the male often has greater difficulty adjusting to the role of a more vulnerable life. The stronger the macho image, the greater the adjustment. He may be well up the ladder of his career, but he also must realize that there will be limits to his achievements. Perhaps his shift from father to spouse may not be as traumatic as the wife's since the kids were only one of the claims on his time. But he may also realize that he missed his kids' childhood. They have left the nest, and he has spent more time in his career than with his children. It is an opportunity that cannot be retrieved. There can be much regret.

With the kids gone, mommy and daddy must turn toward each other and say hi. That is a difficult thing to do given all the other struggles they are going through. Fortunately, they have some things going for them which the young marrieds do not. They have a history together. They have a bonding in which their identities are intertwined. They hopefully have learned much about each other. They hopefully have developed skills in relating. In other words, if they have not been just mommy and daddy, their desire and their need for each other can carry them through the challenges they face.

Scenario Three: The Twilight Years

The couple are in their late seventies/early eighties. He has a pacemaker. He had a hip replaced in his sixties. She had to help him out of a depression at that time. His gall bladder and appendix are out. There are early signs of Alzheimer's disease.

She is doing rather well, thank you. She needs a little help hearing. Her eyes have faded and work only with the aid of some strong lenses. Fifteen years earlier she had a bout with breast cancer. He stood by her, and they made it through.

Each month finds one or two of their friends or acquaintances passing on. They are afraid as they feel more and more fragile. They feel vulnerable. They are afraid for themselves. They are afraid for each other. They are also bored and annoyed with each other as their world shrinks more and more to the four walls of their apartment. It becomes difficult to remain involved in the many settings that have benefited from their active lives. All the worry, all the time together has led to a lot of argument. They probably snip at each other more now than at any other time of their life. There are even moments when they simply do not like each other.

Their life together, however, is a good example of how intimacy is a deeper reality than just the immediate conscious exchange. Their lives are irreversibly intertwined. The identity of one is locked into the life of the other. They are at least as intimate as the young romantic couple drunk with the look, the presence, the smell, and the feel of each other. Arguably, the older couple is more intimate even though they could use some different company to give variety to their day. They are one with each other at the deepest of levels.

Intimacy, therefore, takes on different dynamics as people pass through different stages of their relationship. There is in fact no one reality called intimacy. The word is used to capture the dance people do with each other in an attempt to draw close.

Before people can draw close to each other, of course, they have to achieve other qualities in their life. They have to like themselves at least to a minimal degree. They have to be able to trust other people. In short, before they can reach out to others in the demands of marriage, they have to have experienced enough love and enough success in their dealings with others and with themselves. A person has to be loved before he or she can love. Marriage is a poor place to learn the basic skills of love and intimacy. It is the place where the advanced lessons take place.

What is most paradoxical about the search for intimacy is that it is a disaster if the spouses give up their own individuality. One marries the other, ideally in our society, because the other is different and interesting. Some people then turn to marriage and spend their efforts trying to become the same. A relationship does not have many healthy prospects, however, if the two do not differentiate themselves at the very same time they are trying to engage in the dance of intimacy.

Edwin Friedman makes this point rather strongly in his book *Generation to Generation:*

Distancing comes about because there is not enough distance to begin with. Marriage partners may separate because they have grown distant, but most couples probably separate because they are not able to achieve any separation at all. Children may wind up undisciplined because their parents pay them no heed, but as many are problemed because they are the objects of too much investment. Emotional distance is perplexing. If there is too much, it is not possible to have a relationship; if there is not enough separation, it is also not possible to have a relationship.

The Christian Perspective

The greatest message that the Christian tradition can bring to the marriage relationship today is a message of failure. It should plead with people to realize that even the most admirable person has significant faults. Every person in the scriptures failed or had doubts in his or her love and service of God. The Christian message should warn people that marriage will not be easy.

The Christian message is not a depressing one. It is not meant to preach doom and despair. Rather, the message of failure is deemed necessary to assure the possibility of success. It becomes a key part of the Christian message today because of contemporary culture's impatience with anything but immediate success. In another place or another time the emphasis might be placed on other aspects of the Christian tradition. Today, however, there is such an intense pursuit of immediate happiness. There is a demand for immediate success. And there is such an impatience with the limitations of life, especially the limitations of others. It is no wonder why marriages are so frail.

The pursuit of self leads to an unhappy narcissism. The pursuit of the other leads to intense joy and intense frustration and anger. The joy cannot be discounted. The frustration and anger must be faced and made productive rather than destructive.

The Christian message does not leave one with the message of defeat, of course. Any caution against unbridled romanticism must be immediately balanced with the sense that people are worth any effort. Not only are people made in the image and likeness of God, but so also is one's lover. The Christian message should cause an excitement about the depth and beauty of the other person. Paradoxically, while the Christian message warns about the limitations of married life, it is at the same time most positive. Nothing is more sensational than the realization that the other is anchored in the deepest mystery of life. Even if the other is fat, gray, and a little slow on the upbeat, the other is seen as residing in God.

Christianity should be one of the forces, then, that combats a certain nervous consumerism. The world is not there to be experienced and used. The world is a community that resides within the ground of all being. It is a community in God. All others — humans, long-haired wambas, white birches, and a fog blanketing a marsh — express the God that is at the base of all creation. They all offer the call of life.

Some, of course, have a greater potential for expressing the depth of life. Humans according to the Christian message have a special place in creation. In fact people become absorbed in each other because it is such a powerful avenue in the search for an intensity in life.

Marriage then is seen as a place where people can find each other if they have the patience, the understanding, and the tolerance to work with each other. Perhaps given the dynamics of the people involved or given the circumstances that deal the cards of life, a couple cannot make it together. If a couple is going to make a success of life, however, they are going to have to be patient, gentle, and forgiving with each other. The God of scripture would have had to walk away from humans many times if patience and understanding were absent.

8.4 "Put Down That Paper and Talk to Me!": Rapport-talk and Report-talk
Deborah Tannen

I WAS SITTING IN A SUBURBAN LIVING ROOM, SPEAKING TO A WOMEN'S GROUP that had invited men to join them for the occasion of my talk about communication between women and men. During the discussion, one man was particularly talkative, full of lengthy comments and explanations. When I made the observation that women often complain that their husbands don't talk to them enough, this man volunteered that he heartily agreed. He gestured toward his wife, who had sat silently beside him on the couch throughout the evening, and said, "She's the talker in our family."

Everyone in the room burst into laughter. The man looked puzzled and hurt. "It's true," he explained. "When I come home from work, I usually have nothing to say, but she never runs out. If it weren't for her, we'd spend the whole evening in silence." Another woman expressed a similar paradox about her husband: "When we go out, he's the life of the party. If I happen to be in another room, I can always hear his voice above the others. But when we're home, he doesn't have that much to say. I do most of the talking."

Who talks more, women or men? According to the stereotype, women talk too much. Linguist Jennifer Coates notes some proverbs:

A woman's tongue wags like a lamb's tail.
Foxes are all tail and women are all tongue.
The North Sea will sooner be found wanting in water than
a woman be at a loss for a word.

Throughout history, women have been punished for talking too much or in the wrong way. Linguist Connie Eble lists a variety of physical punishments used in Colonial America: Women were strapped to ducking stools and held underwater until they nearly drowned, put into the stocks with signs pinned to them, gagged, and silenced by a cleft stick applied to their tongues.

Though such institutionalized corporal punishments have given way to informal, often psychological ones, modern stereotypes are not much different from those expressed in the old proverbs. Women are believed to talk too much. Yet study after study finds that it is men who talk more at meetings, in mixed-group discussions, and in classrooms where girls or young women sit next to boys or young men. For example, communications researchers Barbara and Gene Eakins tape-recorded and studied seven university faculty meetings. They found that, with one exception, men spoke more often and, without exception, spoke for a longer time. The men's turns ranged from 10.66 to 17.07 seconds, while the women's turns ranged from 3 to 10 seconds. In other words, the women's longest turns were still shorter than the men's shortest turns.

When a public lecture is followed by questions from the floor, or a talk show host opens the phones, the first voice to be heard asking a question is almost always a man's. And when they ask questions or offer comments from the audience, men tend to talk longer. Linguist Marjorie Swacker recorded question-and-answer sessions at academic conferences. Women were highly visible as speakers at the conferences studied; they presented 40.7 percent of the papers at the conferences studied and made up 42 percent of the audiences. But when it came to volunteering and being called on to ask questions, women contributed only 27.4 percent. Furthermore, the women's questions, on the average, took less than half as much time as the men's. (The mean was 23.1 seconds for women, 52.7 for men.) This happened, Swacker shows, because men (but not women) tended to preface their questions with statements, ask more than one question, and follow up the speaker's answer with another question or comment.

I have observed this pattern at my own lectures, which concern issues of direct relevance to women. Regardless of the proportion of women and men in the audience, men almost invariably ask the first question, more questions, and longer questions. In these situations, women often feel that men are talking too much. I recall one discussion period following a lecture I gave to a group assembled in a bookstore. The group was composed mostly of women, but most of the discussion was being conducted by men in the audience. At one point, a man sitting in the middle was talking at such great length that several women in the front rows began shifting in their seats and rolling their eyes at me. Ironically, what he was going on about was how frustrated he feels when he has to listen to women going on and on about topics he finds boring and unimportant.

Rapport-Talk and Report-Talk

Who talks more, then, women or men? The seemingly contradictory evidence is reconciled by the difference between what I call *public* and *private speaking*. More men feel comfortable doing "public speaking," while more women feel comfortable doing "private" speaking. Another way of capturing these differences is by using the terms *report-talk* and *rapport-talk*.

For most women, the language of conversation is primarily a language of rapport: a way of establishing connections and negotiating relationships. Emphasis is placed on displaying similarities and matching experiences. From childhood, girls criticize peers who try to stand out or appear better than others. People feel their closest connections at home, or in settings where they *feel* at home — with one or a few people they feel close to and comfortable with — in other words, during private speaking. But even the most public situations can be approached like private speaking.

For most men, talk is primarily a means to preserve independence and negotiate and maintain status in a hierarchical social order. This is done by exhibiting knowledge and skill, and by holding center stage through verbal performance such as storytelling, joking, or imparting information. From childhood, men learn to use talking as a way to get and keep attention. So they are more comfortable speaking in larger groups made up of people they know less well — in the broadest sense, "public speaking." But even the most private situations can be approached like public speaking, more like giving a report than establishing rapport.

Private Speaking: The Wordy Woman and the Mute Man

What is the source of the stereotype that women talk a lot? Dale Spender suggests that most people feel instinctively (if not consciously) that women, like children, should be seen and not heard, so any amount of talk from them seems like too much. Studies have shown that if women and men talk equally in a group, people think the women talked more. So there is truth to Spender's view. But another explanation is that men think women talk a lot because they hear women talking in situations where men would not: on the telephone; or in social situations with friends, when they are not discussing topics that men find inherently interesting; or, like the couple at the women's group, at home alone — in other words, in private speaking.

Home is the setting for an American icon that features the silent man and the talkative woman. And this icon, which grows out of the different goals and habits I have been describing, explains why the complaint most often voiced by women about the men with whom they are intimate is "He doesn't talk to me" — and the second most frequent is "He doesn't listen to me."

A woman who wrote to Ann Landers is typical:

> My husband never speaks to me when he comes home from work. When I ask, "How did everything go today?" he says, "Rough . . ." or "It's a jungle out there." (We live in Jersey and he works in New York City.)
>
> It's a different story when we have guests or go visiting. Paul is the gabbiest guy in the crowd — a real spellbinder. He comes up with the most interesting stories. People hang on every word. I think to myself, "Why doesn't he ever tell *me* these things?"
>
> This has been going on for 38 years. Paul started to go quiet on me after 10 years of marriage. I could never figure out why. Can you solve the mystery?
>
> —The Invisible Woman

Ann Landers suggests that the husband may not want to talk because he is tired when he comes home from work. Yet women who work come home tired too, and they are nonetheless eager to tell their partners or friends everything that happened to them during the day and what these fleeting, daily dramas made them think and feel.

Sources as lofty as studies conducted by psychologists, as down to earth as letters written to advice columnists, and as sophisticated as movies and plays come up with the same insight: Men's silence at home is a disappointment to women. Again and again, women complain, "He seems to have everything to say to everyone else, and nothing to say to me."

The film *Divorce American Style* opens with a conversation in which Debbie Reynolds is claiming that she and Dick Van Dyke don't communicate, and he is protesting that he tells her everything that's on his mind. The doorbell interrupts their quarrel, and husband and wife compose themselves before opening the door to greet their guests with cheerful smiles.

Behind closed doors, many couples are having conversations like this. Like the character played by Debbie Reynolds, women feel men don't communicate. Like the husband played by Dick Van Dyke, men feel wrongly accused. How can she be convinced that he doesn't tell her anything, while he is equally convinced he tells her everything that's on his mind? How can women and men have such different ideas about the same conversations?

When something goes wrong, people look around for a source to blame: either the person they are trying to communicate with ("You're demanding, stubborn, self-centered") or the group that the other person belongs to ("All women are demanding"; "All men are self-centered"). Some generous-minded people blame the relationship ("We just can't communicate"). But underneath, or overlaid on these types of blame cast outward, most people believe that something is wrong with them.

If individual people or particular relationships were to blame, there wouldn't be so many different people having the same problems. The real problem is conversational style. Women and men have different ways of talking. Even with the best intentions, trying to settle the problem through talk can only make things worse if it is ways of talking that are causing trouble in the first place.

Best Friends

Once again, the seeds of women's and men's styles are sown in the ways they learn to use language while growing up. In our culture, most people, but especially women, look to their closest relationships as havens in a hostile world. The center of a little girl's social life is her best friend. Girls' friendships are made and maintained by telling secrets. For grown women too, the essence of friendship is talk, telling each other what they're thinking and feeling, and what happened that day: who was at the bus stop, who called, what they said, how that made them feel. When asked who their best friends are, most women name other women they talk to regularly. When asked the same question, most men will say it's their wives. After that, many men name other men with whom they do things such as play tennis or baseball (but never just sit and talk) or a chum from high school whom they haven't spoken to in a year.

When Debbie Reynolds complained that Dick Van Dyke didn't tell her anything, and he protested that he did, both were right. She felt he didn't tell her anything because he didn't tell her the fleeting thoughts and feelings he experienced throughout the day — the kind of talk she would have with her best friend. He didn't tell her these things because to him they didn't seem like anything to tell. He told her anything that seemed important — anything he would tell his friends.

Men and women often have very different ideas of what's important — and at what point "important" topics should be raised. A woman told me, with lingering incredulity, of a conversation with her boyfriend. Knowing he had seen his friend Oliver, she asked, "What's new with Oliver?" He replied, "Nothing." But later in the conversation it came out that Oliver and his girlfriend had decided to get married. "That's nothing?" the woman gasped in frustration and disbelief.

For men, "Nothing" may be a ritual response at the start of a conversation. A college woman missed her brother but rarely called him because she found it difficult to get talk going. A typical conversation began with her asking, "What's up with you?" and his replying, "Nothing." Hearing his "Nothing" as meaning "There is nothing personal I want to talk about," she supplied talk by filling him in on her news and eventually hung up in frustration. But when she thought back, she remembered that later in the conversation he had mumbled, "Christie and I got into another fight." This came so late and so low that she didn't pick up on it. And he was probably equally frustrated that she didn't.

Many men honestly do not know what women want, and women honestly do not know why men find what they want so hard to comprehend and deliver.

"Talk to Me!"

Women's dissatisfaction with men's silence at home is captured in the stock cartoon setting of a breakfast table at which a husband and wife are sitting: He's reading a newspaper; she's glaring at the back of the newspaper. In a Dagwood strip, Blondie complains, "Every morning all he sees is the newspaper! I'll bet you don't even know I'm here!" Dagwood reassures her, "Of course I know you're here. You're my wonderful wife and I love you very much." With this, he unseeingly pats the paw of the family dog, which the wife has put in her place before leaving the room. The cartoon strip shows that Blondie is justified in feeling like the woman who wrote to Ann Landers: invisible.

Another cartoon shows a husband opening a newspaper and asking his wife, "Is there anything you would like to say to me before I begin reading the newspaper?" The reader knows that there isn't — but that as soon as he begins reading the paper, she will think of something. The cartoon highlights the difference in what women and men think talk is for: To him, talk is for information. So when his wife interrupts his reading, it must be to inform him of something that he needs to know. This being the case, she might as well tell him what she thinks he needs to know before he starts reading. But to her, talk is for interaction. Telling things is a way to show involvement, and listening is a way to show interest and caring. It is not an odd coincidence that she always thinks of things to tell him when he is reading. She feels the need for verbal interaction most keenly when he is (unaccountably, from her point of view) buried in the newspaper instead of talking to her.

Yet another cartoon shows a wedding cake that has, on top, in place of the plastic statues of bride and groom in tuxedo and gown, a breakfast scene in which an unshaven husband reads a newspaper across the table from his disgruntled wife. The cartoon reflects the enormous gulf between the romantic expectations of marriage represented by the plastic couple in traditional wedding costume, and the often disappointing reality represented by the two sides of the newspaper at the breakfast table — the front, which he is reading, and the back, at which she is glaring.

These cartoons, and many others on the same theme, are funny because people recognize their own experience in them. What's not funny is that many women are deeply hurt when men don't talk to them at home, and many men are deeply frustrated by feeling they have disappointed their partners, without understanding how they failed or how else they could have behaved.

Some men are further frustrated because, as one put it, "When in the world am I supposed to read the morning paper?" If many women are incredulous that many men do not exchange personal information with their friends, this man is incredulous that many women do not bother to read the morning paper. To him, reading the paper is an essential part of his morning ritual, and his whole day is awry if he doesn't get to read it. In his words, reading the newspaper in the morning is as important to him as putting on makeup in the morning is to many women he knows. Yet many women, he observed, either don't subscribe to a paper or don't read it until they get home in the evening. "I find this very puzzling," he said. "I can't tell you how often I have picked up a woman's morning newspaper from her front door in the evening and handed it to her when she opened the door for me."

To this man (and I am sure many others), a woman who objects to his reading the morning paper is trying to keep him from doing something essential and harmless. It's a violation of his independence — his freedom of action. But when a woman who expects her partner to talk to her is disappointed that he doesn't, she perceives his behavior as a failure of intimacy: He's keeping things from her; he's lost interest in her; he's pulling away. A woman I will call Rebecca, who is generally quite happily married, told me that this is the one source of serious dissatisfaction with her husband, Stuart. Her term for his taciturnity is *stinginess of spirit.* She tells him what she is thinking, and he listens silently. She asks him what he is thinking, and he takes a long time to answer, "I don't know." In frustration she challenges, "Is there nothing on your mind?"

For Rebecca, who is accustomed to expressing her fleeting thoughts and opinions as they come to her, *saying* nothing means *thinking* nothing. But Stuart does not assume that his passing thoughts are worthy of utterance. He is not in the habit of uttering his fleeting ruminations, so just as Rebecca "naturally" speaks her thoughts, he "naturally" dismisses his as soon as they occur to him. Speaking them would give them more weight and significance than he feels they merit. All her life she has had practice in verbalizing her thoughts and feelings in private conversations with people she is close to; all his life he has had practice in dismissing his and keeping them to himself.

What to Do With Doubts

In the above example, Rebecca was not talking about any particular kind of thoughts or feelings, just whatever Stuart might have had in mind. But the matter of giving voice to thoughts and feelings becomes particularly significant in the case of negative feelings or doubts about a relationship.

This difference was highlighted for me when a fifty-year-old divorced man told me about his experiences in forming new relationships with women. On this matter, he was clear: "I do not value my fleeting thoughts, and I do not value the fleeting thoughts of others." He felt that the relationship he was currently in had been endangered, even permanently weakened, by the woman's practice of tossing out her passing thoughts, because, early in their courtship, many of her thoughts were fears about their relationship. Not surprisingly, since they did not yet know each other well, she worried about whether she could trust him, whether their relationship would destroy her independence, whether this relationship was really right for her. He felt she should have kept these fears and doubts to herself and waited to see how things turned out.

As it happens, things turned out well. The woman decided that the relationship was right for her, she could trust him, and she did not have to give up her independence. But he felt, at the time that he told me of this, that he had still not recovered from the wear and tear of coping with her earlier doubts. As he put it, he was still dizzy from having been bounced around like a yo-yo tied to the string of her stream of consciousness.

In contrast, this man admitted, he himself goes to the other extreme: He never expresses his fears and misgivings about their relationship at all. If he's unhappy but doesn't say anything about it, his unhappiness expresses itself in a kind of distancing coldness. This response is just what women fear most, and just the reason they prefer to express dissatisfactions and doubts — as an antidote to the isolation and distance that would result from keeping them to themselves.

The different perspectives on expressing or concealing dissatisfactions and doubts may reflect a difference in men's and women's awareness of the power of their words to affect others. In repeatedly telling him what she feared about their relationship, this woman spoke as though she assumed he was invulnerable and could not be hurt by what she said; perhaps she was underestimating the power of her words to affect him. For his part, when he refrains from expressing negative thoughts or feelings, he seems to be over-estimating the power of his words to hurt her, when, ironically, she is more likely to be hurt by his silence than his words.

These women and men are talking in ways they learned as children and reinforced as young adults and then adults, in their same-gender friendships. For girls, talk is the glue that holds relationships together. Boys' relationships are held together primarily by activities: doing things together, or talking about activities such as sports or, later, politics. The forums in which men are most inclined to talk are those in which they feel the need to impress, in situations where their status is in question.

Making Adjustments

Such impasses will perhaps never be settled to the complete satisfaction of both parties, but understanding the differing views can help detoxify the situation, and both can make adjustments. Realizing that men and women have different assumptions about the place of talk in relationships, a woman can observe a man's desire to read the morning paper at the breakfast table without interpreting it as a rejection of her or a failure of their relationship. And a man can understand a woman's desire for talk without interpreting it as an unreasonable demand or a manipulative attempt to prevent him from doing what he wants to do.

A woman who had heard my interpretations of these differences between women and men told me how these insights helped her. Early in a promising relationship, a man spent the night at her apartment. It was a weeknight, and they both had to go to work the next day, so she was delighted when he made the rash and romantic suggestion that they have breakfast together and report late for work. She happily prepared breakfast, looking forward to the scene shaped in her mind: They would sit facing each other across her small table, look into each other's eyes, and say how much they liked each other and how happy they were about their growing friendship. It was against the backdrop of this heady expectation that she confronted an entirely different scene: As she placed on the table an array of lovingly prepared eggs, toast, and coffee, the man sat across her small table — and opened the newspaper in front of his face. If suggesting they have breakfast together had seemed like an invitation to get closer, in her view (or obstructing her view) the newspaper was now erected as a paper-thin but nonetheless impenetrable barrier between them.

Had she known nothing of the gender differences I discuss, she would simply have felt hurt and dismissed this man as yet another clunker. She would have concluded that, having enjoyed the night with her, he was now availing himself of her further services as a short-order cook. Instead, she realized that, unlike her, he did not feel the need for talk to reinforce their intimacy. The companionability of her presence was all he needed, and that did not mean that he didn't cherish her presence. By the same token, had he understood the essential role played by talk in women's definition of intimacy, he could have put off reading the paper and avoided putting her off.

The Comfort of Home

For everyone, home is a place to be offstage. But the comfort of home can have opposite and incompatible meanings for women and men. For many men, the comfort of home means freedom from having to prove themselves and impress through verbal display. At last, they are in a situation where talk is not required. They are free to remain silent. But for women, home is a place where they are free to talk, and where they feel the greatest need for talk, with those they are closest to. For them, the comfort of home means the freedom to talk without worrying about how their talk will be judged.

This view emerged in a study by linguist Alice Greenwood of the conversations that took place among her three preadolescent children and their friends. Her daughters and son gave different reasons for their preferences in dinner guests. Her daughter Stacy said she would not want to invite people she didn't know well because then she would have to be "polite and quiet" and put on good manners. Greenwood's other daughter, Denise, said she liked to have her friend Meryl over because she could act crazy with Meryl and didn't have to worry about her manners, as she would with certain other friends who "would go around talking to people probably." But Denise's twin brother, Dennis, said nothing about having to watch his manners or worry about how others would judge his behavior. He simply said that he liked to have over friends with whom he could joke and laugh a lot. The girls' comments show that for them being close means being able to talk freely. And being with relative strangers means having to watch what they say and do. This insight holds a clue to the riddle of who talks more, women or men.

Public Speaking: The Talkative Man and the Silent Woman

So far I have been discussing the private scenes in which many men are silent and many women are talkative. But there are other scenes in which the roles are reversed. Returning to Rebecca and Stuart, we saw that when they are home alone, Rebecca's thoughts find their way into words effortlessly, whereas Stuart finds he can't come up with anything to say. The reverse happens when they are in other situations. For example, at a meeting of the neighborhood council or the parents' association at their children's school, it is Stuart who stands up and speaks. In that situation, it is Rebecca who is silent, her tongue tied by an acute awareness of all the negative reactions people could have to what she might say, all the mistakes she might make in trying to express her ideas. If she musters her courage and prepares to say something, she needs time to formulate it and then waits to be recognized by the chair. She cannot just jump up and start talking the way Stuart and some other men can.

Eleanor Smeal, president of the Fund for the Feminist Majority, was a guest on a call-in radio talk show, discussing abortion. No subject could be of more direct concern to women, yet during the hour-long show, all the callers except two were men. Diane Rehm, host of a radio talk show, expresses puzzlement that although the audience for her show is evenly split between women and men, 90 percent of the callers to the show are men. I am convinced that the reason is not that women are uninterested in the subjects discussed on the show. I would wager that women listeners are bringing up the subjects they heard on *The Diane Rehm Show* to their friends and family over lunch, tea, and dinner. But fewer of them call in because to do so would be putting themselves on display, claiming public attention for what they have to say, catapulting themselves onto center stage.

I myself have been the guest on innumerable radio and television talk shows. Perhaps I am unusual in being completely at ease in this mode of display. But perhaps I am not unusual at all, because, although I am comfortable in the role of invited expert, I have never called in to a talk show I was listening to, although I have often had ideas to contribute. When I am the guest, my position of authority is granted before I begin to speak. Were I to call in, I would be claiming that right on my own. I would have to establish my credibility by explaining who I am, which might seem self-aggrandizing, or not explain who I am and risk having my comments ignored or not valued. For similar reasons, though I am comfortable lecturing to groups numbering in the thousands, I rarely ask questions following another lecturer's talk, unless I know both the subject and the group very well.

My own experience and that of talk show hosts seems to hold a clue to the difference in women's and men's attitudes toward talk: Many men are more comfortable than most women in using talk to claim attention. And this difference lies at the heart of the distinction between report-talk and rapport-talk.

Report-Talk in Private

Report-talk, or what I am calling public speaking, does not arise only in the literally public situation of formal speeches delivered to a listening audience. The more people there are in a conversation, the less well you know them, and the more status differences among them, the more a conversation is *like* public speaking or report-talk. The fewer the people, the more intimately you know them, and the more equal their status, the more it is like private speaking or rapport-talk. Furthermore, women feel a situation is more "public" — in the sense that they have to be on good behavior — if there are men present, except perhaps for family members. Yet even in families, the mother and children may feel their home to be "backstage" when Father is not home, "onstage" when he is: Many children are instructed to be on good behavior when Daddy is home. This may be because he is not home often, or because Mother — or Father — doesn't want the children to disturb him when he is.

The difference between public and private speaking also explains the stereotype that women don't tell jokes. Although some women are great raconteurs who can keep a group spellbound by recounting jokes and funny stories, there are fewer such personalities among women than among men. Many women who do tell jokes to large groups of people come from ethnic backgrounds in which verbal performance is highly valued. For example, many of the great women stand-up comics, such as Fanny Brice and Joan Rivers, came from Jewish backgrounds.

Although it's not true that women don't tell jokes, it is true that many women are less likely than men to tell jokes in large groups, especially groups including men. So it's not surprising that men get the impression that women never tell jokes at all. Folklorist Carol Mitchell studied joke telling on a college campus. She found that men told most of their jokes to other men, but they also told many jokes to mixed groups and to women. Women, however, told most of their jokes to other women, fewer to men, and very few to groups that included men as well as women. Men preferred and were more likely to tell jokes when they had an audience: at least two, often four or more. Women preferred a small audience of one or two, rarely more than three. Unlike men, they were reluctant to tell jokes in front of people they didn't know well. Many women flatly refused to tell jokes they knew if there were four or more in the group, promising to tell them later in private. Men never refused the invitation to tell jokes.

All of Mitchell's results fit in with the picture I have been drawing of public and private speaking. In a situation in which there are more people in the audience, more men, or more strangers, joke telling, like any other form of verbal performance, requires speakers to claim center stage and prove their abilities. These are the situations in which many women are reluctant to talk. In a situation that is more private, because the audience is small, familiar, and perceived to be members of a community (for example, other women), they are more likely to talk.

The idea that telling jokes is a kind of self-display does not imply that it is selfish or self-centered. The situation of joke telling illustrates that status and connection entail each other. Entertaining others is a way of establishing connections with them, and telling jokes can be a kind of gift giving, where the joke is a gift that brings pleasure to receivers. The key issue is asymmetry: One person is the teller and the others are the audience. If these roles are later exchanged — for example, if the joke telling becomes a round in which one person after another takes the role of teller — then there is symmetry on the broad scale, if not in the individual act. However, if women habitually take the role of appreciative audience and never take the role of joke teller, the asymmetry of the individual joke telling is diffused through the larger interaction as well. This is a hazard for women. A hazard for men is that continually telling jokes can be distancing. This is the effect felt by a man who complained that when he talks to his father on the phone, all his father does is tell him jokes. An extreme instance of a similar phenomenon is the class clown, who, according to teachers, is nearly always a boy.

Rapport-Talk in Public

Just as conversations that take place at home among friends can be like public speaking, even a public address can be like private speaking: for example, by giving a lecture full of personal examples and stories.

At the executive committee of a fledgling professional organization, the outgoing president, Fran, suggested that the organization adopt the policy of having presidents deliver a presidential address. To explain and support her proposal, she told a personal anecdote: Her cousin was the president of a more established professional organization at the time that Fran held the same position in this one. Fran's mother had been talking to her cousin's mother on the telephone. Her cousin's mother told Fran's mother that her daughter was preparing her presidential address, and she asked when Fran's presidential address was scheduled to be. Fran was embarrassed to admit to her mother that she was not giving one. This made her wonder whether the organization's professional identity might not be enhanced if it emulated the more established organizations.

Several men on the committee were embarrassed by Fran's reference to her personal situation and were not convinced by her argument. It seemed to them not only irrelevant but unseemly to talk about her mother's telephone conversations at an executive committee meeting. Fran had approached the meeting — a relatively public context — as an extension of the private kind. Many women's tendency to use personal experience and examples, rather than abstract argumentation, can be understood from the perspective of their orientation to language as it is used in private speaking.

A study by Celia Roberts and Tom Jupp of a faculty meeting at a secondary school in England found that the women's arguments did not carry weight with their male colleagues because they tended to use their own experience as evidence, or argue about the effect of policy on individual students. The men at the meeting argued from a completely different perspective, making categorical statements about right and wrong.

The same distinction is found in discussions at home. A man told me that he felt critical of what he perceived as his wife's lack of logic. For example, he recalled a conversation in which he had mentioned an article he had read in *The New York Times* claiming that today's college students are not as idealistic as students were in the 1960s. He was inclined to accept this claim. His wife questioned it, supporting her argument with the observation that her niece and her niece's friends were very idealistic indeed. He was incredulous and scornful of her faulty reasoning; it was obvious to him that a single personal example is neither evidence nor argumentation — it's just anecdote. It did not occur to him that he was dealing with a different logical system, rather than a lack of logic.

The logic this woman was employing was making sense of the world as a more private endeavor — observing and integrating her personal experience and drawing connections to the experiences of others. The logic the husband took for granted was a more public endeavor — more like gathering information, conducting a survey, or devising arguments by rules of formal logic as one might in doing research.

Another man complained about what he and his friends call women's "shifting sands" approach to discussion. These men feel that whereas they try to pursue an argument logically, step by step, until it is settled, women continually change course in midstream. He pointed to the short excerpt from *Divorce American Style* quoted above as a case in point. It seemed to him that when Debbie Reynolds said, "I can't argue now. I have to take the French bread out of the oven," she was evading the argument because she had made an accusation — "All you do is criticize" — that she could not support.

This man also offered an example from his own experience. His girlfriend had told him of a problem she had because her boss wanted her to do one thing and she wanted to do another. Taking the boss's view for the sake of argumentation, he pointed out a negative consequence that would result if she did what she wanted. She countered that the same negative consequence would result if she did what the boss wanted. He complained that she was shifting over to the other field of battle — what would happen if she followed her boss's will — before they had made headway with the first — what would happen if she followed her own.

Speaking for the Team

A final puzzle on the matter of public and private speaking is suggested by the experience I related at the opening of this chapter, in which a woman's group I addressed had invited men to participate, and a talkative man had referred to his silent wife as "the talker in our family." Following their laughter, other women in the group commented that this woman was not usually silent. When their meetings consisted of women only, she did her share of talking. Why, then, was she silent on this occasion?

One possibility is that my presence transformed the private-speaking group into a public-speaking event. Another transformation was that there were men in the group. In a sense, most women feel they are "backstage" when there are no men around. When men are present women are "onstage," insofar as they feel they must watch their behavior more. Another possibility is that it was not the presence of men in general that affected this woman's behavior, but the presence of *her husband*. One interpretation is that she was somehow cowed, or silenced, by her husband's presence. But another is that she felt they were a team. Since he was talking a lot, the team would be taking up too much time if she spoke too. She also may have felt that because he was representing their team, she didn't have to, much as many women let their husbands drive if they are in the car, but do the driving themselves if their husbands are not there.

Obviously, not every woman becomes silent when her husband joins a group; after all, there were many women in the group who talked a lot, and many had brought spouses. But several other couples told me of similar experiences. For example, when one couple took evening classes together, he was always an active participant in class discussion, while she said very little. But one semester they had decided to take different classes, and then she found that she was a talkative member of the class she attended alone.

Such a development can be viewed in two different ways. If talking in a group is a good thing — a privilege and a pleasure — then the silent woman will be seen as deprived of her right to speak, deprived of her voice. But the pleasures of report-talk are not universally admired. There are many who do not wish to speak in a group. In this view, a woman who feels she has no need to speak because her husband is doing it for her might feel privileged, just as a woman who does not like to drive might feel lucky that she doesn't have to when her husband is there — and a man who does not like to drive might feel unlucky that he has to, like it or not.

Avoiding Mutual Blame

The difference between public and private speaking, or report-talk and rapport-talk, can be understood in terms of status and connection. It is not surprising that women are most comfortable talking when they feel safe and close, among friends and equals, whereas men feel comfortable talking when there is a need to establish and maintain their status in a group. But the situation is complex, because status and connection are bought with the same currency. What seems like a bid for status could be intended as a display of closeness, and what seems like distancing may have been intended to avoid the appearance of pulling rank. Hurtful and unjustified misinterpretations can be avoided by understanding the conversational styles of the other gender.

When men do all the talking at meetings, many women — including researchers — see them as "dominating" the meeting, intentionally preventing women from participating, publicly flexing their higher-status muscles. But the *result* that men do most of the talking does not necessarily mean that men *intend* to prevent women from speaking. Those who readily speak up assume that others are as free as they are to take the floor. In this sense, men's speaking out freely can be seen as evidence that they assume women are at the same level of status: "We are all equals," the metamessage of their behavior could be, "competing for the floor." If this is indeed the intention (and I believe it often, though not always, is), a woman can recognize women's lack of participation at meetings and take measures to redress the imbalance, without blaming men for intentionally locking them out.

The culprit, then, is not an individual man or even men's styles alone, but the difference between women's and men's styles. If that is the case, then both can make adjustments. A woman can push herself to speak up without being invited, or begin to speak without waiting for what seems a polite pause. But the adjustment should not be one-sided. A man can learn that a woman who is not accustomed to speaking up in groups is *not* as free as he is to do so. Someone who is waiting for a nice long pause before asking her question does not find the stage set for her appearance, as do those who are not awaiting a pause, the moment after (or before) another speaker stops talking. Someone who expects to be invited to speak ("You haven't said much, Millie. What do you think?") is not accustomed to leaping in and claiming the floor for herself. As in so many areas, being admitted as an equal is not in itself assurance of equal opportunity, if one is not accustomed to playing the game in the way it is being played. Being admitted to a dance does not ensure the participation of someone who has learned to dance to a different rhythm.

Parenting

9.1   The First Child
Kathleen Fischer Hart and Thomas N. Hart

DAVE AND KELLY'S FIRST CHILD BROUGHT A REVOLUTION IN THEIR MARRIAGE which put a real strain on their relationship. Dave and Kelly had known each other for three years, and married in their mid-twenties. Both of them very much enjoyed the bar scene. They liked to drink, dance, and play pool. Dave had become especially adept at pool, and was making a little money at it. He began to get into tournament play. Dave and Kelly had planned to have children sooner or later, but the pregnancy occurred before they were psychologically ready and took them both back a bit.

As the child grew in her, Kelly herself began to change. She felt she was outgrowing the bar scene. As she felt herself becoming a mother, she wanted to drink less and stay home more. She was no longer in much condition for dancing anyway.

When the child was born, she felt a deep joy, and tended the baby with the greatest affection. As far as Dave was concerned, the birth was all right, no big deal. But it began to bother him increasingly that Kelly so seldom wanted to go out to the bars with him. What he had thought was a special problem belonging to the last months of pregnancy and the first months after childbirth began to establish itself as a pattern. Kelly had simply moved on to another stage of life. In outside relationships too, she began to gravitate toward other young mothers rather than to their former bar friends.

Dave could see it only in competitive terms. The baby had taken over the love which used to be his. Fighting increased. Neither seemed to be able to get through to the other. Dave spent little time with the baby, whom he resented, and considerable time away. Since much of the time they spent together went into the argument they could not resolve, Kelly had little appetite for lovemaking. Matters got worse until Kelly and Dave finally parted.

Not all stories of a first child end this way, of course. A child can bring many blessings to a marriage. But Dave and Kelly's story points to some of the factors which need to be considered before a newly married couple is ready for a child, and some of the adjustments which will be required when the child comes. In this chapter we will look both at the challenges and at the blessings. Let us consider the challenges first.

The Challenges of Childbearing
1. Lifestyle.

The adjustment begins early, with the beginning of pregnancy itself. "Your body begins to prepare you," one young mother told us. "Pregnancy starts to cut into your working and social life. You feel like staying home more, which is what you will have to do when the baby comes. You have to watch more carefully what you eat and drink, and that will continue as you breast-feed. You become uncomfortable during the night, and sometimes the baby's movements awaken you, a preparation for nights to come. Already you are losing some of your freedom, and the summons to think beyond yourself and your mate is already there."

During pregnancy, the life of the father is affected too. His wife is tired, and sick more often. Sometimes she is moody or depressed, as pregnancy brings physiological change. In some ways, she grows more inward, focused on the life developing inside. She usually wants to share with him what she is feeling and thinking about during this period, but it takes some evidence of interest, patience, and understanding on his part. In their absence, she may feel unhappily alone and unappreciated, and possibly even resentful. Sickness, fatigue, and moodiness may bring changes to a couple's lovemaking patterns. The emerging mother may feel less interest, at least in intercourse. On the other hand, she may need and appreciate being held and other signs of affection more than ever. She may also need to be assured that her body is still beautiful, in some ways more beautiful than ever.

2. Finances.

The first child makes a financial impact. First there are maternity clothes. Then there are outlays for furniture, clothes, toys, and food for the baby. There are all the medical expenses of pregnancy, childbirth, and followup care. Another expense will become a budget item after the birth — babysitting. Perhaps the greatest impact of all will come from a mother's leaving the workforce near the end of pregnancy and staying out for some months or years to come. If a couple has become accustomed to two incomes, and the woman's identity and life-satisfaction derive heavily from her work outside the home, this will be a major adjustment. "It took me about a year," one mother told us, "to feel I didn't have to work outside the home. It was hard for me to feel I was still a contributing member of the family. The change also meant we had to do without some things we had previously enjoyed."

3. Responsibilities.

Some couples do not discuss parental responsibilities very much beforehand, and developments catch them unprepared. The adjustments are challenging enough even with good preparation. For instance, who will do what after the baby is born? Who will get up during the night, if it is not a question of breast-feeding? Who will get up to take care of the baby or young child on weekend mornings? Will Dad ever take care of the child all day Saturday or Sunday (or both) while Mom goes off to other pursuits? If Mom did all the cooking and housecleaning before the child came, will she simply continue to do so after the birth? If so, resentment is likely to build, because taking care of a baby or young child all day every day is extremely demanding. "What galls me," a new mother told us, "is that he still expects his dinner to be on the table every night when he gets home, including weekends, and when dinner is finished he goes out to the living room to watch TV." Another said, "He still loves his job more than anything else. That's supposed to be his domain, and home and kids are supposed to be mine. It would mean so much to me if we could share both areas more."

Sometimes a husband realizes what an impact a new child has had, and genuinely wants to help his wife. But he comes to her as helper, awaiting his assignment, rather than as someone who is really taking responsibility. If asked, he will shop, do the laundry, or clean the house. But he expects to be thanked when he is finished, and then the responsibility is hers again. What is much more helpful to the new mother is when her husband simply takes over the cleaning, or the shopping, or some of the cooking, and makes them his own. Now he is a collaborator rather than a helper. Now they will be thanking *each other* for taking care of various parenting and household tasks. It is interesting how the bones of contention in unhappy marriages are the gifts which husband and wife freely give one another in marriages that work. This gift-giving is contagious, as well as fun.

> Give, and it will be given to you; good measure, pressed down, shaken together, and running over they will pour into your lap. For the measure you use with others they in turn will use with you (Lk 6:38).

4. The Couple Relationship Itself.

The first child brings some loss of freedom to both husband and wife. No longer can they simply get up and go out whenever they want to. The needs of a third person must always be taken into account. When a fourth is added to the third, all moves become still more complex. But it is not just a question of going out. It becomes more difficult to make time for each other.

Since fatigue is already one of the major factors affecting a couple's sexual relationship, the fatigue that comes with pregnancy and child care will also have to be figured in. Uninterrupted adult conversation will also be harder to manage. And getting away to be together will now involve the difficulty of finding and the cost of paying a babysitter.

And yet a couple has to be creative in continuing to make time for each other and for the relationship, or all family members will suffer. If they are not careful, they will soon know one another only as parents, no longer as friends and lovers. They will have a price to pay for that someday, even if they can manage to stave off payment until the last child leaves home and they are left staring across the living room at one another as strangers. Much anguish can be avoided if they are aware of the danger and taking measures against it all the time. We make time for the things that seem important to us. Can we afford not to make time to remain friends and lovers? Being good parents is important. But if we allow distance to develop between us, we can hardly even be good parents, let alone models of marriage for our children. In any case, our couple relationship remains primary. It will outlive the parenting function by many years.

Sharing time together as a couple, and sharing the parenting, are the best remedies for a husband's developing jealousy over what happens to his wife as she becomes a mother. Then he does not stand outside that new relationship, but inside of it. He has his own relationship to his child, and still a primary relationship to his wife, whom he also supports in her role as mother. "When I hear a man brag that he has never changed a diaper in his life, it pains me," a young mother told us. "What a loss. There is nothing dirty about changing a diaper. It is a great chance to fondle and tickle and kiss and play with your baby. My husband cherishes the chance as much as I do. And the baby loves it."

In light of the various challenges we have considered, when is a couple ready to have their first child? Some couples do not have the leisure to ask the question. They are pregnant when they marry, or they already have children from a previous marriage. For those who do have the leisure to consider the question, the answer is: when they have looked at all the implications and feel ready — that is, when the financial conditions are in place, the impact on the marriage has been measured and plans made for dealing with the new responsibilities, and, above all, when the marital relationship itself is stable and promising. There are plenty of challenges at the beginning of marriage just in terms of living together as a couple, and it seems like a good idea to weather these before taking on the added responsibility of a child. Couples sometimes hope a child will pull a struggling marriage together. That is a very risky bet. A new presence in the home can hardly solve the problems. It will make many of them more acute. Studies are clear on this. When a marriage is in trouble, it is not a good time to have a child.

The Blessings

The challenges to a married couple which come from bringing a child into the world are only part of the story. The blessings also abound. Childbearing is the other part of the mystery and gift of sexuality. It is the power and privilege of being able to co-create with God, to cooperate in generating and fashioning a new human being. Much excitement and happiness attend this process when the stage is properly set for it.

Don and Terri waited longer than many couples do, or need to, before they decided to have a child — four years. Children were in their pre-marriage plans, but career and other considerations counseled delay. In fact, Don and Terri were not that sure of their marriage all through the first three years. Then some breakthroughs occurred in their communication, and a new spirit of concession and cooperation was born. With a fresh confidence in each other and in their ability to make it together for life, they revived their discussion of children and decided it was time.

As they made their plans and began actively to seek conception, Don and Terri noticed a strengthening of the bond between them. For the first time since the days they had planned for their marriage, they felt that they were working together toward the same goal. Then they were greeted with a surprise. Six months went by and there was still no conception. It seemed a very long time to them, and they wondered if it would ever end. It made them doubt their own fertility. As they prayed over it, they came to a deep realization: life is a gift, and it comes from the hand of God. They could do certain things, but the matter ultimately rested with God. Late in the seventh month conception did occur, and Terri and Don rejoiced exceedingly, the way the people of the Old Testament rejoiced when a couple was blessed with a child.

New realizations came to Terri and Don as the pregnancy developed. There were so *many* things outside their control — the sex of the child, the color of its eyes, the makeup of its personality, even its health. They began to see themselves more as caretakers of a human person who would be entrusted to them than as its owners, and in wonder they lived with the gradual hidden fashioning of the body and spirit of this new person. Terri marveled at the preparation of her own body and emotions for this new stage of her life. Along with the wonder and worship went the usual sickness and fatigue, and Terri and Don were challenged to adjust to these developments.

The process of childbirth and the tiny, perfectly formed body of their new little boy were further cause for amazement. The boy knew how to suck at the breast without ever having been taught, and the mother/child bond was deepened through this experience of feeding. Terri reflected on the religious meaning of the gift of the body — hers to Don and his to her in sexual relating, and now her gift of the body to this little infant as physical presence, warmth, and food. She understood more profoundly the meaning of

Christ's gift of the body to us in the Eucharist, the gift of the body being the gift of the self as food and life. Breast-feeding times became for her occasions of this sort of simple contemplation. She found herself quietly marveling at the deep mystery of things.

In the months that followed, Terri and Don watched the gradual emergence of the personality — the grasping of the little hands, the first hesitant smile, the dawning of curiosity. Then came the crawling, the standing on two uncertain legs, and the first faltering steps. Never having watched this development so closely in anyone else before, Don and Terri were amazed at each stage in the process. There were laughs, and there were truly precious moments to share. As the child's life unfolded, their deepest sense was that a real gift had been given to them, and that one of the most important things they had to do the rest of their life was to love that child.

Another young mother told us how she felt a strong desire to clean the house as the day for delivery drew near. She had all the carpets shampooed and the walls washed, so that the baby would have a really clean environment. And then she awoke on a deeper level still. She felt a movement of the Spirit within to do something about her own house, to clean out the locked up room within herself. She took care of some things she had long put off, and ended with the sacrament of reconciliation. After that, she felt ready, at peace with herself and the world.

One of the things children do is show you yourself in a way you have not seen yourself before. In their interaction with you, they reflect you back to yourself. Much of what you see is beautiful, and you didn't know it was in you. Children give you an opportunity to see sides of each other that you had not seen before. The husband watches in amazement as the mother comes out of the wife. The wife watches in joy as the father comes out of the husband. It is often a pleasure to stand back and watch the interaction between the child and your mate; it makes your mate dearer.

There is another side to this mirroring too. "She made us clean up our act," a young couple said. "We started watching our language. We became more aware of patterns of behavior we did not want to model for her. Why, she even got us back to church. We found ourselves examining our whole way of life in the light of our new responsibility, because we really wanted to do right by this child." And so there is a blessed stretching that takes place as a couple becomes generative. Their time is no longer their own. They have to make sacrifices, as they learn to expand their love to embrace each successive newcomer.

Sometimes God is seen and understood in a new way as a result of the parenting experience. The father of a one-year-old boy told us that his son changed his whole image of God. "I look at that little boy and I see myself in him. Every once in a while he gets a look or makes a gesture that is a perfect reproduction of me. And he is so lovable, you know? What has come home to me is that God sees me that way, and loves me the way I love that little boy." A young mother told us her little girl changed her whole outlook on life. "She wakes up every morning eager to greet the new day, with a smile as big as the sun. She is rarin' to go. How can you get out of bed grumpy with someone like that in the house?"

We talked to a couple of parents of many years, whose children were raised. A woman told us she would not have exchanged the experience for anything. Her children, she said, had taught her most of the really valuable things she knew, had made her the person she was. The other was a father of nine, who had raised his children on a tight salary through many years of hard work and sacrifice. On his deathbed, he was asked by one of his children whether it hadn't been a terribly heavy burden all those years, and whether he hadn't had second thoughts about it all from time to time. "Oh, no," he said with a happy smile. "It was all worth it. It was great fun."

9.2   Ten Ingredients of Parenting
Victor M. Parachin

WHEN MICHAEL WAS ONLY SEVEN YEARS OLD, HIS FATHER ABANDONED HIM and his mother leaving them to live in poverty and on the wrong side of the tracks. As a result, the mother had to work all day and hold a second part-time job as a waitress several evenings a week.

In spite of these difficulties and an impoverished economic environment, Michael graduated from college and dental school, earning and paying all of his expenses. He established his own private dental practice which is now the largest in his state.

On the other hand, there is Robert who was raised in a two-parent home. The family income allowed them to live comfortably in a prestigious suburb of Chicago and to send Robert to an expensive private Ivy League school. Three weeks into his first semester Robert attempted suicide. He had failed to get a membership in the school's leading fraternity.

The contrast between these two people is striking. During the last fifteen years as a minister and family counselor, I have worked closely with thousands of families. Often I have asked myself these questions, "What makes the difference? Why do some children adjust and adapt to the changes of life while others give up and give in?"

From experience, I know that the way children evolve and mature has little to do with family income, parental education, and a two-parent or single-parent home. Adults who raise strong, secure, stable children have a parenting style that includes a combination of the following ten important ingredients.

Love. More than anything else, children who grow up well adjusted and able to manage life had a loving parent. Friends of mine learned their one-year-old daughter had a hip dislocation. To correct the problem, the little girl entered the hospital for a week of traction and subsequent surgery.

It was impressive to observe her parents. They both worked outside the home, but they arranged their work schedules so that they could spend twelve-hour shifts at the hospital. For more than a week they ate their meals and slept in their daughter's room. Caroline was never without a parent. She may not remember the hospital confinement, but she will know that her parents loved her so much that everything else became secondary to her care.

Attention. Good parents spend quality time with their children. They will lay the newspaper aside, turn off the television, and listen. Richard Daley, the late mayor of Chicago, had a young family when he was mayor in the 1950s and 1960s. Even though his schedule was crowded and hectic with speeches and meetings, the mayor was home each evening promptly at six o'clock — dinner time with his family. At the dinner table he heard from his children the events of their day, the joys and the disappointments.

Instill persistence. Strong kids almost always come from homes where the parents emphasize perseverance and persistence. They coach and encourage the children not to give up easily.

Here is an example. During lunch with a friend who has a six-year-old son, he mentioned that Michael asked to take a ten-week introductory class in karate. He enrolled in the class but after six lessons Michael wanted to drop it. He didn't like the rigor and discipline. His father encouraged him to complete the remaining four sessions, reminding the lad that ". . . our family never quits."

That lesson in persistence could be invaluable for Michael. When he is an adult and has a setback for some reason or another, he will find creative ways to weather the storm or bring the issue to a healthy resolution.

Nurture faith. Whether parents adhere to the tenets of the Bible, the Koran, the Four Noble Truths of Buddhism, or their own ethical code, they attempt to inculcate values and attitudes that can be an anchor during hard times.

Jan was in her forties when her mother died. The two of them had been extremely close and were not only mother and daughter but also good friends. The loss was a tremendous blow for Jan. When she was a child, she and her family were active in their Jewish faith. Gradually, though, Jan drifted away from regular attendance at the synagogue. Since her mother's death, however, she has returned and worships weekly. The faith her mother instilled in her as a child now sustains her in this time of grief.

242 \ *Topic 9 — Parenting*

Loyalty. Children may face problems that they are unable to resolve. If parents have established a good rapport with them and the children feel secure, they know they can share the issue at home. Sadly this is not always the case.

This is true of a woman who came to me because her marriage was in trouble. Eventually she confided that when she was seventeen and dating the man who later became her husband, she had become pregnant. Frightened and unable to approach either set of parents, she was pressured into having an abortion. To this day she resents him for forcing that decision upon her. Consequently, their marriage is in constant turmoil and struggle.

A parent who raises a self-reliant child conveys to that child that s/he can bring any problem home for discussion and sharing.

Liberty. Healthy parenting is not overprotective. Parents must give children the freedom to make decisions on their own and to deal with the challenges of life in their own way.

I recall Sally, a junior in high school, who had to tell her mother she was pregnant. The mother was upset, but she wisely asked Sally what she planned to do. Together they talked about the pregnancy. Sally chose to have the baby and give it up for adoption. Her mother really wanted to keep the baby and raise the child, but she acquiesced to Sally's decision and respected her choice.

Provide information. Involved parents provide their children with information. Such parents know information is power and that knowledge allows children to master their universe.

9.3   Stepmothers
Bobbie Reed

"HAVING A STEPFATHER IS OK," SAID 10-YEAR-OLD JAY EMPHATICALLY, "BUT A stepmother is yucky!"

This from a boy who has had two stepmothers and who has been very close and loving with both!

Stepmotherhood as a general concept has been much maligned. Fairy tales tell of "wicked" stepmothers. Shakespeare wrote of cruelty and dishonesty in steprelationships. And the classics show the various adversities that befall children who have the misfortune of having a stepmother! Since little has been done to force some reality into the general connotation of stepmotherhood, it is no wonder that the negative perception persists.

True, there are wicked, cruel, uncaring stepmothers, just as there are wicked, cruel, and unfeeling mothers. But both are in the minority when compared to the total population of women raising children.

In fact, sometimes a stepmother is in a better position than the natural mother to have a positive influence on the development of a child.

- If the stepmother is married to a noncustodial father, her contact is probably limited to short-term visits during which it is possible to maintain calm consistency. The custodial parent can be so bogged down with the day-to-day problems that survival becomes more critical than teaching the child.

- If the stepmother does not have a career outside of the home, she has more time to interact with children than does a mother who must work to support her family.

- Some people are better at parenting than others. A stepmother may be one of those people who has just the right blend of patience, wisdom, and humor to make parenting a joy.

- If children, especially adolescents, are resentfully struggling with their mother for independence, they sometimes turn to their stepmother for the nurturing they still desire and need.

Whether or not the relationship between the stepmother and the children works out depends on so many variables that neither success nor failure can be credited to the stepmother alone.

So Many Resentments

Most stepmothers find their first year mined with hidden resentments, and they seem to explode at the worst possible times. These unexpected hostilities are difficult to resolve before a major explosion because they are often repressed until the pressure becomes too much to control. Some are only nebulous feelings rather than identified, specific objections. Here are typical resentments.

1. From the ex-wife

New wives are often accused of having broken up the previous marriage, whether or not there is any basis in fact for the allegation. Protective of their "territorial rights," ex-wives may operate on a I-may-not-want-him-but-I-don't-want-anyone-else-to-have-him premise. Therefore, new wives are to be resented. Or perhaps the problem is envy of the new wife who is making a marriage work which the ex-wife couldn't. All too often the basis of the hostility is the terrifying fear that the children will come to love the stepmother more than their own mother.

Sometimes the two women can get together and honestly talk over their roles and relationships to each other. Even without becoming close friends, the women can allay one another's secret fears and often eliminate resentments. Such communication may be impossible or unprofitable. But as long as the new wife can maintain a healthy perspective toward the ex-wife, these resentments can be treated as minor problems rather than major disasters.

2. From her own children

A mother who remarries a man with children faces the possibility of resentment from her own children. Having to share a mother's love, time, and attention with a stepfather and stepsiblings is not always a pleasant prospect to children who may have had their mother to themselves for several years.

Recognizing ahead of time that her children may feel left out in the new relationship, a mother will want to take time to openly discuss fears and expectations with her children. A little understanding and a lot of reassurance that they are still loved as much as before will go a long way in helping children adjust to having a stepfather in the home.

3. From her husband

Fathers who have not resolved their guilt over the "failure" of their former marriage or who are overindulgent with their children tend to resent any conflicts between their children and their new wives. In these situations the new wives are expected to not only support but also to share in the fathers' attempts to "make it up to the children." Any comments about "spoiling the children" or about "overdoing things" may trigger a major marital battle.

A wife can sometimes help her husband see how he is using inappropriate actions to assuage guilt or failure feelings by inviting him to share with her those feelings. However, this conversation is most effective during a quiet, neutral sharing time rather than as part of an emotional conflict over a specific incident. Sometimes a wife cannot help her husband in this area, so she must commit him to the Lord's care and let the Holy Spirit work out the healing of old wounds.

4. From the stepchildren

Stepchildren perceive, or dream up, many excuses for resenting dad's new wife.

- Because she broke up their home (whether or not she did);
- Because she's keeping dad from remarrying mom (whether or not he ever would);

- Because she's too young (or old);

- Because she does things differently from mom (whether or not mom's way is desirable);

- Because she makes dad happy and is important to him;

- Because she shares dad's time, love, and attention;

- Because she can . . .;

- Because she can't. . . .

A resentful, hateful child is difficult to love, even when one understands some of the fears and insecurities behind the negativism. Building that bridge of communication often seems a one-sided effort from the adult to a nonresponsive child.

Children who are responsive to a prospective stepmother sometimes change suddenly when dad marries her. Before the marriage she is perceived as a special friend of theirs and dad's. She is fun to be with as they do special things together. When she tells them to do something or asks them not to do other things, she is obeyed because they want to please this special friend. Even though she is an adult, she is often viewed as an equal. Then she marries dad, and suddenly she is no longer an equal or a friend. She is a parent with full authority to give orders and withhold pleasures. This shift in roles may be experienced by the children as a betrayal of trust, to be deeply resented.

5. From within

"I have a few resentments myself," Rhoda admits. "I try so hard to live up the expectations of my husband, stepchildren, and myself, but I get so tired. I have rights in this family, too!"

She's correct. She does have rights. Deep within that inner person even the best of us experience resentments when we feel that our wants or needs are not being met. Stepmothers are given many opportunities to feel left out, forgotten, and not valued in the same way as others:

- When part of her paycheck goes to support his ex-wife and children;

- When the ex-wife makes excessive demands on her husband and he meets them;

- When the children (his, hers, or theirs) intrude;

- When she is continually compared unfavorably to the ex-wife;

- When there is never enough time to meet all of the demands;

- When her husband fails to support her in front of his children;

- When she is expected to assume total responsibility for his children while he abdicates his share.

Unresolved resentments, like termites in a house, eat away at the relationship weakening its structure. These resentments bring bitterness and anger and alienate people one from the other. Thus, as resentments are recognized and owned, they must be openly confronted in an attempt to free the relationships from these destructive forces. Each family member's needs and desires must be given considered attention. In an atmosphere of loving acceptance, fears can be allayed, constructive criticism can be accepted, and hurts healed through forgiveness. Paul urges this course of action in Ephesians 4:31-32: "Let all bitterness and wrath and anger and clamor and evil speaking be put away from you, with all malice. And be ye kind one to another, tenderhearted, forgiving one another, even as God for Christ's sake hath forgiven you."

A wise stepmother will recognize that at times she is going to be caught in the middle of situations she didn't anticipate. As a result her responses may be overwhelmingly negative. But in marrying into a stepfamily, she has taken a vow before God to give of herself to this new relationship. She will need to be able to:

- openly discuss her feelings with her husband;

- ensure that her relationship with the Lord is kept open and strong; and

- be willing to try alternate approaches to resolve problems.

Reaping Rewards

"Wally is well behaved, obedient, happy, and doesn't use baby talk anymore," boasts Fay with pardonable pride.

Six-year-old Wally had come to live with her just a couple of months after her marriage to his dad. As the baby of the family Wally had never been required to abide by the standards of behavior expected of his older brothers, and therefore he was never disciplined. Through long hours of loving instruction and patient reinforcement of positive actions, Fay had helped Wally prepare for the realities of first grade. She had disproved his kindergarten teacher's assertion that Wally had a serious learning disability. "The only reason that Wally didn't know colors or the alphabet and didn't have a large vocabulary was that no one had taken time to teach him," Fay explained. When Wally excelled in school, Fay felt rewarded for her efforts.

The rewards of being a stepparent are the same as those of being a parent. We are rewarded (often belatedly) when our children appreciate us, respect us, love us, or imitate us. We are rewarded when our children succeed in their lives because of our investment in their development. The difference between parenthood and stepparenthood lies in the fact that in the latter case one is investing in the lives of someone else's children.

No matter how wonderful the stepmother is, she never takes the place of the biological mother. This fact may hurt the stepmother who feels she has been far more of a "mother" than the natural mother ever was. But one must keep in mind that the tie between child and parent goes beyond the surface interactions between them. That people want to identify with their natural parents is evident by the fact that many adults who were adopted children expend much time and money searching out their biological parents.

However, just because a stepparent cannot take the place of a natural parent does not mean that the steprelationship cannot be loving, strong, and fulfilling.

Healthy Relationships

Keeping the relationships healthy challenges a stepparent's resourcefulness at times; and juggling priorities, mediating conflicts, and keeping the homelife operational significantly drains one's energy. Still, each individual relationship must be carefully nurtured if the family unit is to be strong.

In the following discussion of relationships that the stepmother must attend to, many of the principles also apply to stepfathers.

1. With self

When Jill remarried, she kept on with her graduate studies and her teaching job. She felt it was important to continue to fulfill her intellectual needs.

Assuming responsibility for personal needs is appropriate behavior, as long as this does not violate another's rights. A sense of personal worth enables interaction with others in a positive way. Several people who were interviewed offered ideas for taking care of self.

- Diane keeps a studio where she can paint in the solitude she requires.

- Marge joined a health spa and works out a couple of evenings a week.

- Irene belongs to a reading discussion club that meets one evening a week.

- Elizabeth is a guest lecturer, which sometimes takes her out of town for a couple of days.

Whatever it takes to reinforce the inner self without damaging the family relationship is worth the investment. For a person who is not whole, and needs to reinforce the inner self, it may be a matter of looking to others to fill in the gaps. People with no self-confidence want others to be confident for them. Shy people depend on others to draw them into conversation and activities. People with poor self-images need others to reinforce their worth. Expecting someone else to take the responsibility for personal deficiencies sets up a dependency in the relationship which is an unfair burden to the partner. Those who take responsibility for their own growth and personal development can relate to their partners as whole people.

2. With the Lord

A man tried to explain his problem to a psychiatrist.

"My wife and I live in a $200,000 house, drive new Cadillacs, entertain lavishly, both at home and on our yacht, travel all around the world . . ." he paused to breathe.

"That's quite a life-style," the psychiatrist commented thoughtfully. "What's wrong with it?"

"There's no problem with our life-style," the man replied. "My problem is that I only earn $150 a week!"

How ridiculous! To try to live a $1,500-a-week life on a $150-a-week income! And yet, people often do — overcommitting themselves by trying to live superhuman lives with only natural strength, and consequently failing. God's strength is needed to live the victorious life as new creatures in Christ. In Ephesians 6, Paul urges putting on the whole armor of God in order to withstand attack. In John 15, Christ asserts that without Him, people can do nothing. Truly, successful human relationships are only possible when people are right with God.

Communicating with God on a regular basis provides insights that are helpful in resolving the problems of everyday life. Personal assurance of God's love is revealed. And the success promised in Psalm 1:1-3 is experienced.

3. With the Mate

"I never dreamed there was anyone like Tim," Sara sighed happily. Eagerly she adopted her new husband's habits, ideas, preferences, and hobbies. If ever her desires conflicted with his, she gave in without a murmur. She seemed to live for Tim.

Nine years later they were divorced.

Within a few months Sara remarried. Still bitter over Tim's rejection "after all she had given him," Sara promised herself she would never be the "giver" again. And so she staunchly held her ground on even the smallest disagreement. She never initiated reconciliations. True to her promise, she did not give of herself to her new husband.

They were divorced within two years.

If any marriage is to work, both partners must be willing to love one another freely and be sincerely committed to submitting one to the other.

This mutual commitment must not be overlooked in the hectic family schedule.

Research studies show that the husband-wife relationship has a profound effect on the children. "Children act out the marriage," says counselor Tom Russell. "If the relationship is good, the children tend to be well adjusted. If the relationship is faulty, children tend to exhibit behavior problems."

Successful couples have made sure they took the time to be romantic and affectionate with each other. They enjoyed being alone together. Because thoughtfulness and courtesy go a long way in a marriage, they remember birthdays, anniversaries, special interests, or preferred foods.

4. With the children

There are three types of stepmothers:

a. those who do not have children of their own;

b. those who have children of their own, living with them; and

c. those whose children live elsewhere (i. e., with their father, or in their own homes). Previous experiences with developing successful parent-child relationships will influence the way a stepparent interacts with the stepchildren.

Learning to live with other people's children is indeed a challenge. Nancy often fought the urge to leave during the first two years of her remarriage. For seven years she had lived alone with her sons (who were 11 and 15 by the time she remarried Marvin). A regular family schedule had evolved which suited all three. The boys, like most children, understood mom well enough to know when to leave her alone and when to ask for special favors. Then homelife was fairly free from conflicting needs or wants.

Marvin's children, all four of whom were under ten years of age, were totally unfamiliar with house rules, schedules, or the signs of a mother who is at the end of her strength. When Marvin took a second job to relieve the financial strain, Nancy's determination to overcome all obstacles in her new marriage was put to the test. Four years passed before Nancy felt able to relax somewhat. The marriage and the family relationships survived.

Although each family situation is unique, young stepmothers whose stepchildren are under 10 years old do tend to develop close relationships. On the other hand, blended families where both mates have adolescents are the least successful for the obvious reasons. The greatest period of stress for a biological family is the children's adolescence. Combining two adults and one or more adolescents from two different families to form a new family is to attempt stepkinship under the most adverse conditions possible.

Stepparents with children of their own may find it difficult to be impartial. Regardless of their feelings (for some people are more lovable than others), stepparents should be careful to keep their "courtroom decisions" as fair and equal as possible. And yet, it is imperative that they take time out to be alone with their own children who must not suffer a loss of intimacy just because others have joined the family group.

Weekend stepparents face a double challenge — to develop two life-styles that are expected to interface smoothly. For most of the time the non-custodial couple's homelife routine is adult centered. Then, at least twice a month the children arrive for the weekend, and the alternate life-style begins.

At least part of the weekend, the children usually want to be alone with their parent, which excludes the stepparent. Some times this is resented. "Since we both work all week I look forward to my weekends with Roger. I don't want him to take off with his kids without me!" one young stepmother shared. But other women view these "alone times" as opportunities to do the things they've been wanting to do.

- Velma has lunch with a single woman friend.
- Wanda goes to a romantic movie (her husband hates them).
- Trisha curls up in front of the fire with a good book.
- Kim does her housecleaning with no one under foot.
- Phyllis goes window shopping.

Designing the relationship that will work between stepparent and stepchild is a very individual undertaking, for people are so different that what works for one person doesn't always work for another.

5. With the ex-spouses

Ex-spouses have a way of intruding into new marriages, partly because they are still co-parents of children who share both homes. A second reason is that the years spent together cannot be erased. Emotional ties (both loving and antagonistic) are difficult to completely sever. Also, unresolved issues from former marriages have a tendency to carry over into new marriages. Consequently the relationship with both of the ex-spouses requires consideration.

Ideally a cooperative arrangement can be developed for sharing the children and making decisions related to their welfare, while maintaining a hands off attitude toward the other aspects of each other's lives. However, the very reasons why a couple got divorced (differing values, priorities, life-styles and ideas) often preclude the totally cooperative approach.

6. *With a friend*

Everyone needs a best friend of the same sex, someone who will listen without judging or proffering instant solutions to the major perplexities. That person is one who keeps confidences, in short is an empathizing, accepting, loving confidant.

A best friend is needed when the inner well of strength has run dry or when affirmation from someone outside the marriage is needed. There come times when a person isn't ready to talk things over with the spouse yet because the anger is too intense or the pain is too deep. Talking over feelings with this friend first helps clarify the thoughts and sort out the feelings. Ranting, raving, yelling, or weeping is safe because there will be no repercussions. As the feelings are expressed and brought under control, personal strength is renewed and the problems are kept in perspective. Return to the family and problem resolution is then possible.

A Promise for Stepmothers

On those difficult days, stepmothers may want to consider the following paraphrase of Luke 6:27-38:

> Love all those who seem to be your enemies, and do good to those that hate you. Bless those who resent you, and pray for those who are angry and hateful toward you. When your husband's ex-wife or children take that which is rightfully yours, give it freely without demanding equal compensation. Treat each member of your family the way you would like them to treat you. Loving your husband is easy, because he loves you in return. Anyone can love those who are loving. But if you will love and be kind to those who are unloving and hurtful, your reward will be great. If you are not judgmental and condemning, you will not be judged or condemned. Forgive and you will be forgiven. If you will give freely, you shall receive good measure pressed down, shaken together, and running over. For what and how you give, you shall receive in kind.

9.4 Stepfathers
Bobbie Reed

DINNER HAD BEEN A GOURMET'S DELIGHT IN AN ELEGANT RESTAURANT. IN muted tones, the orchestra provided the romantic mood. The lights in the couple's eyes were more than a reflection of the candle flames. They were in love, and Larry had just proposed marriage.

As much as she loved Larry, Sandy was hesitant to verbalize the Yes in her heart. In the two years that she and Larry had been dating, he had yet to build a strong relationship with her three young sons. On occasion she had heard him make remarks which strongly implied that children were not part of his planned life-style. How then could he propose? Had he considered all of the ramifications of marrying the mother of three boys?

Sandy voiced these questions gently, not wanting to dampen the ardor of the moment, or to seem unromantic.

"The kids are no problem, Honey." Larry assured her. "I love you enough to accept the fact that you have kids. They're just part of the package!"

Although not completely reassured, Sandy accepted the proposal. The engagement lasted two months during which Larry made a conscious effort to incorporate Sandy's boys into his life. "I'm too self-centered to enjoy taking the responsibility for nurturing, instructing, and developing children. I don't want to lose you, but if we go through with our wedding plans, we are all going to be hurt later on. So I guess this is good-bye," he told Sandy one night.

A painful, but wise decision.

A Package Deal

Stepchildren are more than just "part of the package" that comes with a new spouse. They are people, new, individual members of the intimate family.

However, the fact that there are stepchildren is more often than not a given in second marriages. And, because our country's judicial system has traditionally given physical custody of minor children to the mother in divorce or dissolution cases, stepfathers can usually expect that their stepchildren will be in residence.

Living with someone else's children may be a difficult adjustment for a new husband for several reasons:

1. If he has never had children and has been living alone, how can he anticipate the new situation accurately?

He probably expects the house to be as neat in the evening as when he left in the morning. He may expect special snacks to still be in the kitchen cupboards when he wants them five days after they were purchased. He may not understand about the "mysterious, unknown stranger" who causes all of the household damages when parents aren't around. And he, reasonably, may want to be alone with his wife more than seems possible with children in the house.

"It's not exactly the children themselves I resent. It's their constant presence. I mean, they're always there. Even when we're sitting alone after they are in bed asleep, we're not alone. Am I making any sense?" Harold asks.

Of course you are, Harold. Adjusting to living with another person is a process of dovetailing needs, wants, and priorities through continued interaction, until the motion becomes smoothly operational, much like two cog wheels in a mechanical apparatus. Because the friction of metal against metal could cause mechanical failure, cog wheels are kept well lubricated for as long as they are in motion. Just so relationships must be kept well protected with love to minimize the possibility of friction resulting in a family disaster. When the other person one is living with is a new spouse, the process is facilitated by the ecstasy of romantic love, something that is not a factor in the relationship with new stepchildren.

Easing into living in a family unit after living alone is facilitated when expectations are discussed with all members ahead of time. The man should feel free enough to explain that there are some considerations he really needs to cope effectively. These may include getting to read the paper first, shower first, or even having 20 minutes of quiet, uninterrupted alone time immediately upon returning home. Such seemingly small considerations cost other family members very little effort, but they can go a long way toward making a new stepfamily work.

2. If a man's own children live with the ex-spouse, his stepchildren may serve as constant reminders of his loss and trigger any number of inner responses.

Earl feels remorse that he never developed a close bond with his own children before his divorce.

Isaac tries too hard to have a perfect relationship with his stepchildren, who are substitutes for the sons he never sees. (They live 2,000 miles away, and the mother refuses him any contact, even though the court order reads "reasonable visitation.")

Fred tends to hold back a little from his three-year-old stepdaughter. The pain of losing his close relationship with his own daughter is too recent to allow him the freedom to risk another loss.

Sam finds that he must constantly remind himself that his style of communicating with children is unfamiliar to his stepchildren. His own children had learned to understand him well but it had taken years to achieve!

Vince recognizes that his own children have suffered the loss of him as part of their daily homelife. So when they come to visit, he makes a special effort to reassure them of his continued love and support. He goes out of his way to listen to and share with them.

This common attempt to squeeze a couple of weeks' worth (or even more) of attention into a two-day weekend is sometimes resented by stepchildren. They consider it unfair.

Once again the solution to these different situations is for the family members to be understanding of the problem for the man involved. NOT trying to understand exactly how he feels and why he does what he does may imply disagreement with his reasoning and a judgment that he is behaving inappropriately. So, instead, try to be understanding and accepting, allowing him to work through his conflicting feelings, finding the behaviors with which he can accept his new relationships.

On the other hand, family members do have a responsibility to provide feedback to the man on their responses to his behaviors. Saying "You shouldn't do . . ." is judgmental. Saying "When you do thus and so, I feel . . ." is providing valuable feedback that helps a man decide on the behaviors he chooses to adopt.

3. If a man's children live with him and his new family, he may feel his relationships with the two sets of children being constantly compared by all members of the group.

It is unrealistic to expect that the relationships will be completely the same. A father has a history of relating to his own offspring. Between them, they have developed a workable system. On the other hand, his stepchildren have their own well-developed system of interacting with a parent. The two systems are probably different. Therefore, while the man may continue relating to his own children according to their system, the system which becomes operational with the stepchildren tends to be a compromise between the two systems — his and theirs.

The adjustment to living with other people's children is one which most stepfathers make successfully. In fact, one study revealed that a greater percentage of stepfathers had excellent relationships with their stepchildren than did stepmothers. Some sociologists explain that because men usually have careers outside of the home, their opportunities for interacting with stepchildren are limited, and therefore conflicts are minimized. However this argument seems somewhat invalid in a society where working wives are the norm.

Crime and Punishment

Even when the prenuptial discussions include child rearing and discipline, a couple will often find that they sometimes disagree on the proper way to respond to less-than-ideal behavior.

In steprelationships, natural parents usually give permission to their mates to discipline the children. However, that permission is often conditional as it is mentally qualified with "as long as I agree with the way you discipline at the time." Children are quick to sense division between their parents and to press their advantage with the more lenient adult in any given situation. Agreeing as a couple and family on standards of behavior and appropriate consequences for failure to meet those standards is one way to minimize discipline conflicts.

Discipline is the key word. A family is not a judicial system charged with meting out punishments for crimes. A family serves as an instructional institution for teaching children to be functional adults. The Scriptures give repeated admonitions for parents to train their children in the ways of the Lord. The learning process involves trying new behaviors and checking the outcomes to see if the desired goals were accomplished. Thus, training children and adolescents to assume the responsibility for their own behavior by accepting the natural consequences of the behavior is the key to effective disciplining. The ineffectiveness of punishment and the principle of natural consequences is clearly defined and illustrated in Dave and Jan Stoop's *The Total(ed) Parent* (Irvine, CA: Harvest House Publishers, 1978).

The Farmer Takes a Wife

Why do men marry?

To find companionship. To have their housekeeping needs met. To take care of a woman. To rescue children from being raised in a one-parent home. To have children. To replace a family lost through death or divorce. To be fulfilled. To be special to significant others who will love and care for them. To . . .

Many are the reasons for marriage. But perhaps the basic one is God's own observation that it is not good for a man to be alone. We have all discovered that life seems to have more meaning, and pleasures bring more joy when shared with a special friend. A spouse is intended to be that special friend.

"Sometimes I feel as if our friendship ended when we got married," George comments. "Before we were married, Ann and I used to collaborate on writing projects. She would get a sitter for her children and come over to my apartment. We each had our own desks and supplies. The quiet intimacy of creating together would be broken by heated discussion as we would struggle to help each other communicate complex concepts in a clear writing style. We always had a pot of coffee brewing — we drank gallons! Sometimes we would take a break and just sit in front of the fire and share. Hours would fly by unnoticed. It was a wonderful time.

"Then we got married. We set up a writing space in the family room. That didn't work because when we wanted to write, the kids wanted to watch TV. We tried writing at night after the children were asleep, but we were too tired to be creative. Right now we're set up in the corner of our bedroom, but we are often interrupted. Besides it's pretty crowded in there with all of our bedroom furniture as well as our writing supplies. I really miss those writing sessions."

As difficult as it may sometimes be to find ways to be alone together, the couple must strive to do so. For the strength of the family lies in the unity of the couple.

The Farmer Leaves a Wife

A man's relationship to his ex-wife affects his relationship with his new wife.

Any hostility between a man and his ex-spouse over support payments, custody, or visitation usually includes his new wife.

Sometimes the relationship with the ex seems "too good," Lori shares. "Paul was always running back to his ex-wife's house to repair the plumbing, trim the trees, or repair the car. I couldn't help myself. I began to feel jealous!"

Counselor Richard Baker explains this common situation. An ex-wife may continue to make demands on her husband after their divorce. As long as she hasn't found someone else to depend on, she may want to make him pay for having left her, or she may feel he owes her his continued assistance. The demands may be for household repairs, extra money, a change in the visitation plans, or any number of other things. The ex-wife (or ex-husband) learned how to manipulate her husband during their marriage, through such devices as threats, acting helpless, appealing to his love of the children. She knows how to get him to do what she wants.

So she calls, and he goes. Result: The ex-wife is rewarded for her manipulation and will probably continue to make demands.

The new wife receives mixed messages. Her husband says he loves her and is happy with their game-free relationship. And yet, he continues to respond to the ex-wife's obvious game-playing. The ex-wife gets away with things the husband would never tolerate in the new wife. The man's actions seem to belie his words. Which is to be believed? Sometimes the new wife comes to wonder if her husband will leave her for his ex-wife, since he continues to return to her on demand.

The husband believes the situation to be perfectly clear. He continues to relate to his ex-wife as he did during their marriage because those were the ground rules of their relationship. He "can't" change the rules unilaterally. "She couldn't handle it." Or, "It's less disruptive to just do what she asks and get it over with" are typical explanations. And, contrary to his new wife's fears, the husband is not usually tempted to return to his former wife.

Roy comments, "I love my wife. We have the kind of open and honest relationship I've always wanted, but have never had before. Anytime I have to go over to my ex-wife's for one of her little jobs, I thank God for giving me my new wife."

Roy (and other husbands in similar situations) needs to delineate his responsibilities. Continued financial responsibility for spousal and child support, and ongoing responsibility for parenting his child, is not responsibility for taking care of the ex-wife's other needs. He is free from his commitment to cherish, protect, and care for her. His new commitment is to his new wife and to their new life together.

Follow the Leader

As the head of the house, the husband is charged with setting the spiritual pace for the family. A close relationship with God provides the strength to be a good role model and the wisdom to make good decisions.

In some respects, if he is to have a significant influence on the children, a stepfather is required to be a better leader than a natural father. Children tend to forgive natural parents for failing to be everything they should be. But stepparents don't always get that same level of acceptance. However, in both cases, the actions speak more clearly than the words. And so, a goal of stepfathers (and fathers) would be to say with Paul, "Follow me, even as I am a follower of Christ."

Stepchildren

Children
The challenge
The beloved intruders
Those who put the "step" into a remarriage

The way children respond to the remarriage of one of their natural parents (and the subsequent gain of a new stepparent) depends on the perceived impact of the marriage on their own lives. If the anticipated impact is positive, then the response is positive. But if the impact seems threatening or disruptive, the response will be somewhat negative.

Conflicting Feelings

When a biological family is divided by a divorce, all members experience the loss. Gone is the intimate security of the family, never to be completely regained. The loss must be mourned as part of the healing process.

One of the first responses to a loss is to deny reality. The children in a divorce situation are almost always convinced that they were somehow responsible. Therefore, they conclude that if they were powerful enough to break up the family, then they are also powerful enough to reunite it again. And most children try to do just that — against all odds. When their efforts are unsuccessful, they experience guilt, frustration, anxiety, and other negative feelings.

A second mourning emotion is anger. Often children have a deep-seated anger toward the noncustodial parent for having "deserted" them. But because anger toward one's own parent is not always easy to accept in one-self, children frequently transfer this anger to the stepparent.

Sometimes children express their sense of loss through sudden behavior changes: weeping, tantrums, a decline in scholastic achievement, antisocial mannerisms, or quiet withdrawal.

As the mourning experience is completed, the children find the wounds of loss are in the process of being healed. Because healing is an individual process, the mourning period varies in length from child to child. With healing comes the ability to form a modified relationship with the custodial parent, and also the noncustodial parent when contact is maintained.

Then one day the children are told that one of their parents is going to remarry. Immediately comes the recognition that the family life is about to change again. Instant fear! Will the change mean a loss of the child's importance to the parent?

I'm Scared!

Expecting to become less important to the parent after a remarriage, the child tries to regain the parents' attention. A child's resistance to the new marriage sometimes take the form of a one-person war against the couple. The cries for reassurance of personal importance can be very annoying to say the least.

- Jamie gets a fever (slight, but real) every time mom goes out with her husband-to-be.

- Tom quizzes his mom's dates to determine their intentions of marrying his mother.

- Jeff said to the woman his father loves, "My mom is very successful. She says Dad can't take a woman who's successful and beautiful, because he feels it intimidates him. I guess that's why he dates you."

- Tim is openly rude.

- Patty committed a misdemeanor and wound up in Juvenile Hall.

Extremely hostile behaviors toward the (future) stepparent are indicative of a need for professional assistance to overcome irrational fears. Some of the fears which may be terrifying to children are:

1. Fear of disloyalty

Loving a stepparent may seem an act of disloyalty to the natural parent of the same sex, a concept which may be supported by an insecure parent.

Children experiencing this fear need to be reassured that the stepparent is not a replacement but an additional parent. Loving one does not preclude loving the other.

2. Fear of losing again

When children lose a parent through death or when one parent completely disappears after a divorce, children may become afraid to risk loving for fear of losing again. If their own parent deserted them, they reason, might not the stepparent?

As children learn to trust the stepparent, their fears should subside and allow them to reach out in love.

3. Fear of losing the parents' love

"Now that Mom (or Dad) has a new spouse, some of the time which used to be mine is now theirs. Is some of the love which was mine, now being channeled to the new spouse?" a child wonders.

A sensitive couple will ensure that the child has the attention needed from the biological parent to reaffirm the love between them.

Power, Power, Who's Got the Power?

Children, especially adolescents, are super at power plays. The favorite game of pitting one parent against the other is infinitely more challenging as children have the opportunity of playing one home (and set of parents) against the other home (and set of parents). Add in four sets of grandparents, and you can have a very destructive human chess game.

Parents who buy into the games find that children are more than willing to spy on, tattle, gossip, and tell stories about one home to the other. But children need to learn that each of their families has the right to privacy. Each home has a set of behavior standards and consequences for inappropriate behaviors. Neither home is 100 percent right nor 100 percent wrong; the homes are simply different models.

Another power ploy is testing the limits of acceptable behavior. With so many changes in the life-style because of a remarriage, children often attempt to renegotiate all of the standards of behavior from their single-parent home.

- "Do I still have to eat my carrots?"
- "Do I still have to go to bed at 9:30 p.m.?"

As difficult as the testing attempts may be, parents must not give up and remove the limits, because children need limits. They fight rules, but even as they attack, they depend on the security of knowing where the limits are. Consistency of standards and discipline has proven most significant in parenting well-adjusted children.

I Need You!

Besides their basic food, clothing, and shelter needs, children have other needs.

A physical space of their very own is very important to children. The dimensions of the space will vary from family to family depending on available resources. Ideally, children would have a room of their own in each home. But if this is impractical, then a designated space will work: a bed, a corner, a drawer, or a closet. Having a specific, personal space gives a sense of belongingness to the child.

Spatial needs also include room to grow intellectually and emotionally. A child has the right to individual ideas, opinions, values and preferences which may not be consistent with those of the parent. Giving children intellectual and emotional space includes encouraging disclosure and discussion without condemnation.

2. Affirmation

Educator Ed Reed discusses the importance of parental affirmation and gives ideas for its use in the home.

To affirm someone communicates individual value and acceptance as a person — imperfections and all. To affirm builds positive relationships. To affirm reinforces a person's sense of self-worth. Affirmation feels good! Both to the receiver and the giver.

Parents have a responsibility before God to affirm their children. To show by actions that they are valuable and important as individuals. Only then can positive relationships develop, based on mutual trust, concern, and love. Only in an affirming home atmosphere can children open up and share their deepest thoughts, concerns, fears, and feelings. Then, lasting spiritual growth can occur.

Children remember the times a parent gives affirmation — and the times they don't!

One way to use affirmation is to assist a child in setting goals, then affirming any progress which is made. Specific behaviors that parents may decide to affirm might include: sharing, obeying, praying, studying God's Word, winning a spiritual battle, kindness, loving sweetness, doing extra chores, taking a bath without being told to, or even just getting through the evening without a brother-sister quarrel!

Jesus affirmed people in His life for a variety of behaviors. He affirmed Mary of Bethany as she worshiped at His feet. He affirmed the widow who cast her mite into the temple treasury. He affirmed the faith of the centurion whose servant was healed. He affirmed His disciple Zacchaeus and the woman at the well by spending time with them.

Effective opportunities for affirming children include:

- Affirming the value of their ideas and encouraging creative thinking through listening attentively.

- Affirming their right to enjoyment by letting them share in the planning of family leisure time.

- Affirming their friendship by doing things together such as projects, working, playing, and talking.

- Affirming growing experiences by allowing risk taking without recriminations over resultant failures.

- Affirming their humanity by being fully human parents. (Free to be wrong sometimes. Unafraid to apologize).

- Affirming positive character traits by concentrating on one characteristic as a family for several weeks. (For example, if the trait is kindness, each family member would look for opportunities to be kind each day. During the dinner hour, individuals share their experiences and celebrate one another's acts of kindness).

- Affirming love by frequent hugging and touching one another.

3. Spiritual guidance.

As children grow up, they need to be guided into spiritual development. A guide is a person who knows the path because of having walked it before. A guide leads those who follow. Parents who worship with their families in church, who let the children observe their searching God's Word for answers and comfort, and who share their prayer life with the children are effective guides.

Children in stepfamilies are confronted with some hard-to-accept realities. They have suffered a loss of their natural family unit. Their identity is shaken. Stepparents have entered the picture. Their lives have been disrupted several times in different ways. Someone is to blame. Only through forgiveness comes the healing. And parents need to teach forgiveness by modeling an understanding spirit and a loving heart, ready to forgive.

4. Special help

Some children are unable to work through the fears, the hostilities, and the insecurities on their own. Sometimes more than parental love and guidance is required. Children who are having difficulty coping with the pressures in their world may become extremely possessive of their natural parent, resenting any attention given to someone else — especially the new stepparent. Or children may fantasize with great exaggeration about the non-custodial (or dead) parent or the family life prior to the divorce (or death of a parent). Hyperactivity, extreme nervousness, ultrasensitivity, and aggression are other signs of a need for special help. Whenever one family member needs professional help, the whole family is involved. The problem is not the individual's, it belongs to the family. When a lack of money prevents a family from seeing a counselor, they may find other community resources available.

- School districts often have family counseling services, or a psychologist on staff who may be consulted. Since children who act *out* at home often also act *out* at school, counseling services through the school may be appropriate.

- Many pastors have found key spiritual leaders in the church who also have professional counseling backgrounds, and are willing to be of assistance to members of the body who are in need.

- Local state, county, or city social service agencies provide crisis intervention services to families in need.

- Self-help groups such as those formed by the Stepfamily Foundation are becoming increasingly available in many of our cities.

Seeking professional assistance when needed is the wisest move a parent can make to help children living in steprelationships.

Who's Who?

Most children call their stepparents by their first names. In other families children select a nickname or an affectionate term of address. In some a form of mother or father is encouraged. Forcing children to identify the stepparent as mom or dad is not recommended; however, some children do so spontaneously and naturally. The important thing to remember is that stepparents' authority does not depend on what they are called.

Introductions are best kept simple. There is no need to emphasize the steprelationship by saying, "This is my stepson." Rather, "This is our son, Will." Insisting on specifying that a relationship is a "step" may give children the impression that the stepparent does not consider them as a real part of the family.

The Grass is Always Greener

Fantasizing about a better life than the present one is a common human habit. Wanting to go live with the other parent is common among children whose time with their noncustodial parents is limited. That other home takes on all of the lure of Fantasy Island. Life there would certainly be far superior to what they have now!

Rarely are these fantasies diminished by parental reminders of realities. Neither should a parent belittle the other, for in tearing down the image of a parent, the child's self-image is also damaged. Most fantasies disappear as the children grow up, but sometimes they must be allowed to experience their dreams, because their obsession with it has caused them to develop antisocial behaviors to express their frustration with thwarted desires.

Jesus Was a Stepchild

Every boy or girl who experiences the emotional turmoil inherent in steprelationships has an understanding Lord. Jesus was a stepchild. He knew the feelings of having an earthly father question Him as He went about His Father's work in the temple. He knows today the kinds of problems a family encounters when all of the children do not share the same set of parents. He understands and cares.

9.5 Strong Families
Nicholas Stinnett

ABSTRACT: To improve family life, it is more helpful to look at what makes families strong than at what is wrong with them. Using state, national, and international samples, the author studied "strong" families: intact families that have a high degree of marital happiness and high parent-child satisfactions and that do a good job of meeting each other's needs. Strong families consistently show appreciation of one another, spend time together, are committed to one another, use good communications, are religious, and take a constructive approach to crises. On the basis of these six qualities, the author suggests recommendations designed to help strengthen families.

The quest for self-fulfillment during the twentieth century has developed into a major goal in American culture (Yankelovich, 1981). However, in our preoccupation with this objective we have neglected the family and lost sight of the fact that so much of the foundation necessary to facilitate the life-long process of individual self-fulfillment (such as the development of interpersonal competence, self-confidence, self-esteem, respect for self and others, and the vision and knowledge that life can be enriched) is developed within strong, healthy families.

We have considerable evidence that the quality of family life is extremely important to our emotional well-being, our happiness, and our mental health as individuals. We know that poor relationships within the family are very closely related to many problems in society (such as juvenile delinquency and domestic abuse).

As we look back in history we see that the quality of family life is very important to the strength of nations. There is a pattern in the rise and fall of great societies such as ancient Rome, Greece, and Egypt. When these societies were at the peak of their power and prosperity, the family was strong and highly valued. When family life became weak in these societies, when the family was not valued — when goals became extremely individualistic — the society began to deteriorate and eventually fell.

Obviously, it is to our benefit to do what we can to strengthen family life; this should be one of our nation's top priorities, but unfortunately it has not been.

So much of what is written about families has focused on problems and pathology. On the newsstand we see many books and magazine articles about what's wrong with families and the problems that families have. There are those who like to predict that the family will soon disappear and that it no longer meets our needs.

Certainly we need information about positive family models and what strong families are like. We need to learn how to strengthen families. We don't learn how to do anything by looking only at what *shouldn't* be done. We learn most effectively by examining how to do something correctly and studying a positive model. We have not had this positive model as much as we need it in the area of family life. Understanding what a strong family is provides educators, counselors, and families with a positive model. Getting this knowledge first-hand from those who have created a successful family situation gives us a good picture of how families become strong.

We have many strong families throughout this nation and the world. There has been little written about them because there has been very little research focusing on family strengths. It was with this in mind that we launched the Family Strengths Research Project, a search that has taken us throughout our nation as well as to other parts of the world. This research was inspired in part by the pioneer work in family strengths of Otto (1962, 1964).

Our search began in Oklahoma where we studied 130 families identified as strong. More recently, we have completed a national study of strong families representing all regions of the nation, an investigation of strong Russian immigrant families, a study of strong black families and an examination of strong families from various countries in South America.

The research method varied. For example, one approach was represented by the Oklahoma study. In this project we had the assistance of the Cooperative Extension Service to help identify the strong families We asked the Home Economics Extension Agent in each of the counties of Oklahoma to recommend a few families that the agent considered particularly strong. The Home Economics Extension Agents were suited to this task for three reasons — their background training in family life, their concern for improving family life as part of their work, and the great amount of contact they have with families in the community. Also we gave the agents some guidelines for selecting the families. The guidelines were that the families demonstrated a high degree of marital happiness, a high degree of parent-child satisfaction as perceived by the Extension Agent, and that the family members appeared to meet each other's needs to a high degree.

For purposes of this study, all the families were intact with husband wife, and at least one child living at home. The first requirement for inclusion in this sample of strong families was the recommendation of the Extension Agent. The second requirement was that the families rate themselves very high in terms of marriage satisfaction and parent-child relationship satisfaction. The 130 families that met these two conditions were included in the sample. Both urban and rural families were represented in the sample, although there were more families from small cities, towns, and rural areas than from large urban areas. In most instances, we found very little difference between the urban and rural families.

A second research technique was demonstrated by the national study. The strong families in this study responded to an article sent to various daily and weekly papers across the nation. The 41 newspapers asked to run the article were selected to ensure a sample from all regions of the country, and from both rural and urban areas. The news release described the national study and asked families who felt they qualified as strong families to send their names and addresses to the researchers. The philosophy behind this approach can be debated almost endlessly. In short, we believed that rather than we as professionals defining what a strong family is, we would let families make the decision themselves

The response to the news release was tremendous. Each family that responded was sent copies of the Family Strengths Inventory for the husband and wife. Many families also sent elaborate stories describing their family and its characteristics and activities in detail. The inventory focused on both the husband-wife and parent-child relationships and collected demographic information. Only families that rated themselves very high on marriage happiness and parent-child satisfaction were included in the final sample. This was similar to the screening procedure used in the Oklahoma study. The final sample size for the national study was 350 families.

In summary, we researched 130 families in the Oklahoma study, 350 families in the National Project, and 180 families in the South American study. In addition, smaller studies of Russian immigrant families and black families have been completed. In all of these research projects the families completed questionnaires and later a few of them were interviewed. Our questions covered a broad range of factors concerning their relationship patterns. For example, we asked how they deal with conflict, about communication patterns, and about power structure. When we analyzed the vast quantity of information, we found six qualities that stood out among these strong families. Six qualities they had in common seemed to play a very important role in their strength and their happiness. It is interesting that the same six qualities were found to characterize strong families in all of the research studies we conducted.

The Six Qualities of the Strong Families

Appreciation

The first quality of the strong families was certainly one of the most important. It emerged from many different questions and in many ways that we were not expecting. The results were permeated by this characteristic. That quality is appreciation. The members of these families expressed a great deal of appreciation for each other. They built each other up psychologically, they gave each other many positive psychological strokes; everyone was made to feel good about themselves.

All of us like to be with people who make us feel good about ourselves; we don't like to be with people who make us feel bad. One of the tasks of family counselors who are working with family members who make each other feel terrible is to get them out of that pattern of interaction and into a pattern where they can make each other feel good. William James, considered by many people to be the greatest psychologist our country has ever produced, wrote a book on human needs. Some years after that book was published he remarked that he had forgotten to include the most important need of all — the need to be appreciated. There are so many things that we do for which we receive no reward other than appreciation; perhaps we all need to work on our ability to express appreciation. One difficulty in this is that we sometimes fear that people will think we're not sincere or that it's empty flattery. This need not be a concern. We *can* be sincere. Every person has many good qualities, many strengths. All we have to do is look for them, and be aware of them.

There are many ways in which we can develop the ability to express appreciation and thus make our human relationships better and certainly improve the quality of our family life. One widely used technique is one that Dr. Herbert Otto, Chairman of the National Center for Exploration of Human Potential, has used and written about a great deal. It has also been a tool for many counselors and is now being used by families on their own. This is called the "strength bombardment" technique. Here is the way it operates: The entire family comes together. There may be a group leader or counselor, or some member of the family can act as a leader. One person in the family is designated as the target person. For example, the mother may begin as target person. She is asked to list the strengths that she feels she has as a person. If she lists only two or three because she's modest, the leader can urge her to list others. After she has finished the list, her husband is asked to add to her list of strengths. Or he may elaborate on the strengths that she has already listed. When he has finished, each of the children is asked to add to mother's list of strengths. When this process is finished, the husband becomes the target person. The same procedure is repeated for him. Then each of the children becomes the target person.

The "strengths bombardment" technique is very simple, but the results have been amazing. When families do this exercise, they become more aware of each other's strengths, and more aware of their strengths as a family. They get into a pattern of looking for each other's good qualities and they also get into the habit of expressing appreciation. The result of this with so many families is that it makes their interaction with each other more positive. Some follow-up studies done with families who have gone through this activity show that the increased level of positive interaction is maintained for a period of time after the exercise has been completed. Many families are now using this technique periodically on their own.

Spending Time Together

A second quality found among strong families is that they did a lot of things together. It was not a "false" togetherness or a "smothering" type of togetherness — they genuinely enjoyed being together. Another important point here is that these families structured their life-styles so that they could spend time together. It did not "just happen"; they *made* it happen. And this togetherness was in all areas of their lives — eating meals, recreation, and work.

One interesting pattern which has emerged from our research is the high frequency with which the strong families participate in outdoor activities together such as walking, jogging, bird watching, camping, canoeing, horseback riding, and outdoor games. While there are many strong families who are not particularly fond of outdoor activities, the finding in our research that so many strong families employed this as an important source of enjoyment and of their strength as a family raises the question of how the participation in outdoor activities as a family might contribute to family strengths. One logical possibility is that when families are participating in outdoor activities together they have fewer distractions — the family members are away from the telephone and the never-ending array of household tasks — and can concentrate more upon each other, thus encouraging a good communication experience. Another possibility is that physical exercise is often one benefit of participation in outdoor activities and the exercise itself contributes to personal feelings of well-being, health, and vitality.

Commitment

A third quality of these strong families was a high degree of commitment. These families were deeply committed to promoting each other's happiness and welfare. They were also very committed to the family group, as reflected by the fact that they invested much of their time and energies in it. We have not had very much research on commitment, and perhaps in recent years it has not been fashionable to talk about it. Yet, Yankelovich (1981) observes that our society is now in the process of leaving behind an excessive self-centered orientation and moving toward a new "ethic of commitment" with emphasis upon new rules of living that support self-fulfillment through deeper personal relationships. Also, as David and Vera Mace (1980) have noted, only if you have produced a commitment to behavior change have you done anything to improve the life of a person or the life of a marriage or family. Some of the best research on commitment has been done in communes.

Some communes have been successful and others have not. One of the main differences found between the two groups is commitment. Those communes that are the most successful, that last the longest, and that are the most satisfying in terms of the relationships, are those in which there is a great deal of commitment — among individuals and to the group. Again, commitment in the communes was reflected in the amount of time the members spent together. The same was true with the strong families.

All of us are busy and we sometimes feel that we have so many things to do that we are pulled in a thousand different directions at the same time. Strong families experience the same problem. One interesting action that these families expressed was that when life got too hectic — to the extent that they were not spending as much time with their families as they wanted — they would sit down and make a list of the different activities in which they were involved. They would go over that list critically and inevitably there were some things that they really did not want to be doing, or that did not give much happiness, or that really were not very important to them. So they would scratch those activities and involvements off their lists. This would free time for their families and would relieve some of the pressure. As a result they were happier with their lives in general and more satisfied with their family relationships.

This sounds very simple, but how many of us do it? We get involved too often and it's not always because we want to be. We act so often as if we *cannot* change the situation. We *do* have a choice. An important point about these families is that they took the initiative in structuring their lifestyle in a way that enhanced the quality of their family relationships and their satisfaction. They were on the "offensive." We may have talked too much about families as simply reactors in society, being at the mercy of the environment. In fact, there is a great deal that families can do to make life more enjoyable. These strong families exercised that ability.

Good Communication Patterns

The fourth quality was not a surprise. Strong families have very good communication patterns. They spend time talking with each other. This is closely related to the fact that they spend a lot of time together. It's hard for people to communicate unless they spend time with each other. One of the big problems facing families today is not spending enough time together. Dr. Virginia Satir, a prominent family therapist, has stated that often families are so fragmented, so busy, and spend so little time together that they only communicate with each other through rumor. Unfortunately, too often that is exactly what happens.

Another important aspect of communication is that these families also listen well. They reported that their family members were good listeners and that this was important to them. The fact that family members listen to one another communicates a very important message — respect. They are saying to one another, "You respect me enough to listen to what I have to say. I'm interested enough to listen too."

Another factor related to communication is that these families do fight. They get mad at each other, but they get conflict out in the open and they are able to talk it over, to discuss the problem. They share their feelings about alternative ways to deal with the problem and in selecting a solution that is best for everybody. These strong families have learned to do what David and Vera Mace (1980) have reported to be essential for a successful marriage — making creative use of conflict.

High Degree of Religious Orientation

The fifth quality that these families expressed was a high degree of religious orientation. This agrees with research from the past forty years that shows a positive relationship of religion to marriage happiness and successful family relationships. Of course, we know that there are persons who are not religious who have very happy marriages and good family relationships. Nevertheless a positive relationship between marriage happiness and religion exists according to the research of many years. These strong families went to church together often and they participated in religious activities together. Most of them, although not all of them, were members of organized churches. All of them were very religious.

There are indications that this religious quality went deeper than going to church or participating in religious activities together. It could most appropriately be called a commitment to a spiritual life-style. Words are inadequate to communicate this, but what many of these families said was that they had an awareness of God or a higher power that gave them a sense of purpose and gave their family a sense of support and strength. The awareness of this higher power in their lives helped them to be more patient with each other, more forgiving, quicker to get over anger, more positive, and more supportive in their relationships. Many of the values emphasized by religion, when put into action, can certainly enhance the quality of human relationships. Dr. Herbert Otto has observed that we could spend more time looking at the spiritual aspect of developing human potential, and perhaps we could benefit by exploring more about the spiritual aspects of developing family strengths. For these strong families, religion played a major role.

Ability to Deal with Crises in a Positive Manner

The final quality that these families had was the ability to deal with crises and problems in a positive way. Not that they enjoyed crises, but they were able to deal with them constructively. They managed, even in the darkest of situations, to see some positive element, no matter how tiny, and to focus on it. It may have been, for example, that in a particular crisis they simply had to rely to a greater extent on each other and a developed trust that they had in each other. They were able to unite in dealing with the crisis instead of being fragmented by it. They dealt with the problem and were supportive of each other.

![decorative banner]

Topic Ten

Interfaith –
Interrace Marriages

10.1 The December Dilemma
Claire Berman

BEFORE GAIL MARKS[1] AND STEVEN BUCKLEY WERE MARRIED, THEY ENTERED
into an agreement. Although Steven planned to remain an Episcopalian, any
children they had would be raised in their mother's religion, Judaism.

When the couple's daughter, Jessica, was born four years later, there
was no religious ceremony to welcome her. Holidays such as Passover and
Easter were celebrated by the family at the homes of the respective grandparents. Then, when Jessica turned three, she was enrolled in a nursery school
that was affiliated with a Reform Jewish temple. "At that time, I began to
feel some stirrings about my own religious affiliation and beliefs," says Gail.
She found herself attending children's services with Jessica at the temple
from time to time. Once in a while, Steven would join them.

"Everything seemed to be going smoothly," Gail said, "until our family
got zapped by the December Dilemma." She laughs. "If you don't know
what that is, you're *not* in an interfaith marriage."

Those who *are* in an interfaith marriage, however, know full well the
tensions involved in deciding what to do about Christmas – which is essentially what the December Dilemma is all about. "Should we acknowledge
Christmas?" asks Gail. "Should we create a 'fairness' contest by making
much ado about Hanukkah, which is basically a minor Jewish holiday, just
because it falls during this time of year? Should we exchange gifts?"

---

1. Pseudonyms have been used for some family members' names.

271

The December Dilemma brings to the forefront of a marriage issues reflecting partners' different backgrounds that have remained submerged the rest of the year. Frequently, in fact, the difference in religion doesn't really matter to the couple while they are childless. "Without question," says Gail, "the problem of Christmas has increased in importance for us as Jessica has grown older."

Calendar-Cycle Events.

Christmas and other holidays create tension for many an interfaith family. "I know that I agreed to have our daughter brought up Jewish," says Steven, "but I didn't realize how I would feel about not being able to give her Christmas." For this couple – as for many others – the single most emotional issue of the December Dilemma is whether or not to have a Christmas tree. "Around the time that Jessica was five," Gail recalls, "Steven suddenly announced that he didn't want us to celebrate Christmas only with his parents. He wanted there to be a tree in *our* house, too. I found myself saying no, absolutely not."

To couples-and-family therapist Esther Perel, of New York City, Gail and Steven's experience is fairly typical of the interfaith couples she sees. "Christmas often crystallized the whole issue [of religious differences] between Jewish and Christian partners," she says, *especially* as it concerns the children, because so much of Christmas involves childhood memories." For the Christian partner, Christmas can be a family or secular event as well as, or even instead of, a religious holiday. Even if the tree has only secular meaning for the Christian partner, however, it may remain a Christian symbol in the Jewish partner's eyes.

Interfaith Marriages on the Increase.

Although there are no national statistics on the number of couples marrying across religious lines, even the most casual observer may have noticed that marriage between partners of different faiths is on the rise. The phenomenon is not limited to Jewish-gentile marriages, of course, but this combination presents a particular challenge because of the great differences in basic beliefs.

A report studying marriages between Jews and Christians in ten different communities from coast to coast – the closest thing we have to a national sample – provides some indication of how commonplace intermarriage has become.

"Until 1970 we were looking at intermarriage rates in the Jewish community of 10 to 14 percent," says Egon Mayer, Ph.D., professor of sociology at Brooklyn College, in New York, and an author of that report. "In 1989 that figure rose to 38 percent for Jewish males up to age 40 in first marriages, while 22 percent of Jewish women married non-Jewish spouses." Interfaith alliances in second marriages are even more prevalent.

There was a time when such liaisons were likely to result in the young couple's being disinherited by their families and expelled from their faiths. Although ostracism of those who "marry out" still takes place in certain families and within the more zealously religious communities, a more liberal atmosphere currently prevails. Hence, the *big* question facing many men and women caught up in dual-religion romances today seems to be not whether to intermarry but, rather, how to raise their children.

Life-Cycle Events.

Once a child is born, decisions must be made that are likely to bring the question of religion quickly to the fore. Will the baby be baptized? If a boy, will he be circumcised? Such life-cycle events continue to crop up as the child grows older. Will the child attend religious school? If yes, in what faith? The family may also feel pressures from outside the home. Grandparents who have kept their counsel regarding the interfaith marriage are likely to be far more outspoken concerning the religious upbringing of their grandchildren. If a grandparent requests it, will the child be confirmed? Have a bar mitzvah?

Participants in an interfaith marriage are sometimes surprised by their own feelings. One man who, before becoming a parent, had agreed not to raise children in *any* organized religion later found himself wanting to attend services with his daughter. "What draws me to organized religion now," he says, "is that I'd like my child to be exposed to some structure in which morality is taken seriously."

The following are some of the diverse answers I received to the question of how to raise the children, offered by couples who intermarried. It is evident that what works for one family is not necessarily right for another. It is also clear that the parents' search for answers is a thoughtful and ongoing pursuit.

Seeking Agreement – Finding a Unifying Faith.

Linda Frank has fond memories of growing up in Avon, Connecticut, where much of her family's life revolved around their Congregational church. Her husband, Paul, attended Sunday school at a Reform Jewish congregation in Forest Hills, New York, where he grew up, but, he says, "It was much more a social than a religious activity. All of my friends were there."

"I could never have become Jewish," Linda says. "I don't feel comfortable with it. It's steeped in ceremony and tradition that I don't know." Paul, on the other hand, did not feel at home in Linda's church. "There was a large cross at the front," he says, "and a lot of the Trinity in the ceremony, which made me uneasy."

Until their son, David, was four, Linda Frank attended a Unitarian church periodically. "Then, when David was about to enter Sunday school, we were asked if he could be an angel in the Christmas pageant," Paul says. "We said yes. In taking him to rehearsals, I found that I liked the involvement and the people I met. From then on, the church quickly became our special community, our village in the city."

Choosing to Convert.

In contrast with the Franks, some interfaith couples solve the problem of how to raise their children by having one of the partners convert to the religion of the other.

There is no question, according to Carol Levithan, that the intention to have children was *the* factor motivating her decision to convert from Methodism to Judaism, her husband Jack's faith. "Jack did not ask me to convert," says Carol. "It was clear, however, that Jack's religious commitment was stronger than mine. On a pragmatic level, I knew that any children we had were likely to be identified as Jews, and I didn't think it was possible to raise them in the Jewish faith with only one parent being Jewish."

But there's more to identity than adhering to one system of religious beliefs over another, families quickly discover. Interfaith issues are often also intercultural – the foods we eat, the songs we sing, the holidays we acknowledge – and the ways that we celebrate them are all tied up with our heritage.

"Although I underwent a formal conversion," says Carol, "I wondered about whether one could truly feel identified with a religion that one converts into. I've learned that it *can* happen, that you can become part of the collective consciousness of another people, but it takes a long time and a strong commitment."

Selecting One Religion, Incorporating Another.

Mary Friedman, a Roman Catholic, discussed religion with her husband, Donald, who is Jewish, on their third date. "I told Donald I had very strong feelings for him," Mary recalls, "and that I didn't want to continue the relationship if religion was going to be a problem." Donald did not have difficulty with the idea of raising his children as Catholics, but he also wanted to introduce Jewish traditions into their upbringing.

The couple married and had three daughters, now all in their twenties, who regard themselves as "interfaith children who belong to the Catholic community." Although the family observes the rites and rituals of the Roman Catholic church, the Friedmans also incorporate certain Judaic rituals into their family observances. "Our Passover seder is second to none," says Mary with pride. "This is, after all, the same meal that the Lord was celebrating before he died. What Don and I have conveyed to our daughters is that we have to respect the different ways that people bring ritual into their lives."

When people intermarry, and even if a dominant religion is chosen for the family, it is imperative that each parent be informed about the other's religion and respectful of the other's heritage, according to those who deal with family relationships. "Children are used to seeing differences between their parents," says Mel Hawthorne, chaplain of the Church Center for the United Nations, in New York City. "They recognize, for example, that one parent is skilled in music while the other is knowledgeable about sports. Children can handle differences. What they cannot handle between their parents is conflict."

Double Exposure.

Parents who choose to raise their children in two religions find that they not only have to gain an understanding of and respect for their spouse's faith but, in many cases, also have to become more knowledgeable about their own religion. "The more people examine their religion and learn about their spouse's, the more likely they are to understand the similarities and the very real differences between them," writes Rabbi Lavey Derby in his foreword to *Raising Your Jewish/Christian Child*, by Lee F. Gruzen (Newmarket Press). "That growing understanding will contribute to an authentic approach to family religious experience, not the interchangeability of religious symbols. ('Please don't hang your Happy Hanukkah sign from the Christmas tree.')"

Elizabeth O'Brian, a woman whose Catholic education extended through college, found Stanley Rosen's willingness to have their children baptized critical to accepting his marriage proposal. "Baptism essentially meant that I would be giving life, in a Christian sense, to any children we had," she says.

"If you agree to have our children baptized," Elizabeth remembers telling her then suitor, "I'll agree to raise them Jewish."

Replied Stanley, "If you agree to raise them Jewish, I'll agree to have them baptized."

"I came home and thought to myself, What in the world are we doing?" says Elizabeth, laughing as she looks back. "When you baptize your children, you agree to raise them as Catholics. We asked our religious leaders what their thoughts were. Fortunately, I consulted a priest who told me, 'My suggestion is to baptize them and to leave the rest to God.' It was our first encounter with the nitty-gritty of raising children in an interfaith marriage."

The true intermingling of faiths in this family did not occur until it was time for the children to begin their formal religious education. Until then, the entire family's synagogue attendance had pretty much been limited to the High Holidays. Elizabeth attended mass alone. Then, unable to find a local synagogue that would accept their children as students, because they had not been converted to Judaism, Stanley became active in founding a new, more liberal congregation. For a time he served as its spiritual and educational director. To this day, he teaches in the religious school. Because of this new involvement, the family (including Elizabeth) began to attend Friday-night services every week.

"Somewhere along the line," Stanley says, "I decided to reciprocate. The children and I started to accompany Elizabeth to church, where she serves as a Eucharistic minister. It gradually became acceptable to me that they also attend church Sunday school. It was no longer a case of 'This is what Daddy does; this is what Mommy does.' What we were now saying to our children was, 'This is what *we* do.'"

"Stanley and I felt it was our responsibility to offer God to our children in the ways that we know God, and then let them make their own, informed choice," Elizabeth says.

Their daughter, Beverly, sixteen, says she'll have a tough time deciding. Brian, fourteen, says, "I think it will depend on who I marry."

"The thing that's exciting to me," says Elizabeth, "is that both of them are planning to be *something* when they grow up. I think *that's* what we've accomplished. And the thing that has happened to Stanley and me over the years is that *we* have come to accept that whatever they decide is all right with us."

10.2 The Advantages and Contributions of Intermarriage
Man Keung Ho, Ph.D.

INTERMARRIAGE HAS BEEN TREATED IN THE PAST AS AN ABNORMALITY, defiance, or disgrace. Those who openly object to intermarriage for racial, ethnic, or religious reasons unfairly criticize it as a matrimonial "mismatch" or disaster. They feel it holds virtually no potential for growth and is doomed to failure. The truth is intermarriage, like any other marriage, in itself is neither good nor bad, right or wrong, successful or unsuccessful; it all depends on the couple involved to make it or not to make it succeed.

To make an intermarriage work, the couple needs a positive attitude that recognizes that intermarriage, if properly maintained, can be satisfying and advantageous to the intermarried couple, as well as to others who are around them. A couple who feels uncertain, insecure, and defensive of their involvement in an intermarriage has little chance of success. The affirmation of the intermarriage and the security found in each other are perhaps the most important ingredients in the building of a successful intermarriage.

The primary purpose of this chapter is to discuss the advantages of intermarriage and the contributions that a successful intermarriage can provide to society at large. The following discussion is based on my fifteen-year practice as a marriage counselor, personal contacts with hundreds of intermarried couples, and my own seventeen-year experience of intermarriage. The following discussion consists of three parts. First, the benefits found in preparing for an intermarriage; second, the many advantages intermarried couples experience in their relationship; third, the contributions intermarriage can make to others as the couple's relationship grows and matures.

Advantages of Intermarriage Preparation
1. More Thorough Preparation.

Due to society's attitudes, the individual contemplating intermarriage can be expected to encounter a fair amount of unsolicited advice and opposition from close friends and relatives. Despite original resentment toward this opposition, the individual will at least begin to think more seriously about intermarriage. When my wife and I were contemplating our marriage, during a one-week period, her parents, relatives, close friends, and her nursing instructors all talked to her about the negative implications of her impending marriage. In addition to resenting their unsolicited advice and discouragement, my wife felt uncertain, unloved, and exceedingly alone. In between prayers for God's guidance, my wife spent many hours considering the genuine care and concern evident in her family's and friends' suggestions, as she pondered the validity of their advice. She told me after our marriage that she had never given so much thought to anything in her whole life as she did to our marriage.

Although I did not encounter the same degree of opposition, I, too, devoted considerable time and energy thinking about our forthcoming marriage. As a graduate student in social work, I realized intellectually the importance sociological factors play in the success or failure of an intermarriage. Two years' courtship with my wife had thoroughly convinced me that we were psychologically and emotionally compatible. However, I was not certain how my parents, relatives, and close friends would accept my Caucasian wife. In addition to getting input from a few close friends who were intermarried, I consulted with two of my social work professors whose expertise was in marriage and family living. Their unbiased attitudes and concerned feedback provided me a greater degree of certainty and positive feelings about my plans for intermarriage.

Many successful intermarried couples report that the unenthusiastic attitude on the part of relatives and close friends toward their intermarriage helped them search harder for the motives behind their desire to intermarry. They more carefully assessed the degree of compatibility they felt with their partner. "I picked up every article and book I could possibly find regarding intermarriage. Although most of what I read discouraged such marriages, they started me thinking and rethinking all the time," one intermarried wife commented. "As a matter of fact, we once postponed our wedding. We had to be absolutely sure," echoed her husband. "Our one-year-long engagement provided us and our relatives ample time and opportunity to interact, to know, and to adjust to each other. I would suggest a long engagement period to every couple considering intermarriage," volunteered Mary, a Catholic whose husband is a Protestant.

As couples struggle to convince themselves — as well as others — of the suitability and desirability of their intermarriage, they are likely to take time to consider seriously the future of their interaction and relationship. Such projection and serious discussion can help the couple think, feel, and plan beyond their present romantic feelings. Thus they deepen their commitment and increase the likelihood of permanence in their marriage. Obviously, not every couple responds to parental or external opposition with thoughtful considerations. Sometimes opposition actually prompts couples into making a quick decision that may result in a dissatisfying marriage. Those who take others' opinions and opposition thoughtfully and take time to contemplate seriously their own actions are more likely to have a successful intermarriage.

2. Greater Degree of Commitment.

Commitment in a marriage refers to an agreement or understanding between husband and wife that their marital union is for a lifetime. A committed couple gives top priority to resolving difficulties and problems that come up in their marriage. Couples of the same religious or cultural background, who have encountered relatively mild or no opposition (perhaps even encouragement) from parents, clergy, or friends, will likely not have the realistic appreciation of commitment as will intermarried couples who have had to struggle every step to make their marriage a reality.

"Our ten-month engagement period was the most trying period for our relationship," commented Jack who is a Mormon married to a Baptist. "During those ten months everybody seemed to be against us. My own parents took every possible opportunity to discourage me from marrying a non-Mormon. Our Mormon bishop tried to convince me with literature and studies showing why marriage to a non-Mormon would not work. My own beloved sister cried and urged me not to upset our parents. On several occasions, she even brought home some Mormon girl friends, hoping that I might develop an interest in one of them," continued Jack. "I admit that I was in turmoil when my fiancee shared with me that she also experienced similar opposition and discouragement from her family. I really had doubts if we should continue with our marriage plans. After many hours of frank and honest discussion, we were sure that our love was not just infatuation. Our discussions enabled us to deepen our understanding of each other and further clarify our motives for intermarriage. With all the opposition from those who cared about us, it would have been easier for us to call it quits. We didn't; we stuck with each other instead. Our struggles during the engagement period gave us a lot of confidence in our marriage later. This is what commitment does," concluded Jack.

Since intermarriages often develop in a rather hostile environment, the couple find themselves forced into a more self-reliant position. Upon making the decision to intermarry, the individual realizes that he or she can no longer depend upon sympathetic supporters to make the marriage work. Whether the intermarriage succeeds or not will be contingent mainly upon the couple's determination and willingness to make it work. Such couples, having faced opposition, are usually strengthened in their commitment to make their marriage succeed.

The greater degree of commitment displayed by intermarrieds is documented by a study recently conducted in Hawaii.[1] The purpose of the study was to compare the strengths of homocultural and intercultural marriages under stress. The population selected for this study consisted of fifty-six couples who had completed home hemodialysis training at least six months prior to the study. Data regarding these fifty-six couples were obtained by reviewing medical records and social service summaries and also by interviewing nursing staff who knew the couples. Success of home hemodialysis was defined as the patient's being maintained at home for a minimum of six months. Failures were those who could not be maintained for six months at home and had to return to a hospital-based dialysis program. The ethnic group of both the patient and the spouse was known for fifty-one of the couples. Thirty-seven were homocultural couples; of these, twenty-eight were successful at home hemodialysis and nine were failures. Fourteen were intercultural couples, and they experienced no failures. The probability that this difference could be explained by chance is less than five percent. The results of this study support the hypothesis that an intercultural marriage requires stronger bonds and commitment and, therefore, will tolerate an external stress more readily.

1. Streltzer, J., "Intercultural Marriages Under Stress: The Effect of Chronic Illness." *Adjustment in Intercultural Marriage.* Honolulu, Hawaii: The University Press of Hawaii, 1977.

3. Greater Degree of Self-Other Differentiation.

Among the many benefits marriage provides is the opportunity to better understand and to accept oneself. For couples of the same cultural and religious backgrounds, this process of self-acceptance and self-differentiation is often difficult. Janet, a divorcee, explained that the major problem in her previous marriage was caused by the fact that both she and her ex-husband, David, shared practically everything in common. Janet and David are Caucasian and Protestant. Both grew up in the same town and graduated from the same high school. Both are from middle class families and share the same values on practically every subject. "We could not have been happier when we first married. Our parents and close friends thought our marriage was made in heaven. We loved each other so much; we were always together. For a while, we felt we were the luckiest, most compatible and admired couple in town," commented Janet. "But our relationship began to change when we realized one day we were just tired and bored with each other. We knew each other's background, beliefs, and interests too well. We ran out of topics to share with each other. Instead, we picked fights about minor things, and we seemed to get on each other's nerves all the time. We could not understand why we could know each other so well and depend on each other so completely, but at the same time come to a point where we could not even tolerate each other's presence," explained Janet.

After the divorce, Janet spent ten months in therapy. During this period, she met Jerry, who is a Catholic. The couple has been dating for five months. Janet reflected that her relationship with Jerry was very different from her relationship with David. "The fact that Jerry is a Catholic made me guarded in my dealings with him at the beginning of our relationship. After we got to know each other, we began to discuss important matters — including our own faith — honestly and openly. Through the mutual sharing of our faith, we came to know each other much better. We now realize we have a lot of commonalities in our beliefs, and I specifically like the manner in which we mutually respect and accept our religious differences. Although we care about each other a lot and spend a great deal of time with each other, we have separate friends, and we occasionally do things separately according to our own individual interests. Because of our mutual respect and acceptance of our religious differences, I feel I am gaining a stronger personal identity. We have no plans to marry yet, but the feeling of being oneself and having a separate identity is something I definitely need in my next marriage," concluded Janet.

Obviously, Janet's experience does not apply to all couples who share a religious or cultural background, but it clearly reflects the advantage intermarriage can hold for couples. When we are surrounded by others, including our spouse, whose religion or cultural experiences are like ours, we tend to take our value orientation, beliefs, and individuality for granted. The commonalities we share with our spouse provide us with comfort and complacence, which does little to challenge our individuality and identity. When our partner is of a different ethnicity, race, or religion, this difference forces us to be more aware of and to work toward gaining recognition and acceptance of our own identity. Only through respecting and accepting our own identity can we genuinely respect and accept our partner's identity.

Advantages to the Intermarried
4. Greater Degree of Acceptance, Tolerance, and Respect.

A couple's recognition of cultural and religious differences is one important step toward building a successful intermarriage. Marriage between individuals of the same cultural or religious backgrounds often leaves both spouses with little physical, psychological, and emotional space between them. Since they are seen and expected to function as one entity, they may be reluctant to acknowledge differences. When one spouse thinks, feels, or behaves differently from the other, tension and feelings of rejection may develop. In defense of one's self-righteousness, a spouse may attack the other who is expressing differences. The one attacked will naturally become defensive, and the virtues of acceptance, tolerance, and respect, essential to a successful marriage, may disappear. What begins as a trivial issue may end in unresolvable conflict between the couple.

An intermarried couple usually has a high degree of awareness and acceptance of their cultural or religious differences. These differences are constantly visible and are usually reinforced by those around them. The couple feels little threat to their sense of individuality when one partner is confronted by the other who thinks, feels, and behaves differently. In some instances, intermarried couples actually are surprised when their partners behave no differently in a situation than they do. Allen, a Reformed Jew, asked his Protestant wife, Debbie, on Christmas Eve if she was bothered by something, for this was the first Christmas in their five-year marriage that Debbie was not playing Christmas music. Debbie replied smilingly that since she was filled with joy, warmth, and appreciation of God's presence in their marriage, she wanted to share this with Allen in a special quiet way. Allen was touched by Debbie's generosity. He replied that as his love grew stronger for her, he was no longer bothered by Christmas music as he once was.

As we accept the other's differences, we have no need to be critical of our partner. We no longer feel pressured to defend ourselves. Our mutual acceptance frees us to truly be ourselves. In this freedom, we become secure and comfortable enough to take risks and make changes in our attitudes, feelings, and behavior. Jennifer, a Caucasian, confessed that when she married Phillip, an American Indian, she was feeling insecure about herself. "I never was comfortable with myself when I was growing up. I dropped out of the sorority house when I was a junior in college. The pressure to conform and to be like the other girls on campus got to me. When I met Phillip, I felt very comfortable with him. He did not expect me to conform as white guys did. It felt refreshing to be with Phillip, who allowed and encouraged me to be myself," added Jennifer.

When asked to comment on the adjustment problems of intermarriage, Sovann, a Vietnamese wife, admitted that after spending two years convincing her parents to approve her marriage to Mike, who is black, she considered the daily husband-wife hassles too trivial to be bothered with. "Our struggle to be married had convinced me that we really loved each other. We indulge each other by letting the other "get by" with a lot of little things. We don't agree with each other all the time, but that's no big deal. Whenever we get bogged down in some silly argument, we remind each other of the obstacles and struggles we overcame to marry. That gives us strength to go on and plenty of love to respect, accept, and indulge each other," added Sovann.

5. Broader Opportunities for Learning and Growth.

The fact that a couple comes from different religions or cultures provides them with ample opportunities to learn from each other. To mature as an individual, we can never cease to learn; but real learning can take place only if one is allowed and encouraged to be different. Additionally, real learning requires a conducive environment and challenging stimuli, and these are often provided by a partner with a different background from ours. Rivera, a noted Hispanic educator and community organizer, admits that he attributes a great deal of his professional success to his helpful and inspiring Caucasian wife. "I've learned so much from Jeannie about how white folks think and feel toward certain ideas and issues. In my dealings with whites, I've been successful in bridging the communications and cultural gap. I've been surprised how wrong I was in stereotyping them. Although occasionally I'm still annoyed by Jeannie who persistently corrects my misconceptions of the white culture, I trust and appreciate her honesty and sincerity in helping me to relate to whites on an individual basis," explained Rivera.

One partner's different religious practices or observances can also be a stimulating and inspiring learning experience for the other. Dollie, an Irish Catholic, related that at the beginning of her marriage, she was somewhat threatened by her Jewish husband, Herb, who was an active supporter of Israel and a generous contributor to Jewish philanthropic causes. Herb always conducted Passover Seder at home and visited the synagogue on Yom Kippur, the Day of Atonement, and the holiest day of the Jewish year. Through continued discussions with her husband, Dollie learned the significance of these Jewish religious observances and in the process became more aware of her own religious heritage. As Dollie became interested in her husband's religious and ethnic practices, Herb, in turn, volunteered to attend mass and St. Patrick's Day celebrations with her. "Being a 'nondevout' Irish Catholic, I was sure I would not take my faith seriously the moment I left my parents' home and got married; but because of Herb's strong identity with Judaism, I've been forced to examine my own roots. Now, I not only have rediscovered my own faith and ethnicity, I also have discovered my husband's religious faith and ethnicity. I feel my marriage over the past two years has helped me grow up rapidly," reflected Dollie.

As we grow up, most of us are "wounded" by some unpleasant experience that will affect us in adult life. Some of these wounds may be healed by a partner who has a different religious or cultural orientation.

Peter, a socially conscious and highly motivated Caucasian, was frustrated by the fact that he was approaching mid-life but still had to struggle daily to provide for his family. His childhood dream of becoming a noted architect had faded long ago, and he was now working as an assistant to a city planner. His disappointment in his career and his inability to provide the affluence he wished for his family gradually drove him into depression and divorce. After some months Peter remarried. His present wife, Karen, an American Indian, has had a profound and positive influence on Peter and has helped him overcome his depression. When asked to elaborate on his wife's influence on him, Peter explained that Karen had taught him to live noncompetitively and happily. Through her influence, he learned that one of the virtues in life for the American Indian is sharing with others instead of accumulating material goods. He came to realize that to attain maturity, he had to learn to live with life, its evil as well as its good. He learned that in the midst of abject poverty can come the courage to face life as it is, and he came to appreciate the importance of a sense of humor. With help from Karen, Peter also learned to believe that no matter where he stands, he is an integral part of the universe. Because every person is fulfilling a purpose, no one should have the power to impose on another. For this reason, each person is to be respected, and each should have reverence for all others. The security Peter found in this sense of inner fulfillment provided him with a sense of serenity that he was missing prior to marrying Karen.

6. Greater Opportunities and Perspectives for Children.

Through exposure to both parents' religious and ethnic cultures, children from a successful intermarriage tend to have a greater opportunity to learn and to express themselves. They are likely to have a heightened awareness, a harmonious integration of themselves and their environment, a satisfying relationship with themselves, and enriched relationships with others. The opportunity for assimilation and integration of both their parents' backgrounds can make children of intermarriages more "cultured" than children of parents from the same religious, ethnic, or racial background.

Tyroon's father is Caucasian Protestant; his mother is Black Moslem. As a young child growing up in a white neighborhood, Tyroon had the opportunity to spend every summer in a black neighborhood where his grandparents resided. Tyroon accumulated many fond memories of playing ball and just "messing around" with the black kids while staying with his grandparents. "I particularly liked the soul music, the laughter, and the spontaneity of living among blacks. Being with the black folks helped me mature very early. My grandparents refused to do things for me which I could do for myself. First, I resented having to do so many chores, but I later appreciated the opportunity to learn to be self-sufficient," recalled Tyroon.

Naomi, a second generation Japanese-American who is a top scholar in her senior high school class, volunteered that she would not trade her childhood experiences for anything. Naomi's father is an immigrant from Japan and her mother is a Caucasian of Polish descent. "While my mother tended to be protective of me and keep me from anxiety-provoking situations, my father would gently explain to me the value of learning how to cope with a stressful event. I benefited so much from my mother's positive unconditional love which made me feel secure. Additionally, I learned from my father discipline and determination to get a difficult task accomplished. My parents never tried to conceal the fact that they are racially and culturally different. They wanted me to learn from their differences. As a matter of fact, my physical appearance and my identity made me unique among my peers. My classmates' curiosity about my ethnic background makes me feel they really are interested in me as a unique person and as their special friend," commented Naomi.

While the majority of his friends in senior high school show up at school in fashionable jeans and ride in relatively new cars, David, a Quaker and president of the Social Action Club, is content with wearing plain clothes and riding his bicycle to school. When asked the reason behind his nonconformist style, David explained calmly that he likes simplicity and the virtue of quality living, and he is perplexed by social injustice. "My father is a Quaker who taught me the virtue of simplicity. My conscientiousness about social injustice stems from the influence of my mother who is a devout Catholic. She believes to be a Catholic is to mirror the image of God who is fair and just," volunteered David.

7. Children More Accepting of Differences in Others.

A child's relationship with others depends a great deal upon his or her ability to accept differences in others. If parents with the same religious and cultural backgrounds do not expose their child to different ways of thinking, he/she may find it difficult to accept differences in others. For a child of an intermarriage, on the other hand, living and interacting with differences become facts of life. When this child is faced with strange and new ideas or behavior in others, he or she is not surprised and can accept and react positively to these differences.

When the rest of the third graders were ridiculing and running away from Kireen, an Arab-American who had brought a lamb chop for lunch, Kwok-Hong, a Chinese-American, remained seated and behaved calmly. When he was asked by one of the students how he could stand seeing and smelling Kireen's lamb chop, Kwok-Hong replied matter of factly that strange foods and diets never bothered him. "When I was in Hong Kong visiting my grandparents last Christmas, my uncle took us to a Chinese restaurant where we had snake meat. Since I like the taste of snake meat, why should I make fun of Kireen's lamb chop?" quipped Kwok-Hong. In response to Kwok-Hong's support, Kireen commented affectionately, "You're my pal."

When Gary, an American Indian student, was demonstrating the rain dance to his class, a majority of the students laughed with disbelief. Somaly, a Vietnamese Buddhist, was one of the students who refused to laugh and ridicule Gary. The teacher asked Somaly's feelings and impressions about the rain dance. Somaly explained that growing up in a Buddhist family in Vietnam, she had been exposed to a variety of Buddhist practices. "Some of these practices may seem strange to foreigners, but they are the Buddhist's way of relating to God." She added that she appreciated the opportunity to learn about American Indian ways of relating to God and would never consider the rain dance a laughing matter.

Nancy, a second generation Pole and a college junior majoring in special education, was exceptional in working with elementary students with reading difficulties. "I have a special feeling for individuals who cannot read and speak English well. My mother is a Polish immigrant and has had difficulty reading English for years. Even now, when she gets emotional, she prefers to speak in Polish. I recall many times my mother telling me that her deficiency in English makes her very self-conscious. I acquired a sensitivity from my mother toward those who cannot speak and read English well," explained Nancy.

8. Greater Vitality in Family Living.

There is clear evidence that families plagued by problems are families in which there are few activities and little excitement in the home environment. Since family members do not engage in fun and pleasurable activities together, they become more vulnerable to and intolerant of family conflict and crises. The diversity in an intermarriage often assures that there is no lack of activity in the family. With a variety of interests and pursuits, such a family's life rarely becomes a boring routine.

Despite being raised as a Lutheran, which is the religious faith of his mother, Tom related that some of his most pleasant memories were of times he spent with his Jewish father. In addition to practicing Christianity at home, Tom always looked forward to participating in Passover Seder with his father. His visits to the synagogue with his father on Yom Kippur were highlights of his childhood.

Similarly, my wife's Irish Catholic background and my Chinese cultural heritage have produced an exciting blend and mixture in our family's activities. In addition to enjoying delicious Irish meals, we all look forward to St. Patrick's Day celebrations and Irish dancing. Our meals may offer American or Chinese food with the option of using flatware or chopsticks. Our family also blends American and Chinese style clothing. In addition to practicing American customs and traditions such as celebrating Christmas, Independence Day, and New Year's, we celebrate the Chinese New Year and other festivals like Chung-Chow-git (Mid-Autumn Moon) and Ching-Ming (Early Spring). The Chung-Chow-git is a reminder of people's relationship to nature (God), and Ching-Ming is a reminder of people's relationship with ancestors. These observances have added a great deal of cohesion and vitality to our family. I remember listening to a conversation between our older son and his friend when our son was four. As he was patiently explaining to his friend about the lucky money (Li-See) he received from his grandparents in Hong Kong for Chinese New Year, his friend abruptly interjected and complained, "It is not fair; you have two New Years. I have only one. You have lucky money and I don't."

The richness of an intermarriage provides the family with planned and structured times and activities in which family members can freely and openly engage and express their affection for each other. Such experiences provide family members with a sense of belonging, stability, identity, and continuity that are essential to their social, psychological, emotional, and spiritual development.

Advantages and Contributions to Others
1. A Model of Acceptance to Families and Friends.

A successful intermarriage offers benefits to those who are close to the couple. When Judy, a Caucasian Protestant, and Armando, a Philippino Catholic, were married, parents of both spouses displayed little enthusiasm or support. The couple's parents respected their children, but they were uncertain how the interracial and interfaith aspects of their marriage were going to fare. Judy and Armando's marriage has had its share of adjustment problems, but the couple usually settle their differences remarkably well. They have two elementary school-age children who have been a pride and joy to their grandparents. One year ago, Judy's parents (both Caucasian), after thirty-two years of marriage, experienced marital conflicts which nearly ended in divorce. "When I was seriously wondering whether to get a divorce or not, I caught myself thinking about my daughter's marriage. What impressed me most about her marriage was their ability to accept each other and to work out their cultural and religious differences. When I think of the many adjustments Judy and Armando have had to make during the course of their marriage, I feel embarrassed about my rigidity and my unwillingness to compromise with my wife," explained Judy's father.

An interfaith marriage can provide relatives with an example and inspiration to strengthen their own spirituality. "I had no idea that my son's interfaith marriage could have such positive effects on my spirituality. Our son's continued and exhaustive study of Catholicism and his efforts to understand Judaism, the religion of his wife Barbara, made me realize that both mine and my husband's Catholic faith had not grown since the day we married. Since both my husband and I are Catholic, we tend to take our faith for granted. There is a great deal about Catholic beliefs which we have not studied and, therefore, do not know much about. Neither one of us likes to discuss this subject because we hate to admit we are ignorant. John and Barbara have been married for only one year but she studied Catholicism diligently and probably knows more about it than my husband and I," explained John's mother when she was asked in a religious education class the reason behind her enrolling. "Interestingly enough, the opportunity for my husband and me to study Catholicism together has shown us that we can disagree agreeably. We owe this gift to our son and daughter-in-law," she added.

A successful intermarriage can be a challenge to others' ethnocentrism, their subjective, emotional belief that their ethnicity, race, or religion is superior to others. Abdul, a Black Moslem, and Sharon, a Caucasian Protestant, have a very successful marriage. Although Abdul is a successful businessman and a devoted husband and father, Sharon's father had difficulty accepting him. Five years after the couple's marriage, Abdul's father-in-law finally felt comfortable in introducing Abdul to his friends as his son-in-law. "I have learned a lot about myself through my daughter's intermarriage. I could not believe I was so prejudiced toward blacks; I was very hostile to my own daughter whom I felt subjected me to this personal predicament and embarrassment. As I witnessed the love my son-in-law showed to my daughter, I became grateful to him and accepted him. As I gradually changed my attitude toward blacks, I discovered that I was also changing my attitude toward other ethnic groups and nationalities. Many of my old attitudes towards things in general have also changed, and my wife and other people find me a lot easier to live with and to be with. I owe this to Abdul and Sharon's intermarriage," concluded Sharon's father.

2. Enrichment of Community Life.

If an intermarried couple is successfully married, they usually are active in community affairs. The unique talents of intermarried couples and the love they both share easily and readily spill over to others with whom they have contact in the community. Pedro, a Cuban immigrant, was instrumental in organizing soccer leagues for school-age children. In addition to his many hours of organizational work, Pedro headed the coaching staff. His friendly personality and extensive knowledge of soccer were readily appreciated in the community. One of the parents volunteered that Pedro's contribution extended beyond his sharing of his knowledge of soccer. His generous sharing of himself made him a walking advertisement for the people of Cuba. Through their interaction with Pedro, many children were exposed to Cuban culture. The children's respect and acceptance of Pedro enabled them to accept differences more easily. When Pedro was asked the reason behind his active involvement in the community, his reply was, "I was blessed with the acceptance of my wife who is American Caucasian; my involvement with the community is only an extension of our happy marriage."

Although a Protestant himself, James was the guitarist for his wife's Catholic church. When the church honored him for his contribution, James explained that his acceptance by Catholics meant a great deal to him as a person and a Protestant. Through his musical involvement with the Catholic church and the parishioners' acceptance of him, he felt the presence of God. Those parishioners who are close to James shared with him this same sentiment.

As an intermarried couple, my wife's and my involvement with our community has also been very meaningful to us. Our last five years' active involvement with our parish's marriage preparation program is a living example to the engaged that intermarriage can work. Our continued involvement with the program also witnesses to the engaged couples that constant work and learning from each other will be needed to keep their marriage alive and their lives productive.

We are involved in religious education, Big Brothers and Big Sisters, Boy Scouts of America, a children's home, and our son's soccer program. But our involvement and contributions to community life are not limited to us as an intermarried couple; our children are also involved. The visible difference in our children's physical appearance and their bicultural background have contributed significantly to the schools they attend and to the children with whom they interact. They are often asked by their teachers to share with their classmates the various cultural practices of our family. Our children have been asked to demonstrate the use of chopsticks and to display calligraphy for their classes. We have been told repeatedly by our children's teachers that their bicultural background has added an enlightening educational dimension to their classes and to the school environment as a whole.

3. An Example of God's Love for All Mankind.

Despite our differences, all of us are God's children. We are God's creation. It is God who creates us different from one another. To be different does not imply good or bad, right or wrong, superior or inferior. It does not imply that we cannot or should not love each other. Instead, our differences can complement each other's needs, heal past wounds, and help each of us to be more whole. Despite religious teaching that we are to love each other regardless of our differences, many racial, ethnic, and religious groups and their followers do just the opposite. Intermarriage can be like a lighthouse for all to see that God's love and plan for unity between races, ethnicities, and religions can be lived out in a world of spilled milk and dirty diapers, and in the crisis-stricken, conflict-laden world that family life can be.

I recall twelve years ago when I first took my wife to visit my parents in Hong Kong, they commented on the strong affection and bonds of love they witnessed in both of us. My father remarked that because of my wife's relationship to him as her father-in-law, he felt less suspicious and more trusting of foreigners, including Americans. The warm and sincere reception which my wife received from my parents and hundreds of relatives and close friends made us believe that our marriage had the same positive impact on all of our relatives and close friends. Likewise, my wife's family and relatives have expressed to us that our intermarriage has enlightened their respect and acceptance of others who are different from them.

As an educator, marriage counselor, and an active member of our church and community, I have close contact with individuals who have various family and marital problems. Their willingness to share with me their intimate family and marital difficulties is influenced partly by my intermarried status. Occasionally, clients who are of the same cultural and religious background inform me that they are inspired by my intermarriage. "If you and your wife can make it as a married couple despite all of your cultural differences, I should give my marriage a chance. After all, both my wife and I are white Americans and share the same religious faith," commented one of my clients.

My racial identity and the fact that I speak with a Chinese accent have created curiosity and sometimes initial animosity in some adults and children my wife and I have met. But after they get to know us and we get to know them, we relate to each other as friends. In so many instances, I have had adults and children tell me that they were pleasantly surprised to learn I am no different from them. They say they appreciate my warmth, acceptance, friendliness, and respect for them. My response to them is that we are all God's children. Perhaps, God is using me and my marriage to remind them of this simple fact.

Applications and Suggestions
1. Intermarried Couples.

Recognizing that intermarriage has added advantages and makes unique contributions to others should be reassuring to those of us involved in intermarriage. Our certainty and confidence in intermarriage can help us to be less defensive and more confident in our relationship with our spouse and with others.

Aware of the advantages in an intermarriage and the contributions it can make, our next step is to ensure that our own intermarriage achieves its full potential. The advantages and contributions of intermarriage are not givens; a great deal of awareness and hard work are required of a couple prior to and after their wedding to realize these advantages and make these contributions. But just having a conviction of the potential of an intermarriage is the first positive step toward making the marriage successful.

2. Individuals Interested in Intermarriage.

It is important to keep in mind that the advantages of intermarriage that we have been discussing stem from a successful intermarriage. It would be a mistake to intermarry thinking that these advantages are automatic. Intermarriage may sound intriguing to you, but you should not overlook the many potential problem areas inherent in intermarriage. If you are considering intermarriage, it is imperative that you carefully evaluate your motives, assess your compatibility, and double your determination if you are to be successfully intermarried. As a couple prepares for intermarriage, they can likely anticipate considerable opposition and unsolicited advice from relatives and friends. You need to be patient and considerate toward families' and friends' concerns and suggestions, remembering that to a certain extent the success of your marriage depends on their support. It is important that your relationship with relatives and close friends not be jeopardized just because they have different perspectives on intermarriage. They still have a sincere interest and concern for you and your future happiness.

3. Relatives and Friends.

The advantages and contributions described in this chapter are real facts of life for many intermarried couples. But still these couples or couples contemplating intermarriage can anticipate strong opposition and resentment from loved ones who believe the old myth that intermarriage holds no promises and advantages but automatically spells disaster. As relatives or close friends, it is not for us to decide whether our loved one should intermarry. Instead, our responsibility is to assist the couple to have a successful marriage, intermarriage included. To do this one must first give support and cooperation. We may not agree with our loved one's decision, but we need to be respectful of his or her intentions. Upon sensing our respect and genuine concern, the individual will come to trust us enough to engage us in mutual exploration of his or her desires and motivations. If we show that we appreciate the advantages and contributions of intermarriage, our loved one may respect and trust us more. An accepting and trusting atmosphere will, in turn, encourage him or her to explore comfortably and nondefensively with us potential problem areas inherent in intermarriage.

Relatives and close friends do play a vital role in making or breaking a loved one's marriage. Regardless of our feelings about intermarriage, it is our loved one's happiness that should be our utmost concern. The individual is not asking us to make the decision. Instead, our loved one is asking us to be interested and supportive of his or her decision or indecision. As described in this chapter, the success of our loved one's intermarriage can bring enrichment to our own lives.

4. Clergy and Counselors.

Recognizing the potential richness of intermarriage is essential in successfully counseling individuals involved in intermarriage. By conveying to the couple an awareness of the potential richness of intermarriage, the counselor can gain the counselee's trust and openness that are essential to successful counseling. When the counselor acknowledges the potential richness of intermarriage, the counselee is made to feel that he or she is not making (or has not made) an unreasonable or foolish mistake. The counselee then is free to express concerns reflecting potential problems or real problems in the relationship. The role of the clergy or counselor is not to encourage or discourage intermarriage. Instead, the counselor is to assist the counselee in making a thoughtful and wise decision.

Generally, couples recognize society's unfavorable attitude toward intermarriage. The counselor's positive attitude may provide the support the couple needs to help them arrive at a mutually beneficial decision. If the counselor shares society's negative view of intermarriage, then he or she needs to refer the couple to other professionals who have a more positive and objective view of intermarriage. The attitudes of the counseling minister, priest, or rabbi and his or her interaction with the couple can have an enormous effect on their happiness and their future relationship with God.

Summary

Intermarriage provides couples with advantages which may include more thorough premarital preparation, a greater degree of commitment, and a greater degree of self-other differentiation. When the intermarriage is successful, it enables the couple to tolerate and respect each other's cultural differences. Successful intermarriage can also provide greater opportunities for learning and growth as an individual and as a married couple. Broader cultural perspectives can also produce gifted children who learn to accept differences in others. Successful intermarriage provides greater diversity and vitality in family living and can benefit other people. It provides a model of mutual acceptance to the families of origin; it brings enrichment to community life; and it exemplifies God's love of all mankind.

10.3 Problems in Intermarriage
Man Keung Ho, Ph.D.

INTERMARRIAGE, LIKE ANY OTHER MARRIAGE, IS A CONTINUOUS PROCESS IN which two persons learn to live together and adjust to each other in order to work toward common goals and achievements. When persons of different ethnic, racial, or religious backgrounds marry, their adjustment difficulties are likely to greatly exceed those of couples of the same background. To the normal differences in personality, social class, education, and life experiences must be added the differences in values, customs, and traditions associated with differing ethnicities, races, and religions. The main objective of this chapter is to explore some of the problems which are particularly relevant to intermarried couples.

Generally, adjustment problems in intermarriage can be traced to one of three sources: (1) the total cultural milieu; (2) the social factors contributing to the intermarried's adjustment problems; and (3) the couple's interaction as husband and wife and as parents. These three problem areas will serve as our outline in discussing difficulties normally encountered by intermarried couples.

Major Cultural Conflicts

Culture, in one of its simplest meanings, refers to the widely shared customs and traditions of a specific homogeneous population, be it an ethnic, racial, or religious group. In such a social entity, marriage is established according to customs which specify eligible partners, ways of negotiating the marriage, and behaviors and relationships appropriate for marriage. Presumably, all marriages in such social groups take place within the same population. In the case of intermarriage, husband and wife from differing cultures involving various customs, traditions, thoughts, and behavior, will naturally encounter adjustment difficulties with each other. Additionally, some cultures have antithetical, almost mutually exclusive, concepts of marriage.

Bruce, a Caucasian, was extremely frustrated by the fact that his Taiwan-born wife, Le-Yang, didn't seem to be bothered by their lack of intimacy toward each other. Bruce was operating from a modern Western concept of marriage which emphasizes romantic love and mutual self-realization as important marriage goals. Le-Yang came from a cultural background that placed greater emphasis on economic security and subservience to husband as major goals in marriage.

Differing concepts of marriage are also responsible for Jennifer's and John's disillusionment. Jennifer is a Mormon and John is a Methodist. "I don't understand why John is unhappy. I'm always home when he arrives. Everybody says I'm an excellent housewife, and I wait on him hand and foot. What is wrong with letting my husband be in charge?" asked Jennifer. John's complaint was that he no longer was happy in a "father-daughter" type of marriage and preferred instead an egalitarian husband-wife relationship. But Jennifer seemed unable to reciprocate. "I don't like to be in charge. Besides that, my mother was never in charge and she and father got along beautifully," explained Jennifer.

Clearly Jennifer's comment is a reflection of the cultural values she obtained from her Mormon home while growing up as a child. Differing cultural values are a major problem in intermarriage because most of us tend to feel that our particular culturally ordained values are incontestably "right" or "true" or "the best." This quality of essential rightness is inherent in value systems, for each culture tends to teach its particular value system as representing the most appropriate way to conduct one's life. We usually do not recognize that we subscribe to a particular set of values until they are challenged — perhaps when we encounter someone whose values differ from ours. Once our value system is challenged, especially by our spouse, we become uncertain and react defensively. We may lose objectivity and become offensive, which could result in increased marital problems.

Problems Caused By Outside Sources
1. Influence from Relatives.

In addition to problems caused by the clash of cultures, problems in intermarriage may emanate from our family members, including parents, grandparents, siblings, uncles, aunts, cousins, and so on.

Sophia, an Italian Catholic, and Jay, an Irish Catholic, had not been speaking to each other for days since the couple's recent visit to Sophia's family. Jay was annoyed by the "kissing and hugging" behavior displayed by Sophia's family members. "It would be okay if they were affectionate toward each other all the time, but they fight like hell when they disagree," complained Jay. "What's more, when they insist that both Sophia and I attend their Italian Catholic church, I cannot take it," continued Jay.

Karen, a Caucasian, was upset because over the past months she had hardly seen her husband, Sung-Boo, a Korean, and their three-month-old son. Sung-Boo got off work earlier than Karen so he picked up their son from the nursery and went to his parent's home. His parents openly criticized Karen for returning to work after the baby was born. Although Sung-Boo realized the financial necessity behind Karen's working, he still felt guilty that his parents' wishes were unmet. His uncertainty about his priorities, whether to please his parents or his wife, caused him considerable personal misery and threatened his relationship with his wife and young son. As the couple was struggling with their problems, in-laws from both families contended that because of their cultural differences, the couple should never have married.

2. Churches' and Religious Groups' Attitudes.

After a two-year courtship with her Catholic boyfriend, John, Edie finally convinced her Jewish (Reformed) parents to approve of an interfaith wedding ceremony at which a priest and a rabbi would jointly officiate. To avoid offending Edie's parents and the rabbi, John was successful in getting his priest to delete certain Christological references in the ritual. To everybody's dismay, the rabbi from the synagogue Edie's parents attended refused to perform the ceremony.

A review of the history of Judaism reveals that from the beginning Jews have looked with disfavor upon intermarriage with non-Jews, and for centuries their survival as a distinct religious and ethnic group has been due in large measure to their refraining from intermarriage with other groups. The language of Deuteronomy (7:1-4) is direct and clear: "When the Lord your God brings you into the land which you are to enter and occupy, and dislodges great nations before you . . . make no covenant with them. . . . You shall not intermarry with them, neither giving your daughters to their sons nor taking their daughters for your sons. For they would turn your sons from following me to serving other gods, and then the wrath of the Lord would flare up against you and quickly destroy you."

Rabbi Sol Roth, president of the Rabbinical Council of America, recently recommended that Jews who marry outside the faith and rabbis who perform the ceremonies be denied all "leadership roles in Jewish life." Rabbi Sanford Seltzer, Director of Research and Planning of the Union of American Hebrew Congregations, explained recently that a rabbi's refusal to participate in an interfaith marriage ceremony is in no way intended as a deliberate slight to the engaged. Their stand is based upon Judaism's view of marriage which essentially states that a wedding ceremony is the symbolic prelude to the commitment of a couple to live as Jews, to raise children in the Jewish faith and, thereby, to preserve the future of the Jewish people. An interfaith marriage by definition means the existence of two faiths, side by side, in one family. Most Jews, especially the Orthodox, feel that the Jewish religion is being seriously threatened by secular forces, and one way to combat these forces is to discourage marriage outside the faith.

Judaism's negative stand toward intermarriage may not be shared by other religious groups, but each has its practices that directly or indirectly discourage intermarriage. For a Roman Catholic to marry a non-Catholic, special permission from the bishop is required. To obtain this dispensation, the Catholic party must reaffirm, to the priest or deacon preparing him or her for marriage, faith in Christ and must state the intention to continue living that faith in the Catholic church. Prior to the wedding ceremony, the Catholic partner must also promise verbally or on paper "to do all in my power to share the faith I have received with our children by having them baptized and reared as Catholics." The non-Catholic partner must be informed of this promise. Many Catholic dioceses permit interfaith marriage outside of a Catholic church building provided the couple completes a four- to six-month marriage preparation program. Often the priest and the non-Catholic minister will jointly celebrate the wedding service.

Most Protestant Christian churches do not have the same stringent policies regarding intermarriage, but all encourage their members to marry other Christians. St. Paul advises in his Second Epistle to the Corinthians, 6:14: "Do not be mismated with unbelievers. For what partnership have righteousness and iniquity? Or what fellowship has light with darkness?"

With the increase in intermarriage, religious groups are having more contacts with each other. As understanding grows, there is a gradual but slow shift of attitude toward accepting or tolerating intermarriage. Yet, those who have chosen to marry outside their own group still are made at times to feel that they are the outcast. This feeling of isolation and guilt can easily create problems between husband and wife.

3. Housing Discrimination.

Horace, a Caucasian, and Janet, a black, married right after graduation from college. In his new job, Horace had to move immediately to another city while Janet stayed behind to complete last-minute packing and moving details. Horace found a lovely apartment in a nice section of town where he worked. One week later Janet moved into the apartment with him. While relaxing by herself at the apartment's swimming pool, the apartment manager acted surprised to see her there and asked if she was a guest of one of the tenants. Janet replied that she was Horace's wife. Early next day, the manager asked to see Horace privately. He said he had mistakenly rented the apartment which he had previously promised to another person. As a means of compensating for his mistake, the manager volunteered to refund Horace's money and not charge him for the week's rent.

As Horace was innocently explaining to Janet what had happened, she became furious and charged the manager with racial discrimination. While Horace was trying to help Janet make sense, Janet got angry with him also. "I give up. How can I expect a 'honky' to really understand racial discrimination!" screamed Janet.

4. Employment and Job Promotion Discrimination.

Neal, a Jew, and Renee, a Protestant, were both trained as public school teachers. After moving to a predominantly Protestant neighborhood, Neal, despite having a master's degree, was unable to get a teaching job in the local school, whereas Renee, who had only a bachelor's degree, was hired immediately. The reason for hiring Renee but not Neal, according to the principal, was that Neal was overqualified. When Neal told the principal that he was willing to take a bachelor's degree salary for his work so that he could teach in the neighborhood, the principal replied, "You will regret it later and quit us in no time." Due to the school's teacher shortage, the principal finally agreed to hire Neal as a temporary substitute. After two full years of substituting, Neal's application to be a full-time teacher still was denied. "I don't want you to think I have anything against you Jewish people, even though you're the first Jew I've dealt with," suggested the principal.

Problems Caused by Husband-Wife Interaction

Thus far, discussion has centered around cultural differences and social factors that contribute to intermarrieds' problems. There are also problems that come from the couple's daily interactions with each other. Such problems usually can be traced back to each individual's ethnic, racial, or religious background differences.

1. Food and Dining Etiquette.

On their one-month wedding anniversary Oi-Ching, a Chinese wife, was upset when her Japanese husband, Yoko, prepared raw fish for the special celebration. After her initial shock and disbelief, Oi-Ching decided Yoko intentionally prepared raw fish as a means to express his resentment for having to cook for her that particular evening. In return, Yoko criticized Oi-Ching for being too provincial and refusing to try anything non-Chinese. As their argument progressed, Yoko also criticized Oi-Ching for her bad table manners. He said that on several occasions she had used her own chopsticks to pass and serve food to their house guests. Oi-Ching was flabbergasted and explained that she used her own chopsticks to pass and serve food to family members and guests to demonstrate kindness, graciousness, intimacy, and respect. "How could it be?" responded Yoko. "The use of chopsticks to serve food is dirty and disrespectful. Chopsticks are frequently used to transfer the bones of the dead during Japanese funeral ceremonies and, therefore, should never be used to serve food to guests or family members in my house," added Yoko. The dietary and dining etiquette differences between Oi-Ching and Yoko clearly reflect their ethnic cultural backgrounds.

Many religious customs govern the eating habits of people, such as no pork, fish on Friday, fasting on certain days, dietary observances during Lent, and the like. Such religious requirements may not be a problem during courtship when romantic emotions run high and interaction between the couple usually is courteous and limited. They may loom as irreconcilable sore spots after the couple marries and begins to interact daily and intensely with each other.

2. Festivities and Observances.

Allen, a reformed Jew, and Cindy, a Presbyterian, vowed that they would not allow their religious differences to affect their marriage. Both are highly educated professionals in the health field, and they believed any problem could be overcome by rational discussion. To insure their own individuality, they each have separate hobbies and separate circles of friends in addition to their mutual friends. Allen sometimes attends synagogue, but Cindy has not attended church for sometime because she usually works on Sundays. Occasionally, she attends synagogue with Allen.

A week before Christmas, Cindy's brother brought her a Christmas tree, explaining that he happened to stumble on a good buy — two trees for the price of one. Cindy placed the tree next to the fireplace in the family room and decorated it nicely. When Allen came home that evening, Cindy jovially told him that the tree was a gift from her brother and that it reminded her of the warmth and pleasure of her childhood. Instead of sharing her excitement, Allen asked if he could move the tree from the family room to Cindy's sewing room. Cindy insisted that the Christmas tree was not meant as a religious symbol and that Allen should not be offended so easily and behave so immaturely. The couple did not speak to each other the rest of the evening. Next morning at breakfast, Allen finally broke the silence by relating to Cindy the anti-Semitism which he had experienced as a child in a predominantly Christian neighborhood. Despite his constant struggle to keep things in proper perspective, the memories of harassment were still a vivid part of him. Consequently, Allen found Christmas a very taxing and uncomfortable time of year. As Allen was expressing his feelings, Cindy burst into tears. "As much as I sympathize with you and your Jewish experience, I find it difficult to give up part of me, for celebrating Christmas with the persons I love, apart from any religious implications, has been a warm and dear tradition for me," explained Cindy.

3. Friendships.

While intermarriage is a personal matter between two people, their continuing relationship and happiness depend also on their interaction with others, including their friends. Through interacting with friends, the couple satisfies their social need for sharing and enrichment and avoids becoming too self-centered. Nevertheless, making friends and maintaining friendships present peculiar difficulties for many intermarried couples.

Nita, an American Indian, and Jerry, a Caucasian, had not socialized with friends for some time. Nita commented she was bored to death sitting at home doing nothing except complaining to Jerry that he shouldn't be watching television on weekends. Jerry replied that not leaving the house to socialize with friends was not his fault, for if Nita's American Indian friends would accept him he would be happy to go with her to visit them. "I always enjoyed visiting with friends before we married," added Jerry. Nita was curious about Jerry's comments regarding her Indian friends, and she asked if Jerry would elaborate on that statement. Jerry explained that on numerous occasions when the couple had been out with Indian friends, they would stop laughing or talking every time he approached them. "They were not impolite or disrespectful to me, but my presence just makes them stop talking or feeling comfortable," added Jerry. "Interestingly enough, this is exactly how I feel when I am with your white friends," echoed Nita.

The couple's discomfort with their friends and their friends' discomfort with them is real and common in intermarriages. The couple's mutual understanding and acceptance of each other does not imply that their friends will do the same. Friendship begins with common values, interests, and backgrounds. Friends of intermarrieds usually find that one partner in the marriage does not share their commonalities. Differences in background generate uncertainty, distrust, and discomfort, which destroy social relationships.

Some couples choose to relinquish their individual friends to make new friends with whom they feel compatible as a couple. This arrangement works only if the couple can agree on the meaning of compatibility. Also, the friends the couple selects must want to reciprocate friendship. This is not always the case, due to diverse cultural and religious backgrounds. The intermarried couple's difficulty in making and maintaining friendships also affects their leisure-time recreation and activities. Their isolation from friends forces them to interact more with each other and to depend more on each other for recreation and enjoyment. Thus, the couple's relationship may become too close, leaving no space for individuality and creativity. Soon, both parties in such a situation may feel stifled and begin to resent the constant presence of the other.

4. Financial Management.

Most marriage counselors agree that money is one of the major problem areas in a marriage. The couple's financial difficulty can involve both the question of not having enough money and the question of managing the funds they have. The proper management of money is a skill that must be learned and which will be defined differently by different cultures or religions.

Ireen, a Lutheran, was shocked and upset that her husband Mike, a Mormon, had actually committed one third of their total yearly income to the Mormon church. "You wouldn't take me to a movie because you said we don't have enough money; now you decide to give one third of our yearly earnings to your church. Are you married to your church or to me?" Ireen asked angrily. Mike's decision as to how the money should be spent was guided by the Mormon teaching on church support. This obviously conflicted with Ireen's religious belief and upbringing.

Theresa, a Caucasian, was very upset by her Chinese husband, Wai-Hong, who sent a monthly check to his widowed mother in Hong Kong. "What bugs me the most is that his mother does not even need the money. Besides, Wai-Hong would not buy me a gift for my birthday which he considers no big deal," complained Theresa. Again, the manner in which Wai-Hong chose to spend money was culturally determined. Despite the financial status of his mother, Wai-Hong considered it his duty as a son to remember and to honor his mother by sending her money. Furthermore, birthdays (other than one-month, thirtieth, and sixtieth) are not considered eventful according to traditional Chinese customs. While his wife was criticizing his way of spending money, Wai-Hong was puzzled by her lack of respect for him as an honorable son and a thrifty husband.

5. Pract :e of Religious Faith.

Different religious teachings and practices often provide the basis for misunderstandings and disagreements between an interfaith couple. It is one thing to recognize the fact that differences do exist. It is quite another thing to live with these differences day in and day out as intermarrieds must do. Differences in religious practices persist even when a couple believes that the problems arising out of such differences have been resolved. The roots of religion are planted deep, and they are not easily uprooted or neutralized.

Joan, a Quaker, decided to marry John, a Catholic, claiming that John was exactly the kind of husband she needed despite their religious differences. Because of her true and total love for him, Joan was willing to give up attending her own church and attend John's church instead. This arrangement lasted for several months after their marriage, but gradually Joan lost interest in attending Mass with John. Both Joan and John were very sensitive about this issue so to avoid an argument, they avoided discussing the topic altogether. Joan began to feel a sense of alienation from God and her feelings toward her husband grew ambivalent. Because of Joan's indifferent attitude toward the Mass and religion as a whole, John also began to get a feeling of incompleteness in his marriage.

Steve, a Southern Baptist, and Mary Ann, a Unitarian, discovered soon after their marriage that despite their both being Protestant, the beliefs and practices of their respective churches were quite different. Steve, as a Baptist, insisted upon adhering to the Bible as "the supreme standard by which all human conduct, creeds, and opinions should be tried." As a Unitarian, Mary Ann insisted that truth cannot be reduced to a single creed and that to live is to continue questioning. As a form of compromise, they agreed to attend their own churches separately, and to avoid influencing each other's religious beliefs, the couple decided not to discuss religion. Steve and Mary Ann agreed that although their compromise seemed to work for them, each missed the companionship and spiritual sharing. They agreed that they had not foreseen this problem before marriage. "I hate to be apart from him, especially during fun social activities at my church," complained Mary Ann. "I don't like our 'Sunday split' either, and I worry about what we will do when we have children," Steve commented.

When Christopher, a Catholic, and Barbara, a Jew, married, they experienced a great deal of opposition from their parents and relatives. The priest and the rabbi could not agree on the interfaith ceremony and the couple ended up having a civil wedding ceremony. After their wedding, Christopher and Barbara both harbored hostility toward organized religions. They moved away from their parents and decided to have nothing to do with religion. "Organized religion did not accept us; why should we accept it?" complained Christopher. "So far religion has been a splitting force instead of a cementing element in our marriage," volunteered Barbara.

Rejecting one's religion as a means to make an intermarriage work may be too big a price for an individual or any couple to pay. Without faith, an individual is weakened in his or her internal strength, spirit, and commitment essential to becoming a happy individual and to achieving a successful intermarriage. Statistics on divorce consistently reveal that divorced couples show more religious indifference than married couples. Marriage counselors agree that religious couples tend to work harder to solve their marital problems than nonreligious couples.

6. Sexual Adjustment.

Since religious orientation has a strong impact on an individual's life, it should come as no surprise that it also affects an individual's sexual relationship with a marital partner.

Mark, a Catholic, and Kathy, an Episcopalian, were married two years ago. Mark graduated from college a year ago and works in a children's home as a social worker. Kathy, a psychology major, will be graduating at the end of the semester. While they both love children, they decided before marriage to wait until Kathy obtains her college degree before starting a family. They decided to use a natural family planning method to delay having children. Two weeks ago, Kathy was informed that in view of her excellent academic performance she would likely be awarded a graduate scholarship in clinical psychology. Mark and Kathy were delighted by the good news, but in order for Kathy to complete her graduate degree in the specified two-year period, the couple had to further delay their plans to have children. Although showing signs of ambivalence, Mark finally conceded. But when Kathy explained to him that she would need to take some kind of contraceptive due to her recent irregular menstrual cycle, Mark objected. Kathy felt that Mark's objection resulted not from his Catholic beliefs, but more from his unwillingness to accept the fact that she would have a master's degree and he would not. Mark insisted that he was quite comfortable with his academic accomplishment but that he just could not live with the fact that he would be consciously participating in the prevention of the birth of a child. "I refuse to cooperate with you in this immoral act," insisted Mark.

When one marital partner is Roman Catholic, most discussions of sex in intermarriage center on the issue of birth control. However, the role of sex in intermarriage is far broader than that of reproduction and contraception. The sex act is a form of marital behavior by which and through which the married couple develop, express, and enrich their spiritual, physical, and emotional relationship with each other. Our attitudes toward sex and its role in marriage are derived in very large part from our religious beliefs. Throughout history, religious codes have regulated in considerable detail the conditions under which intercourse may occur, the times on the church calendar when it is discouraged or forbidden, positions to be assumed, and various other aspects of the marital relationship. In addition to religious restrictions, different ethnic and racial groups have specific codes regulating the sexual behavior of their members.

Carla, a Caucasian, was puzzled and annoyed by her Japanese husband who refused to display any physical affection toward her in public. "As a matter of fact, sometimes I get the impression that he is ashamed to be seen with me when other people are around," complained Carla.

Vila, a Latino, was distressed by his Caucasian wife, Wanda, who hardly responded to him sexually, especially in public. Vila complained to his wife, "You complain that I am not affectionate toward you, but you always turn me down when I want to make love to you." Wanda explained, "I want you to make love to me with words as well as actions. I can't respond affectionately when I don't feel good toward you and toward our relationship." The couple's sexual problems were related to their communications problem. Despite Vila's display of physical closeness, he was unaccustomed to expressing deep personal feelings verbally, as Wanda desired. Vila and Wanda's individual cultures determined the manner in which they expressed their affection, and their differences in expression interfered with their sexual adjustment.

7. Childrearing Practices.

Every couple brings to marriage the religion and culture of their own nuclear families. If they share the same basic religious, ethnic, and cultural backgrounds, their differences are usually minor and present fewer difficulties. However, if they come from different religious, ethnic, and racial backgrounds, their differences may be more fundamental or complex. Intermarried couples may work out their differences and maintain a stable marriage until children enter the picture. At that point, previously determined arrangements and compromises may not be adequate to accommodate new demands and stresses brought on by the child. The arrival of a child reactivates the couple's memories of their own early childhood and underscores their childrearing beliefs. Such beliefs can produce new conflict between spouses. Sometimes this results in the child's becoming the symptom of this conflict when he or she begins to display uncertainty, anxiety, rebellion, and difficulty in learning or making friends.

Tanya, a hyperactive ten year old, is intelligent but behind in her school performance. Tanya's mother, a school teacher herself, is white and Tanya's father is black. Tanya is very fond of her parents but has difficulty in following their instructions. For instance, whenever Tanya misbehaves at home, her mother usually reprimands her verbally and then forgets about the incident. Her father takes a much stricter approach, which may include sending her to her room and withholding her weekly allowance.

The behavior of Tanya's parents in disciplining their daughter represents a typical pattern for intermarried families. Intermarried parents consistently emphasize different values and employ different approaches in disciplining children. Having to respond to two different sets of instructions, children in this type of family often become confused and easily distracted.

In order to avoid conflicts with a spouse, some intermarried couples adopt a "one-partner-taking-over" policy. Mary, a Catholic, took her Catholic commitment to do all in her power to rear the children Catholic seriously. In addition to insuring that their son, John, got the proper Catholic education at church and at home, Mary carefully screened his friends. On one occasion, Mary forbade John to join a baseball team because she did not want her son to be the only Catholic on the team. Mary's husband, Bob, is non-Catholic and disapproves of his wife's overcontrolling behavior, but he says nothing in order to preserve their harmonious relationship. To maintain his noninterference strategy, Bob withdrew from the family, joined the Bass Fishing Club and became a weekend fisherman. Bob's detachment from the family necessitated his wife's taking full control of the home, including raising their son. Mary complained that she was tired of functioning as a single parent, and John resented seldom seeing his father. Recently, he said that he could not stand his mother. "She won't let me breathe. She embarrasses me. I hate going places with her, including church," complained John.

As an alternative to one spouse being in charge, some intermarried couples handle raising children by a compartmentalized arrangement. Orando, a Mexican-American, believes that boys should be interested in sports, especially soccer which he played extensively as a child. Three times a week, Orando takes his son Tommy to soccer and T-ball practices and games. The rest of the time, Orando does nothing with his son. The son refuses to attend church activities and is having difficulty at school. "Church and school are Janet's (his Caucasian wife) responsibility," declared Orando. "I don't think Daddy really cares as long as I do well in sports," expressed Tommy. "The school personnel thought I was a single parent, for they had never seen my husband," complained Janet.

Partly due to the magnitude of their cultural differences or their unwillingness to accept disharmony in their relationship, some intermarried couples raise their children by adopting a total hands-off attitude. If neither parent wants to impose values in deference to the other, the children are left in a vacuum with no model or guidance.

Ron, a Protestant, and Sara, a Catholic, decided since they were not practicing members of their churches they would leave it up to their daughter, Dollie, to choose her own religion. Until her senior high school year, Dollie never expressed any interest in church or in religion, although most of her classmates belonged to some religious organization. Dollie's moral values were severely tested when a boy she dated insisted on having sexual relations with her. Searching for guidance, Dollie became interested in religion and attended three separate churches with friends of different faiths over a two-month period. In the midst of her uncertainty, Dollie was disappointed that her mother and father showed no interest in spirituality and did not provide her with meaningful help in selecting a religion.

Obviously, the problems of intermarried couples presented in this chapter could easily be problems experienced by married couples of the same racial, ethnic, or religious backgrounds. However, because of their cultural and religious differences, intermarried couples tend to have more built-in handicaps to overcome in their relationship with each other. The following are suggestions meant to help those involved in intermarriage.

Applications And Suggestions
1. Married Couples.

By recognizing that certain marital problems stem from our cultural or religious differences, we should not be defensive in relating to our spouse during a conflict. Since our thinking, feelings, and behavior are culturally determined and learned, they can be unlearned and relearned. The process of unlearning and relearning requires objectivity, adaptability, and an ability to communicate fully, all of which is necessary for achieving a successful intermarriage. Due to their differences, the couple is provided with ample opportunity for new learning. Once we make a commitment to intermarriage, we have the opportunity and responsibility to make the marriage work. Success in intermarriage does not imply that we should bargain for less than what we are culturally and spiritually. On the contrary, success in intermarriage can be inspiring and enriching as we learn and adopt new ways and ideas.

2. Individuals Interested in Intermarriage.

Love between two individuals may not overcome long-standing social prejudices and religious antagonisms that intermarriage can bring to the forefront. It may happen that an individual in intermarriage may feel that making the marriage work requires too many changes and sacrifices that would diminish himself or herself as a person. When we are romantically in love, it is easy to overlook all the potential obstacles involved in intermarriage. But as our marriage settles into reality, our intense romantic feelings toward each other may subside and problems between us may grow to be unmanageable. Prior to a final commitment to intermarriage, it is advisable that we set aside temporarily our intense romantic and subjective feelings and review with each other, as objectively as possible, problems we may encounter as an intermarried couple. Since our parents, relatives, and close friends have a longtime involvement and investment of interest in us, we need to consider their feelings and not automatically regard their opinions or oppositions as prejudices. In considering an ecumenical marriage, it is advisable that we consult with a priest, minister, rabbi, or religious leader about our proposed intermarriage and the adjustments that will be necessary.

It is normal and to be expected that you will experience uncertainty about a planned intermarriage. This is true in planning any marriage. However, if you continue to have doubts as you plan your intermarriage, it is critically important to examine and reexamine closely your motives. Remember, the best route to a successful marriage is sound preparation. In view of the potential problems and complexities in intermarriage, it is mandatory that there be an objective, thorough, and thoughtful preparation.

3. Relatives and Friends.

Relatives and close friends have the responsibility to advise the loved one of the potential problems he or she might encounter in intermarriage. The manner in which we share this information is important. Most individuals involved in or contemplating intermarriage, feel uncomfortable in broaching the topic of intermarriage. They sense the negative attitude many people have toward marrying outside "one's group." As relatives and close friends, we need to be particularly sensitive to the engaged couple's needs. Accordingly, we may initiate the contact and express our desire and willingness to discuss intermarriage at a time and place most convenient for them. We need to suggest questions relating to the couple's actual knowledge of intermarriage. It is important that we display objectivity about intermarriage and make it clear that we do not think it necessarily spells failure or disaster. Especially communicate your awareness that intermarriage can offer unique advantages and make significant contributions to the couple and to others. Ask if there are areas of intermarriage they wish to discuss. Your nonjudgmental attitude will be appreciated by the couple who usually understand, at least intellectually, that they will face unique problems in intermarriage.

Don't hesitate to discuss the problem areas you see in an intermarriage but do so without presumption. Keep a proper perspective on your relationship with your loved one and respect his or her ultimate decision. The couple's desire to intermarry should not be interpreted as a personal rejection of you as parents, relatives, or friends. Remember that the couple planning intermarriage are individuals who have their own right to choose a marriage partner and who are ultimately responsible for whatever decision they make. If their decision contradicts your personal wishes, try to accept it lovingly. The one you love will always remain your son or daughter, nephew or niece, relative or friend. He or she will need you throughout married life, especially during periods of stress. Your support or lack thereof could be a major factor in their successful or unsuccessful intermarriage.

If your loved one is already intermarried and chooses to share marital problems with you, sensitively help him or her to recognize that the problem may be cultural instead of personal. Encourage the couple to capitalize upon what they have in common rather than emphasizing their cultural differences. Your sincere loving involvement in assisting an intermarried couple may even help you enrich your own marriage and life in general.

4. Clergy and Counselors.

Helping a person who is intermarried or contemplating intermarriage recognize potential problems is no easy task. Because of the dim view so many churches and religious groups have toward intermarriage, persons involved or interested in intermarriage usually feel defensive during their initial encounter with clergy. It is important that the clergy recognize this built-in attitude in the couple, otherwise it can become a communications barrier. It can be helpful for the clergy to inquire about the individual's or couple's opinion of the member of the clergy as a representative from a religious organization. Such a discussion can help the couple realize that clergy, although representing a religious faith, can be individuals of genuine warmth and positive regard for the couple's situation. An individual's trust in the clergy will pave the way for open and honest discussion about potential problems in intermarriage.

As a representative of a particular religious faith, it is the clergy's responsibility to share with the intermarried, or persons interested in intermarriage, the current precise position or regulations that particular faith has regarding intermarriage. A self-righteous, dogmatic, and insensitive attitude toward the couple may drive them further away from the religious organization, and clergy should guard against this.

It is essential that the clergy examine their attitudes toward intermarriage in general and particularly persons involved in intermarriage. Should an individual still harbor negative, uncompromising attitudes toward intermarriage, that person should excuse him or herself from counseling persons intermarried or considering intermarriage. Instead, the couple should be referred to other clergy or counselors who have a more objective attitude, who can help the couple openly and fully explore potential problems, and who will accept the uniqueness of each couple seeking to respond to God's call to marriage.

10.4 Mixed Blessings: Ten Lessons Learned from Interfaith Couples
Robert T. Reilly

THIRTY-FIVE YEARS AGO AN ARTICLE ON "MIXED MARRIAGES" IN A CATHOLIC magazine began this way:

> A short time ago I asked my wife if she would marry me if she had to do it all over again. She thought the question over briefly and answered, "No, I don't think so." Normally, I suppose I would be expected to feel hurt and angry at this reply, but I wasn't. Ours is not a normal situation. You see, we are the one-in-a-thousand couple who are enjoying a very successful mixed marriage.

Both husband and wife tell their stories in this piece. He laments that he feels uncomfortable with the sacrifices his Protestant wife must make, with his own reluctance to continue practices like the family rosary, and even with their diverse sets of friends. She complains of Catholic smugness, the awkward attempts at conversion by her husband's friends, and of the general resentment she experiences as an outsider.

"I have learned to agree with the Catholic Church in only one thing," she concluded 35 years ago. "Mixed marriages are undesirable. They carry so many added burdens that it is no wonder most of them fail . . . . We must live with this as with a stranger in the house. And no one relaxes when there are strangers in the house."

The grim odds of 1000 to 1 have certainly improved. Good thing, too, since well over half — perhaps 60 percent — of marriages by Catholics are to people of another faith or no faith at all. In the United States, the numbers have doubled in the last 40 years, fueled by mobility, economic gains by Catholics, the weakening of ethnic ties, and an increasing tolerance for diverging religious viewpoints. Conservatives might add a perceived decline in traditional Catholic values. According to a recent Gallup Poll, three out of four Americans approve of interfaith marriages, with Catholics demonstrating more acceptance than Protestants. The age of the couple is a factor in interfaith marriages, as is family background, the amount of religious education, the ethnic mix of the community, and even whether this is a first or second marriage. Interfaith marriages are more common the second time around.

Whatever the cause, the statistics can't be ignored, especially when paired with other considerations. Interfaith (or ecumenical) marriages remain the greatest single source of Catholic converts — and also the prime cause of Catholic defections. However, there seems to be a trend away from conversion. At least half of the marriages between Catholics and Protestants remain "mixed." Young people today don't seem to feel the same need to unify a marriage in this way as did their parents.

"Religious peace is part of our culture," says Kathy Nelson, a Catholic married to a Lutheran. "Taking this away is a loss."

True, but Nelson and others have discovered ways to deal with this loss and with the pressures of the ecumenical marriage. Not surprisingly, certain concerns surface in most of these unions.

Lynn Wragge, a Catholic, says, "I would like to have us receive Communion together. That bothers him. And it bothers me, too."

Her husband, Doug, a Lutheran, adds, "If I could receive Communion, I believe I would be happy."

Although discussions about inter-communion continue, and although some priests freely dispense the sacrament without undue concern over the religious status of the communicant, the official church position doesn't sanction the practice. In addition, the Catholic Church has modified the expectations it imposes on the Catholic partner in an interfaith marriage, but it still expects the Catholic to do all he or she can to see that their children are brought up Catholic.

There are also disagreements over the veneration of Mary, the sacrament of Reconciliation, liturgy, the quality of the sermons, music, holy days, and especially the spiritual training for the children.

"It's simple to deal with a theoretical child and simple to share theoretically," says Don Dean. He and his wife's first child wasn't born until they were married five years. After that, Don, a Presbyterian, confesses that all sorts of hidden fears surfaced.

Cold Shoulders

There can be numerous religious snags to threaten an ecumenical marriage, and they arise even among couples who are not particularly devout. Perhaps they are symptomatic of other wedded ills, but they find their focus in spiritual matters.

So the problems are there, and they spill over into other areas of the marriage. Still, some couples overcome these difficulties and survive. How do they manage it?

Claudia, a child of the '60s, somewhat of a rebel, married a Muslim, a man whose parents came from Pakistan. As a result, she felt ostracized by her friends and her church. In response, she joined a Christian Fundamentalist sect. More fervent than ever, she now tries to evangelize her classmates, but they all avoid her.

The institutional church, too, is not always as sensitive as it might be. Divorced persons have complained about this, even when they haven't remarried. And when they do wed, the reaction can be decidedly cold.

"His synagogue wouldn't let us marry because I was a Catholic," says Ruth Mendelson, "and my church wouldn't marry us because he was divorced. We finally married in his synagogue and had a kosher reception. More Jews than Catholics attended.

"Before I announced my plans to marry Bert," she continues, "everyone seemed happy, or at least tolerant, about our relationship. When we said we intended to marry, after two years of dating, I was told I couldn't lector anymore and that I'd have to drop out of the liturgy committee. I guess that's understandable. You have to have peace in your own church. I'm involved again now, but certain roles in the Catholic Church remain closed to me."

For six months after the marriage, Ruth did not receive Communion. Now she does. The resistance seems to be melting away on both sides.

In the book *Happily Intermarried,* authored by a priest, minister, and rabbi, the topic of the Jewish-Christian marriage is explored in depth:

> Most people do not reject either Jewish or Christian theology. (Some people take theology more seriously than others, but very few become convinced that the religious convictions with which they were raised are wrong.) Most people feel at home in the religious community in which they grew up and don't want to reject their family heritage.

Joanne Hultman is an exception. "I was never very devout, and I wasn't involved in religion in high school or college. It was my decision to convert to Judaism, even before I married. I never had any doubts. I made a conscious choice. I grew up seeing my parents together in church, and I wanted that for my children, too. My daughter needs to know who she is. I don't want her to be a wash."

Conversion was also the answer for Dean Sitzmann, brought up a Catholic. For the first six years of his marriage to Susan, who was active in her Lutheran church, they alternated between the Sunday services.

"We struggled with our beliefs for a long time, and not just with things like the Catholic veneration of Mary but also about the better music in the Lutheran tradition and what I saw as more social activism in the Catholic Church."

Before they were married (they dated for two years), Dean and Susan had discussed children.

"I wanted our children to go to one church," says Dean. "So I settled on the Lutheran Church. I was comfortable there. Now I'm on the church council, but I bring a lot of Catholic ideas to our deliberations."

Sometimes ecumenical couples settle on a "neutral" religion. Sometimes they merely stop going to church altogether.

Some insist that each interfaith couple must find its own way, but these couples reveal that they derive strength from certain practices, from attitudes and activities that might be emulated. Ten of these categories include:

1. Talk it out

Interfaith couples need to discuss problems before they become big problems. Every parent trying to reason with a smitten offspring knows that it's virtually impossible to depict the thorny side of marriage. No problem seems insurmountable and no warnings carry weight. Pastoral counselors encounter similar difficulties. They've learned to discuss rather than preach.

"Any pressure and you lose," says Father James Fitzgerald, an Omaha, Nebraska pastor. "I think I can encourage the believing individuals to be true to their consciences and to their own religion. If one of the parties is indifferent, then I can offer help, then or later. And I can also help each person see the riches of the other's background."

Along with this quiet understanding, a counselor may also explore some of the likely areas of conflict — but not in a dogmatic way.

"Let them know you offer support, not criticism," suggests Pastor Frank Reisinger, a Lutheran minister. "I try to educate them about the other's faith, to help them find a place where they can grow."

Reisinger reviews their options. Will they attend separate services, the same church, or will they find another compromise? What plans have they made for their children? And to make the discussion deal with immediate issues, he asks, "And where do you plan to go to church the Sunday after the wedding?"

This sort of frank dialogue should continue between the married couple, concentrating on areas where disagreement is likely or areas where one's sensitivity detects potential hurt.

For example, Dean and Susan Sitzmann dated for two years and took classes at the Newman Center at a South Dakota university and then attended classes in the Lutheran Center. They carefully talked about children before they were married, and they agreed they didn't want them going to different churches.

But others fear that too many Protestants marrying Catholics fail to speak up or ask questions. Yet, it seems, those who took time to look ahead have had fewer surprises and fewer destructive conflicts.

2. *Live Your Own Faith*

According to Sister Janice Mengenhauser of the Chicago Family Life Office, "Couples who come in strong, stay strong. What we learn is that it's possible to have unity if the individuals will sacrifice, work, forgive, learn, and keep their own faith meaningful."

The Catholic Church has always promoted the notion of setting a good example. Converts are made by observation rather than by argument. Research demonstrates that the stronger partner in an interfaith marriage frequently brings the other to that same view.

Conversion, in this context, becomes more of a by-product than a goal. Compatibility is the aim; and intensity of belief helps achieve this if both partners are equally devout.

"I was brought up with a narrow Catholic view," says Kathy Nelson, "and while in college in Colorado, I backed away from this. When I met Paul, he was more religious than I."

"Maybe," interjects Paul, "but I came from a Scandinavian tradition where everyone goes his own way. You didn't worry much about others, and you concluded you weren't worth very much yourself. You were struggling against . . . "

"I think it's called impending doom," interrupts Kathy.

Paul laughs, then continues, "But despite those drawbacks, I preferred the Lutheran tradition; and I began figuring out what my spiritual needs were. I still feel that what we do for ourselves and others transcends religion."

Jim Johnson was raised a Presbyterian. His wife, Bev, spent twelve years in Catholic schools.

"Still," she admits, "Jim's views broadened my religious outlook. He is much more likely to see commonality in our beliefs. We never saw each other's religion as enemy territory. In the first years of our marriage I didn't go to Mass regularly. I'd say our children brought me back. I rediscovered the fact that I was a better person for this."

3. Learn Your Way In

People in interfaith marriages could take a long look at Ruth Mendelson. An active Catholic, she married again after the death of her husband, this time to a Jew. Her ability to blend the two traditions is remarkable but she's worked at it.

Ruth brought five of her children to the marriage, and her husband had four. She read, she talked, she listened. Through her example, her husband became a more active Jew.

"He would ask me questions," she says. "And his kids say I'm a better Jew than their mother was. And my children (who are being raised Catholics) can see where their roots were. They can recite the wine blessing in Hebrew, and they observe Hanukkah and participate in the Seder. When my husband's mother died, I sat *shiva* for her for three days. His eldest son told me he couldn't believe I would do that and asked me why. 'Because I love your father,' I told him. If you love someone, you want to be into his life and faith."

Mendelson was also a pall bearer at the funeral of her husband's uncle. She shoveled dirt on the grave and read the graveside prayer in Hebrew. "That's my niece," said another uncle, proudly.

When Joanne Hultman married into the Jewish faith, she first spent a whole year with a rabbi, attended all the High Holiday services, and learned Hebrew. Eventually, she converted to Judaism.

"I don't think you can do both," she explains. "It confuses the children. I grew up seeing my parents together in church, and I want this for my children. When we visit my family at Christmastime, it's like going to a birthday party, except it's their birthday and not yours."

Among the interfaith Christian couples, Jim and Deanna Fuller say they talk about religion a lot, do Bible readings together, and go to each other's church. So do Paul and Kathy Nelson, who have baptized their children in both faiths. Many couples attempt to understand the beliefs of their spouses. And some of them note this cross-fertilization affecting not only their lives but also the conduct of the denominational rites.

"Lutherans are encouraging more frequent Communion," says Susan Sitzmann, "and I see people making the sign of the cross. I'd like to see a merger some day."

4. Show Some Respect

One thing that will doom an ecumenical marriage is for one person to continually downgrade the creed of the other. Successful interfaith couples often confess there are doctrines they don't understand or don't believe in their spouses' religion, but they never try to undermine those tenets.

"There are very few clear issues that separate Catholics and Episcopalians," says the Rev. Michael J. Tan Creti, an Episcopal priest. "But you can't assume that the interfaith couple has worked these out. Sometimes the couple is dealing with divisive issues in silence, and the resentment grows. There's every reason why they can keep their own beliefs, but it takes work and energy."

"Compassion, tolerance, patience," adds Father James Scholz, a Catholic pastor at an inner-city parish. "Each person has to be willing to be edified by the other."

Winnie Callahan, a Methodist married to a Catholic, resisted the notion of Confession as being an invasion of privacy. And the method of Baptism was a big issue between her and her husband. But they talked things over, and she spoke with various priests, and she tried. He tried, too.

"I'd say he was a lukewarm Catholic before our first baby was born," says Winnie. "He felt religion had been crammed down his throat. And he was depressed after Vietnam. Then came the desire to show me what he knew about Catholicism. He reached back a little harder."

"It amazed me what I learned," agrees John Callahan. "I grew up in a factory Catholic Church. Fast Mass, mumbo-jumbo, nothing for families, no community. I started to go to other services, like Winnie's Methodist service. I picked up things that I could look for in my own church. I came to believe that, as long as you believe and do what's right, you'll get to heaven."

5. Give it a Try

Participating in anything but the Mass may be difficult for Catholics, especially older Catholics, those brought up in a tradition of avoiding contact with the rituals of another faith. Today this is changing. Many churches exchange congregations periodically or invite neighboring parishes to co-worship. Interfaith couples seemed to have worked this out even earlier.

"When our daughter was confirmed," recalls Bev Johnson, "my husband and I volunteered to serve as a sponsoring couple who invited other children to our home. Some people brought up the fact that my husband wasn't a Catholic, but they let us do it anyway."

Jean Linerski's attempts to find a new home in the Catholic Church didn't work. She struggled with her conscience for several years and watched her children being baptized Catholics, one by one. She went to Mass, served on parish committees. But she felt empty. Finally she stopped going to church altogether until a chance meeting with an Episcopal priest, a childhood friend, caused her to return to being an Episcopalian.

"I'm glad I made that decision," she says. "I'm on my way back to feeling whole again. My husband is a traditional Catholic. He wants to be more open, but another part of him makes it tough to break the mold. I've had a spiritual homecoming, but we go to separate churches now. We're in a process. But we're still talking."

Ruth Mendelson knows how to share her time and energy between two faiths. Her husband helps her decorate the Christmas tree and worked on her parish's centennial committee. She's a lector in her own church but also a source of advice to Jewish women about their rituals.

"Last Good Friday," she says, "we had a Seder at our house. There were more Catholics than Jews in attendance. A priest said some of the prayers. And we all went to the synagogue first to get in the right spirit."

6. Pray Together

"Group prayer is not comfortable for most people," admits Sister Janice Mengenhauser. "It takes practice."

Except with charismatic individuals, spontaneous prayers have not been as popular for Catholics as learned prayers. And some forms of Catholic prayer make the Protestant partner a bit edgy.

"I don't feel comfortable praying to saints," confesses Doug Wragge. "But we do pray as a family at meals. After the regular grace, we sometimes try spontaneous prayer. Even our 4-year-old does this. And sometimes we also hold hands, something our little girl brought to the ritual. At night Lynn and I don't pray together; but we do pray, and our kids know we pray."

Don Dean figures that anything that brings you closer to God is the right step, and he says learning to pray together was the answer for him and his wife.

"This was difficult," he says, "because my prayer wasn't spoken, wasn't shared. As we learned to pray together, we extended this to our children. These two component pieces gave us the little church. The other church is just a building."

7. Watch Your Words

Avoiding arguments is good advice in any relationship, but religious arguments tend to be particularly bitter and hurtful, especially for the spouse who is deeply religious. Even barroom debaters are urged to steer clear of religion and politics.

"I suppose we just don't discuss religion a lot," says Doug Wragge. "We spent time studying each other's beliefs; and I think that, essentially, we believe the same things."

According to Jim Johnson, "We talk about religion a lot. We just don't have any long theological discussions. Those can get nasty. The fact that she has strong beliefs actually strengthens me."

Interfaith couples have to learn how to talk about their diverse feelings, but always in the spirit of love and understanding. Otherwise, they lose.

I remember being asked by a student to talk with her fiancée about the Catholic Church. I tried to shift the job to a Newman Club chaplain or a Jesuit friend. She would have none of it. So I visited with the couple. He

314 \ *Topic 10 — Interfaith – Interrace Marriages*

came armed with every complaint against the Catholic Church, from the Inquisition to contraception. After about twenty minutes of this contention, I said, "Hey, hold it! I'm not marrying this woman, you are. I thought you wanted to know what she believed. You have to live with her." That settled him down, and we got along well after that.

It's true. There are numerous points of potential conflict. The question is whether one wants to be informed or wants to be right.

8. Give a Little

Catholics aren't too good at negotiating They tend to feel that very little is negotiable. Actually, there are many compromises that can be made without invading the conscience or practice of the Catholic partner.

"My wife is not as willing to give," asserts Doug Wragge. "I go to her church and she goes to mine, but I know she wouldn't even consider joining the Lutheran Church. I don't know if her feelings are really acceptance or if they are sacrifices."

Lynn Wragge doesn't disagree. "He's willing to compromise; I'm not. That makes it hard."

Thus far, their young daughter hasn't created any extra tension. She alternates between their two churches. But Doug and Lynn realize problems may arise in the future. "We have a long way to grow yet," Doug says.

Jim Johnson thinks the solution lies in "the willingness of one partner to negotiate within the spirit of the other." Bev Johnson, a Presbyterian, has seen to the religious education of the children and takes them to CCD classes. She also attends Mass with Jim. Both have chosen to attend a parish other than their geographically assigned church because they find this elected parish more free and less divisive.

The Nelsons send their children to public schools rather than face some of the family demands imposed by having children in parochial schools. They also monitor what their children are taught in religion classes and attempt to temper what they consider the more radical doctrines.

9. Yell for Help

Many difficult situations are eased by the knowledge that others are suffering similar pain. Sensitive clergy and pastoral ministers are beneficial, and many interfaith couples eventually find someone who can address their needs. Ecumenical support groups have been convened in many denominations. Often these are staffed by older interfaith couples, and the give and take of experiences proves to be helpful therapy.

"What we talk about," says Tan Creti, "are common experiences. Participation was slow at first but has grown."

"Where there is love, there can be unity," insists Father Thomas McDermott, a pastor in a small Midwestern town. "Meetings provide the incentive to search out more unity. We look at differences with the presumption, based on love, that there is meaning and legitimacy in all Christian faiths."

Other groups may help, too.

"We belonged to the Christian Family Movement," says Bev Johnson. "That organization allowed us to share faith where denomination didn't matter. It was neutral ground. It gave us a forum to explore the ideas of others."

The Johnsons also made a Marriage Encounter together but were a little put off because they were not eligible to be presenters, since one was a Protestant, and because, at the conclusion of the weekend, Jim was given Communion while she was given a blessing.

The Wragges, the Fullers, and others have been in support groups for years. They now find themselves sources of counsel for younger members. Some interfaith couples also attend interfaith sessions at the Protestant churches.

Besides support groups and pastoral counseling, many books and pamphlets are available. Most of these are short and focused, containing everything from instructions for engaged couples to case histories of interfaith couples.

10. Keep Your Chin Up

A lot of pressure comes from family members. This varies according to locale and family structure, but it can be an extra burden on an interfaith marriage.

One ecumenical bride, frustrated by the criticism of both families, delivered an ultimatum to them: either shut up or stay home. Most of them came to the wedding, but they all had little hope of the success of this Catholic-Methodist union. Eighteen years later, the Methodist wife derives some comfort from the fact that the marriage her mother-in-law constantly threw up to her, one between her brother-in-law and another Catholic, has since ended in divorce.

"He remarried after that, and his parents had a tough time swallowing this. What it boils down to, I think, is two people and whether or not they want the marriage to work."

Joanne, who converted from Catholicism to Judaism, found her family very supportive: "There was no grief, no arguments. In fact, they've asked me for books on Judaism, so they can be better informed."

Nowadays, people of all faiths seem to be more tolerant of ecumenical marriages; but some difficulties still exist. One woman who would like to convert to Catholicism hesitates to do so while her mother is still alive. Another woman who enrolled her children in a parochial school gets frequent calls from her mother who is convinced the nuns will place the youngsters under some sort of medieval spell. And there are the situations where the families boycott the weddings and regret it ever after. All of these heartaches can strain the couple's relationship, so the couple must put them aside and work through its own problems.

These are merely ten suggestions. There are many others. Possessing a sense of humor might be an excellent addendum. Concentrating on the essential holiness of the married state might be another. And some modern theologians are also reminding the interfaith couple that their union can serve as a sign for the closer ties between denominations, letting the larger church mirror the smaller church.

Lynn Wragge sees all of this activity as a hopeful sign. "Instead of highlighting differences," she says, "we have to discover a better way to worship together, a way to highlight our sameness . . . perhaps a new way to worship that no one else has yet thought of."

Marriage and Family – Here to Stay?

11.1 The Church as the Context for the Family
Robert N. Bellah

*Ed. Note: In our March issue, we published a symposium on Roman Ca-
tholicism and "American exceptionalism." Among the 11 contributions,
some views were expressed that were not in harmony with the editorial
stance of the* NEW OXFORD REVIEW, *as might be expected in any symposium. For example, Robert N. Bellah, an Episcopalian, wrote approvingly
of practicing homosexuals living together when they sustain a "stable,
permanent, and faithful" – i.e., non promiscuous – relationship. In our
June issue, we printed four letters – the substance of which we agree with –
critiquing Bellah's position. In response, Bellah, an* NOR *Contributing
Editor and esteemed colleague, sent us the article printed below in the
interests of clarifying his views on marriage, sex, and family in general.
We believe that it is a marvelous defense and explication of the Christian
view of the family, although we continue to disagree with his position –
very briefly restated – on homosexuality. The article is adapted from a
talk given to the Southern Baptist Convention's Christian Life Commission
Seminar on the Family in Charlotte, North Carolina, on March 24, 1987.
Prof. Bellah wished to note that some issues discussed, such as the
question of the teaching office of the church, would have been phrased
differently for a Roman Catholic or an Episcopalian audience, but that the
issues are nonetheless faced by all Christians.*

IN THIS AUDIENCE I THINK I CAN TAKE IT FOR GRANTED THAT WE BELIEVE
in the family. We see it as a basic unit in both social life and spiritual life.
We can say this without any nostalgia for an allegedly perfect "traditional

317

family," knowing that the family, like all other human institutions, is subject to sin and corruption and always in need of thoughtful reform. But just the simple idea of a man and a woman vowing to stay with each other "till death do us part" and trying to raise children together seems daunting. Marriage is difficult. A recent *New Yorker* cartoon showed a clergyman celebrating the marriage service and saying to the couple, "till death do you part or the going gets hairy." And how is one to bring children into a world such as ours? How can we transmit to them a sense of moral responsibility and a religious understanding of life? How can we create within the family a moral and religious atmosphere that can withstand the pressures of the larger world in which we live?

It is bad enough that television programs like "Dallas" and "Dynasty" come into our homes with their sordid tales of ambition, corruption, and cruelty. But these days the newspapers and television news bring into our homes real stories that make "Dallas" and "Dynasty" seem like fairy tales. We read about Ivan Boesky and other inside traders in the top investment banking firms on Wall Street. And we read about the National Security Advisor and the Director of the CIA undertaking or condoning actions Congress had not authorized and which are at variance with our expressed policy. And we read about officials all the way up to the President trying to deny what has plainly happened. The family seems like a very fragile institution if it is expected to adhere to a higher morality than that of our central economic and political institutions.

Let me say at once that I believe the family, or to give it a physical location, the home, is too small and too vulnerable to sustain the moral life of its members unassisted. If it is to succeed over time in providing meaning and coherence it will have to be included in and supported by larger social structures. I want to emphasize the church in particular as a context for family life, but it is not the only institution that is necessary for the immediate support of the family. We must include the school, the neighborhood, and the larger public realm as well. What all these institutions have in common, if I may borrow some terminology from Jurgen Habermas, is that they are part of what he calls the life-world. What is distinctive about the life-world is that its medium of communication, what he sometimes calls its steering mechanism, is language.

In contrast to the life-world, Habermas speaks of the systems, in particular the market economy and administrative bureaucracy. It is characteristic of the systems that their medium of communication, their steering mechanism, is nonlinguistic. In the case of the economy it is money; in the case of bureaucracy it is power. Ideally money and power are means that should be used to attain ends established through linguistic communication, through discussion, in the life-world. But as we know, these particular means easily become ends in themselves. Those devoted to them become obsessed with them. In our recent scandals we have seen how certain investment bankers sought to accumulate money beyond any capacity to spend it and how certain administrators sought power without any restraint by law or Congress. These are possibilities deeply rooted in the human soul, in what Christians call sin. St. Augustine, in his masterly analysis of the disorders of the soul, spoke of concupiscence, that is, wishes that are out of control, and *libido dominandi*, the desire to dominate. These are endemic possibilities for human beings, but the powerful systems of the modern world have the capacity to objectify these disordered motives, and to tempt individuals, sometimes almost irresistibly, in the direction of inordinate desires for wealth and/or power. Finally, Habermas argues, the systems become so powerful in our modern society that they begin to, as he puts it, colonize the life-world, that is subordinate the life-world to the nonlinguistic steering mechanism of money and power.

A number of incidents reported in *Habits of the Heart* can be interpreted in these terms. Brian Palmer (we do not use real names) was so preoccupied with rising in status and income in his corporation that he badly neglected his wife and children to the point where his marriage broke up and he had to rethink everything about his life. Jim Reichert, had for several years raised money for the local YMCA in order to build recreation facilities for Chicano youngsters with nowhere else to play, an activity that gave him a great sense of fulfillment in contributing to the life of his community. But now he finds the bank for which he works requires him to leave the community of which he has come to feel so much a part or sacrifice monetary advancement and a sense of achievement in his occupation.

One need not turn to *Habits of the Heart* to think of examples of how pervasively the systems colonize the life-world. I am thinking of the constant anxiety about achievement and competition our society fosters almost from nursery school. Will my grades be good enough to get me into a good college? Will I get a good job? Will I get promoted? Will I become CEO? Or, in my own profession, will I get tenure? Will I be recognized in the profession? Will I get a named chair? And I am sure there are comparable pressures on the clergy. Under these conditions it is not surprising that our society offers so many palliatives for anxiety. We turn to drugs when we need relief, to alcohol, tobacco, or cocaine, all of which are enormously profitable businesses. Or we turn to television or music, whose only redeeming features are that they distract us from our worries. Or we think that one more purchase of one more commodity will make us feel better. Both the anxiety and the common palliatives we use to fight it undermine our capacity to function adequately in the family and other parts of our life-world.

Much in the way our society is organized makes us think the pressures we feel are beyond our capacity to resist. Competition is a powerful force and survival a powerful motive. Dare we turn down a monetary advancement, given the high cost of college education for our children and the uncertainty of retirement plans, just because our husband or wife and children would be better off in the place where we presently live? And how can we control what our children are doing? Do we have the authority? Can we set guidelines on the television they watch, or, perish forbid, the music they listen to? And how do we know what they are up to anyway? Powerful outside pressures fragment and atomize the family so that each member goes his or her own way and the home is only a temporary stopping point between lives that are basically unconnected.

There are three ways of dealing with this situation, in ascending order of difficulty, and I think you can already guess that I will be advocating the third. The first is essentially to surrender, and allow the family to be buffeted by whatever waves from the larger society sweep over it. This indeed does not take much effort, but we can hardly be surprised if it produces broken marriages and neglected or abused children.

The second solution is harder and requires considerable institutional support beyond the family. This is the fundamentalist response. It attempts to create a separate culture in the family with as little penetration from the larger society as possible. Certainly the church will be necessary for this solution and probably "Christian schools" as well. The trouble with this solution is that it is undiscriminating with respect to what it keeps out and ultimately with respect to what it lets in as well. It settles for easy and superficial absolutes, believing, for example, that the Bible speaks for itself and needs no interpretation. And it accepts stereotypical views of "traditional values" and the "traditional family," which turn out to date back only to the 19th century, or even to the 1950s, and represent only an earlier version of American values – not necessarily more validly Christian than our current values.

The third response to the pressures on the family coming from the larger society is more difficult, for it neither surrenders to those pressures nor imagines that one can simply erect a wall to keep them out. This third alternative involves a much more active process of discussion and discrimination, one which involves certain basic understandings and then a great deal of negotiation about particular cases. Because this alternative is so difficult, the family alone is not likely to be able to sustain it. Here, as in the second response, the church will be of decisive importance, that is, the church as context for discussion, decision, and commitment.

I can only suggest some of the things this third alternative means to me. To begin with, we have to realize that the idea of Christian marriage is not very well understood in our society. Love is a central word in the Christian vocabulary and it is a central word in the vocabulary of romantic love in our society, but though the meaning of the term overlaps in the two contexts it is certainly not identical. In the culture of romantic love, love is primarily a feeling — indeed, an overwhelming feeling that sweeps us away. But unfortunately, it is a rather fragile feeling that often disappears rapidly; according to some social scientists, in its acute form it lasts 90 days and in its more attenuated form about a year.

Jesus tells us to love God and our neighbor. Indeed, he tells us to love our enemies. It is not that Christian love is not a matter of feeling, but it is certainly not only a matter of feeling. You cannot command a feeling, so that cannot be all that Jesus meant by love. And certainly we are not overwhelmed by an emotion of love toward our enemies. Without beginning to exhaust the idea of Christian love, we can see that it involves an element of intention and will that are largely absent in the idea of romantic love. Love intends the good of the loved one. It is more focused on the other than on the self and its transient feelings. Love is prepared to persist in the face of adversity. (Think of the classic phrases in the marriage service in the Book of Common Prayer.)

If we think of love as the basis of marriage, and I think we should, then these two different conceptions of love will imply two very different conceptions of marriage. If marriage is based only on the idea of romantic love, then when the intensity of the feeling begins to diminish, as it inevitably does, the basis of the marriage is threatened. Popular psychology tells us that marriage partners can be friends and that that is an important basis of a good marriage. That is fine and may help things survive for a while, but what if a third party comes along who rouses the intense feelings of romantic love? In the ideology of romantic love, not only is it all right to leave the original partner and go off with the new love, it is actually immoral not to. I believe that this ideology has much to do with the high divorce rate in our society. If romantic love is the chief basis of marriage and intense romantic love is inevitably transient, then marriage will inevitably be transient. This is what is called serial monogamy, but perhaps it should better be called serial polygamy.

The idea of Christian marriage is quite different. For Christians marriage is a contract to a noncontractual relationship. Most Christians believe this so strongly that they consider marriage a sacrament. In any case, its intention is indissolubility; not for as long as the excitement lasts, but till death do us part. Yet, Christian marriages can fail, not because we see marriage as inherently transient but because we know that we are sinners, that we do those things we ought not to do and do not do those things we ought to do. In a society saturated with the idea of romantic love, of course Christian marriage cannot ignore romance. We can be grateful for all the therapeutic advice as to how to bring a little romance back into a longstanding marriage. And we must also face the fact that romantic feelings toward third parties will occur in most marriages, and sometimes more than feelings. And not only sexual feelings, but also feelings of anger and hostility, often justified by the behavior of the other partner, are normal in any long-lasting close relationship. But in a genuine marriage, feelings of rejection, normal enough, will be moderated by understanding and forgiveness. Forgiveness is a central component of the Christian idea of love, and certainly forgiveness is essential in any marriage that will endure.

Forgiveness, acceptance, and understanding are essential components of Christian marriage, but it is not a one-sided forgiveness, acceptance, and understanding. "Traditional marriage" often expected these virtues from women but not from men. There is nothing Christian about that. If they are wonderful qualities in women they are wonderful enough to be shared by men.

But a marriage based not only on subjective feeling, but also on concern for the good of the other and on the intention of indissolubility, requires more than the commitment of two individuals, particularly in a culture that is not particularly sympathetic to those ideas and doesn't even understand them very well. Family and friends are important, but only if they understand and support this conception of marriage. A tradition and a community that embody these ideals, such as the church, are ultimately indispensable. This is all the more the case when the marriage fulfills itself by becoming a family, by bringing children into the world.

Although I will define the archetypal family as consisting of a married couple and their children, and I believe a kind of primary dignity belongs to that form of the family, I want to say strongly that that is not the only form of family that exists, or that needs to be affirmed and supported by the church. Indeed these archetypal families are probably in the minority in sheer numbers. Single parent families are common and need our special care and support. Pairs of adults of the same sex who have committed themselves to live together as a family, and groups of adults who have agreed to do so for whatever reason, are frequent in our larger cities. Wherever we find relationships of faithful mutual care and support it will be important to include them in the larger pattern of family life. It does not detract from the worth of such relationships, however, to give a certain primacy to the relation of a married couple and their children and to see the health of the family in that sense as vital for all other forms of family life as well.

All I have said about relations between the spouses applies to relations between parents and children. Often we must care for our children when we don't feel like it, or when we don't feel like it at a particular time. If we only cared for children when we feel like it they probably would not survive. We may love our children deeply and yet when they are angry, unreasonable, or inordinately greedy, as at times they inevitably are, we may thoroughly dislike them. And however much we may intend not to, from time to time we let them down. So here too understanding, acceptance and forgiveness are essential. Especially forgiveness, including the capacity to forgive ourselves.

Things really become difficult when children start school and become to a degree independent. Then it is all too easy for each member of the family to go his or her own way. At this time peer group, television, and school begin to have dominant influence on the life of children, and parents may give up the struggle to have any effect on their characters. The only way for the family to have a formative influence is for the family to create a common culture with common symbols and practices. Though the parents must lead in this process, from an early age children can be included in the creation of the common culture, can contribute their own symbols and meanings, and help shape common practices.

The core of the common culture is ritual, what we might call "family sacraments." Perhaps the most central family sacrament is the common meal. Yet today when everyone is so busy and schedules do not mesh, it is very easy to abandon the common meal altogether, which happens in many families. Each individual drifts into the kitchen when he or she needs a bite to eat and then hastens off to the next event. Such eating cannot even be called a meal but has recently become known as grazing. Resisting this tendency is the beginning of the effort to maintain a family culture.

One should probably try to have a common meal at least once a day and at least several common dinners a week. Family meals are not always pleasant. They may be the occasion of conflict between siblings or between parents and children. But they are one of the few places where family members can find out what each other is doing and thinking. Meals should not be a time only for children to show and tell. Parents should express their own concerns and tell of their activities outside the home. But meals should not be an occasion where only the parents talk to each other and the children listen. All should be included. It is on such occasions that children learn to listen respectfully to others and to express what is important to them. The dinner table is a place to learn the rules of civil discourse, and I can assure you that if they are not learned there they are not likely to be learned in school.

But meals are for eating and not just talking. Grabbing a Big Mac on the run is not a meal. Essential to the ritual is the preparation and enjoyment of wholesome food. The preparation of the food, serving it, and cleaning up after the meal are all part of a cooperative effort which makes the meal festive and sacramental. These are not activities that should devolve only on the wife and mother. Father and children should play an essential part, especially when, as is usually the case today, the mother is employed outside the home.

In a Christian family it will be normal for the meal to begin with a prayer. This need not be tedious but should be more than perfunctory. It is appropriate to mention in the prayer some major event in the life of the family (such as a birthday), an event in the larger world, or some aspect of the liturgical year, and then to include some discussion of this in the following conversation.

It may be possible to have common prayer, perhaps including a Bible reading, at some time other than meals, perhaps at the children's bedtime.

Biblical literacy is threatened everywhere in America today, and not only among children. Thus parents should consciously try to bring in Bible stories and verses, perhaps some lines from a psalm or a parable or saying of Jesus', not only on solemn occasions but as part of the daily discourse of family life. What is learned in Sunday School or religious education classes will not be retained if it is not reflected in family life. And without biblical literacy a genuine Christian community cannot survive these days.

Other family rituals include recreation and holidays. Trying to make time for family outings, picnics, or shared sports strengthens the family culture. If these are a natural part of family life, then the annual vacation will be more enriching and less of a trial. It is particularly important for the family to redeem the great Christian holidays from their distorted commercial form. This is especially difficult at Christmas time, but where Advent is used as a time of preparation, Christmas may take on quite a different meaning. At Easter time it is important to remember Good Friday, something Protestants have not always done. The secular culture does not want to think of Good Friday, for it wants resurrection without crucifixion. Children love holidays, and the great Christian feast days can be the occasion of much joyful learning.

On these occasions, as well as on Sundays, family observances ought to be combined with church observances. The family should understand itself as a cell in the body of Christ, mirroring the local congregation as the local congregation mirrors the whole of God's people. But the kind of integration of family and congregation I am advocating may imply a kind of parish life that is no commoner than the Christian family for which I am hoping. Richard Osmer vividly paints the picture that concerns me:

> Noticing what is absent is more difficult than we commonly suppose. If a person grows up in a suburb in which all the trees were leveled when the houses were built, it is highly unlikely that he or she will miss the massive beauty of an old oak or the splendor of a large maple in fall. What is missing remains hidden, for it has never been a part of the person's experience.
>
> The contemporary Protestant church faces the difficult task of noticing the absence of an authentic teaching office in its life. The fact that this essential ministry of the church has been missing for so long makes it even more difficult to recognize what is not present. Its absence, however, is felt in an increasingly widespread sense that something is missing; something of great importance is not present in the church's life.

What Osmer means by the "teaching office" includes sermons and more informal instruction by the pastor and all forms of Christian education, so it is not literally missing in any local church. What Osmer means by the teaching office, however, involves the whole congregation in the whole of its life searching for God's will in the light of Scripture and the experience of the Christian people, and trying to discern what to do. For most of us most of the time, when we leave church on Sunday morning we are no longer concerned or only subliminally concerned with the teachings of Christ, which leaves not only our work life but even our family life highly vulnerable to the prevailing winds of the surrounding secular culture. What would a more vigorous teaching office look like?

I was recently talking to a leader in the Mennonite Church about the practice in his congregation. It is a bit rigorous, but it is instructive. Sunday service lasts for three hours. First there is an hour of hymn, prayer, and thanksgiving; then there is an hour devoted to the word of God, including the sermon; then there is an hour of discernment, which perhaps has the most to teach us. This Mennonite group believes the worshiping community should be no larger than 100 people, so when the congregation grows beyond that it splits into two separate worshiping groups. This is precisely because of the importance of discernment, for everyone is included in that part of the service. During the period of discernment what has been sung in the hymns and read in the Scripture and spoken in the sermon is thrown open for discussion as to what it means for those assembled. There is the assumption that what has been taught has authority, but that it is a difficult task to discern what that means and that it requires the effort of all to find the way. This particular group breaks down into still smaller segments that meet one night a week in the homes of members. In this smaller prayer and discussion group the teen-age children are encouraged to attend, to learn from the efforts of their seniors, and to add their own comments when appropriate. This idea of teaching by inclusion rather than through one-way instruction is worth pondering.

The point I want to make is that the church as a context for family life as well as the church as a vital point for the transformation of the world cannot operate without what the Mennonites call discernment. We need to know what is in Scripture, tradition, and history and we also need to think together about what that means to us here and now in this confusing and rapidly changing world. In our individualistic culture it is easy to assume that discernment and application can be left to the individual. All he or she needs is an inspiring or "motivating" church service and the rest can take care of itself. But very often either nothing gets carried away at all or only very halting or even distorted ideas get taken away and the individual has no real idea of what to do about it. This is why we need the church not just as a group of passive listeners but as an active community of interpreters able to carry the message into the whole of our lives. And the family too should be, as a microcosm of the church, a community of interpreters.

It is this notion of the church as a community of interpreters that makes the third response to the challenge of culture that I mentioned earlier different from the second or fundamentalist type. The fundamentalist response to all the problems of life is that "Christ is the answer." In practice this means relying on a very superficial reading of the Bible or on the words of an authoritarian pastor. But if Christ is the answer, he is also the question. If the answer to our problems is to follow him, and I think it is, then we find, if we are serious, that Christ is challenging us very hard to think about what following him actually means under these particular circumstances of our lives. He does not expect us to sink into passivity, but to take up our cross, to take up the way of the servant, and to discern in the midst of all our suffering and confusion what to do. And mercifully he has given us his church to help us in that task. We need to uphold and sustain each other and we need all the wisdom we can gather from our brothers and sisters in Christ. But the answer is almost never obvious or easy. And we will find that we make many false starts and must begin again or correct our direction.

But let us try to be a bit more specific in thinking about the process of discernment, which, by the way, can also be called practical theology or the theology of the laity, or, as far as I am concerned, just theology. Richard Mouw has called attention to a useful set of criteria developed by Gerald Vandezande in a book entitled *Christians in the Crisis*. These are guidelines for what Vandezande calls "biblically faithful stewardship" and were developed initially with an eye to investment policies, but, as Mouw suggests, have much broader implications. Christians, Vandezande says, must attempt: first to be *gentle* in the way we treat the environment; second, *just* in the way we treat our fellow workers; third, *wise* in the use of the creation's resources; fourth, *sensitive* to the needs of our neighbors as they pursue their vocations and tasks; fifth, *careful* in the way we use technology, so that we do not idolize technical know-how, but use it as a way of serving legitimate human goals; sixth, *frugal* in our patterns of energy consumption, so that we do not waste the building blocks of the good life; seventh, *vigilant* in the prevention of waste; eighth, *fair* in the determination of prices; ninth, *honest* in the way we promote the sales of our products; and tenth, *equitable* in the earning of profit.

Actually that would be an excellent list to begin a discussion group on Christian vocation, on the way we can think about being Christians in our occupations. But it could just as well be the beginning of quite a few good discussions in the family. How do we in the home, as well as in the church and the larger world, show forth the gentleness, the justice, the wisdom, the sensitivity, the care, the frugality, the vigilance, the fairness, the honesty, and the equity God requires of us?

Another way to look at Vandezande's list is to see that he is advocating what Albert Borgmann calls "careful power." Borgmann points out that in much of the world today we are devoted to the exploitation of what he calls "regardless power." When we cut down rain forests for short-term profits even though there may be long-term deleterious effects on the world's climate, that is regardless power. When we support military insurrection without exhausting the possibility of negotiation, that is regardless power. When a corporate headquarters in New York closes down a plant in Oklahoma where 200 women make slacks at $6 an hour in order to open one in Mexico where the women will make 60 cents an hour, that is regardless power. Or when we load our homes with expensive appliances that are used only a few times a week, if then, that is regardless power. Jesus reminds us again and again, in the Beatitudes, in the whole of the Sermon on the Mount, in many of the sayings and parables, that his way is the way of careful power, not of passivity, but of the gentle persistence of love. But in a culture obsessed with what is called "regaining the competitive edge," with winning and dominating and being number one, it is easy for Christians to forget about Jesus or, even worse, to imagine him as a "member of a winning team" devoted to regardless power, and so turn him into our image rather than conform ourselves to his. We need the family and the church working together to help us discern a more truly Christian way.

Yet I do not want to give the impression that the family and the church together can provide a little oasis in the larger society where we can maintain a decent Christian life whatever happens. There are societies where that strategy is the only one possible and then it must be carried out as best one can. But in a society where free institutions still survive, institutions to which Christians have made enormous contributions even though we have never come near creating a "Christian society," I believe we have an obligation of citizenship as well as discipleship. Or, I would say, following Fr. John Coleman, that citizenship is part of our discipleship. It will take more than the church to nurture the family, even though I have tried to argue for the church as the primary context for the family. The family is terribly vulnerable to pressures from the larger society that the church itself cannot control. Tax laws, the welfare system, the cost of housing, work schedules, and patterns of remuneration in business and industry all have enormous consequences for family life. The family will be colonized and strip-mined by the systems controlled by money and power unless we can reinvigorate a political life dedicated to the common good.

Not only must the church defend and strengthen the family, it must also lead us into a vigorous discussion of public life so that we can discern those measures that will limit the destructive consequences of regardless power and will shape our lives in accord with the dictates of careful power. It will not always be easy. We must expect to be rejected and persecuted as Jesus was. But if we follow his way we also know that we are the salt of the earth, the light of the world, that we have lost our lives in order to find them in the most joyous fellowship of all.

11.2 Marriages Made to Last

Jeanette Lauer and Robert Lauer

ABSTRACT: The authors studied 351 couples who had been married for 15 years or more. They found 300 happily married, 32 mixed (only one partner was happy), and 19 unhappily married. Happy couples agreed that the two most significant reasons for their happy marriages were a positive attitude toward the spouse (liking that person as a friend) and the belief that marriage is a long-term commitment to something sacred. They also agreed that sharing the aims and goals of life, feeling that the spouse has grown more interesting, and wanting the relationship to succeed were the next important reasons. The authors discuss such other factors as the couples' laughing together, philosophy of life, showing affection, sex, and exchanging ideas.

We recently completed a survey of couples with enduring marriages to explore how marriages survive and satisfy in this turbulent world. Through colleagues and students we located and questioned 351 couples married for 15 years or more.

Of the 351 couples, 300 said they were happily married, 19 said they were unhappily married (but were staying together for a variety of reasons, including "the sake of the children"), and among the remaining 32 couples only one partner said he or she was unhappy in the marriage.

Each husband and wife responded individually to our questionnaire, which included 39 statements and questions about marriage — ranging from agreement about sex, money and goals in life to attitudes toward spouses and marriage in general. We asked couples to select from their answers the ones that best explained why their marriages had lasted. Men and women showed remarkable agreement on the keys to an enduring relationship (see box).

The most frequently named reason for an enduring and happy marriage was having a generally positive attitude toward one's spouse: viewing one's partner as one's best friend and liking him or her "as a person."

As one wife summed it up, "I feel that liking a person in marriage is as important as loving that person. Friends enjoy each other's company. We spend an unusually large amount of time together. We work at the same institution, offices just a few feet apart. But we still have things to do and to say to each other on a positive note after being together through the day."

It may seem almost trite to say that "my spouse is my best friend," but the couples in our survey underscored the importance of feeling that way. Moreover, they told us some specific things that they liked about their mates — why, as one woman said, "I would want to have him as a friend even if I weren't married to him." For one thing, many happily married people said that their mates become more interesting to them in time. A man married for 30 years said that it was almost like being married to a series of different women: "I have watched her grow and I find her more fascinating now than when we were first married."

A common theme among couples in our study was that the things they really liked in each other were qualities of caring, giving, integrity, and a sense of humor. In essence, they said, "I am married to someone who cares about me, who is concerned for my well-being, who gives as much or more than he or she gets, who is open and trustworthy and who is not mired down in a somber, bleak outlook on life." The redemption of difficult people through selfless devotion may make good fiction, but the happily married people in our sample expressed no such sense of mission. Rather, they said, they are grateful to have married someone who is basically appealing and likable.

Are lovers blind to each other's faults? No, according to our findings. They are aware of the flaws in their mates and acknowledge the rough times, but they believe that the likable qualities are more important than the deficiencies and the difficulties. "She isn't perfect," said a husband of 24 years. "But I don't worry about her weak points, which are very few. Her strong points overcome them too much."

A second key to a lasting marriage was a belief in marriage as a long-term commitment and a sacred institution. Many of our respondents thought that the present generation takes the vow, "till death us do part" too lightly and is unwilling to work through difficult times. Successful couples viewed marriage as a task that sometimes demands that you grit your teeth and plunge ahead in spite of the difficulties. "I'll tell you why we've stayed together," said a Texas woman married for 18 years. "I'm just too damned stubborn to give up."

Some of the people in the survey indicated that they would stay together no matter what. Divorce was simply not an option. Others viewed commitment somewhat differently. They saw it not as a chain that inexorably binds people together despite intense misery but rather as a determination to work through difficult times. "You can't run home to mother when the first sign of trouble appears," said a woman married for 35 years.

"Commitment means a willingness to be unhappy for a while," said a man married for more than 20 years. "I wouldn't go on for years and years being wretched in my marriage. But you can't avoid troubled times. You're not going to be happy with each other all the time. That's when commitment is really important."

In addition to sharing attitudes toward the spouse and toward marriage, our respondents indicated that agreement about aims and goals in life, the desire to make the marriage succeed, and laughing together were all important. One surprising result was that agreement about sex was far down the list of reasons for a happy marriage. Fewer than 10 percent of the spouses thought that good sexual relations kept their marriage together. Is sex relatively unimportant to a happy marriage? Yes and no.

330 \ *Topic 11 — Marriage and Family – Here to Stay?*

Although not many happily married respondents listed it as a major reason for their happiness, most were still generally satisfied with their sex lives. Seventy percent said that they always or almost always agreed about sex. And indeed for many, "satisfied" seems too mild a term. A woman married for 19 years said: "Our sexual desire is strong, and we are very much in love." One man said that sex with his wife was like "a revival of youth." Another noted that for various reasons he and his wife did not have sex as frequently as they would like, but when they do "it is a beautiful act of giving and sharing as deeply emotional as it is physical."

While some reported a diminishing sex life, others described a relatively stable pattern and a number indicated improvement over time. "Thank God, the passion hasn't died," a wife said. "In fact, it has gotten more intense. The only thing that has died is the element of doubt or uncertainty that one experiences while dating or in the beginning of a marriage."

On the other hand, some couples said they were satisfied despite a less-than-ideal sex life. A number of people told us that they were happy with their marriage even though they did not have sex as frequently as they would like. Generally, men complained of this more than women, although a number of wives desired sex more than did their husbands.

There were various reasons for having less sex than desired, generally involving one partner's exhaustion from work or family circumstances ("We are very busy and very involved," reported a husband, "and have a teenager who stays up late. So we don't make love as often as we would like to.")

Does this dissatisfaction with sex life lead to affairs? We did not ask about fidelity directly, but the high value that most of our subjects placed on friendship and commitment strikes us as incongruous with infidelity. And in fact only two of those we questioned volunteered that they had had brief affairs. One husband's view might explain the faithfulness of the group: "I get tempted when we don't have sex. But I don't think I could ever have an affair. I would feel like a traitor."

Such treason, in fact, may be the one taboo in enduring relationships. A wife of 27 years said that although she could work out almost any problem with her husband given enough time, infidelity "would probably not be something I could forget and forgive." The couples in our sample appear to take their commitment to each other seriously.

Those with a less-than-ideal sex life talked about adjusting to it rather than seeking relief in an affair. A woman married 25 years rated her marriage as extremely happy even though she and her husband had had no sexual relations for the past 10 years. "I was married once before and the marriage was almost totally sex and little else," she said. "So I suppose a kind of trade-off exists here — I like absolutely everything else about my current marriage."

Many others agreed that they would rather be married to their spouse and have a less-than-ideal sex life than be married to someone else and have

---

What Keeps a Marriage Going?

Here are the top reasons respondents gave, listed in order of frequency.

Men	Women
My spouse is my best friend.	My spouse is my best friend.
I like my spouse as a person.	I like my spouse as a person.
Marriage is a long-term commitment.	Marriage is a long-term commitment.
Marriage is sacred.	Marriage is sacred.
We agree on aims and goals.	We agree on aims and goals.
My spouse has grown more interesting.	My spouse has grown more interesting.
I want the relationship to succeed.	I want the relationship to succeed.
An enduring marriage is important to social stability.	We laugh together.
We laugh together.	We agree on a philosophy of life.
I am proud of my spouse's achievements.	We agree on how and how often to show affection.
We agree on a philosophy of life.	An enduring marriage is important to social stability.
We agree about our sex life.	We have a stimulating exchange of ideas.
We agree on how and how often to show affection.	We discuss things calmly.
I confide in my spouse.	We agree about our sex life.
We share outside hobbies and interests.	I am proud of my spouse's achievements.

---

a better sex life. As one wife put it, "I feel marriages can survive and flourish without today's emphasis on sex. I had a much stronger sex drive than my husband and it was a point of weakness in our marriage. However, it was not as important as friendship, understanding, and respect. That we had lots of, and still do."

We found a few beliefs and practices among our couples that contradict what some therapists believe is important to a marriage. One involves conflict. Some marriage counselors stress the importance of expressing feelings with abandon — spouses should freely vent their anger with each other, letting out all the stops short of physical violence. According to them, aggression is a catharsis that gets rid of hostility and restores harmony in the marital relationship. But some social scientists argue that intense expressions of anger, resentment, and dislike tend to corrode the relationship and increase the likelihood of future aggression.

Happily married couples in our survey came down squarely on the side of those who emphasize the damaging effects of intensely expressed anger. A salesman with a 36-year marriage advised, "Discuss your problems in a normal voice. If a voice is raised, stop. Return after a short period of time.

Start again. After a period of time both parties will be able to deal with their problems and not say things that they will be sorry about later."

Only one couple said that they typically yelled at each other. The rest emphasized the importance of restraint. They felt that a certain calmness is necessary in dealing constructively with conflict.

Another commonly held belief that contradicts conventional wisdom concerns equality in marriage. Most social scientists note the value of an egalitarian relationship. But according to the couples in our sample, the attitude that marriage is a 50-50 proposition can be damaging. One husband said that a successful marriage demands that you "give 60 percent of the time. You have to be willing to put in more than you take out." A wife happily married for 44 years said she would advise all young couples "to be willing to give 70 percent and expect 30 percent."

In the long run, the giving and taking should balance out. If either partner enters a marriage determined that all transactions must be equal, the marriage will suffer. As one husband put it, "Sometimes I give far more than I receive, and sometimes I receive far more than I give. But my wife does the same. If we weren't willing to do that, we would have broken up long ago."

Finally, some marriage experts have strongly advocated that spouses maintain separate as well as shared interests. It is important, they argue, to avoid the merging of identities. But those in our survey with enduring, happy marriages disagree. They try to spend as much time together and share as many activities as possible. "Jen is just the best friend I have," said a husband who rated his marriage as extremely happy. "I would rather spend time with her, talk with her, be with her than with anyone else."

"We try to share everything," said another. "We even work together now. In spite of that, we often feel that we have too little time together."

We did not detect any loss of individuality in these people. In fact, they disagreed to some extent on many of the questions. Their intense intimacy — their preference for shared rather than separate activities — seems to reflect a richness and fulfillment in the relationship rather than a loss of identity. "On occasion she has something else to do, and I enjoy the time alone. But it strikes me that I can enjoy it because I know that soon she will be home, and we will be together again."

Our results seem to underscore Leo Tolstoy's observation that "Happy families are all alike." Those who have long-term, happy marriages share a number of attitudes and behavioral patterns that combine to create an enduring relationship. For them, "till death us do part" is not a binding clause but a gratifying reality.

11.3 Coming Apart: Radical Departures since 1960

Steven Mintz and Susan Kellogg

A GENERATION AGO OZZIE, HARRIET, DAVID, AND RICKY NELSON EPITOMIZED the American family. Over 70 percent of all American households in 1960 were like the Nelsons: made up of dad the breadwinner, mom the home-maker, and their children. Today, less than three decades later, "traditional" families consisting of a breadwinner father, a housewife mother, and one or more dependent children account for less than 15 percent of the nation's households. As American families have changed, the image of the family portrayed on television has changed accordingly. Today's television families vary enormously, running the gamut from traditional families like "The Wal-tons" to two-career families like the Huxtables on "The Cosby Show" or the Keatons on "Family Ties"; "blended" families like the Bradys on "The Brady Bunch," with children from previous marriages; two single mothers and their children on "Kate and Allie"; a homosexual who serves as a surrogate father on "Love, Sidney"; an unmarried couple who cohabit in the same house on "Who's the Boss?"; and a circle of friends, who think of themselves as a family, congregating at a Boston bar on "Cheers."

Since 1960 U.S. families have undergone a historical transformation as dramatic and far reaching as the one that took place at the beginning of the nineteenth century. Even a casual familiarity with census statistics suggest the profundity of the changes that have taken place in family life. Birthrates plummeted. The average number of children per family fell from 3.8 at the peak of the baby boom to less than 2 today. At the same time, the divorce rate soared. Today the number of divorces each year is twice as high as it was in 1966 and three times higher than in 1950. The rapid upsurge in the divorce rate contributed to a dramatic increase in the number of single-parent households, or what used to be known as "broken homes." The number of households consisting of a single woman and her children has doubled since 1960. A sharp increase in female-headed homes was accompanied by a steep increase in the number of couples cohabiting outside marriage; their numbers have quadrupled since 1960.

Almost every aspect of family life seems to have changed before our eyes. Sexual codes were revised radically. Today only about one American woman in five waits until marriage to become sexually active, compared to nearly half in 1960 who postponed intercourse. Meanwhile, the proportion of births occurring among unmarried women quadrupled. At the same time, millions of wives entered the labor force. The old stereotype of the bread-winner-father and housewife-mother broke down as the number of working wives climbed. In 1950, 25 percent of married woman living with their hus-bands, worked outside the home; in the late 1980s the figure is nearly 60 percent. The influx of married women entering the labor force was particularly rapid among mothers of young children. Now more than half of all mothers of school-age children hold jobs. As a result, fewer young children can claim their mother's exclusive attention. What Americans have witnessed since 1960 are fundamental challenges to the forms, ideals, and role expectations that have defined the family for the last century and a half.

Profound and far-reaching changes have occurred in the American family in behavior and in values. Contemporary Americans are much more likely than their predecessors to postpone or forego marriage, to live alone outside familial units, to engage in intercourse prior to marriage, to permit marriages to end in divorce, to permit mothers of young children to work outside the home, and to allow children to live in families with only one parent and no adult male present. Earlier family norms of a working father, a housewife, and children have undergone major alterations. The term "family" had gradually been redefined to include any group of people living together, including such variations as single mothers and children, unmarried couples, and gay couples.

All these changes have generated a profound sense of uncertainty and ambivalence. Many Americans fear that the rapid decline in the birthrates, the dramatic upsurge in divorce rates, and the proliferation of loose, noncontractual sexual relationships are symptoms of increasing selfishness and self-centeredness incompatible with strong family attachments. They also fear that an increased proportion of working mothers has caused more children to be neglected, resulting in climbing rates of teenage pregnancy, delinquency, suicide, drug and alcohol abuse, and failure in school.

Today fear for the family's future is widespread. In 1978 author Clare Boothe Luce succinctly summarized fears about the fragility of the family that continue to haunt Americans today:

> Today 50% of all marriages end in divorce, separation, or desertion . . . . The marriage rate and birth rate are falling. The numbers of one-parent and one-child families are rising. More and more young people are living together without benefit of marriage . . . . Premarital and extra-marital sex no longer raises parental or conjugal eyebrows . . . . The rate of reported incest, child molestation, rape, and child and wife abuse, is steadily mounting . . . . Run-away children, teenage prostitution, youthful drug addiction and alcoholism have become great, ugly, new phenomena.

What are the forces that lie behind these changes in family life? And what are the implications of these transformations?

New Morality

The key to understanding the recent upheavals in family life lies in a profound shift in cultural values. Three decades ago most Americans shared certain strong attitudes about the family. Public opinion polls showed that they endorsed marriage as a prerequisite of well-being, social adjustment, and maturity and agreed on the proper roles of husband and wife. Men and women who failed to marry or who resented their family roles were denigrated as maladjusted or neurotic. The message conveyed by the broader culture was that happiness was a by-product of living by the accepted values of hard work and family obligation.

Values and norms have shifted. The watchwords of contemporary society are "growth," "self-realization," and "fulfillment." Expectations of personal happiness have risen and collided with a more traditional concern (and sacrifice) for the family. At the same time, in addition to its traditional functions of caring for children, providing economic security, and meeting its members' emotional needs, the family has become the focus for new expectations of sexual fulfillment intimacy, and companionship.

Today a broad spectrum of family norms that prevailed during the 1950s and early 1960s is no longer widely accepted. Divorce is not stigmatized as it used to be; a large majority of the public now rejects the idea that an unhappily married couple should stay together for their children's sake. Similarly, the older view that anyone who rejected marriage is "sick," "neurotic," or "immoral" has declined sharply, as has the view that people who do not have children are "selfish." Opinion surveys show that most Americans no longer believe that a woman should not work if she has a husband who can support her, that a bride should always be a virgin when she marries, or that premarital sex is always wrong.

Economic affluence played a major role in the emergence of a new outlook. Couples who married in the 1940s and 1950s had spent their early childhood years in the depression and formed relatively modest material aspirations. Born in the late 1920s or 1930s, when birthrates were depressed, they faced little competition for jobs at maturity and were financially secure enough to marry and have children at a relatively young age. Their children, however, who came of age during the 1960s and 1970s, spent their childhoods during an era of unprecedented affluence. Between 1950 and 1970, median family income tripled. Increased affluence increased opportunities for education, travel, and leisure, all of which helped to heighten expectations of self-fulfillment. Unlike their parents, they had considerable expectations for their own material and emotional well-being.

In keeping with the mood of an era of rising affluence, philosophies stressing individual self-realization flourished. Beginning in the 1950s, "humanistic" psychologies, stressing growth and self-actualization, triumphed over earlier theories that had emphasized adjustment as the solution to individual problems. The underlying assumption of the new "third force" psychologies – a name chosen to distinguish them from the more pessimistic psychoanalytic and behaviorist psychologies – of Abraham Maslow, Carl Rogers, and Erich Fromm is that a person's spontaneous impulses are intrinsically good and that maturity is not a process of "settling down" and suppressing instinctual needs but of achieving one's potential.

Even in the early 1960s, marriage and family ties were regarded by the "human potential movement" as potential threats to individual fulfillment as a man or a woman. The highest forms of human needs, contended proponents of the new psychologies, were autonomy, independence, growth, and creativity, all of which could be thwarted by "existing relationships and interactions." Unlike the earlier psychology of adjustment, associated with Alfred Adler and Dale Carnegie, which had counseled compromise, suppression of instinctual impulses, avoidance of confrontations, and the desirability of acceding to the wishes of others, the new humanistic psychologies advised individuals to "get in touch" with their feelings and freely voice their opinions, even if this generated feelings of guilt.

The impulse toward self-fulfillment and liberation was further advanced by the prophets of the 1960s counterculture and New Left, Norman O. Brown and Herbert Marcuse. Both Brown and Marcuse transformed Sigmund Freud's psychoanalytic insights into a critique of the constraints of liberal society. They were primarily concerned not with political or economic repression but rather with what they perceived as the psychological repression of the individual's instinctual needs. Brown located the source of repression in the ego mechanisms that controlled each person's instincts. Marcuse, in a broader social critique, believed that repression was at least partially imposed by society.

For both Brown and Marcuse, the goal of social change was the liberation of eros, the agglomeration of an individual's pleasure-seeking life instincts, or, as Marcuse put it, the "free gratification of man's instinctual needs." Brown went so far as to challenge openly the basic tenets of "civilized sexual morality," with its stress on genital, heterosexual, monogamous sex, and extolled a new ideal of bisexualism and "polymorphous perversity" (total sexual gratification). For a younger, affluent, middle-class generation in revolt against liberal values, the ideas of Brown and Marcuse provided a rationale for youthful rebellion.

An even more thoroughgoing challenge to traditional family values was mounted by the women's liberation movement, which attacked the family's exploitation of women. Feminists denounced the societal expectation that women defer to the needs of spouses and children as part of their social roles as wives and mothers. Militant feminist activists like Ti-Grace Atkinson called marriage "slavery," "legalized rape," and "unpaid labor" and denounced heterosexual love as "tied up with a sense of dependency." The larger mainstream of the women's movement articulated a powerful critique of the idea that child care and housework was the apex of a woman's accomplishments or her sole means of fulfillment. Feminists uncovered unsettling evidence of harsher conditions behind conventional familial togetherness, such as child abuse and wife beating, wasted lives and exploited labor. Instead of giving the highest priority to their families, women were urged to raise their consciousness of their own needs and abilities. From this vantage point, marriage increasingly came to be described as a trap, circumscribing a woman's social and intellectual horizons and lowering her sense of self-esteem. Homemaking, which as recently as the early 1960s had been celebrated on such television shows as "Queen for a Day," came under attack as an unrecognized and unpaid form of work in contrast to more "serious" occupations outside the home. And, as for marital bliss forevermore, feminists warned that divorce – so common and so economically difficult for women – was an occurrence for which every married woman had to be prepared. In general the feminists awakened American women to what they viewed as the worst form of social and political oppression – sexism. The introduction of this new awareness would go far beyond the feminists themselves.

The challenge to older family values was not confined to radical members of the counterculture, the New Left, or the women's liberation movement. Broad segments of society were influenced by, and participated in, this fundamental shift in values.

Although only a small minority of American women ever openly declared themselves to be feminists, there can be no doubt that the arguments of the women's movement dramatically altered women's attitudes toward family roles, child care, marital relationships, femininity, and housework. This is true even among many women who claim to reject feminism. Polls have shown a sharp decline in the proportion of women favoring large families and a far greater unwillingness to subordinate personal needs and interests to the demands of husbands and children. A growing majority of women now believe that both husband and wife should have jobs, both do housework, and both take care of children. This represents a stunning shift of opinion in a decade and a half. A new perception of woman in the family has taken hold. In extreme imagery she is a superwoman, doing a full-time job while managing her home and family well. The more realistic image is of the wife and mother who works and struggles to manage job and family with the help of spouse, day care, and employer. Thus, as women increasingly seek employment outside the home, the family itself shifts to adjust to the changing conditions of its members while striving to provide the stability and continuity it has traditionally afforded.

During the 1960s a sexual revolution that predated the counterculture swept the nation's literature, movies, theater, advertising, and fashion. In 1962, Grossinger's resort in New York State's Catskill mountains introduced its first singles-only weekend, thereby publicly acknowledging couples outside marriage. That same year, Illinois became the first state to decriminalize all forms of private sexual conduct between consenting adults. Two years later, in 1964, the first singles bar opened on New York's Upper East Side; the musical *Hair* introduced nudity to the Broadway stage; California designer Rudi Gernreich created the topless bathing suit; and bars featuring topless waitresses and dancers sprouted. By the end of the decade, a growing number of the nation's colleges had abolished regulations specifying how late students could stay outside their dormitories and when and under what circumstances male and female students could visit with each other.

One of the most important aspects of this latter-day revolution in morals was the growth of a "singles culture" – evident in a proliferation of singles bars, apartment houses, and clubs. The sources of the singles culture were varied and complex, owing as much to demographic shifts as to the ready availability of birth control, cures for venereal diseases, and liberalized abortion laws. The trend toward postponement of marriage, combined with increased rates of college attendance and divorce, meant that growing numbers of adults spent protracted periods of their sexually mature lives outside marriage. The result was that it became far easier than in the past to maintain an active social and sex life outside marriage. It also became more acceptable, as its patterns became grist for the popular media and imagination.

Sexually oriented magazines started to display pubic hair and filmmakers began to show simulated sexual acts. *I Am Curious (Yellow)* depicted coitus on the screen. *Deep Throat* released in the 1970s, showed cunnilingus and fellatio. Other manifestations of a relaxation of traditional mores included a growing public tolerance of homosexuality, a blurring of male and female sex roles, increasing public acceptance of abortion, the growing visibility of pornography, a marked trend away from female virginity until marriage, and a sharp increase in the proportion of women engaging in extramarital sex. Within one decade the cherished privacy of sexuality had been overturned and an era of public sexuality had been ushered in.

Increasingly, values championed by the women's movement and the counterculture were adopted in a milder form by large segments of the American population. A significant majority of Americans adopted permissive attitudes on such matters as premarital sex, cohabitation outside of marriage, and abortion. Fewer women aspired to motherhood and homemaking as a full-time career and instead joined the labor force as much for independence and self-fulfillment as from economic motives. The preferred number of children declined sharply, and to limit births, the number of abortions and sterilizations increased sharply. A revolution had occurred in values and behavior.

Black Families in Poverty

At the same time as the attitudes and behavior of middle-class white Americans were transformed as a result of increasing affluence, the impact of feminism, and a revolution in sexual mores, the circumstances of the black family also shifted, but in very different ways. The situation of poor black families significantly worsened during the 1960s and 1970s. Illegitimate births increased dramatically, and the proportion of young blacks living in poverty climbed steeply. Today, half of all black children grow up in poverty, more than half are born outside wedlock, and nearly half live in female-headed households.

The plight of the black family came to public attention early in the fall of 1965, when the federal government released a confidential report written by Daniel Patrick Moynihan, then an obscure assistant secretary of labor, called *The Negro Family: The Case for National Action.* In his report Moynihan argued that the major obstacle to the advancement of the black community lay in a vicious and self-perpetuating cycle of despair in the urban ghettos. "The fundamental problem," Moynihan maintained, was the breakdown of the black family. "The evidence – not final, but powerfully persuasive – is that the Negro family in the urban ghettos is crumbling." The black middle class had managed to create stable families, "but for the vast numbers of the unskilled, poorly educated city working class, the fabric of conventional social relationships has all but disintegrated."

To support his thesis, Moynihan cited startling statistics. Nearly 25 percent of all black women were divorced, separated, or living apart from their husbands, compared to 7.9 percent of white women. Illegitimacy among blacks had risen from 16.8 percent in 1940 to 23.6 percent in 1963, while the white rate had only climbed from 2 to 3 percent. The proportion of black families headed by women had climbed from 8 percent in 1950 to 21 percent in 1960, while the white rate had remained steady at 9 percent. The breakdown of the black family, Moynihan contended, had led to a sharp increase in welfare dependency, delinquency, unemployment, drug addiction, and failure in school.

The Moynihan Report attributed the instability of the black family to the effects of slavery, Reconstruction, poor education, rapid urbanization, and thirty-five years of severe unemployment, which had undermined the role of the black man in the family. Unable to support their families, many black fathers simply disappeared, leaving the women to cope and rule. In Moynihan's view, children raised in female-headed families, deprived of a male role model and authority figure, tended to remain trapped in a cycle of poverty and disadvantage:

> From the wild Irish slums of the 19th-century Eastern seaboard, to the riot-torn suburbs of Los Angeles, there is one unmistakable lesson in American history; a community that allows a large number of men to grow up in broken homes, dominated by women, never acquiring any stable relationship to male authority, never acquiring any set of rational expectations about the future – that community asks for and gets chaos.

The report concluded with a call for national action to strengthen the black family through programs of jobs, family allowances, and birth control. It did not support the belief that enforcement of civil rights laws would be sufficient to bring about equality. Only new and special efforts by the federal government could alleviate conditions within urban ghettos and strengthen the black family.

Release of the Moynihan Report in August 1965 unleashed a storm of public criticism. Critics feared that the report would reinforce white prejudice by suggesting that sexual promiscuity and illegitimacy were socially acceptable within the black community and that the instability of the black family was the basic cause of racial inequality. Others accused the report of diverting attention from the underlying problems of racism and poverty and of blaming the victims for their own distress.

How accurate was Moynihan's assessment of the black family? On the one hand, he was prescient in identifying single-parenthood, illegitimacy, and poverty among children as major social issues. Indeed, these problems have so worsened since Moynihan wrote his report that they now affect the entire society and can no longer be addressed solely in terms of race. At the same time, however, in important respects Moynihan's analysis was flawed. The problems of illegitimacy and absent fathers were exaggerated, the strengths of the black family were ignored, and the differences between the black family and the white family were overestimated.

Contrary to the impression conveyed by the report of the prevalence of "matriarchy," "deviance," and "family disorganization" among blacks, the overwhelming majority of black families during the 1960s, 1970s, and 1980s were composed of two spouses. In 1960, 75 percent of black children lived with two parents; a decade later, 67 percent did. Today six out of every ten black families have two parents, and two-parent families remain the norm in the black community. The report's discussion of illegitimacy also seriously distorted the facts. Far from increasing, as Moynihan implied, the black illegitimacy rate – the proportion of unmarried women bearing children – had actually been declining consistently since 1961 and has, in fact, continued to decline up until today. In 1960, ninety-eight out of every thousand single black women gave birth to a baby. In 1980 only seventy-seven did. The proportion of black births that were illegitimate increased, but this was the result of a sharp drop in the birthrate of married black women. The report further exaggerated the difference between black and white illegitimacy rates by ignoring the fact that white women were much more likely than black women to use contraceptives, to have premarital pregnancies terminated by abortion, or to put babies born out of wedlock up for adoption.

Moynihan tended to downplay the role of unemployment and the welfare system in producing family instability. Low wages and the unstable, dead-end occupations available to black men contributed to a sense of frustration and powerlessness that prevented many lower-class men from becoming stable husbands and fathers. And the welfare system added to the breakup of families since in half the states welfare benefits could only begin after a father deserted his family.

Much of the disparity between white and black family patterns – in 1965 and today – is simply a result of poverty. The statistical gap between the races largely disappears when one compares blacks and whites of the same economic level. Blacks with incomes above the poverty line differ little from white families in their proportion of female-headed households. Furthermore, a significant part of the disparity in family patterns is explained by the skewed sex ratio of the black population: The number of black men of marriageable age is significantly smaller than the number of black women of marriageable age. The 1970 census indicated that there were only 86 black males for every 100 black females aged twenty to twenty-four and just 84 black males for every 100 females aged twenty-five to thirty-four.

Although many poor families do not conform in structure to middle-class norms, it is important not to underestimate the strength and durability of the lower-class black kinship system. By focusing on the instability, weakness, and pathology of lower-class black families, the Moynihan Report failed to recognize that lower-class black family patterns were a rational response to conditions of severe deprivation. Moynihan underestimated the competence of black mothers in rearing and supporting their children and the support black families received from an extended kinship network. Although Moynihan regarded lower-class black families as "disorganized" and "father-deprived" because they failed to conform to middle-class ideals of the nuclear family, later researchers found an extensive network of kin and friends supporting and reinforcing the lower-class black family. In urban ghettos, destitution and the inability of individual households to fulfill basic needs led lower-class blacks to form "domestic networks," which tended to replace the nuclear family as the fundamental unit of social organization. Friends and relatives helped mothers, took the place of fathers, provided child care, and shared resources.

When President Lyndon B. Johnson announced the War on Poverty in 1964, his diagnosis of the problem of poverty was profoundly influenced by the Moynihan Report. Drawing on Moynihan's argument that poverty and unemployment had undermined the black family and that family disorganization perpetuated social and economic inequality, President Johnson pledged that a primary goal of federal antipoverty programs would be "to strengthen the family and create conditions under which most parents will stay together." Unless the family was strengthened, the president declared, all other legislation "will never be enough to cut completely the circles of despair and deprivation." A unique political commitment to the family had been made by the federal government.

When Lyndon Johnson left the presidency in 1969, he left behind a legacy of a transformed federal government. At the end of the Eisenhower presidency in 1961, there were only 45 domestic social programs. By 1969 the number had climbed to 435. Federal social spending, excluding Social Security, had risen from $9.9 billion in 1960 to $25.6 billion in 1968.

Johnson's "Great Society" represented the broadest attack Americans had ever waged on the special problems facing poor and disadvantaged families. It declared decisively that the family-related problems of the poor problems of housing, income, employment, and health – were ultimately a federal responsibility.

During the 1960s the federal government showed an increasing commitment to improving the welfare of the nation's poor families. To improve their economic status, government greatly expanded public assistance programs. In 1959 there was essentially only a single welfare program providing public assistance to the poor – Aid to Families with Dependent Children (AFDC). Payments were small, amounting to only about a quarter of the median income, and relatively few poor families participated in the program. During the 1960s and early 1970s, AFDC rolls grew rapidly as a result of a sharp increase in the number of female-headed families and changes in eligibility requirements, including a 1961 law that allowed states to grant assistance to families containing an unemployed father and a 1968 Supreme Court ruling that it was unconstitutional for states to deny AFDC benefits to households containing a live-in adult male.

To assure adequate health care coverage to persons receiving federally supported public assistance, in 1965 Congress established Medicaid and in 1968 enacted the Child Health Improvement and Protection Act providing for prenatal and postnatal care. To combat hunger and malnutrition among the poor while disposing of surplus agricultural commodities, the federal government created the Food Stamp program in 1961 and subsequently added school breakfast and lunch programs. To address the problems of crowded and dilapidated housing, Congress in 1961 began to subsidize builders of low-income housing and in 1965 made rent supplements available to poor families. To reduce infant and maternal mortality, the numbers of unwanted children, and physical and mental handicaps among the poor, Congress in 1967 extended Medicaid coverage to include family planning services and required that they be provided to AFDC mothers. To train poorer Americans for new and better jobs, Congress adopted the Manpower Development and Training Act in 1962 and the Economic Opportunity Act in 1964 to provide vocational training, basic education, and summer employment for disadvantaged youth. To encourage adult AFDC recipients to enroll in job-training programs and seek work, Congress in 1967 required states to provide day care or child development facilities for the children of such women. To promote education in 1964 Congress established Head Start, a program of compensatory preschool education for poor children.

Johnson promised to reduce poverty, alleviate hunger and malnutrition, expand community medical care, provide adequate housing, and enhance the employability of the poor. When he left office in 1969, he could legitimately argue that he had kept his promise. Contrary to the widespread view that "in the war on poverty, poverty won," substantial progress had been made. During the 1960s the incidence of poverty was reduced, infant mortality was cut, and blighted housing was demolished. In 1960, 40 million persons, 20 percent of the population, were classified by the government as poor. By 1969, their number had been reduced to 24 million, 12 percent of the population. Infant mortality among the poor, which had barely declined between 1950 and 1965, fell by one-third in the decade after 1965 as a result of the expansion of federal medical and nutritional programs. Implementation of Medicaid and Medicare helped to improve the health of the poor. Before 1965, 20 percent of the poor had never been examined by a physician; by 1970 the figure had been cut to 8 percent. The proportion of families living in substandard housing – usually defined as housing lacking indoor plumbing – also declined steeply, from 20 percent in 1960 to 11 percent a decade later.

Few questions of public policy have evoked greater controversy than the impact of government welfare programs on the families of the poor. Political conservatives have generally argued that public assistance, food subsidies, health programs, and child care programs weakened poorer families. President Ronald Reagan voiced a common conservative viewpoint when he declared, "There is no question that many well-intentioned Great Society-type programs contributed to family breakups, welfare dependency, and a large increase in births out of wedlock."

Belief in a causal connection between increased government welfare expenditures and family breakdown rests on a close chronological correlation between rising welfare spending and dramatic increases in female-headed households and illegitimacy among the poor. Back in 1959, just 10 percent of low-income black Americans lived in a single-parent household. By 1980 the figure had climbed to 44 percent. It was during the late 1960s, a time of rapid economic growth and increasing antipoverty expenditures, that the prevalence of two-parent black families declined most steeply, from 72 percent in 1967 to 69 percent in 1968 to just 63 percent in 1973. Today 59 percent of black families have two parents present. At the same time, the number of illegitimate births among the poor grew substantially. Had the number of single-parent families remained at the 1970 level, the number of poor families in 1980 would have been 32 percent lower than it was.

What was the impact of massive federal intervention on the families of the poor? Did the expansion of state services contribute to rising rates of illegitimacy and single-parent families? The answers to these questions are still uncertain. On the one hand, there is little empirical evidence that welfare policies encourage family breakup. Statistical studies have found no correlation between the level of AFDC benefits and the proportion of black children in single-parent households. What other studies have shown is that increases in wages produce a sharp drop in female-headed households, reinforcing the view that low wages and unstable employment are major contributors to family instability.

It seems clear that some of the apparent deterioration in black family patterns is illusory. The dramatic increase in black single-parent families living on welfare is not so much a result of a dramatic increase in the number of unmarried women having illegitimate babies as that fewer unmarried mothers live with their parents or other relatives than was the case in the past. Nearly two-fifths of the increase in female-headed households between 1950 and 1972 is explained by the movement of existing single-parent families out of households of parents or other relatives. Public assistance allowed female heads of poor families greater opportunity to set up independent homes. If female-headed families made up a growing proportion of the poor, this partly reflected a sharp reduction in poverty among other groups. One of the consequences of government policy was to alter dramatically the profile of the poor. Increases in Social Security payments dramatically reduced the incidence of poverty among the elderly. The Supplemental Social Security program introduced in 1973 sharply reduced poverty among the disabled. As a result of reductions in poverty among the elderly and disabled and increases in the number of single-parent, female-headed households, poverty has been increasingly feminized.

The Feminization of Poverty

Today families headed by women are four and a half times as likely to be poor as families headed by males. Teenagers who have children out of wedlock are seven times as likely to be in poverty. Although female-headed families constitute only 15 percent of the U.S. population, they account for over 50 percent of the poor population. Teenagers and women in their early twenties who bear illegitimate children constitute a large segment of the population that remains poor and dependent on welfare for long periods of time.

And yet the picture is not quite so bleak as it might seem at first glimpse. Although a majority of poor families are female-headed, it is no longer true that most female-headed families are poor. Over the past two decades, the poverty rate of female-headed families has declined steeply, as women have succeeded in obtaining better-paying jobs in the labor force. Back in 1960, 50 percent of all female-headed families lived in poverty. By 1970 the figure had fallen to 38 percent and down to 19 percent in 1980. Meanwhile, few female-headed families remain in poverty for very long. Most mothers who receive public assistance are self-supporting individuals who have recently experienced a sudden divorce or separation. Most of these women leave the welfare rolls within two years. And finally, many poor women eventually marry, leaving poverty. Nearly three-quarters of young black women who bear a child out of wedlock marry by the age of twenty-four, usually ending their poverty.

Still, there can be little doubt that the nation's welfare policies actually provide incentives to the poor to avoid marriage. Under present law, if an AFDC mother marries, the stepfather assumes financial responsibility for supporting her children, which may deter the couple from marrying. In twenty-nine states, unemployed fathers are ineligible for assistance, which may encourage an unemployed father to desert his family so that his wife and children can obtain AFDC benefits. The discouragement of marriage in American welfare law contrasts sharply with European policies. In such countries as France, Hungary, Sweden, and East and West Germany, which have adopted explicit "family policies," the national government subsidizes families in a variety of ways, including the provision of family allowances to supplement parents' income and direct cash payments to parents when they have children.

Children in a New Age

Along with a mounting federal commitment to shore up the nation's poor families came another domestic revolution, a radical new self-consciousness about child rearing. Over the past quarter century, Americans have grown progressively more concerned about the plight of the nation's young people. Alarmed by sharp increases in delinquency, alcohol and drug abuse, pregnancy, and suicides among children and adolescents, parents became uneasy about the proper way to raise children. They also worried about the effects of day care, the impact of divorce, and the consequences of growing up in a permissive society in which premarital sex, abortion, and drugs are prevalent.

The past two decades have witnessed significant changes in the experience of childhood and adolescence. Since 1960 the proportion of children growing up in "traditional families" in which the father is the breadwinner and the mother is a full-time homemaker has fallen dramatically while the number growing up in single-parent, female-headed households or in two-worker, two-parent households has risen steeply. Before 1960 divorce was an occurrence experienced by relatively few children. Of children born during the 1970s, in contrast, 40 percent will experience a divorce before their sixteenth birthdays, and nearly 50 percent will spend at least part of their childhood in a single-parent home.

At the same time as marriages grew less stable, unprecedented changes took place within families. The proportion of married women with pre-schoolers who were in the labor force jumped from 12 percent in 1950 to 45 percent in 1980. Families grew smaller and, as a result, children have fewer siblings. Families also became more mobile, and hence children have less and less contact with relatives outside the immediate family. According to one estimate, just 5 percent of American children see a grandparent regularly. Young children spend more of their time in front of the television set or in the care of individuals other than their parents – in day-care centers, preschool programs, or the homes of other families – and more and more teenagers take part-time work.

Each of these changes has evoked anxiety for the well-being of children. Many adults worry that a high divorce rate undermines the psychological and financial security of children. Others fear that children who live with a single female parent will have no father figure with whom to identify or to emulate and no firm source of guidance. Many are concerned that two-career parents with demanding jobs substitute money for affection, freedom for supervision, and abdicate their parental roles to surrogates. Still others fret that teenage jobs undermine school attendance and involvement and leave young people with too much money to spend on clothing, records, a car, or drugs. Today's children and adolescents many believe, are caught between two difficult trends – decreasing parental commitment to child nurture and an increasingly perilous social environment saturated with sex, addictive drugs, and alcohol – that make it more difficult to achieve a well-adjusted adulthood.

According to many Americans, children have paid a high price for the social transformations of the 1960s and 1970s – spiraling divorce rates, the rapid influx of mothers into the work force, a more relaxed attitude toward sex, and the widespread use of television as a form of child care. They are afraid that these patterns have eroded an earlier ideal of childhood as a special, protected state – a carefree period of innocence – and that today's permissive culture encourages a "new precocity" that thrusts children into the adult world before they are mature enough to deal with it. They worry about the deleterious effects of divorce, day care, and overexposure – through television, movies, music, and advertisement – to drugs, violence, sex, and pornography. They are concerned that parents have absorbed a far too egalitarian view of their relationship with their children and have become incapable of exercising authority and discipline.

Giving credence to these fears are a variety of social indicators that appear to show an erosion in the parent-child bond and a precipitous decline in children's well-being. Public opinion polls indicate that two-thirds of all parents believe that they are less willing to make sacrifices for their children than their parents were. Other social statistics – ranging from college entrance examination results to teenage suicide rates – suggest that the decline in parental commitment to children has been accompanied by a sharp increase in problems among young people. Since 1960 the high-school dropout rate has increased until roughly one student in four drops out before graduation; juvenile delinquency rates have jumped 130 percent; the suicide rate for young people fifteen to nineteen years old has more than tripled; illegitimate births among white adolescent females have more than doubled; and the death rate from accidents and homicides has grown sixteenfold. Half a million adolescent females suffer from such eating disorders as anorexia nervosa or bulimia. American teenagers have the highest pregnancy rate of any industrialized nation, a high abortion rate and a high incidence of such venereal diseases as syphilis, gonorrhea, and genital herpes.

Of course, it is easy to exaggerate the depravity of today's youth. Such problems as drug abuse, illegitimacy, and suicide affect only a small fraction of young people, and millions of others are raised in strong, caring homes by supportive and loving parents. Despite this, however, there is a widespread perception that American society is experiencing great difficulty in preparing children for adulthood.

To a growing number of Americans, parenthood has become an increasingly frightening prospect. Fathers who once drag raced in hot rods and guzzled beer illegally are frightened by the idea of their children using drugs. Mothers who once made out with their boyfriends in parked cars are alarmed by statistics showing that teenage girls run a 40 percent chance of becoming pregnant and run three times the risk of contracting venereal disease than they did. One result is that parents have become progressively more self-conscious, anxious, and guilt-ridden about child rearing; fearful that even a single mistake in parenting might inflict scars that could last a lifetime. To address parents' mounting anxiety, a veritable torrent of child-rearing manuals has appeared.

Although most discussions of child rearing in the 1960s and 1970s dwell on Dr. Benjamin Spock, his era of influence was even then coming to an end. Until 1960, American child-rearing literature was dominated by a handful of manuals, notably Spock's *Baby and Child Care* and the publications of Dr. Arnold Gesell and the Yale Child Development Clinic, which traced the stages of children's physical, cognitive, and emotional development. The arena rapidly grew more crowded and confused during the 1960s with the publication of a spate of new child-rearing books. By 1981 more than 600 books were in print on the subject of child development. These new manuals tended to convey a sense of urgency absent in earlier child care books, rejecting the easy going approach championed by Dr. Spock. One child care expert, Dr. Lee Salk, addressed the subject in words typical of the new child-rearing literature: "Taking parenthood for granted can have disastrous results."

As the number of child-rearing books multiplied during the 1960s, a fundamental schism became increasingly apparent. At one pole were those echoing concerns voiced by Vice President Spiro T. Agnew that overpermissiveness – that is, too much coddling of children and overresponsiveness to their demands – resulted in adolescents who were anarchic, disrespectful and undisciplined. An extreme example of this viewpoint could be found in James Dobson's *Dare to Discipline,* which called on parents to exercise firm control of their children through the use of corporal punishment. At the other pole were writers like Mark Gerzon, author of *A Childhood for Every Child,* who took the position that the characteristic American child-rearing techniques stifled creativity, generated dependence, instilled sexist biases, and produced repressed and conformist personalities. Authors like Gerzon called on parents to reject control through power and authority and to foster an environment based on warmth and understanding. Most child-rearing books, however, fell between the two, calling on parents to balance firmness and love and to adapt their methods to the unique temperament, needs, and feelings of each child.

Although the authors of the burgeoning new child-rearing literature disagreed vehemently on such specific issues as the desirability of day care or whether mothers of young children should work outside the home, they did agree that successful child raising presents a much more difficult challenge today than it did in the past, noting that even parents with a deep commitment to their offspring confront difficulties that their parents did not have to face.

Among the most potent new forces that intrude between parents and children is television. The single most important caretaker of children in the United States today is not a child's mother or a babysitter or even a day-care center but the television set in each child's home. Young children spend more time watching television than they do in any other activity other than sleep. The typical child between the ages of two and five spends about thirty hours a week viewing television, nearly a third of the child's waking time. Older children spend almost as much time in front of the TV. Indeed, children aged six to eleven average twenty-five hours a week watching TV, almost as much time as they spend in school. Since 1960 the tendency has been for children to become heavier and heavier television viewers.

The debate about television's impact on children has raged furiously since the early 1950s. Critics are worried about parents' use of the television set as a babysitter and pacifier and as a substitute for an active parental role in socialization. They argue that excessive television viewing is detrimental because it encourages passivity and inhibits communication among family members. They express concern that children who watch large amounts of television tend to develop poor language skills, an inability to concentrate, and a disinclination to read. Moreover, they feel that television viewing tends to replace hours previously devoted to playtime either alone or with others. And, most worrisome, they believe that violence on TV provokes children to emulate aggressive behavior and acquire distorted views of adult relationships and communication.

Research into the impact of television on children has substantiated some of these concerns and invalidated others. Television does appear to be a cause of cognitive and behavioral disturbances. Heavy television viewing is associated with reduced reading skills, less verbal fluency, and lower academic effort. Exposure to violence on television tends to make children more willing to hurt people and more aggressive in their play and in their methods of resolving conflicts. Time spent in front of the TV set does displace time previously spent on other activities and, as a result, many games and activities – marbles, jacks and trading cards, for example – are rapidly disappearing from American childhood.

However, television also introduces children to new experiences easily and painlessly and stimulates interest in issues to which they might not otherwise be exposed. For many disadvantaged children, it provides a form of intellectual enhancement that deprived homes lacking books and newspapers could not afford. And, for many children, television programs provide a semblance of extended kinship attachments and outlets for their fantasies and unexpressed emotions.

While some television shows, such as *Sesame Street* and *Mr. Rogers' Neighborhood,* do appear to improve children's vocabularies, teach them basic concepts, and help them verbalize their feelings, overwhelming evidence suggests that most television programs convey racial and sexual stereotypes, desensitize children to violence, and discourage the kinds of sustained concentration necessary for reading comprehension. On balance, it seems clear that television cannot adequately take the place of parental or adult involvement and supervision of children and that the tendency for it to do so is a justifiable reason for increased public concern.

The single most profound change that has taken place in children's lives since 1960 is the rapid movement of millions of mothers into the labor force. In the space of just twelve years, the number of mothers of children five or under who work outside the home tripled. Today nearly half of all children under the age of six have a mother who works. Many factors have contributed to this trend, including a rising cost of living and a declining rate of growth in real family income; increased control of fertility through contraception and abortion, which has meant that careers are less likely to be disrupted by unplanned pregnancies; and women's rising level of educational achievement, which has led many women to seek work not only as a way of getting a paycheck but as a way of obtaining personal independence and intellectual stimulation.

The massive movement of mothers into the work force presented a major social problem: How should young children be cared for when their mothers work outside the home? This question gave rise to more controversy than almost any other family-related issue during the late 1960s and early 1970s.

The event that first precipitated this debate was the publication in 1964 of a Department of Labor study that found almost one million latchkey children in the United States, unsupervised by adults for significant portions of the day. As the number of working mothers climbed in the late 1960s, many family experts advocated day care as a necessary response to the large number of mothers who had gone to work. At first the national debate focused on the child care problems of single mothers – widowed, divorced, and unmarried – and on whether they should be encouraged to enter the labor force.

Liberals, led by Senator Walter Mondale, argued on behalf of a national system of comprehensive child development and day-care centers. Building on the model of the Head Start program, Mondale proposed in 1971 that the federal government establish a national system of services that included day-care programs, nutritional aid for pregnant mothers, medical and dental care, and after-school programs for teenagers. President Richard Nixon vetoed the bill in a stinging message that called the proposal fiscally irresponsible, administratively unworkable, and a threat to "diminish both parental authority and parental involvement with children." The president warned against committing "the vast authority of the national government to the side of communal approaches to child rearing over against the family-centered approach."

Following the presidential veto, congressional support for a federally funded system of day care evaporated. Nevertheless the actual number of children enrolled in nursery schools or group day-care centers grew dramatically. At the time of the president's veto, less than one-third of all mothers with children one year old or younger held jobs. Today half of such women work, three-quarters of them full-time. As a result a majority of all children now spend some of their preschool years in the care of someone other than their mother.

The trend is toward formal group day-care programs. Back in 1970 just 21 percent of all three- and four-year-olds were cared for in day-care centers or nursery schools. But between 1970 and 1983 the proportion virtually doubled, climbing to 38 percent. Today over two-thirds of all three- to four-year-olds are in a day-care, nursery school, or prekindergarten program.

The single largest provider of day care now is the federal government, which offers child care, health, and educational services to some 400,000 low-income children through the Head Start program and which subsidizes private day-care facilities through child care tax credits, state block grants, and tax breaks for employers who subsidize day-care services. Nonetheless, the great majority of preschool child care arrangements in the United States are private, ranging from informal baby-sitting arrangements to private day-care centers run by national chains. Today two-thirds of all children are cared for in private facilities, and day care is an eleven-billion-dollar industry. The largest private corporation, KinderCare, has more than a thousand centers licensed to care for as many as a hundred thousand children.

The drive for expanded day-care programs has its principal roots in the growing number of working mothers, the proliferation of single-parent homes, and the belief that access to day care is necessary to guarantee women's equal right to pursue a career. But the trend has also been fueled by new theories of child development, which emphasize the psychologically beneficial effects of a stimulating peer environment, by mounting evidence that children can assimilate information earlier than previously thought, and by research that has shown that disadvantaged children who participated in Head Start were more likely to graduate from high school, enroll in college, and obtain self-supporting jobs and were less likely to be arrested or register for welfare than were other children from low-income families.

As formal child care programs proliferated, parents, educators, and social scientists began to examine the impact of day care on children's social and psychological growth, their intellectual development, and their emotional bond with their mother. The effects of day care remain the subject of intense controversy. Expert opinion varies widely, from those who fear that such programs provide an inadequate and unsatisfactory substitute for the full-time care and devotion of a mother to those who stress the resilience and adaptability of children. On one side, Jerome Kagan, a Harvard developmental psychologist, concludes that recent research reveals "that group care for young children does not seem to have much effect, either facilitating or debilitating, on the cognitive, social or affective development of most children." On the other side of the debate, Michael Rutter, a child psychologist at London's Institute for Psychiatry, states that "although day care for very young children is not likely to result in serious emotional disturbance, it would be misleading to conclude that it is without risks or effects."

At present, knowledge about the impact of day care in children's intellectual social, and emotional development remains limited. Research has suggested that quality day care has "neither salutary nor adverse effects on the intellectual development of most children"; that early entry into full-time day care may interfere with "the formation of a close attachment to the parents"; and that children in group day care are somewhat more aggressive, more independent, more involved with other children, more physically active, and less cooperative with adults than mother-raised children.

The most pressing problem for parents at the moment is an inadequate supply of quality day care. The quality of day-care centers varies widely. The nature of care ranges from family day care, in which a woman takes children into her home for a fee, and cooperatives staffed or administered by parents, to on-site company nurseries, instituted by approximately one hundred corporations, and child care chains. High-quality centers, which can charge as much as $500 a month to care for a child, usually enroll only a small group of children and provide a great deal of individual attention. Low-quality centers, in contrast, tend to have a high ratio of children to caretakers, a high level of staff turnover, a low level of parental involvement, and a high noise level.

Another serious problem is the lack of access to day care on the part of poorer children. Access to day care varies enormously according to family income. Seventy-five percent of all children from families with incomes of more than $25,000 a year participate in day-care or preschool programs by the age of six, compared to just a third of children from families with incomes of less than $15,000. Today, as a result of limited public funding, just a fifth of all eligible children are enrolled in Head Start. Children from poorer families are also less likely to participate in programs with an educational component.

The United States lags far behind major European nations in assuming public responsibility for children's welfare. Today most European countries offer a variety of programs designed to assist working mothers, including paid maternity and paternity leaves for mothers and fathers who hold jobs, financial allowances for families with children, and subsidized public nurseries and kindergartens. Finland and Hungary go even further, paying mothers who stay at home with their children. The United States, with its long tradition of private-sector approaches to public problems and ingrained hostility toward state intervention in the family, has yet to come to terms with the problems presented by the massive influx of mothers into the workplace. The burden of coping with child care remains with the individual family.

Of all the dramatic changes that have taken place in children's lives in recent years, the one that has aroused the deepest public concern is the spiraling divorce rate. Since 1960 the number of children involved in divorce has tripled, and in every year since 1972, more than a million children have had their homes disrupted by divorce. Of the children born in the 1970s, 40 percent will experience the dissolution of their parents' marriage before they themselves are sixteen. As one expert noted, "Children are becoming less and less of a deterrent to divorce."

As divorce became a more pervasive part of the American scene, researchers began to ask penetrating questions about the psychological and emotional implications of divorce for children. Back in the 1920s, authorities on the family, using the case-study method, had concluded that children experienced the divorce of their parents as a devastating blow that stunted their psychological and emotional growth and caused maladjustments that persisted for years. Beginning in the late 1950s and continuing into the early 1970s, a new generation of researchers argued that children were better off when their parents divorced than when they had an unstable marriage; that divorce disrupted children's lives no more painfully than the death of a parent, which used to break up families just as frequently; and that the adverse effects of divorce were generally of short duration.

Recent research has thrown both of these points of view into question. On the one hand, it appears that conflict-laden, tension-filled marriages have more adverse effects on children than divorce. Children from discordant homes permeated by tension and instability are more likely to suffer psychosomatic illnesses, suicide attempts, delinquency, and other social maladjustments than are children whose parents divorce. As of now, there is no clear-cut empirical evidence to suggest that children from "broken" homes suffer more health or mental problems, personality disorders, or lower school grades than children from "intact" homes.

On the other hand, it is clear that divorce is severely disruptive, at least initially, for a majority of children, and a significant minority of children continue to suffer from the psychological and economic repercussions of divorce for many years after the breakup of their parents' marriage. It is also apparent that children respond very differently to a divorce and to a parent's death. When a father dies children are often moody and despairing. During a divorce, many children, and especially sons, exhibit anger, hostility, and conflicting loyalties.

Children's reactions to divorce vary enormously, depending on their age and gender and, most important of all, their perception of their parents' marriage. Children who viewed their parents' marriage as unhappy tend to adjust more easily to divorce than those who regarded their home life as basically happy.

For many children initial acceptance of their parents' separation is followed by a deep sense of shock. Although some children react calmly on learning that their parents are divorcing, a majority of children of all ages are vulnerable to feelings of pain, anger, depression, and insecurity. Family breakups often result in regressive behavior and developmental setbacks that last at least a year.

Studies that followed children five years after a divorce found that a majority of children show resilience and increased maturity and independence. But, for a significant minority, the emotional turmoil produced by divorce proves to be long standing, evident in persistent feelings of hostility, depression, sexual anxiety, and concern about being unloved. Among a minority of children, the apparent consequences of divorce include alcohol and drug abuse, outward-directed despair and aggression, and sexual promiscuity.

Clearly, divorce is an extremely stressful experience for children, whose economic and emotional costs continue to run high long after the parents' separation. Economic disruption is the most obvious consequence of a divorce. In the immediate aftermath of a divorce, the income of the divorced woman and her children falls sharply, by 73 percent in the year following divorce, while the father's income rises by 42 percent. Adding to the financial pressures facing children of divorce is the fact that a majority of divorced men evade court orders to support their children. Recent surveys indicate that only 40 percent of support orders are fully complied with during the first year after a divorce and that by the tenth year after separation, the figure falls to 13 percent.

Other sources of stress result from the mother's new financial responsibilities as her family's breadwinner, additional demands on her time as she tries to balance economic and child-rearing responsibilities, and, frequently, adjustment to unfamiliar and less comfortable living arrangements. Burdened by her new responsibilities as head of her household, a mother often devotes less time to child rearing, forcing her to rely more heavily on neighbors, relatives, and older children.

The emotional and psychological upheavals caused by divorce are often aggravated by a series of readjustments children must deal with, such as loss of contact with the noncustodial parent. Many children of divorce have to deal with feelings of abandonment by their natural fathers. More than nine of every ten children are placed in their mother's custody, and recent studies have found that two months following a divorce fewer than half the fathers see their children as often as once a week and, after three years, half the fathers do not visit their children at all.

Further complicating children's adjustment to their parents' divorce is the impact of remarriage. Roughly half of all mothers are remarried within approximately two years of their dionly briefly in single-parent homes. Today there are over 4 million households – one of every seven with children – in which one parent has remarried and at least one child is from a previous union. These reconstituted families often confront jealousies and conflicts of loyalty not found in families untouched by divorce, leading a number of investigators to conclude that "homes involving step-relationships proved more likely to have stress, ambivalence, and low cohesiveness" than did two-parent homes. At the same time, other researchers have found that most children of divorce favored remarriage.

Today's children are growing up in an unstable and threatening environment in which earlier sources of support have eroded. They live in a permissive culture that exposes them from an early age to drugs, sex, alcohol, and violence. The increasing divorce rate, the entry of many mothers into the full-time work force, high rates of mobility, and the declining importance of the extended family all contribute to a decline in support and guidance. As a society the United States has largely failed to come to grips with the major issues facing children, such as the need for quality care while parents work and the need for a stable emotional environment in which to grow up.

Revolution in Family Law

As the nation's families have changed, America's courts have become increasingly embroiled in disputes that pit wives against husbands and children against parents. Today nearly half of all civil court cases in the United States involve questions of family law. The courts are struggling with such questions as whether, in cases of divorce, the mother should be presumed to be the parent best suited to rear young children or whether grandparents should be granted visitation rights to a grandchild whose parents have divorced. The courts have also had to decide whether a husband can give the couple's children his surname over his wife's objections, whether husbands and wives should be permitted to sue each other, and whether children have a right to "divorce" their parents or to choose where they will live, independent of their parents' wishes.

A revolution has taken place in the field of family law, and equally sweeping changes have occurred in divorce law. State legislatures, responding to the sharp upsurge in divorce rates during the 1960s and 1970s, radically liberalized their divorce statutes, making it possible to end a marriage without establishing specific grounds, and, in many states, allowing one spouse to terminate a marriage without the consent of the other. As the number of divorces mounted, every state adopted reforms designed to reduce the acrimony and shame that accompanied the divorce process.

Until 1970, when California adopted the nation's first "no-fault" divorce law, a basic legal assumption was that marital relationships could only be ended for serious cause. Under fault statutes, divorce could only be granted on such grounds as desertion, nonsupport, cruel and abusive treatment, adultery, alcoholism, or a long prison term, and the division of property in a divorce was to reflect the share of guilt attributed to each partner. A man who wanted a divorce was expected to pay lifetime alimony to his wife, the purpose of which was to reward the woman's devotion to her family and to punish the husband who would abandon his wife.

Within a span of just five years, all but five states adopted the principle of no-fault divorce. Today every state except South Dakota has enacted some kind of no-fault statute. Under no-fault divorce laws, a couple can institute divorce proceedings without first proving that either was at fault for the breakup. Rather than sue the other marriage partner, a husband or wife can obtain a divorce simply by mutual consent or on such grounds as incompatibility, living apart for a specified period, or "irretrievable breakdown" of the marriage. In complete no-fault states, a single partner can obtain a divorce unilaterally, without regard for the wishes of the other partner.

The goal of no-fault divorce was to provide couples with a way to avoid long acrimonious legal battles over who was to blame for a failed marriage and how marital property was to be divided. In an effort to reduce the bitterness associated with divorce, many states changed the terminology used in divorce proceedings, substituting the term "dissolution" for the word "divorce" and eliminating any terms denoting fault or guilt.

Recently courts have also sought to overturn the so-called "tender years" doctrine that a young child is better off with the mother unless the mother is proved to be unfit. The current trend is for the courts not to presume in favor of mothers in custody disputes over young children. Most judges now only make custody awards after considering psychological reports and the wishes of the children. To spare children the trauma of custody conflict, many judges award divorced parents joint custody, in which both parents have equal legal rights and responsibilities in decisions affecting the child's welfare.

Likewise, courts have moved away from the concept of alimony and replaced it with a new concept called "spousal support" or "maintenance." In the past, courts regarded marriage as a lifelong commitment and, in cases in which the husband was found guilty of marital misconduct, held that the wife was entitled to lifelong support. Now maintenance can be awarded to either the husband or the wife, and it can be granted for a limited time to permit a spouse to go to school, acquire skills, and become self-supporting.

As the legal system has moved away from the principle of lifelong alimony, growing attention has been placed on the distribution of a couple's assets at the time of divorce. One state, Mississippi, still awards property on the basis of the name of the title to the property. Four "community property" states divide property acquired during the marriage equally, while the remaining states allow judges to award property "equitably." In dividing up property, a majority of states now require the courts to place monetary value on the wife's contribution as homemaker and mother and require judges to consider such sources of family wealth as insurance policies, pensions, deferred income, and licenses to practice a profession.

Today many women's groups, which initially favored no-fault divorce, are calling for sharp modifications of such laws. They maintain that under present law "divorce is a financial catastrophe for most women." Legal rules that treat men and women equally, critics argue, tend to deprive women of the financial support they need. Under no-fault laws, many older women, who would have been entitled to lifelong alimony or substantial child support payments under the old fault statutes, find it extremely difficult to support their families. Today, the courts award only 15 percent of divorced women alimony, and in most cases the amounts are small (averaging approximately $250 a month) and granted temporarily until a wife reenters the work force. Also, courts, following the principle of equality, generally require ex-husbands to pay only half of what is needed to raise the children, on the assumption that the wife will provide the remainder. To make matters worse, many men are remiss on court-ordered alimony or child support payments.

Another problem results from the expectation that women will reenter the labor force. Courts generally assume that a woman will be able to support herself following a divorce. In reality, however, the earning capacity of many divorced women is quite limited, especially if they have been longtime housewives and mothers. According to one study, only about one-third of wives worked regularly before the divorce, many part-time or sporadically for relatively low incomes. Many of these women find it difficult or impossible to obtain jobs that will allow them to maintain a standard of living approaching the one they had while married.

Cases in which husbands and wives are pitted against each other have increasingly found their way onto the nation's court dockets. Among the issues facing the courts are these: Can a husband be criminally prosecuted for raping his wife? Can a husband give his children his surname over his wife's objections? Can an expectant mother obtain an abortion despite her husband's opposition? Until recently the law considered the father to be "head and master" of his family. His surname became his children's surname, his residence was the family's legal residence, he was immune from lawsuits instituted by his wife, and he was entitled to sexual relations with his spouse. Today the nation's courts have called all of these legal presumptions into question. The Massachusetts Supreme Court has ruled that husbands and wives can sue each other, the supreme courts of Massachusetts and New Jersey have said that husbands can be prosecuted for raping their wives, and the California Supreme Court has ruled that a husband cannot give his children his surname without his wife's agreement.

Another dramatic change in the field of family law is the courts' tendency to grant legal rights to minor children. In the past, parents enjoyed wide discretionary authority over the details of their children's upbringing. More recently the nation's courts have held that minors do have independent rights that can override parental authority. The issues being brought before the courts include these:

> Should an unmarried fifteen-year-old Utah girl be able to obtain an abortion without her parents' knowledge?
>
> Should a twelve-year-old Ukrainian boy and a fifteen-year-old Cuban girl have a right to choose where they will live, even if this means living apart from their natural parents?
>
> Should a fifteen-year-old Washington State girl, unhappy with her parents' restrictions on her smoking, dating, and choice of friends, be allowed to have herself placed in a foster home against her parents' wishes?
>
> Should children be encouraged to turn in their parents for drug use, as in a recent California case?

In deciding such cases, the courts have sought to balance two conflicting traditions: the historic right of parents to control their childrens' upbringing and the right of all individuals, including children, to privacy, due process, and equal rights. In some cases the courts have sided with the parents; in other cases they have supported children; in still others the rulings have been mixed. The U.S. Supreme Court has struck down state laws that give parents an absolute veto over whether a minor girl can obtain an abortion but upheld a Utah statute that required doctors to notify parents before performing an abortion. The Court ruled in the Utah case that a compelling state interest in maintaining the integrity of the family was more important than the girl's right to privacy. Two states – Iowa and Utah – have enacted laws greatly expanding minors' rights. These states permit children to seek temporary placement in another home if serious conflict exists between the children and their parents, even if the parents are not guilty of abuse or neglect.

Recent decisions in family law have been characterized by two seemingly contradictory trends. On the one hand, courts have modified or struck down many traditional infringements on the right to privacy. They have prohibited laws regulating consenting sexual relations between spouses and restricting the right of parents to obtain contraceptive information or pass it on to their children. Since 1970, twenty states have decriminalized all forms of private sexual conduct between consenting adults, and in four other states, judicial decisions have invalidated statutes making such conduct a crime.

On the other hand, courts have permitted government intrusion into areas traditionally regarded as bastions of family autonomy. Shocked by reports of abuse against children, wives, and the elderly, state legislatures have strengthened penalties for domestic violence and sexual abuse. Courts have reversed traditional precedents and ruled that husbands can be prosecuted for raping their wives. A 1984 federal law gave states new authority to seize property, wages, dividends, and tax refunds from parents who fail to make court ordered child support payments. Other court decisions have relaxed traditional prohibitions against spouses testifying against each other.

What links these two apparently contradictory trends is a growing sensitivity on the part of the courts toward the individual and individual rights even when family privacy is at stake. Many recent court decisions are consistent with a greater regard for the autonomy of the individual. Thus, in recent cases, the courts have held that a husband cannot legally prevent his wife from having an abortion, since it is the wife who must bear the burden of pregnancy, and have also ruled that a wife's legal domicile is not necessarily her husband's home. Court decisions on marital rape reflect a growing recognition that a wife is not her husband's property.

One ironic effect of these legal decisions has been a gradual erosion of the traditional conception of the family as a legal unit. In the collision between two sets of conflicting values – individualism and the family – the courts have tended to stress individual rights. For example, the Supreme Court recently struck down a Wisconsin law that forbids remarriage by divorced spouses until they have made arrangements for the financial care of their children on the grounds that it would encourage the birth of children out of wedlock, discriminate against the poor, and violate rights to personal freedom. Earlier in time the law was used to reinforce relationships between spouses and parents and children, but the current trend is to emphasize the separateness and autonomy of family members. The Supreme Court has repeatedly overturned state laws that require minor children to receive parental consent before obtaining contraceptive information or an abortion, and the lower courts have been unwilling to grant parents immunity from testifying against their own children. Similarly, state legislatures have weakened or abolished earlier laws that made children legally responsible for the support of indigent parents, while statutes that hold parents accountable for crimes committed by their minor children have been ruled unconstitutional.

The nation's courts did not choose to become involved in family questions. The current legal ferment is a legacy of dramatic changes that have occurred in the nature of family life as divorce rates have soared, family patterns have grown less uniform, and the bonds connecting parents and children have loosened. These changes have resulted in novel disputes that have found their way into lawyers' offices. What is clear is that in a wide range of areas – including child custody, children's rights, spousal support, and property division – the nation's courts will continue to wrestle with a host of problems spawned by America's changing families.

The Pro-Family Movement

Recent changes in family life have produced bewilderment, apprehension, and alarm, and many Americans believe that the consequences of these changes have been disastrous. A Gallup poll conducted in 1977 found that almost half of all Americans surveyed believed that family life has deteriorated in recent years. This sense of unease has generated a political crusade among Americans who fear that climbing rates of divorce, working mothers, and single parents represent a breakdown of family values. These people, who have adopted the label "pro-family," have built a powerful political coalition out of a series of disparate elements including religious conservatives, such as the Moral Majority, the Religious Roundtable, and Christian Voice; traditional political conservatives, and single-issue groups concerned about a variety of family-related issues such as legalized abortion, ratification of the Equal Rights amendment to the Constitution, feminism, access of teenagers to contraception, sex education in schools, homosexuality, pornography, school busing for racial integration, and eroticism on television.

Although the pro-family movement has drawn support from men and women of every social and economic background, it has appealed largely to women of lower economic and educational status who hold strong religious beliefs, whose self-esteem and self-image are bound up with being mothers and housewives and who want to ensure that women who devote their lives to the family are not accorded lower status than women who work outside the home.

Despite many disagreements in strategy and belief, the pro-family movement is united in its assessment of blame for the purported deterioration of family life. The issues that ignite the most passionate outrage on the part of the pro-family movement include feminism, which is viewed as primarily responsible for encouraging women to work outside the home; "secular humanism," believed to be responsible for eliminating all traces of religious values in public life; and the youth movement of the 1960s, which is held responsible for propagating a gospel of erotic experimentalism and self-gratification, sanctioning any form of behavior no matter how unconventional. The pro-family movement is also united in agreement on how the beleaguered American family can be helped. Among other things, the movement has sought the restoration of prayer in schools, screening of textbooks, limits on teenagers' access to contraceptives, and reversal of the Supreme Court's decisions on abortion.

The pro-family movement has waged political battles on several fronts. One part of its strategy has been an effort to overturn the landmark 1973 *Roe v. Wade* ruling, in which the Supreme Court declared that the decision to have an abortion was a private matter of concern to a woman and her physician and that only in the later stages of pregnancy could the government limit the right to abortion. Opposition to abortion has taken many forms, from calls for a constitutional amendment that would declare that from the moment of conception a fetus is a full human being entitled to constitutional protections, to efforts to restrict the use of government funds for abortions, to lobbying for local statutes limiting access to abortion by requiring waiting periods before abortions could be performed and parental consent for abortions for minors The major legislative success of the "right to life" movement was adoption by Congress of the so-called Hyde amendment, which permitted states to refuse to fund abortions for indigent women. Despite this legislative effort, some fifteen states and the District of Columbia continue to fund abortions for poorer women.

Another goal of the pro-family movement is to limit teenagers' access to contraceptive information. One proposal, put forward by the Reagan administration, was the "squeal rule," which would require family planning agencies that receive federal funds to notify the parents of minor children of requests for contraceptives. Another battle has been fought over the Equal Rights Amendment. Those who oppose the amendment have argued that it poses a threat to the family because it would eliminate all discrimination on the basis of sex, including the prohibition of marriages between persons of the same sex, and guarantee access to abortion and family planning services.

The major legislative aim of the pro-family movement has been enactment of the Family Protection Act, which combines the disparate concerns of the movement into a single piece of legislation. This act would prohibit the use of legal aid funds in cases dealing with abortion, divorce, and gay rights and would restore prayer to the public schools.

Arguments between the pro-family movement and its critics reached a peak in 1978, when President Jimmy Carter convened a White House Conference on Families to develop coherent policies to assist American families. The conference quickly became a battleground over such issues as legalized abortion, the Equal Rights Amendment, and gay rights and revealed the deep schism of values that had developed around family issues. The pro-family movement charged that feminists and ethnic minorities had won a disproportionate share of slots at the conference and accused the delegates of a bias against "traditional Judeo-Christian values concerning the family." At the conclusion of the conference, the White House issued a report recommending ways that government could strengthen American family life. Among the proposals were calls for the ratification of the Equal Rights Amendment, the right to abortion, and sex education in the schools, but, because of the opposition spearheaded by the pro-family movement, implementation of these measures proved impossible.

A Deep Sense of Ambivalence

As the 1978 White House Conference on Families dramatically illustrated, American society today is deeply divided by conflicting conceptions of what constitutes a family and how government can best strengthen families to deal with contemporary problems. Yet, despite the furor generated by these disputes, an important point should not be missed. Public opinion polls indicate that while only a minority of Americans supports the legislative proposals of the pro-family movement, a large majority agrees with their belief that the family is an institution in deep trouble.

Recent transformations in American family life have left Americans with a deep ambivalence about their familial roles. A substantial majority of Americans today say that they are less willing to make sacrifices for their children than their parents were and believe that unhappy parents should not remain married simply for the sake of the children. Yet, at the same time, an almost equal majority believes that "parents now have a reduced commitment to their children and their children to them" and want "a return to more traditional standards of family life." Unable to assimilate fully the domestic revolution of the past two decades, Americans are struggling to find a fair way to juggle individual, familial, and social demands.

The American family today, like the family at the end of the eighteenth century and again at the end of the nineteenth, is in the midst of a profound historical transformation. Older assumptions – such as the idea that marriage is a lifetime commitment and that a proper family contains a breadwinner father and a housewife mother – have eroded. The older definition of the paternal role that equated a "real man" with a "good provider" who single-handedly supported his family has increasingly given way to a new ideal – honored as much in the breach as in the observance – that he should take an active role in family life, child care, and housework. Similarly, the older ideal of womanhood that defined a "real woman" as a good mother, wife, and hostess has been diluted by a sharp decline in the number of children in each family and women's growing participation in the world of wage work. Meanwhile, new notions of "children's rights" have challenged traditional assumptions that parents should, rightly or wrongly, dictate important decisions in their children's lives.

Ours is an age of transition. Our families have grown less stable and uniform; traditional family role definitions and expectations have been thrown into question. And, like earlier ages of transition, ours is also an age of conflict. This includes conflicts between groups that hold competing ideals of a proper family but also deep internal conflicts that rage within individuals. Today a large majority of Americans feel torn between a continuing commitment to and nostalgia for older ideals of family life, stressing lifelong marriage and full-time mothering of children, and a newer, more flexible but less dependable conception of the family that allows for greater freedom and self-absorption.

There is little point in looking nostalgically to the past for a solution to current problems. The 1950s pattern of family life – characterized by high rates of marriage, high fertility, and stable rates of divorce – which many continue to regard as an ideal, was the product of a convergence of an unusual series of historical, demographic, and economic circumstances unlikely to return again. Every barometer indicates that families in the future will be small, fragile, and characterized by late marriage and low birthrates. Today about half of all married women with minor children participate in the labor force. Today most working wives are part-time workers; in the future, many more will be likely to be full-time workers, as families become increasingly dependent on a wife's income.

The challenge facing Americans in the years to come is not to hope wistfully for a return to the "normality" of the 1950s – which was actually inconsistent with long-term trends – but a much more difficult and much more concrete predicament. This challenge is to institute new social arrangements that will help moderate the effects of women's entry into the work force, of divorce, and of women's increasing need for autonomy. Possible solutions lie before us. These range from flexible working arrangements to enable employees to be effective parents to adequate supplies of affordable quality substitute care when parents work, maternity and paternity leaves to assist parents who are starting families, revision of welfare policies that encourage the flight of husbands, custody and visitation agreements that will facilitate continuing contact between divorced parents and their children, legal guarantees that children of divorce will receive an adequate and secure income, and monetary incentives for parents who stay home with their children. Americans agree on the desirability of strong families; the ultimate question is whether the nation has the political will to create conditions that will foster stronger families.

11.4 Myths and Reality
Lenore E. Walker

THE BATTERING OF WOMEN, LIKE OTHER CRIMES OF VIOLENCE AGAINST women, has been shrouded in myths. All of the myths have perpetuated the mistaken notion that the victim has precipitated her own assault. Some of them served as a protection against embarrassment. Others were created to protect rescuers from their own discouragement when they were unsuccessful in stopping the brutality. It is important to refute all the myths surrounding battered women in order to understand fully why battering happens, how it affects people, and how it can be stopped.

The battered woman is pictured by most people as a small, fragile, haggard person who might once have been pretty. She has several small children, no job skills, and is economically dependent on her husband. It is frequently assumed she is poor and from a minority group. She is accustomed to living in violence, and her fearfulness and passivity are emphasized above all. Although some battered women do fit this description, research proves it to be a false stereotype.

Most battered women are from middle-class and higher income homes where the power of their wealth is in the hands of their husbands. Many of them are large women who could attempt to defend themselves physically. Not all of them have children; those who do do not necessarily have them in any particular age group. Although some battered women are jobless, many more are highly competent workers and successful career women. They include doctors, lawyers, corporation executives, nurses, secretaries, full-time homemakers, and others. Battered women are found in all age groups, races, ethnic and religious groups, educational levels, and socioeconomic groups. Who are the battered women? If you are a woman, there is a 50 percent chance it could be you!

Myth No. 1: The Battered Woman Syndrome Affects Only a Small Percentage of the Population.

Like rape, the battering of American women is a seriously underreported crime. Data on wife beating are difficult to obtain because battering generally occurs at night, in the home, without witnesses. The statistics on battered women are buried in the records of family domestic disturbance calls to police departments, in emergency room records in hospitals, and in the records of social service agencies, private psychologists, and counselors. The United States Commission on Civil Rights recently completed an investigation which supports the suspicion that police records on battered women are inaccurately low owing to poor police reporting techniques. My personal estimate is that only one in ten women report battering assaults.

364 \ *Topic 11 — Marriage and Family – Here to Stay?*

Marjory Fields, a New York City attorney who specializes in battered women, reports that of 500 women represented in divorce actions in Brooklyn in 1976, 57.4 percent complained of physical assaults by their husbands. They had suffered these assaults for approximately four years prior to seeking the divorce. Of 600 divorcing wives in Cleveland, according to a study by Levinger, 36.8 percent reported physical abuse by their husbands. The first epidemiological study of battered women undertaken in this country, by sociologists Murray Straus, Richard Gelles, and Susan Steinmetz, reported that a physical assault occurred in 28 percent of all American homes during 1976. This statistic, nearly one third of all families, is certainly evidence that the battered woman problem is a widespread one.

Myth No. 2: Battered Women Are Masochistic.

The prevailing belief has always been that only women who "liked it and deserved it" were beaten. In a study of battered wives as recently as twenty years ago, it was suggested that beatings are solicited by women who suffer from negative personality characteristics, including masochism. "Good wives" were taught that the way to stop assaults was to examine their behavior and try to change it to please men: to be less provocative, less aggressive, and less frigid. There was no suggestion that provocation might occur from other than masochistic reasons, that aggressiveness might be an attempt to ward off further assault, and that frigidity might be a very natural result of subjection to severe physical and psychological pain. The burden of guilt for battering has fallen on the woman, and the violent behavior of the male has been perpetuated. The myth of the masochistic woman is a favorite of all who endeavor to understand the battered woman. No matter how sympathetic people may be, they frequently come to the conclusion that the reason a battered woman remains in such a relationship is that she is masochistic. By masochism, it is meant that she experiences some pleasure, often akin to sexual pleasure, through being beaten by the man she loves. Because this has been such a prevailing stereotype, many battered women begin to wonder if they are indeed masochistic.

Myth No. 3: Battered Women Are Crazy.

This myth is related to the masochism myth in that it places the blame for the battering on the woman's negative personality characteristics. Battered women's survival behaviors have often earned them the misdiagnosis of being crazy. Unusual actions which may help them to survive in the battering relationship have been taken out of context by unenlightened medical and mental health workers. Several of the women in this sample reported being hospitalized for schizophrenia, paranoia, and severe depression. One woman who told of hearing voices which told her to kill her husband had received numerous electroshock therapy treatments. But just listening to her

describe her husband's brutal treatment made her hallucination very understandable. Many women reported being given heavy doses of anti-psychotic
medications by doctors who were responding to their overt symptoms rather
than attempting to understand their family situations. It is not clear whether
these women were overtly psychotic at the time of their reported diagnoses.
As a clinical psychologist, I can state that at the time I interviewed these
women, there was insufficient evidence of such disorders. One woman was
interviewed shortly after being released from a state hospital. Arrangements
had been made for her to go to a temporary shelter, legal assistance was
provided to initiate divorce proceedings, and her batterer was refused knowledge of her whereabouts. Her mental health improved markedly within days.
I wonder how many other women who have been mislabeled as mentally ill
were really attempting to cope with a batterer. After listening to their stories,
I can only applaud their strength in retaining their sanity.

*Myth No. 4: Middle-Class Women Do Not Get Battered as Frequently or as
Violently as Do Poorer Women.*

Most previously recorded statistics of battering have come from lower-
class families. However, lower-class women are more likely to come in contact with community agencies and so their problems are more visible. Mid-
dle- and upper-class women do not want to make their batterings public.
They fear social embarrassment and harming their husbands' careers. Many
also believe the respect in which their husbands are held in the community
will cast doubt upon the credibility of their battering stories. The recent public focus on battered women has brought many of these middle- and upper-
class women out of hiding. The publicity being given the problem is creating
a climate in which they think they will finally be believed. They report an
overwhelming sense of relief once they have told their stories and find that
others will now believe them.

*Myth No. 5: Minority-Group Women Are Battered More Frequently than
Anglos.*

The battered women interviewed in this study were Hispanic, native
American, black, Asian, and Pacific American, as well as Anglo. Although
each grew up in a culture with different values and different attitudes about
male and female roles, none of them was able to make any impact on the
kind of violence she experienced. Anglo and minority women alike told
similar battering stories and experienced similar embarrassment, guilt, and
the inability to halt their men's assaults. Minority women, however, spoke of
having even fewer resources than Anglos to turn to for assistance.

Myth No. 6: Religious Beliefs Will Prevent Battering.

The Catholic, Protestant, Mormon, Jewish, Eastern, and other religious women in this study all indicated that their religious beliefs did not protect them from their assaultive men. Most of the women in my study held religious beliefs. For some, belief in a deity helped them endure their suffering, offering comfort and solace. Sometimes attending services was the only safe outside contact they had. However, other women indicated they no longer practiced their religion, because giving it up eliminated a point of conflict with their batterer. Still others gave up their religion in disillusionment, feeling that a just and merciful God would not have let them suffer so. Others reported losing faith after having unsuccessfully sought help from a religious or spiritual leader.

Some women told stories in which their religious adviser suggested they pray for guidance, become better women, and go home and help their husbands "become more spiritual and find the Lord." Needless to say, these women did not have time to wait for their husbands to "find the Lord" while they continued to receive brutal beatings. Other women joyfully told of humane religious advisers who understood their problems and helped them break out of their disastrous relationships.

Myth No. 7: Battered Women Are Uneducated and Have Few Job Skills.

The education level of the women interviewed ranged from fifth grade through completion of professional and doctoral degrees. They were homemakers, teachers, real estate agents, lawyers, psychologists, nurses, physicians, businesswomen, politicians, and successful corporation executives. Some did well at their jobs and some performed poorly. Although many were successful career women, they stated they would give up their careers if it would eliminate the battering in their relationships. Most had tried changing jobs or staying home without any effect on their husbands' behavior. Those women who chose to be homemakers tried heroically to keep their lives from falling apart: they struggled to make financial ends meet, kept family chaos at a minimum, and tried to smooth life for their batterer. Most of them sought status in their home lives rather than in their careers. Thus, their self-esteem was dependent on their ability to be good wives and homemakers and was not well integrated with their successful professional activities.

Myth No. 8: Batterers Are Violent in All Their Relationships.

Based on the women in my study, I estimate that only about 20 percent of battered women live with men who are violent not only to them but also to anyone else who gets in their way. Unfortunately, this violent group of men has been the most studied. They tend to be poorer and to live outside the mainstream of society's norms. They often have fewer resources or skills with which to cope with the world. Most street crime is committed by such men. They also have the most contact with society's institutions and seem always to be in trouble with the police. They often subsist on welfare payments; their children have behavioral and learning problems in school; they use hospital clinics. Courts send them to treatment facilities in lieu of jail sentences. Because so much of our resources is spent in dealing with these people, it often seems that they are representative of all of the violence in our culture. When it comes to battered women, this is simply not true. Most men who batter their wives are generally not violent in other aspects of their lives.

Myth No. 9: Batterers Are Unsuccessful and Lack Resources to Cope With the World.

It has been suggested that men who feel less capable than their women resort to violence. Contrary findings were reported in England, where physicians, service professionals, and police had the highest incidence of wife beating. Most of the professionally successful volunteers in this study have similarly successful husbands. Among the affluent batterers were physicians, attorneys, public officials, corporation executives, scientists, college professors, and salesmen. Many of these men donated a good deal of time and energy to community activities. Often they would be unable to maintain their high productivity level were it not for the support of their wives. In one town, the mayor's wife, whose layers of make-up concealed the serious bruises he had inflicted upon her, regularly assisted him with all his official duties. In some cases, previously successful men lost their effectiveness because of alcohol or emotional problems. Many men were reported as erratic in performance by the women. As a group, however, the batterers in this sample would be indistinguishable from any other group of men in terms of capability.

Myth No. 10: Drinking Causes Battering Behavior.

Over half the battered women in this sample indicated a relationship between alcohol use and battering. Many tended to blame the battering incidents on their men's drinking. Upon further questioning, however, it became clear that the men beat them whether or not they had been drinking. But some association between drinking and battering cannot be denied. Exactly what it is, is still not known. It does seem reasonable, however, to suggest that in many cases alcohol is blamed as the precipitating factor, whereas it is only a component in the battering relationship. But it is psychologically easier for the battered woman to blame the violence on the batterer's drunkenness. Often the men in this study drank as a way of calming their anxieties. Drinking seemed to give them a sense of power. Many of the women felt that if they could only get their men to stop drinking, the battering would cease. Unfortunately, it just did not happen.

The most violent physical abuse *was* suffered by women whose men were consistent drinkers. Much work still needs to be done on the association between drinking and battering. I strongly suspect that there are specific blood chemistry changes that occur under a generalized stress reaction such as battering. Furthermore, these may be the same chemicals that are found in the blood of alcoholics. It is entirely possible that fundamental changes in brain chemistry cause both cycles. It is hoped that as our scientific technology becomes more precise, we will be able to measure these chemical changes with more accuracy.

Myth No. 11: Batterers Are Psychopathic Personalities.

If batterers could be considered antisocial and psychopathic personalities, then individual psychopathology could be used to differentiate batterers from normal men. Unfortunately, it is not that simple. The batterers in this sample were reported to have many kinds of personality disturbances other than just being psychopathic. One trait they *do* have in common with diagnosed psychopaths is their extraordinary ability to use charm as a manipulative technique.

The women interviewed all described their batterers as having a dual personality, much like Dr. Jekyll and Mr. Hyde. The batterer can be either very, very good or very, very horrid. Furthermore, he can swing back and forth between the two characters with the smoothness of a con artist. But, unlike the psychopath, the batterer feels a sense of guilt and shame at his uncontrollable actions. If he were able to cease his violence, he would.

Myth No. 12: Police Can Protect the Battered Women.

The women in this study manifestly do not believe this to be true. Only 10 percent ever called the police for help. Of these, most stated that the police were ineffective: when the police left, the assault was renewed with added vigor.

Sociologist Murray Straus, in his studies on violence in the family, labeled such assaults a crime and declared that were the violence to occur in any setting other than the home, it would warrant prosecution. He cites studies indicating that somewhere between 25 and 67 percent of all homicides occur within the family in all societies.

A recently completed study in Kansas City and Detroit indicates that in 80 percent of all homicides in those cities, the police had intervened from one to five times previously. Thus, homicide between man and woman is not a "crime of passion," but rather the end result of unchecked, long-standing violence.

Myth No. 13: The Batterer Is Not a Loving Partner.

This myth has spawned others, most particularly that of the masochistic wife. Women have been accused of loving the batterers' brutality rather than their kindness because it has been difficult for society to comprehend the loving behavior of batterers. But batterers are often described by their victims as fun-loving little boys when they are not being coercive. They are playful, attentive, sensitive, exciting, and affectionate to their women. The cycle theory of battering described later on explains how the batterers' loving behavior keeps these women in the battering relationship.

Myth No. 14: A Wife Batterer Also Beats His Children.

This myth has some foundation in fact. In my sample, approximately one third of the batterers beat their children. These men were also suspected of seductive sexual behavior toward their daughters. In another third of the cases, battered women beat their children. Although the children of the final third were not physically abused, they suffered a more insidious form of child abuse because of living in a home where the fathers battered the mothers. Those women in my sample who had seen their fathers beat their mothers report psychological scars which never healed. Children whom I encountered while doing this study seemed to be undergoing similar traumas. The National Center for Child Abuse and Neglect has reported a higher percentage of men in battering relationships who also beat their children than those who do not. Their data show that when there is concurrent child abuse in these families, 70 percent is committed by the violent man.

Myth No. 15: Once a Battered Woman, Always a Battered Woman.

This myth is the reason why many people have not encouraged women to leave their battering relationships. They think she will only seek out another violent man. Though several of the women in this sample had a series of violent relationships, this pattern did not hold true for most of those interviewed. While they wanted another intimate relationship with a man, they were extremely careful not to choose another violent one. There was a low rate of remarriage for older women who had left battering relationships. Most of them had left a marriage by going against the advice of their families and friends. They preferred being single rather than trying to make the male-female relationship work again. Women who had received some beneficial intervention rarely remarried another batterer.

Myth No. 16: Once a Batterer, Always a Batterer.

If the psychosocial-learning theory of violent behavior is accurate, then batterers can be taught to relearn their aggressive responses. Assertion rather than aggression, negotiation rather than coercion, is the goal. My theoretical perspective, then, indicates that this myth of once a batterer, always a batterer is just that. The data have not yet been analyzed to prove it false.

Myth No. 17: Long-Standing Battering Relationships Can Change for the Better.

Although everyone who believes in the positive nature of behavior change wants to believe this myth, my research has not shown it to be true. Relationships that have been maintained by the man having power over the woman are stubbornly resistant to an equal power-sharing arrangement. Thus, even with the best help available, these relationships do not become battering free. At best, the violent assaults are reduced in frequency and severity. Unassisted, they simply escalate to homicidal and suicidal proportions. The best hope for such couples is to terminate the relationship. There is a better chance that with another partner they can reorder the power structure and as equals can live in a nonviolent relationship.

Myth No. 18: Battered Women Deserve to Get Beaten.

The myth that battered women provoke their beatings by pushing their men beyond the breaking point is a popular one. Everyone can recount a story where the woman seemed to deserve what she got: she was too bossy, too insulting, too sloppy, too uppity, too angry, too obnoxious, too provocative, or too something else. In a culture where everyone takes sides between winners and losers, women who continuously get beaten are thought to deserve it. It is assumed that if only they would change their behavior, the batterer could regain his self-control. The stories of the women in this study indicate that batterers lose self-control because of their own internal reasons, not because of what the women did or did not do. Furthermore, philosophically this myth robs the men of responsibility for their own actions. No one could deserve the kind of brutality reported in these pages.

Myth No. 19: Battered Women Can Always Leave Home.

In a society where women are culturally indoctrinated to believe that love and marriage are their true fulfillment, nothing is lost by pretending that they are free to leave home whenever the violence becomes too great. In truth, battered women do not have the freedom to leave after being assaulted. A battered woman is not free to end her victimization without assistance.

Myth No. 20: Batterers Will Cease Their Violence "When We Get Married."

A small number of women in this sample reported violence in their premarital relationships. They thought that their men would cease their abuse once they were married, because the men would then feel more secure and more confident of the women's exclusive love for them. In every case, the expected marital bliss did not happen. Rather, the batterer's suspiciousness and possessiveness increased along with his escalating rate of violence.

Myth No. 21: Children Need Their Father Even If He Is Violent

This myth shatters faster than some of the others when confronted with the data on the high number of children who are physically and sexually abused in homes where there is such domestic violence. There is no doubt that the ideal family includes both a mother and a father for their children. However, children of abusive parents, compared with children of single parents, all say they would choose to live with just one parent. The enormous relief in living with a single parent expressed by children who formerly lived in violent homes where the father beat the mother had severe emotional and educational problems. The women in this sample remained with their batterers long after the children left home, putting to rest the myth that they were staying because it was better for the children. They remained because of the symbiotic bonds of love established over a period of time in such relationships.

Who, then, are the battered women?

Common Characteristics of Battered Women

As indicated earlier, the battered women interviewed for this book were a mixed group, representing all ages, races, religions (including no religion), educational levels, cultures, and socioeconomic groups. The youngest was seventeen years old, and the oldest was seventy-six years old. The shortest battering relationship was two months and the longest lasted fifty-three years, when the batterer died from natural causes.

The battered woman in this study commonly:

1. Has low self-esteem.

2. Believes all the myths about battering relationships.

3. Is a traditionalist about the home, strongly believes in family unity and the prescribed feminine sex-role stereotype.

4. Accepts responsibility for the batterer's actions.

5. Suffers from guilt, yet denies the terror and anger she feels.

6. Presents a passive face to the world but has the strength to manipulate her environment enough to prevent further violence and being killed.

7. Has severe stress reactions, with psychophysiological complaints.

8. Uses sex as a way to establish intimacy.

9. Believes that no one will be able to help her resolve her predicament except herself.

Although a few of the women were unmarried and not living with their batterers, most either lived with their batterers or had been legally married to them. Many women reported living with their batterers prior to marriage without experiencing abuse. Abuse usually began in the first six months of marriage. Some women had no children; several had seven or more; a few were interviewed during pregnancy. For many, this was their first marriage; for others, it was their second, third, and, in one case, her fifth. While some of the women were still living with the batterers, others had left the relationship prior to participating in this study. A number of the women began the process of terminating a battering relationship while the interviewers were still in contact with them. Several of the women interviewed were referred while in the hospital recuperating from injuries inflicted by the batterer. To the best of my knowledge, none of the women has died. Four killed their husbands and several others were arrested for assault on their men. The women who talked with us lived in urban environments, in suburbia, and in isolated rural areas. There seemed to be a high concentration of women living in areas which afford anonymity. Many Metropolitan Denver women lived in the foothills of the mountains, where they were isolated, especially in winter.

Low Self-esteem

Because of their lowered sense of self-esteem, these women typically underestimated their abilities to do anything. They doubted their competence and underplayed any successes they had. Those battered women with activities outside the home evaluated their outside performance and skills more realistically than they could their wifely duties. They were in constant doubt about their abilities as housekeepers, cooks, or lovers. Thus, the man's constant criticism of them in these areas adversely affected their judgment. Women in general have not learned how to integrate their home lives and outside lives as men do. They tend to evaluate their performances at home and outside the home according to separate criteria. Battered women tend to be traditionalists about home performance, since that is the basis of their self-esteem. Activities outside the home simply do not figure in their evaluation of how they feel about themselves. Thus, when things are not going well at home, the battered woman considers herself a failure. She has internalized all the cultural myths and stereotypes and assumes the guilt for the batterer's behavior. She agrees with society's belief that the batterer would change his behavior if only she could change her behavior. If she has lived with him for a while, she is aware that although she can often manipulate him to some degree, she has, in truth, little control over his behavior. This makes her feel even more of a failure. Most of the women interviewed eventually got around to saying that they were still not completely sure that there was not something they could have done differently that might have made the batterer cease his abusive behavior.

Traditionalists

The traditionalist orientation of the battered woman is evident in her view of the woman's role in marriage. First, she readily accepts the notion that "a woman's proper place is in the home." No matter how important her career might be to her, she is ready to give it up if it will make the batterer happy. Often she does just that, resulting in economic hardship to the family. Even those who believe that women have a right to a career suspect that that very career might be causing the batterer's difficulties. Those women who cannot give up working feel guilty. Although many of the women work because the family needs the money, they also state that the time spent on the job provides a brief respite from the batterer's domination. But the batterer's need to possess his woman totally often causes her to lose or leave her job. The batterer batters her with a litany of suspicions about her supposed behavior on the job. Usually, he is jealous of her work relationships, especially those with other men.

Battered women who work often turn their money over to their husbands. Even those women who provide the family's financial stability feel their income belongs to their husband. Ultimately, she gives the man the right to make the final decisions as to how the family income is spent. The battered woman views the man as the head of the family, even though often she is the one actually keeping the family together; she makes the decisions concerning financial matters and the children's welfare; and she maintains the house and often a job as well. She goes out of her way to make sure that her man feels he is the head of the home. Some of the women interviewed revealed elaborate deceptions they resorted to to put aside some money – money they saved secretly in order to leave the marriage. Often they did not follow through, but their nest egg helped them cope. Others left the relationship when they had enough money.

Keepers of the Peace

Another behavior common among battered women is the attempt to control other people and events in the environment to keep the batterer from losing his temper. The woman believes that if she can control all the factors in his life, she can keep him from becoming angry. She makes herself responsible for creating a safe environment for everyone. One woman interviewed spent an enormous amount of time talking about her efforts to control her mother, his mother, and their children so that none of them would upset her husband. She found that if she kept all these people in check through some interesting manipulations, life was pleasant in their home. The moment someone got out of line, her man began his beatings.

Severe Stress Reaction

The battered women in this sample were hard workers who lived under constant stress and fear. This had physical and psychological effects on them. Although most battered women report being able to withstand enormous amounts of pain during a battering incident, at other times they are often seen by their doctors for a variety of minor physiological ailments. Battered women often complain of fatigue, backaches, headaches, general restlessness, and inability to sleep. Psychological complaints are, frequently, depression, anxiety, and general suspiciousness. Being suspicious and secretive often helps a battered woman to avoid further beatings. Many battered women go to great lengths to find a few moments of privacy from their very intrusive battering husbands. They will often hide things from their men that they fear might precipitate another battering incident.

Childhood Violence and Sex-Role Stereotyping

I was curious to learn whether or not the women who lived in battering relationships with their husbands had also lived in battering relationships with their parents. Although this was true in a small number of cases, many more women reported that their first exposure to violent men was their husbands. Their fathers were described as traditionalists who treated their daughters like fragile dolls. The daughters were expected to be pretty and ladylike and to grow up to marry nice young men who would care for them as their fathers had. Doted upon as little girls, these women, in their fathers' eyes, could do no wrong. Such pampering and sex-role stereotyping unfortunately taught them that they were incompetent to take care of themselves and had to be dependent on men.

Common Characteristics of Men Who Batter

Who are the batterers?

The batterers described were also a mixed group. They represented all ages, races, religions (including no religion), educational levels, cultures, and socioeconomic groups. The youngest was described as sixteen years old and the oldest was seventy-six. They were unrecognizable to the uninformed observer and not distinguished by demographic data.

The batterer, according to the women in this sample, commonly:

1. Has low self-esteem.

2. Believes all the myths about battering relationships.

3. Is a traditionalist believing in male supremacy and the stereotyped masculine sex role in the family.

4. Blames others for his actions.

5. Is pathologically jealous.

6. Presents a dual personality.

7. Has severe stress reactions, during which he uses drinking and wife battering to cope.

8. Frequently uses sex as an act of aggression to enhance self-esteem in view of waning virility. May be bisexual.

9. Does not believe his violent behavior should have negative consequences.

The first three characteristics of the batterers are strikingly similar to those of the battered women. Batterers typically deny that they have a problem, although they are aware of it; and they become enraged if their women should reveal the true situation. These men do not want to discuss the problem, and attempts to learn more about batterers have not been successful. When these men do agree to be interviewed, often as a favor to their women during their contrite and loving phase, they cannot describe the details of an acute battering incident. They evade questions or claim not to remember very much of what did occur. Thus, the knowledge we have of these men comes from the battered women themselves and our few, meager observations.

Researchers Eisenberg and Micklow found 90 percent of the batterers in their study had been in the military. Twenty-five percent received dishonorable discharges. I did not systematically collect such data for this sample, but subjectively it appears that a similarly high percentage were also in the military. Del Martin, feminist author of *Battered Wives,* suggests a correlation between the military as a "school for violence" and subsequent battering behavior in males.

Overkill

There is always an element of overkill in the batterer's behavior. For example, he reports he does not set out to hurt his woman; rather, he sets out to "teach her a lesson." He may begin by slapping her once, twice, three times; before he knows it, he has slapped her ten or twelve times, with punches and kicks as well. Even when the woman is badly injured, the batterer often uncontrollably continues his brutal attack. The same is true for his generosity. During his loving periods, he showers the woman with affection, attention, and gifts. Rather than buying his woman a small bottle of perfume, one batterer bought her a three-ounce bottle. In another instance, the woman asked for a pocket calculator to help her to keep their checkbook balanced. The batterer bought her a calculator capable of performing mathematical computations neither of them understood. Several women complained of their husbands' extravagance, stating that they had to work longer and harder to pay off the charge accounts. This quality of overdoing things tends to be a standard characteristic of battering relationships.

Excessive Possessiveness and Jealousy

Another staple characteristic is the batterer's possessiveness, jealousy, and intrusiveness. In order for him to feel secure, he must become overinvolved in the woman's life. In some instances, he may take her to work, to lunch, and bring her home at the end of the working day. In others, when he goes to work, he may require her to bring him coffee, lunch, his checkbook, and generally to account for every moment of her time. In one extreme case, the batterer escorted his wife to the door of the ladies' room in any public facility they visited. Despite this constant surveillance of her every activity, the batterer is still suspicious of his woman's possible relationships with other men and women.

A frequent subject for the batterer's verbal abuse is his suspicion that the battered woman is having an affair or affairs. Most of the women interviewed had not had other sexual liaisons. If they did engage in affairs, they were generally of very short duration and represented an attempt to alleviate some of their loneliness and stress. Most battered women do not expect another relationship to be any better than the one they are suffering through. If they had any such hopes, they probably would have left the batterer in search of a new Prince Charming long ago.

Childhood Violence and Sex-Role Stereotyping

Although battered women typically do not come from violent homes, batterers frequently do. Many of the batterers saw their fathers beat their mothers; others were themselves beaten. In those homes where overt violence was not reported, a general lack of respect for women and children was evident. These men often experienced emotional deprivation. These reports support the notion of the generational cycle theory that is so popular in our child abuse literature today. Children who were abused or witnessed abuse are more likely to grow up to be tomorrow's abusers.

Batterers' Relationship with Their Mothers

The women also reported that their batterers have unusual relationships with their mothers. It is often characterized as an ambivalent love-hate relationship. The batterer's mother seems to have a good deal of control over his behavior; yet he will often abuse her, too. In fact, many women report that acute battering incidents are triggered by a visit to the batterer's mother. Often their rages are reminiscent of infantile temper tantrums designed by angry little boys to provoke their mommies. Included in this study are several reports from women being battered by young sons. In one such case, a twenty-one-year-old college honor student beat his sixty-five-year-old mother several times a week. When the mother was ill or simply unavailable to him because of previous batterings, he would beat his twenty-year-old girl friend.

Much more research is needed before we can reach any definite conclusions about the relationship between the batterer and his mother. Psychology has done much damage by casting mothers in a negative light as being responsible for the emotional ills of their children. Still, we must look carefully at the role of the batterer's mother in this problem. Also, we must look at the role of the batterer's father and the father-son relationship. The information that we have collected can serve as a beginning to formulate new questions that need to be answered.

Mental Status of Batterers

Psychological distress symptoms were often reported in batterers, particularly prior to an acute battering incident. Alcohol and other drugs were often said to calm his nervousness. Although many of the men seemed to have a need for alcohol, few of them were reported addicted to drugs. Those who were had become addicted to hard drugs while in the military, usually in Vietnam.

Personality distortions were frequently mentioned by the women. They said the batterers had a history of being loners and were socially involved with others only on a superficial level. They were constantly accomplishing feats that others might not be able to. They loved to impress their women. For example, one man took his future bride into a furniture store and handed the salesperson two thousand dollars in cash for a bedroom set she admired. This sort of behavior tended to reinforce their women's viewing them as possessing extraordinary abilities.

The men are further described as being extremely sensitive to nuances in other people's behavior. Their attention to minimal cues from others gives them the ability to predict reactions faster than most of us can. Thus, they are helping their women to deal with others in their world when they share their usually accurate predictions of others' behavior. When these men decompensate under stress, their sensitivity becomes paranoid in nature. When they are comfortable, however, the women appreciate and benefit from this protective behavior, since battered women tend to be overly gullible and trusting of others. Much of this seemingly self-protective behavior becomes homicidal and suicidal when the batterer's violence escalates beyond his control.

Brain Diseases

Many of the battered women felt their husbands' violent behavior approximated some kind of brain seizure and that there might be a relationship between neurological disorders and violence. The most common disorder discussed was psychomotor epilepsy. This is a disorder of the brain manifested by sudden, unexplained outbursts of movement. Persons who suffer from such brain disorder often do not remember their episodes, especially if they result in violence. Sometimes an aura or feeling of an impending attack is identifiable but usually precipitation is unknown. Medication is often useful in controlling onset and frequency of attacks, although a cure is most times impossible.

Neurologists are studying the relationship of such brain diseases and violence. It is interesting, though, that seemingly only men, and not women, are so afflicted with such a physical disorder.

Another disease mentioned that may cause violent outbursts was hypoglycemia. This disease is characterized by low blood-sugar levels that cause starvation among body cells. The brain cells become irritable more rapidly than the rest of the body, and such irritability, it is theorized, can trigger violent outbursts. One woman reported that if she sensed a rising tension, she was able to avoid an acute battering incident by feeding her hypoglycemic husband. Although minor battering incidents still occurred, explosions disappeared. This improvement had been stable over the six months prior to her interview and followed a three-year battering history. I wonder how much her nurturing behavior of feeding him also helped to alleviate his explosiveness.

Further support for the theory of neurological or blood chemistry changes in batterers is found in the geriatric population. Some older women report dramatic changes in their husbands' behavior as they age. Senility or hardening of the arteries can cause previously nonviolent men to begin to abuse their wives. One sixty-eight-year-old woman told of her seventy-year-old husband's attacking her with his cane. Other stories indicate the cruel fate that can befall women who have devoted their lives to pleasing their husbands only to find that aging brings on organic brain syndromes that can impel them to violent behavior.

In conclusion, battered women and batterers come from all walks of life. This sample has indicated that they cannot be distinguished by demographic description or stereotypes. They do have some personality characteristics in common, but it is not known how much the victim/offender roles produce such personalities or whether they sought each other out first. Rather than concentrating on the study of individual personality, it appears that the study of the interrelatedness of the sociological and psychological factors may be the way to a solution.

Choosing a Lifestyle – Coping with Life

12.1 "Guilt"
Barbara Berg

MY ATTACHE CASE WAS ALWAYS THE CATALYST. FOR ALMOST A YEAR, WHEN my children were both toddlers, they would sit or play quietly as I washed up, ate breakfast, and put on my coat. But as soon as I reached for my briefcase, they would burst into inconsolable tears. "Please don't go. Please don't leave us," they would chorus pitifully, sometimes wrapping their little bodies around my legs in an effort to keep me at home.

It made no difference if I explained to them in advance, over breakfast, that Mommy would be leaving for work when I finished my coffee, or if I attempted to sneak out of the door wordlessly, or even if I made four or five trips back from the elevator (which I did all too frequently) to reassure them that I loved them and would be home later. Their reaction was always the same. And so was my response: gut-wrenching guilt – excruciatingly intense when the children were sick or having other problems, a bit lighter when things were going smoothly, but always lurking in the recesses of my mind, its shadowy presence darkening my day.

In my early years of struggling to combine my career and my mothering, I assumed that I was the only one who felt this kind of anguish. Certainly my husband, Arnie, didn't feel any guilt. He was dumbfounded by the suggestion that he could. For him, being both a father and a wage earner are synonymous with being a man. When he had to work late or travel, he missed the children, but guilt entered into neither his vocabulary nor his emotions. And his inability to understand why it pervaded mine was the cause of much friction between us.

Time and again, he would point out all the "certifiable" signs of my good mothering – "the children seem happy," "they love nursery school," "they have lots of friends." Time and again, I tried to explain my guilt to him, but in truth I couldn't comprehend it either, and ironically, the way guilt rules my life made me at least as frustrated and resentful as it made him. It prevented me from doing things that I wanted to do, like going out to dinner with a friend, and it compelled me to do things *I didn't* want to do, like making intricate Halloween costumes on one day's notice. If one of the children was having a problem, I was sure it was because I was working too much; if my writing faltered, it had to be because I was spending too much time with the children. An improvement in one area of my life filled me with worry that I was neglecting another. Like my marriage. Why did the evening conversation between Arnie and me resemble nothing more than two radio dispatchers? "You check the lamb chops," "I'll change the baby," we would shout from opposite ends of the apartment. What happened to *our* quality time? I began to truly need to know if I was the only woman who felt so torn and pulled, who underneath her staunch, unshakable commitment to having children and a career worried that both were being shortchanged.

A Generation of Guilty Mothers

After two years of interviewing nearly 1,000 women of varying backgrounds across the nation, I learned that guilt was their greatest emotional problem. My findings both saddened and surprised me. It saddened me to realize that the present generation of working mothers,[1] the beneficiaries of so much hope and striving, were haunted by such conflict. "The guilt feels deep and almost physical," was how one mother put it, while another labeled it "the most painful experience of my life."

Self-reproach was high and wide: for going back to work, for taking a leave of absence, for leaving the office early to attend a school play, for working late and missing dinner, for being in too pressured a job, for not earning enough, for being short-tempered with the children, for not disciplining more. Whether a woman wanted to work outside the home or was forced to work, whether she loved her job or hated it, whether she was dissatisfied with her children's caregivers or delighted with them, she still felt guilty.

Like me, these women could recognize the gnawing, uneasy feeling guilt brings, but were not *aware* of the real toll it is taking. I had not been

---

1. "Working mother" is not really a satisfactory description of women who work outside the home, since mothers who are at home work also, although in different ways. I use the term here because it has become the generally accepted way of referring to mothers who hold paying jobs.

aware, for example, of the extent to which guilt is responsible for the often self-defeating ways in which we organize our lives. It can affect us at work, making some women stay in low-level jobs too long and others feel that they must be workaholics to justify their working at all. Joyce, for example, a copy chief at a large publishing house for many years, yearned for a promotion. But when she was finally offered a position as head of the department, she didn't accept it, much to everyone's astonishment. "I couldn't bear to leave my daughter," she concluded, "despite the fact that she would be in school all day and I would only get home about one and a half hours later than she."

We end up feeling as though no place is the right place to be. When we are at work, we worry that we should be with our children. When we are with our children, our minds wander to those unfinished reports on our desks. Raima Larter, Ph.D., an assistant professor of chemistry at Purdue University, expressed it this way: "I feel guilty about (a) not spending enough time with my children, (b) not spending enough time at work, but usually (c) guilty about both."

Clearly nothing has changed in the decade since renowned sociologist Jessie Bernard wrote in *The Future of Motherhood* that a "prime requisite for success of the professional mother . . . [was] mastering her feelings of guilt with regard to her children."

Martyrdom

Guilt can also hurt our relationships with our husbands or living partners. Many of us feel that we must "atone" for our working by doing the bulk of child care and housekeeping. Such martyrdom eventually backfires and we become angry at our mates for not helping more. In fact, in my study, the unequal division of household chores emerged as a major cause of arguing between couples, sometimes even leading to a divorce.

Some women feel so guilty that when their husbands do help out, they find themselves undermining their spouses' efforts. "Why did you let her go outside in such a light sweater?" "How did you allow them to make such a mess in the kitchen?" are our all-too-familiar responses to assistance. I found myself engaging in this kind of criticism when I was on a recent out-of-town book tour – a time when my guilt level soars. Each morning I would call home to say hello to the children. On one occasion, my husband told me that they were running late. "No time to make breakfast," he said. He'd pick up some doughnuts for them on the way to school.

"Doughnuts for breakfast?" I screamed into the telephone. "They can't start the day like that!"

Later, when I had time to reflect on my exaggerated response (I should note that in my eight years of mothering there have been times when I, too, have given my children doughnuts for breakfast), I realized that my guilt had made me feel competitive with my husband over who was the better parent – a phenomenon that also can occur between women and their housekeepers or babysitters.

"What Sex Life?"

Guilt can also lead to competitive arguing over such things as money and work, and – it should come as no surprise – all this can erode emotional and sexual intimacy. With pathos, wit, and piercing honesty, an overwhelming majority of the women interviewed confided a loss of sexual spontaneity and closeness in their relationships: "What romance? What sex life?" asked one, while another quipped, "At this rate, we will never have to use birth control again." And a third admitted, "I wish it weren't so, but my love life is a fond memory relegated to my fantasies."

Dr. Merle S. Kroop, associate director of the Human Sexuality Teaching Program at the New York Hospital-Cornell Medical Center, has observed that the lack of desire is common in working mothers. We may attribute diminishing sexual fervor to fatigue, but as Sharon Nathan, Ph.D., also with the Human Sexuality Teaching Program, noted, many of us who are too tired to have sex are not too tired to stay up until midnight watching television. So where is the exhaustion coming from?

Nathan and others suggested that it comes from emotional sources even more than physical ones. Anger can certainly generate feelings of fatigue, says Nathan, who calls anger the flip side of guilt. Our guilt is often expressed in anger toward our partner and against ourselves.

Dr. Alvin Blaustein, who teaches at the Mount Sinai Hospital Human Sexuality Program in New York City, added: "If women are feeling inadequate in the job they are doing as mothers, if they are feeling that they are not living up to their ideals from childhood, or if their husbands or mothers are making them feel guilty, they may feel that they don't deserve much sexual satisfaction."

The feeling of nonentitlement also makes working mothers reluctant to take any time for themselves. When I asked various groups of women, all of whom are very attentive to the details of their families and their jobs, why their own needs had become the "expendable luxury" of their hectic lives, they answered in one voice: "Guilt." We hardly ever do things just for our own enjoyment or for sheer relaxation, either. And as for attending to our own care, we do it later or not at all. Said one woman, "If I could take an hour for myself, I'd be able to shave both my legs on the same day."

Shortchanging Yourself

Haircuts and buying new clothes get put off until they are beyond the necessity stage, and although we may joke about our out-of-style winter jacket or our unruly locks, the long-term effects of our self-neglect are no laughing matter.

When I asked women about their physical and emotional health, working mothers catalogued a list of ailments that rivaled those in *The Merck Manual*, that vast compendium of human ills. Gastrointestinal complaints, back pains, insomnia, and migraine headaches all plague working mothers, though not as severely as women who stay home. Dr. Morton Leibowitz, an associate professor at the New York University School of Medicine and an internist with a large practice, has observed an increase over the past five years of working mothers who come to him for stress-related complaints.

It seems as though we are really in a double bind. First of all, guilt, which is internal and ongoing, is *itself* a powerful stressor. Second, this guilt prevents us from taking the time to go for a run, spend an hour in the bath, visit with a friend, or just do nothing – all of which could reduce our stress.

Mixed Messages to the Kids

The most vivid way that guilt affects us, however, is in relationships with our children. Strong is our sense of apology. We feel we need to "compensate" for our jobs, and do this in different ways.

"I found myself coming back from business trips loaded with presents for my son," said Susan Hayes, a vice president of marketing from Maryland. Other women told me they tried to make up for being at work by attempting to cram a day's worth of activities – building blocks, doing puzzles, playing games, reading books – into the few hours ("quality time") between the time they got home and their children's bedtime.

Quality time originally began as a concept that was reassuring to working mothers – how we spend our time with our youngsters is obviously more important than the amount of time we are around them – but our guilt has turned the idea of quality time into a rigid imperative, which we must achieve on a daily basis. Women told me that they rated the success or failure of their day according to whether or not they had achieved quality time with their youngsters.

Many working mothers feel that they are too indulgent with their children at home. Psychologist Alan Roland, coeditor of *Career and Motherhood*, found that guilt over working "gives a woman an impulse to do as much as possible for the children." Carolyn, an insurance executive, confessed, "I find myself picking up after them more often when I should be teaching them." Ellen, a private-school director, admits: "I tend to be lax in making them participate in household chores."

In my house, getting my children off to sleep became an incredibly stressful event. I found myself always giving in to their repeated requests for more juice, more stories, more hugs. As their demands increased, so I must confess did my resentment. I was tired; I wanted some time to unwind. But the more resentful and irritable I became, the guiltier I felt. And the guiltier I felt, the more difficulty I had turning off the light and leaving the room.

The children, for their part, became overtired and confused. Did I mean it when I said it was bedtime or didn't I? They weren't sure, and frankly neither was I.

Listening to other women explain their confusion, it seemed to me that however much we may believe in women's right to work in general, and our right to work in particular, however much we may know that our family needs our paycheck, somewhere deep within us is a prohibition against combining both roles. I was struck by the frequency with which they used phrases like, "I feel as though I am breaking with tradition" and "It doesn't feel quite natural to work with young children at home."

Our ambivalence is understandable. The strong pull of our personal pasts (so many of us having been raised by mothers who didn't work), combined with the tenacious grip the cult of traditional motherhood has on the national psyche, makes it easy to forget that *American mothers have always worked.*

Did Rosie the Riveter Feel Guilty?

With the exception of the 1950s, when most middle-class women did not hold jobs, mothers have been working throughout our history. In fact, when female labor was required to keep the economy going, as it was in the Colonial period and during the major wars, women – the majority of them mothers – were encouraged to work.

During World War II, for example, the number of women in the work force rose from about 12,500,000 to about 18,500,000, and while almost all said they planned to quit when the men came home, by the end of the war more than 80 percent preferred to continue working. What's especially interesting is that they do not appear to have felt guilty. (At least no studies have turned up to indicate they did, and women's magazines of the time didn't cover the question.) There are a few good reasons why. First of all, 90 percent of them had the comfort of knowing that their children were being watched by relatives or friends (or, in some cases, paid babysitters) in their own homes. Day care, both federal and local, existed, but it was too scarce to accommodate more than a fraction of the families in need of such services. Second, the women were told that they were "indispensable to national survival." The government, along with the media, lauded the efforts of the "girls left behind." Columnist Max Lerner, referring to the legions of women in factories, wrote, "For all of them, slacks have become the badge of honor."

A 1942 ad for Sanforized clothing came up with the rhyme:

They're running farmers' tractors
They're at a factory bench

The hands that rock the cradle
Wield a nifty monkey wrench.

The situation for today's working mother is quite different. With relatives scattered and friends likely to be as busy as she, the majority have to rely on strangers to watch their children. While many hired caregivers are superb, some are not, particularly those who are themselves underpaid and given the responsibility for watching more children than can be adequately supervised by any one human being. (There are no federal standards regulating the staff-child ratio at daycare centers.)

Moreover, instead of being praised for their efforts, working mothers today are likely to be condemned for being selfish. In spite of the economics forcing women to work, in spite of the fact that about 80 percent of women are still tied to traditional female jobs – file clerk, waitress, nurse – the feeling that working mothers "are getting away with something" is so strong, it is almost palpable. In addition, the Reagan Administration's lack of support for women in the workplace and the growing influence of the fundamentalist movement, which stresses that a woman's role in life is childrearing at home, all do much to exacerbate our sense of guilt.

When we think about how quickly and creatively the consumer sector has responded to working *families* with take-out food services, special clothing stores just for the businesswoman, children's birthday party services, and the like, we can begin to appreciate just how slow and noninnovative our communities, companies, and government have been in respect to child care.

Why, for example, don't corporations sponsor pools of backup child-care people? (Most organizations have pools of temporary office help.) Why can't there be more visiting-nurse services to care for the sick children of employees like the one that the 3M Corporation is presently experimenting with? Why is our typical school day from nine to three? Why aren't more flextime or part-time positions available? Why do only a fraction of our nation's employers offer on- or near-site child-care facilities? Why do we have some states that allow one caregiver to watch as many as 12 toddlers? Why are we still the only industrialized nation without some form of parenting leave?

And why aren't more of us angry about all this instead of misdirecting our anger at our spouses, our children, and mostly ourselves? Why haven't we coalesced around child-care issues? Lack of time and energy must surely be part of the answer, but our guilt and self-recrimination may well be another part of it.

So we need first to pull ourselves out of the vicious cycle. Getting rid of the superwoman myth and the many demands she makes on us is a good place to begin. Just how unrealistic that mythical creature is becomes clear when we talk with other women and learn that none of us is able to be all things to all people all the time.

It isn't surprising that those working mothers who have a chance to discuss their common problems with one another at their jobs find themselves less conflicted. A woman who is a member of Financial Mothers, one of the support groups for working mothers being formed within different companies and professions, told me that just knowing how many others share her concerns and doubts has helped her to feel less guilty.

These organizations, important as they are, affect only a small number of working mothers. For the kinds of structural changes we need, women must join together with men to strive for corporate and public policies sensitive to our needs. Only then will we be freed from the tyranny of guilt.

12.2 Phase One: The First Five Years
Jack Dominian

The first five years of marriage constitute the first phase of marriage. These years are significant in three ways. 1) They are the important years of adjustment and are loaded with difficulties. 2) It has been found that these years are very important in laying the foundations of the relationship. When a marriage breaks down, people often locate the causes in these early years. 3) It has been found that between thirty and forty percent of all marital breakdown occurs in the first five years. So they are important, and they should be supported. Let us consider the five dimensions in this phase.

1. Social Factors

Separation from parents: At the center of marriage lie the separation of the spouses from their parents and the fusion of a new unity between husband and wife. The parents remain important and are contacted and resorted to. They remain good friends, but the spouses turn to each other for the resolution of their difficulties, management of their affairs, future planning, and the timing of children. It is natural that in all these matters they should consult each other and make mutual decisions, leaving their parents out of the consideration.

This happens with the majority of couples, but there are exceptions and this produces problems. In these instances, one or both spouses remain over-attached to parents. The wife may be over-dependent on her mother, and the husband on his father. The woman may telephone her mother several times a day or visit her at frequent intervals. The mother becomes the confidante of the daughter. The vital secrets of the relationship are entrusted to her. Instead of discussing matters with her husband, she communicates with her mother and the husband is bypassed. His opinions are ignored in favor of her mother's. The husband may turn to his father for advice on economic matters, or worse still, may be employed by his father who plays a dominant role in his son's life. Just as the daughter bypasses the husband, he bypasses her. Such a couple may be married, but they have not put aside dependence on their families.

This is a situation that leads to feelings of exclusion. Repeated requests to abandon dependence on the parent are ignored. The next phase of this problem is that the spouse is criticized, and an alliance is formed between parent and child against the spouse. The situation gets much worse with the formation of triangular tensions between parents and the partners. In the end the marriage may be terminated.

The more common problem is when a spouse is not liked or approved of by in-laws. This puts the other partner in difficulty. They have to choose between their spouse and their parents.

Running the household: When a couple is newly married they have to make arrangements for running the home. Traditionally the wife has had jobs like cooking, cleaning, and the laundry. The husband has had practical, mechanical jobs like mowing the lawn and keeping the car in good repair. Today there is more fluidity of roles. The important thing is that the distribution be fair and be experienced as such. What often happens is that the wife, who also works outside the home, is left with all the household chores and the care of the children. The husband may consider it sufficient to be a provider and do next to nothing in the home. This leads to a common problem. The wife is excessively tired and is not interested in affection and sex.

Money problems: If one listens to a cross-section of opinion, the most common explanation for marriage troubles is money. Money is meant to solve all the problems. The fact that no mention of it has been made up till now is because, while money undoubtedly matters, it is the emotional consequences that are responsible for the conflict. There are plenty of poor people who maintain their marriages and many rich marriages that don't work out. We have to look at the meaning of money and its implications.

Money has three meanings. The first is its economic value; the second is the power it gives to those who have it; and the third is its emotional component.

The first meaning is the one that is usually considered. This often means that there is not enough of it. Since money is essential for buying a house, food, clothing, and other essentials of life, its relative absence leads to tension, quarrels, arguments, and mutual accusations.

The person who controls the checkbook has power over the partner. It is the husband who traditionally controls the money, though this is less and less true today. If a wife is dependent on her husband for her financial survival, if he does not give her enough money for the necessities, she is unable to do anything about it except go to work herself, and then she very often uses the money she earns to supplement the household budget.

In certain marriages the wife or husband may discover that the spouse cannot handle money and is irresponsible with it. This is an enormous strain on a couple. Thirdly, money has an emotional meaning. If one spouse controls it and shortchanges the other, that spouse feels unloved. He or she thinks: "If you loved me, you would share with me equally."

Another cause for conflict is housing. A young couple newly married want a place of their own. When they have to share with their families or with other couples, the scene is set for strain, and it has been found that those who start married life without an independent abode have a greater tendency toward marital breakdown.

The pressures of work: Work is important in the life of a couple for its economic value, social support, and for their self-esteem. There are two problems associated with it, however. These are working excessive hours and unemployment.

Anyone can work long hours, but it is a problem that particularly affects professional people. Doctors, lawyers, accountants, all work long hours and often come home late. This leads to constant arguments that they put their work before their home life. When they come home they are tired and unavailable for conversation. Very often they have their meal, sit in front of the television, and fall asleep. This is exceedingly irritating to the spouse. The other problem is that professional people often have to travel and leave the spouse behind. When this is frequent, it creates an emotional vacuum that is acutely painful.

Another problem is unemployment. Unemployment has a devastating effect on self-esteem and feelings of emotional availability. It is not surprising that it is associated with a high rate of marital breakdown.

Leisure hours: One of the dangers in the early years of marriage is that one of the spouses wants to enjoy the amenities of marriage: an organized household, food, and sex, without contributing to household chores. He or she might tend to use spare time to continue favorite pastimes like golf or tennis, or going to a favorite bar. A bar in particular can become a substitute home, and time spent there can easily lead to neglect of the spouse.

2. Emotional Factors

The emotional factors have been mentioned before in various parts of this book, but here I will mention them briefly again.

Loss of idealization: It has been shown that what holds a couple together in the stage of falling in love is their deep idealization of each other. In brief, each thinks the other is wonderful. Those who are wise begin to accept, even at this stage, that there are limitations to the partner. The limitations are social, as described above, or emotional, that is, in the language already used, they have shortcomings in their emotional availability, capacity to feel, be affectionate or understanding. When limitations are foreseen, their damage is limited. When not foreseen, there is acute disappointment: "This is not the man/woman I fell in love with. I can't recognize him or her." Such feelings herald profound disillusionment.

Restriction of freedom: In some instances the newly married person cannot cope with the limitations imposed on their freedom of movement and/or action. Such a person suddenly feels imprisoned, and within months of the marriage is desperately unhappy and wants to be out of it. When close attention is paid to the period of the courtship and the previous history, it will be found that he or she may have broken off the relationship more than once or been involved with previous relationships. In fact, such men or women may postpone marriage repeatedly, and once they are in it find it intolerable. Within the marriage they become depressed and withdrawn, and all they want is to get out.

Inability to cope with intimacy: The inability to cope with intimacy is another side of the few vulnerable people who marry and then regret it immediately afterward. They form the extreme pattern of avoidant attachment and cannot stand any form of closeness. They made the supreme effort to overcome their difficulty during courtship, but the continuous physical and emotional closeness of marriage is intolerable.

Immaturity: The man or woman who after marriage displays immaturity may come as a shock to the partner. There may have been indications during the courtship, but they were not interpreted correctly. The behavior consists of one or more symptoms of recurrent and acute loss of temper, excessive drinking, aggression with physical and verbal assault, inconsistent and poor work record, sexual excess, rudeness, or possessiveness. Clearly such behavior is extremely immature and endangers a marriage.

3. Sexual Problems

Non-consummation: This is a functional disturbance in which the wife experiences acute pain that makes penetration impossible. It is usually easily corrected.

Birth regulation: Most couples do not have any difficulty with birth control. They use the method most suited to them. If one spouse is a Roman Catholic, he or she may want to restrict birth control to methods acceptable to the church. There is no difficulty in finding suitable training programs to accommodate this special need.

Lovemaking: Women often experience disappointment with sexual intercourse in the first five years of marriage. They may not reach orgasm and/or may experience pain during intercourse. More commonly, there may be disappointment in the quality of lovemaking. One partner may feel that sex is not as rewarding as it was during courtship or that they don't have sex often enough. Men usually complain about frequency, and women about the ambience of the lovemaking.

Difficulty in getting pregnant: A small percentage of couples, approximately eight percent, do not become pregnant when they want to. This leads to the ordeal of examinations, keeping charts, taking fertility pills, and even proceeding to in vitro fertilization. The couple may understand with their head that it is not their fault, but they feel embarrassed about their difficulty. The husband may be found to have a low sperm count which is a blow to his self-esteem, or the wife may have hormonal difficulties. This is often a time when the spontaneity of sexual intercourse is reduced and spouses become mechanically involved in the challenge of reproduction. Their desire to conceive is intermingled with the disappointment and frustration of not being able to. This is a testing time, and the couple need encouragement to get through the difficulties.

Sexual variations: Some partners want to embroider sexual intercourse with some extra-sexual activity, such as a fetish, cross-dressing, or sado-masochistic practices. The wife, who is usually the recipient of such desires, may feel the request surprising or upsetting. The couple should seek help to understand these sexual needs.

Occasionally a homosexual man or woman marries to "cure" their homosexuality, or to prove to themselves that they are not saddled with this difficulty. To their surprise they find they cannot continue with a marriage, and to the dismay of the partner, they separate. Although such an event is exceedingly painful, it is better faced early in the marriage.

Infidelity: The early years of marriage are not usually a time when infidelity occurs. Sometimes it does, however. The affair may involve an ex-girlfriend or ex-boyfriend with whom a relationship was unresolved. As with all affairs, the pain should not stop the process of reconciliation.

4. Intellectual Challenges

A couple usually discovers common interests, outlook, opinion, in the process of the courtship or cohabitation. They will find out whether they have a common background, if their educational outlook coincides, or if they can interest one another apart from in bed. Occasionally a hasty courtship, or one based on infatuation, brings partners together who have little in common. This combination of bodies and not of minds demands an assessment of whether there is sufficient emotional and intellectual affinity to keep the spouses together.

5. Spiritual Difficulties

Couples who share the same faith tradition and who have similar spiritual values are more likely to succeed in a marriage. In mixed marriages, or in marriages in which one spouse is a believer and the other is not, conflicts can more easily arise, especially when children are involved. Couples should discuss the importance of their beliefs and values during courtship and reach a mutual understanding about this before they marry.

12.3 Making Your Dual-Career Marriage Successful

Barbara Chesser

ABSTRACT: Because of their double work load, dual-career couples face several pressing issues. Among them are extra demands on the couple's time and energy, the timing of children, child care, how to spend earnings, changing sex roles and decision making, women being judged by how they succeed in the homemaking role, relative earnings, unrealistic expectations, lack of models for working out satisfactory marital roles, and the superwoman myth. Thirteen advantages of dual-career marriages are listed, as well as ten recommendations for making them better.

Because of the increasing number of dual-career families, all family life education efforts should deal with issues arising in dual-career families. Whether the efforts are preventive, enrichment, or interventional in nature, the marriages of the participants will be strengthened as they become more aware of the issues that arise in dual-career marriages. An increased awareness of these issues and possible ways to handle them constructively will increase the couple's coping skills and problem-solving abilities, thereby building family strengths.

Dual-career family as used in this paper means both husband and wife are pursuing careers and maintaining a family together. The word "career" usually refers to a job which requires a high degree of commitment and a fairly continuous developmental life. A career is different from a job or work, for work may involve any kind of gainful employment. Work may be full-time, part-time, and periodic over the years so that it can be easily changed to accommodate marital and child-rearing responsibilities. Obviously the line of demarcation between a career and a job is not always clear. A career might be placed at one end of a continuum with higher levels of commitment, responsibilities, educational and emotional investment, whereas a job is at the other end of the continuum with lower levels of all these characteristics. The closer one comes to the career end of the continuum, the more likely the issues discussed in this paper will indeed be problematic within the marriage because of the higher level of commitment characteristic of a career as opposed to a job. The closer one approaches the job end of the continuum, the easier, relatively speaking, the issues will be to resolve because of less commitment and investment . . . .

Issues

To work or not to work outside the home may be an issue arising before the couple is married. Many variables will feed into this decision, but for the decision for the wife to work outside the home to be successfully carried out, the wife must really want or need to work. *Want* and *need* may be difficult to differentiate for some persons. For the two million women who head families, there is no choice: they *need* to work. Because of inflation, some wives with working husbands may also feel that they have to work to help pay the rent, buy groceries, and to rear their children. For other women, working may be a way to raise the family's standard of living. Others may work mostly to be with other people. In a society that often measures human worth by how much money you can make or what you do, many women want to feel better about themselves. . . . Being able to sort out why each works may seem too trivial or too philosophical to be practical. But many of the practical decisions in a two-career marriage often rest on why each partner works. Why a farmer's wife works during a drought year may be quite different from why a wife who is a college professor works year after year. Issues and problems may develop on the homefront for each of these couples. And each may require different solutions to keep the marriage on an even keel.

But most couples describe common problems regardless of why they say the wife works. Extra demands on time and energy seem to plague every two-career marriage. The wife may try to do all the housework as well as meet the rigorous demands of a job or career. The husband traditionally views housework as female's work and may have trouble helping with it. He may feel clumsy, or housework may make him feel unmanly, or he may be exhausted from his career. His wife may not want him to help her. She may doubt her own value if he can do "her" work.

Another issue many dual-career couples grapple with is whether or not to have children. An increasing percentage are opting for a childfree marriage, but many career couples merely are postponing the birth of their first child. And most career families have fewer children than couples which include a nonworking wife.

Determination of the "best" time for having a child rests on considerations such as educational plans and establishment of a career and the effects of time-off on these two considerations. Also the availability of maternity leaves may determine the "best" time.

For dual-career couples who have a child, child care becomes a concern. Adequate childcare facilities are still not widely available. Finding a reliable baby-sitter to stay in the home may be a challenge. The financial cost of child care is usually another concern. When the child is older and in school most of the day, child care may not be such a problem. Problems may come when a child does not follow the usual schedule, for example, when he or she is sick. Who stays home? Who takes the child to the doctor? To the dentist? Who leaves work to go to the parent-teacher conference? To the Christmas play? To weekly music lessons? In a traditional marriage, the decision is easy: the mother's job always gives in to the demands of the children. As women increasingly express commitment to their careers, couples are compelled to establish new criteria for decisions regarding child care.

Obviously these criteria are increasingly complicated if a child requires extra care and supervision because of a health problem or a handicap of some kind. Working out satisfactory child care and supervision may also be complicated if the career of one or both of the partners in a dual-career marriage requires travel.

How to handle career relocation if one spouse is offered a promotion which requires moving is another issue confronting some couples at one time or another in their careers. Decision making in this situation may be extra perplexing if it is the wife being offered the promotion. Our culture supports relocations made on the basis of the husband's promotion, not the wife's.

The issue of how to spend the combined earnings of a dual-career marriage confronts most couples. Should the discretionary income be spent on luxuries or travel, or should it be saved or invested? Dual-career families come face to face with this question. Other couples may find that there is no discretionary income. Taxes may take an extraordinary portion of their combined earnings. Transportation expenses for two careers eat up an unreasonable amount of money. Wardrobe demands may gnaw insidiously at the combined earnings. Child care may take its unfair portion. Eating meals out or the purchase of convenience foods may require an undue portion of the paychecks. This is when the couple must scrutinize the value of two careers in one marriage, or they may be challenged to search for desirable ways to economize.

Survival of a two-career family may depend upon the ability of husband and wife to make decisions satisfying to both. Some marriages thrive on the husband making all the major decisions and others depend upon the wife to make them. But partners in most dual-career marriages have to work at learning how to make decisions together. Traditionally, the man made the money, therefore he had the authority to make the decisions. If both husband and wife work to make the money, both have the right to make decisions. Deciding *who* is going to decide and *how* the decisions are made is often more critical than the decisions. Couples able to decide mutually with occasional compromise seem to survive two-career marriages.

Some males egos may be too fragile to survive a two-career marriage. A working wife may signal his failure to make enough money to be considered "successful." Or a wife who makes more money than the husband may threaten a weak male ego. Husband and wife in similar careers may compete too keenly. A wife may occasionally put her husband in a double bind. She may pressure him to succeed in his job while pressuring him to be a terrific husband and father.

Some women may be uncomfortable out of a traditional homemaker role. Society still judges a man by his job and a woman by her homemaking, as a companion, mother, and hostess. Some women may be frustrated if they do better in the work world than their husbands. All husbands and wives it seems are pressured to do more and to do it better. Tensions may really mount in dual-career families if these issues are not dealt with realistically and constructively.

If two-career marriages survive these first few hurdles, they still have not completed the obstacle course. Careers make rugged demands on a husband's and wife's time and energy. So do the children's schedules. Little time and energy remain for friends or recreation. Most couples cannot maintain friendships with all they would like to. So they must make choices – a few friends from his acquaintances, a few from hers, or maybe a few from church, or from parents of their children's friends. Couples need skills in learning to say no to some activities so they can say yes to those they want to do.

Individual partners need to know what they expect of themselves as well as from their mates. They need to examine what they expect of the marriage itself. Couples must communicate these expectations to each other. One husband whose first two-career marriage ended in divorce but who was managing well in a second one shared: "You gotta have lots of heart-to-heart talks of what you want out of marriage and what you are willing to do to accomplish what you want." He explained that not only husband and wife but the kids must have a good understanding of what everyone wants out of the family and the responsibilities each is willing to assume. "Otherwise," he went on, "the family becomes like an explosion in a mattress factory: they never get it all together."

Marriage may be unsafe at any speed, but having unrealistic and unreasonable expectations may be the speed that kills. If this were true for the traditional marriage in which the husband is the breadwinner and the wife is the hearth-warmer, then it certainly is truer for the two-career marriage. Other survival tactics may help, but realistic expectations of self and partner are essential, as one college professor with three young children pointed out:

> You have to be realistic in what you expect of yourself and your marriage partner. It's impossible for one person to be terrific on the job, a terrific husband, a terrific father, and to keep the grass mowed all the time.

An enormous obstacle to two-career couples is the paucity of models of successful two-career marriages. And each two-career couple works through these issues in fairly unique ways that seem best for them. Their solution for a particular problem may not work for another couple.

Another complication is that many couples think other couples have solved most of these problems. Flashes of a superwoman haunt most women. This superwoman who knits marriage, career, and motherhood into a satisfying life without dropping a stitch is overwhelming and gives others miserable feelings of failure.

The foregoing discussion of some of the issues confronting most dual-career marriages may create a foreboding, ominous aura about the dual-career marriage. The marriages of those who do not work successfully through these issues, in fact, may be threatened. However, those who do at least to some extent successfully resolve some of the issues may enjoy some tangible benefits or advantages. Professionals should clearly outline these just as they teach about the issues that usually arise in a dual-career family.

Advantages

Some of the advantages which dual-career families may enjoy are briefly outlined as follows:

1. Dual-career families may enjoy some financial advantages. They may enjoy a higher standard of living. They may be able to accumulate savings. They may be able to provide financial security against possible disasters.

2. The wife may enjoy greater levels of creativity, self-expression, achievement, and recognition. She may enjoy being herself, not an appendage to her husband. This may help her be a better mother and wife.

3. Dual-career marriages provide a greater range of role models for children of both sexes.

4. The husband may be relieved of some of the pressures to succeed and to make money. Thus, he will be able to function more effectively as a husband and/or father.

5. The husband may enjoy his wife more since she will have outside activities and interests to share.

6. Sexual interest in the marriage may heighten in an unstereotyped, dual-career marriage.

7. Parent responsibilities can be shared. Husbands can enjoy their children more, and children can profit from having an available father.

8. Children may learn to be more responsible and more resourceful when their mothers work outside the home. This may reinforce their feelings of achievement, pride, and self-esteem.

9. Children may learn to respect their parents more, especially their mothers, as individuals.

10. The empty-nest syndrome which affects some in later years may be avoided somewhat if the wife is engaged in a meaningful career outside the home.

11. Coping with widowhood may be somewhat easier for the woman who has had a meaningful career in addition to her marriage career.

12. Increased empathy with the demands of the roles of each other may foster mutual respect and facilitate communication.

13. The increased sharing of roles may create feelings of equality, thus strengthening the family.

Recommendations

. . . [G]eneral recommendations that all could work on which would strengthen the American family are as follows:

1. There should be increased knowledge throughout the educational career about role flexibility and/or change. In other words, rigid or stereotyped sex roles should be avoided in textbooks and other learning materials.

2. Mass media should avoid perpetuating stereotypes.

3. Stereotypic assumptions about sex roles should be avoided (for example, "women are absent more from work").

4. Better parent education should be available for all people.

5. There should be more high-quality child care for working parents. Perhaps more neighborhood child care provisions as well as industrial child care should be explored.

6. Business and government could provide more flexible working conditions, including more flexible working hours, sharing of positions, and

more part-time positions without discrimination of benefits, promotions, etc. Increased flexibility would reduce conflict between the demands of parents' employment and the needs of their families. Flexible working hours would also help in battling the war against the traditional 8 to 5 schedule that is based on the assumption that the wife is at home and free to take care of business matters within this time frame.

7. More equitable provisions should be provided for taking time off for childbearing and child care.

8. An integrated network of family services should be developed more fully. All families need easily available preventive services.

9. Marriage and family counseling should continually be developed into a more effective resource for helping members of two-career marriages cope with their stresses and strains.

10. More research is needed on the effects of two-career families. For example, the effects of long-distance marriages on the partners and the children might be explored.

Two-career families are probably a testing ground of things to come as sex roles become more flexible and interchangeable, as inflation continues, and as more careers are open to women. Professionals who are directly involved in activities to help build strengths in families must energetically carry out all of the foregoing suggested recommendations, and they must continue to be supportive and empathic in whatever ways will help strengthen two-career families. And we as professionals need to cherish our own family relationships to provide a model of ways to build strengths in the two-career family.

12.4 Careers and Money, Commitments and Frugality
Anthony Padovano

MARRIAGE IS A SURPRISING COMBINATION OF ROMANCE AND PRACTICALITY.
Love is not an efficient experience. And yet, paradoxically, families are the most efficient units in society. When other agencies attempt to duplicate what families do in the normal course of things, the cost and complication are crushing.
Preparation of meals and housecleaning, birth and dying, child care and nursing for the elderly, sleeping and leisure activities become enormously

expensive, impersonal and sometimes depressing when bureaucracies manage them. Love is often lacking and always less personal as a public service.

We are not suggesting that many of these institutions do not do their best or that dedicated people do not work in them or that they do not bring benefits they alone provide. There are times when families simply cannot cope. We are saying, however, that the family is the model and the norm, the preferred place for all of us, the most humane institution human history knows.

It is ironic that public services are developed for efficiency and yet involve a great deal of waste. Families are not formed with efficiency in mind and yet conserve energy and resources.

Love and Structure

Love happens in a structure even though it eludes all structures. There are rules to play by, assigned by gender or inclination, by choice or convention. There is a specific place one lives, routines of work, rituals of understanding, decisions about children, provisions for eating and sleeping.

Love does not develop in a wilderness but in a cultivated environment. Love is an intimate rather than an outdoor experience, most often a private rather than a public event. Love needs to be housed and restricted; it requires boundaries and parameters; its mathematics, in the beginning, is limited to two people, and later to a few family members. In the context of this circumscription, love becomes universal and reaches out for the whole world.

Even though love is efficient, it becomes nonetheless expensive. Careers and money may not be the sum and substance of love but they are not incidental to the process.

If homemaking is sacred and central to marriage, work outside the home and careers also play their part. The point of work is more profound than the making of money. Although this income allows a couple to function, there are prior values in work and careers which need to be addressed.

Careers are usually a means by which a family joins the larger community. No family is, in its own right, an autonomous culture. It needs the completion which comes from involvement in the social task.

Work, furthermore, is important because it is more than something we do. Work is an expression of ourselves. We are realized in the projects we undertake for the welfare of others.

Work is not a punishment or a discipline, a burden or a curse. It becomes this when people are used for profit, when human beings become merchandise for others, when men and women are made to labor in environments which assault their essential humanity.

In its nature, however, work is a mystical experience, setting up a relationship between the work we do and the product we produce, between ourselves and the others who work with us. We identify ourselves not only by name but also by occupation. We frequently feel an immediate connection with strangers who do the same kind of work we do.

Careers become problematic when the marriage becomes incidental to the demands and dynamics of the workplace. In most marriages, even with the shortened hours and work week of the modern age, more time is expended traveling to and from the workplace, working away from home and in work brought home than is spent on the marriage itself.

Careers may become so absorbing that the marriage is deemed a liability. We can take each other so much for granted that we think everything else is more important. It is a pattern repeated with depressing frequency. There is even social and cultural support for this distortion. Families are often honored for their affluence and occupations rather than for the character of their relationships and the quality of their love.

This absorption with work rather than people is a form of idolatry. We worship the task rather than respect the person. God made human life a unique image and likeness of the divine. Idolatry in the modern age is not so much a formal neglect of God but an indifference to persons.

Careers and money can become addictive. They may lead people to frenzy and neurosis. The mystical experience of work creates madness in those who do not strike a balance between the need for money and the necessity of relationships, between the demands of their careers and the desire for love. No one dies wishing he or she made more money or spent more time at the office. People, at the end, look at the faces and hold the hands of those they are about to leave and wish they had more time with them.

Marriage and Tranquillity

Marriages can profit from contemplation and reflection, from meditation and value clarification, from journal keeping and personal prayer. There are times in the early morning or late at night, alone in a car or traveling in a public vehicle, while dressing or bathing when people ought to take stock of their lives.

Contemplation rescues us from frenzy and madness. It makes us know that careers are valuable and that marriages depend upon them for development. But this is true only if community and relationship, marriage and love, spouses and children are given the time and attention they deserve.

Money may be an asset or a demon. It is an asset when it liberates life from unnecessary burdens, when it allows creative leisure and fosters opportunities for human relationships. It is a demon when it possesses our souls and makes insatiable demands. People seldom believe they have enough money, no matter what the amount. There is always someone richer, someone with more so that we are able to be exceedingly affluent and feel perpetually deprived.

Money becomes addictive as we require greater and greater amounts to satisfy an ever diminishing sensitivity to its pleasure. As with any other addiction, we come to sacrifice everything for money and do things for money we once thought we would never countenance.

As money accumulates, we begin to suffer insecurity. Money was supposed to make us secure and now we find ourselves suspicious of others and threatened by the loss of wealth. Life becomes so unthinkable without vast resources that we contemplate crimes or even suicide if our assets dwindle substantially. Enormous reserves of time and energy, emotion and life investment are devoted to money management. We surround ourselves with security systems and move into neighborhoods where wealth is so conspicuous that they are likely to be burglarized.

We are not suggesting that money is evil or that poverty is not terrifying. We are noting that money demands a price from us in human terms and that it seldom brings the benefits we anticipate. It is most useful when it is kept in perspective. Money easily homogenizes reality, assigning everything a market value, drying up the sources of creativity and diversity which liberate the human spirit.

Money and Human Resources

The more we are invested in people the less money we need. It sounds banal to comment that the best things in life are free. The banality, however, is based on an important truth. The possessions we purchase are valuable and useful only if they are prized less than those gifts which have been freely given. The presence of another person and the love of a child, the grace of God and the sacraments of Christ, the seasons of the year and the stars in the heavens, faith and friendship, music and poetry give life human shape and substance.

Commitment to people leads to creative frugality. By frugality, we do not mean impoverishment but personal enrichment. A certain distance from possessions enhances our humanity and enables us to appreciate the worth of others.

Frugality means that we use what we need but that we do not accumulate those things which blind us to people and suffocate values. In a consumer society, the assumption is that more material goods create more meaning. The good life is defined in terms of possessions, many of which we do not need and all of which require time, attention and care. We sometimes purchase things to prove to others that we are worth noticing and that they are not.

As we become committed to people, we need less of the things money buys. Love rescues us from idolatry. Love's contemplative dimensions create frugality and peace.

If a couple becomes a consuming couple, the marriage itself is eventually consumed, reduced to merchandise and bartered for goods and services that are not worthy of it. The entire theory of consumerism rests on the notions that life is surrounded by scarcity and that commitments limit life. We might discuss each of these ideas in turn.

The assumption that life is a scarce commodity prompts people to accumulate enormous resources. We become identified with what we own, defined by it, so that we are eventually possessed by our possessions.

There is fear that unless we have it all, we have little. We assume that our life is diminished if we have less than we might.

Life, however, is an inexhaustible experience. There is abundance everywhere. Scarcity occurs, for the most part, in those exotic and artificial items which are not necessary. Indeed, scarcity in these areas is fostered so that frenzy increases and market values climb.

Love, however, cannot be depleted and life itself is superabundant. The universe is vast and the mystery of our own planet is more than we can fathom. If some of our brothers and sisters do not have enough to eat or a place to live, if they are without clothing, medical care and education, it is not because there is not sufficient for everyone but because a few refuse to share from the very abundance which has become humanly useless to them.

Some, however, choose to live simply so that others may simply live. This frugality, however, is not even done for this reason alone. Frugality does not mean only that we restrict our ownership and consumption so that there will be more for others. It means, more profoundly, that we neither want nor desire artifacts which assault human life and oppress its spirit.

Commitment, furthermore, is seen by some as a road to impoverishment and deprivation. The assumption is that if we remain committed to a few values and a few people, if our options are limited, we wind up with less.

The truth of the matter is different. A life with no commitments does not open the world to us but closes it. We rush from experience to experience in the desperate hope that we might find peace.

Many of these experiences might bring us peace but fail to do so because we seize them rather than letting them unfold. When we approach reality acquisitively, it loses its capacity to settle us. We plunder life rather than live it. We do not remain long enough to know the meaning of that which we rush by and even destroy in our haste.

Devotion and Mystery

A human person is deeply mysterious. We must be patient a long time before many of the melodies of a human life are played. We must be composed as the other composes the music and harmony of our relationship. We must be attentive with the attention only the contemplative, the frugal and the committed possess.

Jesus once told us that when we find a pearl of great price we devote ourselves to it. Marriage is a pearl of such transcendent and inexhaustible worth that it is fitting to devote a lifetime to its keeping.

There is hardly a man or woman alive who is not moved by the devotion one human being may have for him or her. This devotion, however, must not be taken for granted or received as our due. It must not be a pearl, in another image Jesus gave us, that we cast before swine. It ought not be, in another Gospel reference, the seed we scatter in the brambles and thorns of the careless life we live. It must be cultivated in the good soil of our love. When devotion has been squandered and a marriage is lost, a great pearl is forfeited and we lose the light that might have been reflected on us from it. When devotion is cast away, weeds rather than wheat come from the earth. In the betrayal of every human relationship, an act of treason is directed at the whole human family.

In still another biblical instance, Jesus told us that possession of the entire world is not worth the loss of the human spirit. If we had abundance beyond calculation, all the prestige and affluence one life could hold, all the kingdoms of the earth at our disposal, this would matter little if we squandered along the way the devotion of a loving man or woman or of a needful and happy child.

The leaving of a great fortune to a family seldom does them much good. Bitterness is often intense in the settlement of a large estate.

The great gift to leave behind if we wish our children to flourish and our spouses to have life again is the gift of devotion and commitment. If they remember us as those who thought their life worth our life, then they will know they were pearls of great price. If we leave, not a large fortune, but the memory of our devotion, they will never exhaust it. It will yield a hundredfold in the soil of their hearts.

There is no one who cannot die devoted. Such a person immediately lives again in the life and memories of those to whom he or she gave everything. The first lesson of life is learning how to give the last measure of devotion.

12.5 Spirituality and Lifestyle
Evelyn Eaton Whitehead and James D. Whitehead

THE CHOICES THAT INFLUENCE OUR LIFESTYLE ARE PART OF THE SPIRITUALITY of our marriage. It is in these choices that we express the values that shape our life together. And we sense that Christianity's most significant contribution to our marriage is in the values to which it calls us. That unselfish love is possible, that sacrifice can have value beyond itself, that pleasure is to be celebrated but not idolized, that I am not for myself – alone these profound truths of human life are not always apparent. There is much in contemporary society, perhaps even much in our own experience, to suggest that these convictions are illusory or naive. Alone, we may feel how fragile is their hold on us. In community with other believers, we can face our doubts with less fear because we do not face them alone. We can nourish the religious vision of life that sustains us in our journey of marriage for a lifetime.

Christianity does not give married love its value; rather it celebrates the deeper meaning of married love that can sometimes be lost or obscured in the hectic pace of life. Christianity give us insight, vision into what is ordinarily invisible – the power and presence of God's redeeming love all around us and especially in certain privileged, sacramental experiences. And for most Christians, married love and the life commitments that flow from and surround this love are instances of this privileged experience of the power and presence of God. In this chapter we will explore several of the values which help to shape the lifestyle of Christian marriage.

The lifestyle of our marriage is influenced by many forces. Some of these seem beyond our immediate control – economic factors that bring inflation, political factors that shape national policy on child care, cultural factors that affect what is "expected" of women and men. In some marriages the influence of these external factors is so strong that there seems little room for choice. If I am poor, undereducated or chronically unemployed, it will be difficult for me to feel that I am in control of my own life. These burdens of social inequity weigh heavily on many Americans, adding stress in their marriages. A high incidence of divorce and desertion results.

But for most Americans, the lifestyle of marriage is not simply a product of external forces. We are conscious of ourselves as agents. Within certain limits we choose how we shall live. Some of our "choices" may be illusory, more influenced than we would like to admit by factors outside our awareness, but we are nevertheless conscious of ourselves as making decisions that influence the shape of our marriage.

The choices that are most important for our lifestyle are those that touch on the use of our resources. Our resources of concern, of time and of money are the "stuff" of our life together. The choices we make about these resources are not incidental; they are close to the substance of what our marriage is. What do we care about together? What is our money for? How do we spend the time of our life? It is in our response to these questions that we discover the values of our marriage and express them in our lifestyle.

Prayer and Justice

Prayer is part of the lifestyle of Christian marriage. This will include the ways that we as a couple, as a family, participate in the prayer of the Church, especially the celebration of the Eucharist. But it will involve as well our developing suitable ways for us to pray together, to share – sometimes as a couple, sometimes with the children as well – the intimate experience of coming into the presence of God in prayer. In recent decades the devotional life of many Catholic homes included the family rosary or prayers honoring the Sacred Heart. Family prayer today is more likely to focus on the reading of Scripture, reflecting together on its meaning for our lives and our actions in the world.

Prayer has been urged in marriage as one of the ways for the family to deepen its own unity: "The family that prays together, stays together." To pray together as a couple and as a family can reinforce, sometimes powerfully, our experience of being together in the ways that matter most. But the prayer of Christians is not simply about unity among us; it is about our community with humankind in the presence of God. Liturgical prayer especially celebrates this larger awareness. It is as the people of God that, in the name of Jesus and through the power of his abiding Spirit, we pray. But family prayer, too, should open us beyond "just us." The needs of the world, concretely the ways in which pain and loss and injustice are part of the world that we can influence, are part of our prayer.

In fall 1978 Archbishop Jean Jadot delivered an address on the implementation of the pastoral plan for family ministry that had been developed by the bishops of the United States. In his talk he spoke of prayer, faith and justice as these touch the family. He said, "The prayer I am speaking about is not so much the recitation of prayers as a shared experience of prayer. This finds its origins in a common reading of the Holy Scriptures and in a concern for those who are in need, for justice and peace in the world, for the coming of the Kingdom of God . . . such prayer quite naturally evokes an awareness of the family's mission to service. It also raises the family's social consciousness."

The conviction that we are for more than ourselves is basic to the Christian world view. This value must find its expression not only in our prayer but in our lifestyle. Most of us know that our marriage is about more than "just us." We need more than "just us" if our family is to thrive. We are aware of how much, as a couple and as a family, we depend on contact with certain relatives and support from special friends. But as Christians we go beyond ourselves not just in what we need but also in what we contribute.

Our life as a family and especially our children carry us into the larger world. As our children grow, we sense how much more they belong to the world and its future than they do to us. Thus, our care for them cannot end at our doorstep. Our first movements to contribute to the world beyond may well be for their sake – to make the world a better place for them, a place worthy of their hopes and conducive to their growth. But it is possible for this initial impulse of generative care, our concern for our children and their future, to stagnate. Our preoccupation with what is good for our family can become a new form of selfishness. The boundaries may be broadened slightly, but it is still "us" against "them."

But for many of us the movement of concern for our children invites us into a concern for the children of the world, for the future of humankind. I become more deeply aware that, by emotion and by action, I am involved in the lives of others. As parent, as worker, as citizen, I am in my own way somehow responsible for the future. The world – its hopes and problems – has a claim on me.

As Christians we hear this invitation to generativity reinforced in the call of Jesus. I am not only my brother's keeper; the category of brother and sister has expanded to include whoever is in need. "I was a stranger and you made me welcome, naked and you clothed me, sick and you visited me, in prison and you came to see me" (Matthew 25:35-36). Christianity expands the boundaries of our concern. We find we belong to a larger community. We hold our resources as stewards: these are not simply our "possessions," but the means of our contribution to a more just world.

Most of us sense, increasingly, that the issues of social value and justice that we face in our own lives are complex. There are not many questions where the "one right answer" emerges quickly and clearly. In any particular case, persons of good will and intelligence may come to different conclusions about what should be done. When the issues at stake touch directly on our own lives or our family's welfare – as in questions of job security or property values or tax reform – it can be even more difficult to determine the just response.

In these situations Christian awareness does not give easy answers but it does give us a starting point. We are not for ourselves alone. Action for justice and the transformation of the world is, as Pope Paul VI proclaimed, constitutive of our response to the gospel. We stand under the gospel challenge that we share the burdens of humankind and participate in its liberation. The way in which we, as a couple and as a family, participate in this mission of Christ may well have to be worked out on our own. But it can be expected that our maturing as Christian adults will involve our developing a lifestyle which expresses our understanding of the mission to which Jesus calls us and supports us in our response.

The Meaning of Money

Money is a central issue in marriage. What money means to us influences our relationship; how we use money shapes our lifestyle. And in many marriages decisions about money are among the most complex the couple face. Disagreements about money (how to manage it; how to spend it; who should make these decisions) and distress over money (living beyond our means; bills coming due; not having enough money to meet an unexpected expense) are significant sources of marital strain.

Money issues in marriage are troublesome in part because money carries so many different meanings. What is money for? My response here influences the way I answer the other questions. How much money does our family need? Can we ever have enough? How would we even go about determining what would be "enough" money for us?

For some of us, money is mainly for the practical necessities of life – food, clothing, shelter. For others, it is for enjoyment – for leisure or luxury or fun. Sometimes money is for our children's future, their education or financial security. Sometimes it is for self-esteem: "Surely I am worthwhile, just look at how much money I make." Sometimes money is for power: "I can buy anything and anyone I need." And sometimes it is a resource we have to be used for the good of the world.

Most practical decisions about money carry some larger emotional significance. These decisions say something important to us about who we are in the world. If, as a couple, we see money differently, if we each act out of a different sense of "what our money is for," we can anticipate that money issues will be troublesome to bring up between us and difficult to resolve.

The emotional significance of money is not the only source of strain. Inflation and the threat of economic recession are very real factors in the lifestyle of most families. Young couples find they can no longer afford to buy a house and so delay their decision to have a child. Couples with children realize that they both must bring in a paycheck if they wish to send their children to college. Couples who had resolved to retire early now plan to continue to work, unsure that their retirement benefits will remain adequate to living costs. Faced with rising prices, high interest rates and, for some, even unemployment, many families must make difficult decisions about money – decisions that significantly influence the lifestyle of their marriage.

But admitting the reality of these financially uncertain times, the money strain in many marriages is as much influenced by consumerism as by inflation. Even in this inflationary period, American families enjoy one of the highest levels of affluence in the world. We want and expect "the best that money can buy" for ourselves and our families. Advertising expands our sense of what we need, assuring us that "we owe it to ourselves" because "we're worth it." Perhaps especially as Americans we find ourselves susceptible to the temptation to judge our value by what we have – our material possessions, our standard of living, our buying power. This preoccupation with "the things of this world" has always been in tension with deeper religious intuitions: being is more than having; our worth is not grounded in our wealth; we are not "saved" by what we accumulate. The Christian vision has always called us to a certain detachment from wealth. As believers, we know we hold the goods of this world as stewards. Our responsibility is to care for the person in need, even out of our own substance. Today we see that this challenge has even broader scope. We are more aware of the connections between the prosperity of the United States and the poverty that exists elsewhere. It is often at the expense of other peoples that we have enjoyed, as a nation, the abundant resources of food and energy and technology that constitute "the good life." The patterns of this structural injustice are complicated, to be sure. It is not easy to trace our personal responsibility in this or to determine what we, as a family, can do to right the balance in world economics. But the complexity of the problem does not relieve us of responsibility. As Christians, we need to examine our family's standard of living not only in view of the shrinking dollar but in view of our accountability in the world. How we spend our money and where we invest our savings – for the Christian today these are more than practical financial questions to be resolved in terms of prices and interest rates alone. They are issues of religious significance that give shape to a Christian lifestyle.

Marriage and Ministry

For us as Christians, the question of lifestyle ultimately brings us to a discussion of ministry. Ministry is the action of believers undertaken in pursuit of the mission which Jesus entrusted to the Church – the coming of the Kingdom. Formal ministry is activity that is recognized or commissioned by the community of faith. Alongside this formal ministry is that ministry expected of all believers – the daily efforts to shape the world according to Christian values of love and mercy. Some Catholics who are married are part of the Church's formal ministry. The expanding involvement of lay persons in roles of official ministry is a fruit of the new vitality in the Church since the Second Vatican Council. Lay women and men serve in liturgical ministries in parishes as lectors and musicians and ministers of communion. Increasingly, the teaching ministry of parishes and dioceses is carried out by lay persons, some through full-time careers in religious education programs or Catholic school systems, others serving in a volunteer capacity as catechetists, conveners of an adult discussion group or members of the parish school board. There has been a comparable increase in the number of lay persons staffing the service agencies and social policy programs that operate under Church auspices or support.

This expansion of "approved" or "recognized" ministries over the past two decades has blurred many of the earlier distinctions among religious, clergy and lay persons in our Church. Married men ordained to the permanent diaconate, women religious serving as pastoral associates in parishes, women and married men studying in Catholic seminaries in preparation for careers of full-time ministry – these persons do not fit easily into former categories. In some cases the openness to lay persons in roles of service and leadership has been more a response to personnel shortages ("There just aren't enough brothers, sisters and priests to go around anymore!") than a sign of a deeper appreciation of the scope of the Christian call to ministry. But in any case, a significant number of Catholic lay persons – both married and single – understand their life vocation to be in the formal ministry of the Church.

The involvement of married Catholics as formal ministers in the Church's ministry *to* marriage – as planners and leaders in programs of marriage preparation, marriage enrichment, marriage counseling, and as part of the liturgical celebration of marriage – is on the increase and is good. In our discussion here, however, we wish to look at the relationship of marriage and the general Christian call to ministry.

For some Christians, both those ordained and others who are not, the immediate focus of their own religious action is within the community of faith, a ministry to and through the formal Church. But for most believers the call to live and act in response to the Christian vision will find expression in their family and their work and their other involvements in society. How is the religious experience of marriage related to the religious action or ministry of an adult Christian life? At several places in this book we have discussed this ministry of the mature Christian in terms of religious generativity. Psychological maturity leads me beyond myself and my intimates toward genuine care for the world. So, too, religious generativity leads me beyond the celebration of the "Good News" for myself, toward religious action – ministry – for a world beyond myself and my religious "intimates." We have seen that intimacy can either contribute to generativity (when the experience of our love releases in each of us the psychological resources we need for generosity and self-transcendence) or detract from it (when our love seems so fragile that we must spend our energy and other resources on ourselves, with none to spare for the world beyond). So marriage can have an ambiguous effect in Christian maturity and ministry. There are Christians for whom their own marriage and family occupy their full concern, not only in moments of crisis such as serious illness or the loss of a job, not just during periods of predictable stress like the birth of a child or, for some, the event of retirement – but characteristically. "We are for ourselves – alone." They may take quite seriously their responsibilities as spouses and parents. Their marriage is stable, their children have as many educational opportunities and social advantages as the couple can afford. They may participate actively in the parish. They are regular churchgoers who contribute financially and see to it that their children take part in the religious education program. But through it all, they are "for themselves." They may see the parish in terms of what it has to give them – a satisfying experience of worship, a program of moral education for their children, perhaps even a sense of security and some status in the community. But to be an adult Christian has not brought with it for them the motivating conviction: I am, our family is, for more than our-selves.

Among many other Christians marriage is just such an opening to God and to the world. The lessons of our marriage teach us to care beyond our-selves; our concern for our children links us to the concerns of the world. We sense that our life together as a family not only "uses up" our strengths, but also generates new resources that we can share and spend beyond our-selves. Our home, our love, our joy together, our time, our insights, our concerns, even our money – these resources of our life together do not exist for ourselves alone. At any one point in our marriage we may be over-whelmed with a sense that there is not enough of us to go around, that our resources are deficient, not just in the face of the needs of the world but even for the needs of our own family. But over its life course, if not at every moment, our marriage as maturing Christians will be marked by openness to needs beyond the family and by an active sense of our own contribution to the coming of the Kingdom, the presence of God in justice and love.

There are, of course, many different ways in which this ministry of maturing Christians will be expressed, and so many ways in which the rela-tionship between marriage and ministry will be seen. For some couples, their ministry is through their family life. They open their home to foster children or adopt a handicapped child. In another family the kitchen is always open to the teenagers in the neighborhood and the couple have time to listen to the concerns of their neighbors and friends. A third couple decide in retirement to devote two days a week together to visiting shut-ins or to welcome a recently widowed neighbor to live with them until she can make other plans. Other couples will sense that their involvement in issues of social concern is crucial to the religious education of their children. To take an unpopular stand on a question of racial justice, to become involved in a political cam-paign, to use part of their family's vacation money to assist those who have suffered in a disaster – these couples see such actions as of religious signifi-cance and encourage their children to share this practical understanding of faith.

For many lay Christians the arena of their ministry is the world of their employment. In my professional responsibilities, in my union activities, in a business decision I can influence, in the way I deal with my company subor-dinates and superiors, I try to bring to bear the convictions of my religious faith. On the job I take a stand that I know is right, even at the risk there may be repercussions. Or as a couple we decide to change jobs and move across country, so that we can participate in a project for economic justice. For many of us, then, our efforts to contribute to the world and to justice among people happen here, in the work that we do in the world. It is here that a sense of personal vocation takes shape. It is here that we work to hasten the coming of the Kingdom.

A Playful Marriage

The lifestyle of our marriage has much to do with how we are involved beyond ourselves. But our lifestyle also influences and expresses how we are together. Many of the values of Christianity contribute to the way we live our life together by urging us to take marriage seriously. Marriage is for grown-ups; its responsibilities are significant; the honeymoon does not last forever. These sober truths are important for us to hear and the Church serves us well in giving voice to this wisdom. But Christian wisdom also speaks to another side of marriage – the intimate connections between love and play. As our marriage matures, it becomes more playful. Here we will consider several elements that are part of the lifestyle of a playful marriage.

The Time of Our Life

A playful marriage depends on how we spend time together. The demands of careers, children and other involvements can easily overwhelm a marriage relationship. The fatigue and distraction that result can seriously erode our presence to each other. We learn that the playfulness that marked our carefree relationship at the start of our marriage does not endure easily or automatically. We learn, paradoxically, that if we would have a playful marriage we must work at it. Playfulness between us, like our other experiences of intimacy, will have to be cultivated. It will require a discipline in our lifestyle, especially a discipline of our time.

If marriage is a vocation that begins in a resounding "yes," it matures in many "no's." To have quality time for my partner and our family I find I have to say "no" to many outside demands and requests. This discipline, an "asceticism of time," helps us structure time for these central commitments of our life. Such disciplined planning and foresight can be experienced as cold calculation or as a canny response to life's multiple demands. Without such an asceticism, we become subject to the endless demands (all of them "worthwhile") of contemporary married life. Gradually exhaustion takes the play out of our marriage, both its flexibility and its fun. Our playfulness can be fostered by planning special times for just the two of us. We set aside times and places with protective boundaries. On our vacation, in days of rest or retreat, we give ourselves permission to play again. Apart from the seriousness of the rest of our life, these occasions invite us to play together and enliven our love.

Competition and Play

A playful marriage also recognizes the connection between competition and play. Our competitiveness can be acknowledged. We can accept the fact that marriage is a contact sport, one in which injury, anger and even loss are sometimes to be expected. But our competitiveness can also enliven us. As we identify together how and when we feel competitive toward one another, these feelings lose some of their force over us. We can share more concretely some of our fears about conflict between us and even feel some of the exhilaration of our struggles.

Competition is often an act of intimacy. It brings us "up close" and engages us with one another, however ambiguously. In competition, as in wrestling, we can come in touch with each other in ways that both excite and threaten us. In our competitive encounters we can learn much about ourselves and each other. We can find unsuspected strengths; we can also come upon unacknowledged weaknesses. To compete does not mean that we must use these strengths to dominate or must exploit these weaknesses. My awareness of your weakness can help me love better, help me to protect or at least not take advantage of your vulnerability. Awareness of a strength can help me love better as well, enabling me to use it to foster rather than control our marriage.

The thought of competition in marriage may still disturb us. It may conjure up images of the professional athlete, concerned only with performance and rating, and with coming out ahead in this encounter. But this is only one narrow interpretation of competition. We may also see competition in our marriage as not necessarily setting us against one another but as bringing us closer together. This "closer together" is, of course, threatening. It may well, on occasion, produce hurt and injury. In love and in competition we take the risk of a very close encounter, trusting that we will both play fair. But when we do – overcoming our fear of being crushed and our need to dominate – we are exhilarated *together;* the winner is our marriage and our intimate lifestyle.

Playful Sex

Our sexual life together will be part of a playful marriage. Here the Christian tradition has not always been helpful. A central characteristic of play is its uselessness; it is "just for fun." Christians have learned, on the other hand, that sex is very serious business. It has a specific and (even) exclusive purpose: the begetting of children. Only when this goal is dutifully pursued is our sexual activity to be enjoyed. Thus the seriousness and sacredness of sexuality has, for many Christians, overpowered its playfulness. Is not "playful sex" for playmates and libertines? The ambiguity here parallels that of competition. As competition is neither simply destructive nor simply creative, human sexual activity is neither simply purposeful nor simply playful. As Christians we know that sex is sacred: in our sexual sharing we create more life; through it we confirm and increase our love for one another. But this sacredness does not exclude its playfulness. Sex is for Christians very responsible play. The sexual embrace, sometimes generative of new life and much more often generative of our own love, is also fun.

Christianity has, to be sure, been cautious in recognizing the value of play-fulness in sex. Only recently and even then reluctantly have many of the official voices within the Church been willing to acknowledge the legitimacy of a sexual love whose every act is not intended to bring children into the world. But these developments are happening in our time, in part through the testimony of married Christians. And as they do, it becomes easier for us to celebrate in the lifestyles of Christian marriage the variety and playfulness of sexual love. Sex is not the only place for play in a maturing marriage. But if there is little or no play in our sexual sharing we are likely to find it more difficult to play in the other areas of our common life.

Learning to Play Fair

Another element of a playful marriage is learning to play fair. This means learning the rules that can help our competitiveness and our other intimacies contribute to our marriage, not destroy it. A first rule is that we *need* to contest with one another. To regularly repress our anger, our confu-sion or disagreement will not reduce these feelings but only store them for later use. Being "a good sport" in our marriage does not mean choosing not to compete with or confront my partner. It means actively engaging in this relationship. "Poor sports" are those who choose not to contest anything with their partners. They may stand on the sidelines and complain, but they do not compete. A marriage in which the partners no longer contest, no longer struggle with each other in any significant way, can be called a stalemate. The partners in such a marriage are likely to experience each other as "stale mates."

If the first rule is simply to play – to compete, to get engaged – the second rule is to play fair. This means playing skillfully, knowing when and how to confront my partner. In marriage, as in every other kind of play, timing is important. And our experience of each other in marriage, the years we have been playing together, should help us to determine the timing of our confrontations. I bring up a sensitive issue when I sense the time is right: when *we* can handle it, not just when I want to take it on. Playing fair is likely to be a part of our lifestyle in marriage the more we are each able to display the skillful behaviors of communication and conflict resolution.

Learning to play fair is a complex virtue, one that most of us acquire only gradually as we mature. Its growth is likely to include the discipline of identifying and cutting away habits of ours that are destructive in our mar-riage – belittling the other person, striking back indirectly rather than con-fronting a troublesome issue, using the children as weapons in an effort to win or be right. Finally, play can teach us the importance of compromise and the value of being a good loser. Compromise means finding our way around questions and concerns that threaten a standoff or seem insoluble. The strate-gies of barter and negotiation will, at times, help us sustain our love and commitment. Learning how to be a good loser is also a sign of maturity. Each of us can expect to fail, even repeatedly, in our efforts at love and mutuality. Play reminds us that we need not be ashamed. Love does not mean never having to say I'm sorry; it means becoming good at it.

In all these ways we mature in love. We learn that play is not just for kids, that being able to trust one another is more important than always being right. In his study of adult maturity, *Adaptation to Life,* George Vaillant summarizes these connections among love, trust and play:

> It is hard to separate capacity to trust from capacity to play, for play is dangerous until we can trust both ourselves and our opponents to harness rage. In play, we must trust enough and love enough to risk losing without despair, to bear winning without guilt, and to laugh at error without mockery (p. 309).

In our own marriage we can expect to know winning and losing, risk and error, laughter and love. These are the stuff of a playful marriage, the building blocks of a lifestyle of marriage for a lifetime.